The Militarization of the U.S.–Mexico Border, 1978–1992

CMAS BORDER & MIGRATION STUDIES SERIES
Series editor: Gilberto Cárdenas

The Militarization of the U.S.–Mexico Border, 1978–1992

Low-Intensity Conflict Doctrine Comes Home

TIMOTHY J. DUNN

CMAS Books
The Center for Mexican American Studies
The University of Texas at Austin

A CMAS BOOK
Editor: Víctor J. Guerra
Assistant Editors: Martha Vogel, Jess Jackson

The publication of this book was assisted by a grant from the
Inter-University Program for Latino Research.

Library of Congress Cataloging-in-Publication Data
Dunn, Timothy J., 1961–
    The militarization of the U.S.–Mexico border, 1978–1992 : low-
intensity conflict doctrine comes home / Timothy J. Dunn. — 1st ed.
        p. cm.
    Includes bibliographical references and index.
    ISBN 0–292–71579–X. — ISBN 0–292–71580–3
    1. Mexican-American Border Region. 2. Low-intensity conflicts
(Military science)—Mexican-American Border Region. 3. United
States—Emigration and immigration—Government policy.
4. Narcotics, Control of—Mexican-American Border Region. I. Title.
F787.D46 1995
972′.1—dc20   94-42964

Printed and bound in the United States of America.

First edition (February 1996).
Second paperback impression, January 1997.

Contents

Acknowledgments

Learning is indeed a collaborative endeavor. This principle has been continually reinforced for me throughout my work on this monograph and the various projects that led up to it over the past six and a half years. I am profoundly grateful to the many individuals who have contributed in a variety of ways to the work. First and foremost among them is Professor Gilberto Cárdenas of the Department of Sociology and the Center for Mexican American Studies at the University of Texas at Austin. He helped launch the project in my first semester of graduate school (in the fall of 1988) by encouraging me to pursue my curiosity about U.S. immigration and drug enforcement efforts in the U.S.–Mexico border region. This curiosity sprang from my concern over the various fragmentary signs of militaristic qualities that I had noticed sporadically in those activities in a variety of sources over the previous decade, and over the potential human rights problems that these activities posed. Dr. Cárdenas enabled me to investigate, frame, and refine the unusual topic of border militarization; provided thoughtful supervision of my work on the topic for a 1990 Master's report in Latin American studies; and has guided all of my subsequent efforts to update and rewrite that report into this monograph. I am most grateful for his instrumental guidance, scholarly insight and expertise, collegial exchanges of ideas, unwavering encouragement, and enduring patience in the long process of conceiving and producing this monograph, as well as throughout my graduate studies in sociology and Latin American studies. This project could not have been realized without his ongoing and multifaceted assistance.

I would also like to thank Professors David Montejano and Henry Dietz, both also at the University of Texas at Austin, for their close readings and constructive comments on an earlier draft of this monograph. In their comments, they made very helpful critical suggestions for the editing, updates, and expansions of the monograph, suggestions that greatly improved it.

In addition, two individuals formally located outside of academia have provided invaluable assistance and insight. I am deeply appreciative to María Jiménez, director of the Immigration Law Enforcement Monitoring Project of the American Friends Service Committee, for her interest in and support of my research. She brought her considerable expertise—as a leading border-region human rights activist and analyst of border affairs—to bear on drafts of research reports upon which this monograph is based. She also generously shared information, so much so that I could not acknowledge in my endnotes the great number of occasions that she brought important sources to my attention—I was simply unable to keep track of all those instances. Moreover, she exposed early drafts of my work to broader audiences, which provided me with further important feedback. Likewise, I would like to thank Rogelio Núñez, executive director of the Proyecto Libertad refugee legal assistance project in Harlingen, Texas, for his sharing of information and insights, as a sociologist, human rights activist, and native of the border region.

Numerous friends, colleagues, and interested individuals provided a wide range of additional assistance to this project. I would especially like to thank Daniel Hernández, Kelly Himmel, Jackie Morrel, Beth Sims, David Spener, Michael Stone, and Eduardo Torres for reading all or portions of drafts of this monograph and providing valuable comments and feedback, which in some cases included detailed critiques and editing suggestions. Further, thanks are due to Ron Mader and Manlio Tirado for writing advance book reviews of an earlier draft of the manuscript. I am also very grateful to Melissa Biggs Coupal, Austin Holiday, Jennifer Markley, and Cyrus Reed for their instrumental field-research collaboration and moral support. I would also like to thank the following persons for generously sharing (whether they realized it or not) a wide variety of information, insight, and expertise: Frank Bean, David Berger, Bill Black, Lupe Castillo, Irasema Coronado, Erica Dahl-Bredine, Miriam Davidson, Kirsten Dellinger, Anne Dibble, Ann Dohrmann, Terry English, María Eraña, Isabel García, Chris Gill, Holly Hapke, Joel Heikes, Rubén Hernández, Barbara Hines, Doug Insch, Don Irish, Jeff Jackson, Nancy Campbell Jeffrey, Jonathan Jones, Suzan Kern, Rob Koulish, Ninfa Krueger, Kathryn Kuhn, Jeff Larson, Cynthia Leigh, Martin Markowitz, Roberto Martínez, José Matus, Nelson Mock, Jackie Morrel, Debbie Nathan, Alison Newby, Eric Nichols, Luis Plascencia, Rachel Pooley, José María Ramos, Virginia Raymond, Diana Reynolds, Martín Rocha, Jesús Romo, Nidia Salamanca, Juan Manuel Sandoval, Bill Shelton, Tracy Steele, Dave Stellman, Tom Stellman, Luke Stollings, David Struthers, Mary Swenson,

Winifred Tate, Germán Vega, Pablo Vila, Anne Wallace, Jana Walters, Andrew Wheat, Phil Wingeir, Anne Winkler, and Barbara Younoszai. I was greatly assisted in my research by a variety of other individuals and organizations. The reference staff at the Perry-Castañeda Library and Margo Gutiérrez of the Benson Latin American Collection (both libraries at the University of Texas at Austin), the government documents reference staff at the library of the University of Texas at El Paso, and Charlotte McCann and Cindy Noblitt of the Documentation Exchange in Austin all provided considerable help in my library research for this project. I am also indebted to the Resource Center of the Americas, in Minneapolis, for first introducing me to the concept of low-intensity conflict doctrine. In addition, Proyecto Libertad (in Harlingen, Texas), the Political Asylum Project of Austin, and Casa Marianella (in Austin) provided me with invaluable firsthand exposure to the various concerns of refugees and recent immigrants, and the grassroots activists advocating on their behalf. I am of course extremely grateful to the approximately 30 individuals (mainly federal law enforcement personnel, as well as immigration lawyers and human rights activists) who granted me interviews during various stages of my research on immigration and drug enforcement in the border region.

The Office of Graduate Studies, the C. B. Smith research fund, and the Institute of Latin American Studies, all at the University of Texas at Austin, provided modest yet crucial research grants that enabled me to conduct many of those interviews as well as some limited field observations in the South Texas border region. The final stages of my work on this monograph were made manageable by the library access and miscellaneous support provided by the Center for Inter-American and Border Studies at the University of Texas at El Paso. More generally, my fellow graduate students, as well as the faculty and staff, in the Department of Sociology, the Institute of Latin American Studies, and elsewhere at the University of Texas at Austin helped to create a stimulating and supportive learning and research environment.

I am also very grateful for the patience and diligent, highly skilled work of the CMAS Books editorial staff of Víctor Guerra, Martha Vogel, and Jess Jackson. They brought their considerable talents to bear on a rough manuscript by this novice author, greatly improving the work and bringing it to fruition as a monograph. Relatedly, I deeply appreciate Professor Gideon Sjoberg's instructive counsel on the nature of the editorial process in academic publishing, as well as his persistent encouragement and his broad-ranging scholarly expertise and insights.

On a more personal note, I would like to thank my family for their unflagging, generous, and patient support and encouragement, especially my parents, Robert and Jo Ann Dunn, and my brother Robin Dunn. Likewise, I would like to thank close friends not previously mentioned who have been extremely helpful. I am especially grateful to Amy Liebman for her consistent support, encouragement, and patience, as well as for her insightful and critical discussions of this project and related topics over the past two years. Ken Todd and Phil Crossley have also been especially supportive as I have struggled to complete this monograph. Lastly, I would like to thank all of my friends who have put up with me and offered encouragement of all types as I have gone through this process. I am deeply grateful to them and to everybody who has assisted me in any way in this project. I apologize to any whom I have forgotten to specifically acknowledge.

While all of the aforementioned individuals made important contributions, I alone can be held responsible for the contents of this monograph—the information conveyed, conclusions drawn, opinions expressed, or any errors (factual or of judgment) made therein.

The Militarization of
the U.S.–Mexico Border,
1978–1992

The U.S.–Mexico Border Region

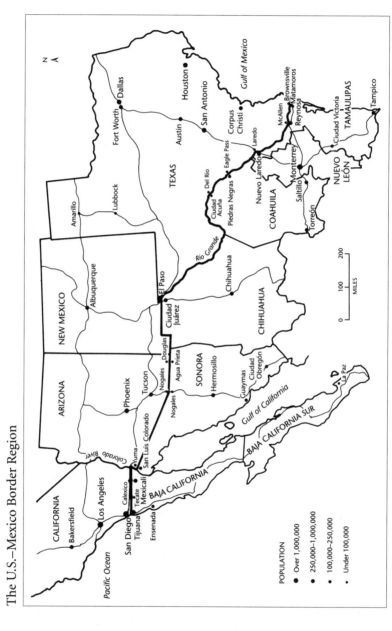

Adapted from Lawrence A. Herzog, *Where North Meets South: Cities, Space, and Politics on the U.S.–Mexico Border* (Austin: CMAS Books, University of Texas at Austin, 1990), 34.

1

Introduction

The U.S.–Mexico border region has been the site of considerable, wide-ranging military and security measures throughout its history. The border itself was established by military force in the Texas Revolution of 1836 and the Mexican War of 1846 to 1848. The cumulative outcome of these conflicts was U.S. conquest, with Mexico forced to surrender approximately half of its national territory, as formalized in the Treaty of Guadalupe Hidalgo in 1848. This coercive annexation left a bitter and complex legacy for *mexicanos* residing in the annexed territories, as well as for those who migrated north from Mexico in subsequent decades, and for the descendants of both groups.[1] Much of this legacy was further shaped by Anglo and state violence against and the dispossession of Mexican-origin and Native American peoples, as contention and conflict in the border region continued for over 80 years. However, with the pacification of the region finally accomplished by the third decade of the twentieth century, less severe means of social control were subsequently employed. Still, the U.S.–Mexico border region (see map, facing page) remained a focal point for special law enforcement and security measures, as is evident, for example, in the deployment of the U.S. Border Patrol in the region from 1924 onward and in the mass deportation efforts focused there during the 1930s and 1954.

In the contemporary period, since the mid-1970s, "border control" has emerged as a salient topic in U.S. politics, with concern for it often spurred on by sensationalistic portrayals of undocumented immigration, drug trafficking, and occasionally even the threat of terrorism as critical issues for the U.S.–Mexico border region. Such depictions by U.S. government officials and the media have fueled a tendency to interpret these issues as potential or actual crises with national security implications. These interpretations, in turn, have helped frame the debate over border enforcement policies.

1

Undocumented immigration was the first of these issues to be portrayed during the contemporary period as a growing crisis with national security implications. This process geared up in the mid-1970s and peaked (for the time being) during the mid-1980s, with the 1986 passage of the landmark Immigration Reform and Control Act (IRCA). The extraordinary Mariel boatlift of some 125,000 Cuban refugees to Miami in the spring of 1980 added greater urgency during and after this period to both U.S. policy debates and media portrayals of immigration enforcement issues with respect to the border region. Relying largely on INS sources, leading U.S. print media, in particular, presented the public with images of an "invasion" of "illegal aliens" from Mexico who were crossing the U.S.–Mexico border in a "steady stream," a stream that was "turning into a flood"—an "illegal tide" overwhelming "the thin green line of the U.S. Border Patrol."[2]

The Reagan administration at times further escalated the rhetoric surrounding undocumented immigration by linking the issue to its controversial interventionist policies in Central America. For example, President Reagan predicted in 1983 that if U.S. military assistance to anticommunist forces in Central America (which had committed numerous human rights atrocities) were halted, the result would be "a tidal wave of refugees—and this time they'll be 'feet people' and not boat people—swarming into our country seeking safe haven from communist repression to our south."[3] In a related vein, in 1982 the Reagan administration's ranking official on refugee affairs in the Department of State asserted:

> Pressures on our borders from the Caribbean and Central America—particularly Mexico—make it certain that in the foreseeable future, as never in the past, the United States is going to have to maintain a foreign policy, including preemptive and prophylactic measures, which has as one of its objectives the protection of our frontiers against excessive illegal immigration.[4]

Following the passage of IRCA in 1986, the issue of illegal drug trafficking gained ascendancy, eclipsing undocumented immigration as the most urgent border-control matter. The issue was formally designated as a threat to national security by President Reagan in 1986, and the ensuing War on Drugs was a prominent element of both U.S. domestic and foreign policy. The issue was also enthusiastically taken up and promoted more broadly by President Bush, particularly early in his term.[5] The U.S.–Mexico border received special attention in government officials' discussions of this "war." For example, in 1988 Congress debated requiring the military to seal U.S. borders against all drug traffic.[6] By 1990 a leading federal drug enforcement official in the southwestern border region characterized the situation thusly: "We are engaged in something akin to a guerrilla war along the border against well-entrenched and well-organized trafficking groups."[7]

To a much lesser extent, even the issue of terrorism has been framed during the contemporary era as a border-control problem. For example, leading border-state and federal officials sometimes drew a link between drug trafficking and terrorist threats, despite the absence of terrorist activities in the border region.[8] In a more hyperbolic vein, President Reagan claimed in 1986 that "terrorists and subversives are just two days' driving time from Harlingen, Texas," during a nationally televised speech to rally public opinion in favor of his administration's belligerent policies in Central America.[9]

The image of the U.S.–Mexico border region that emerges from these sorts of alarmist portrayals is that of a vulnerable zone in urgent need of numerous, serious security measures—to repel an "invasion" of "illegal aliens," to win the War on Drugs, and even to counter the threat of terrorism. Complex international issues such as undocumented immigration and illegal drug trafficking were reduced to one-sided, domestic border-control problems, and framed as potential or actual threats to national security, which in turn required strong law enforcement, or even military, responses. Less coercive approaches were de-emphasized or excluded from consideration in the above portrayals, particularly in the case of the War on Drugs.

Based on the possibility that these dire portrayals of border enforcement issues by leading U.S. government officials and media outlets may have actually influenced border enforcement policies and practices, the present study examines immigration and drug enforcement efforts in the U.S.–Mexico border region from 1978 through 1992. The thesis of this monograph is that the implementation of a wide range of measures during the 1978–1992 period by a variety of U.S. government agencies to address the issues of undocumented immigration and illegal international drug trafficking resulted in the gradual militarization of the U.S.–Mexico border region. "Militarization" in its broadest sense refers to the use of military rhetoric and ideology, as well as military tactics, strategy, technology, equipment, and forces. However, the ideological and rhetorical dimensions of militarization—although important—are generally not examined here. Rather, the scope of this work is limited to the other, more concrete aspects of militarization.

More specifically, militarization is defined in this study as those measures associated with the specific U.S. military doctrine of low-intensity conflict (LIC). While this framework is examined in detail later in this chapter, several key points bear mentioning here at the outset. LIC doctrine was developed during the 1980s to meet a wide variety of perceived threats to U.S. national security in the third world (especially revolutionary insurgencies in Central America). The essence of LIC doctrine is the establishment and maintenance of social control over targeted civilian populations through the implementation of a broad range of sophisticated measures via the coordinated and integrated efforts of police, paramilitary, and military forces. One of the doctrine's distinguishing characteristics is that military forces take on police functions, while police forces take on military characteristics.[10] In theory, low-intensity conflict is a comparatively subtle form of militarization. However, in practice, more severe social-control measures have also often been adopted in the implementation of LIC-style militarizations in Latin America and elsewhere in the third world. Moreover, many of these cases have been accompanied by widespread human rights violations committed by military and security forces, key elements of which have often been trained and advised by U.S. military, security, and intelligence personnel.

An underlying concern for the status of human and civil rights guides this study's admittedly unusual approach of utilizing a military framework to analyze particular law enforcement efforts in the U.S.–Mexico border region. This project has two basic objectives. The first is to provide a detailed examination of immigration and drug enforcement policies and practices in the U.S.–Mexico border region from 1978 through 1992, focusing on the U.S. side and principally, though not exclusively, on the Immigration and Naturalization Service (INS).[11] The second is to compare these efforts with the precepts of LIC doctrine regarding technology, equipment, forces, and operational characteristics, as well as its overall essence. A qualitative case study methodology was used in conducting the research for this project, emphasizing the comparative use of information drawn from a variety of sources. These sources include congressional documents, military press documents, critiques of military doctrine, mainstream and alternative press reports, human rights reports, interviews with 15 South Texas border-area federal law enforcement personnel (mainly INS agents) and 12 human rights advocates, and some limited first-hand observation of Border Patrol enforcement practices and of four border-region detention centers used by the INS. (See appendix 4 for a fuller discussion of related research methods.)

The overall purpose of this work is to bring to light new information and to offer an analysis that may provide additional insight into the developments and shifts in contemporary immigration and drug enforcement efforts in the U.S.–Mexico border region. These topics have by no means been thoroughly examined, as relatively few researchers have addressed them in any substantial detail.[12] In addition, the most in-depth research on the INS as an institution is focused on earlier periods of its immigration enforcement efforts, while investigations of the agency's activities in the contemporary period have typically not emphasized its enforcement endeavors in the border region.[13] Thus, the present study is intended to help fill the gap in the research and analysis of contemporary immigration and drug enforcement efforts in the U.S.–Mexico border region, focusing particularly on the role of the INS. It is hoped that in providing detailed information on and a critical interpretation of these underexamined issues, this study will help to stimulate further debate and research on them.

The remainder of this chapter is devoted to two topics, the discussion of which provides the foundation for the present work. The first is a historical overview of the militarization of the U.S.–Mexico border region, which helps to place current developments in a longer-term perspective. The second is a critical overview of LIC doctrine, leading to the construction of an ideal type of low-intensity conflict doctrine and related practices, which can then be compared with current patterns of immigration and drug enforcement in the U.S.–Mexico border region.

A Historical Overview of the Militarization of the U.S.–Mexico Border

This section provides a selective overview of the history of militarization in the U.S.–Mexico border region since its establishment in 1848, as derived from secondary sources.[14] The focus here is on cases in which the dynamics of border militarization and related social conflicts have been especially graphic, most notably those in South Texas. The establishment and maintenance of the social control of subordinated groups by Anglo groups and the state is a central theme running through the history of the border region. Primary among the subordinated groups were Mexican Americans (or Chicanos or *mexicanos*) and Native Americans. The present discussion is centered on the former group, although militarization was obviously a central issue for the latter group as well.[15]

The history of the militarization of the U.S.–Mexico border can best be understood in terms of one central fact: for many decades, the border was a tenuous social construct, established and maintained by force. The border was in large part either ignored or actively contested by *mexicanos* in the region—both long-term settlers and more recently arrived immigrants—because it was imposed on them and it disrupted their lives. Moreover, *mexicanos* made up the vast majority of the population throughout much of the border region for many decades. The full pacification of the area required some 70 years, and involved the prominent use of a variety of coercive measures both by the state and by Anglo groups.

Barrera's "internal colonization" thesis is a useful point of departure in considering the history of border militarization, for his interpretation provides the key elements of the larger context within which this militarization took place. He proposes that the Chicano population has historically been maintained in a subordinate position through the imposition of a colonial labor system that not only shaped racial and ethnic relations in earlier times but also, to a lesser extent, has endured in the contemporary period. This labor system has been characterized by the segmentation of the labor force largely along racial or ethnic lines.[16] It is important to point out that not only were those *mexicanos* who were living in the border region at the time of annexation treated as a conquered people, but so were those who migrated north across the border in later decades.[17] In addition to serving as a means of exploiting labor, internal colonization enabled U.S. authorities to control what can be considered to be a persistent "ethnic-nationalist problem." That is, it has served to dispossess and subordinate Mexican-origin people, who have a common history and culture as well as a long-standing claim to large portions of territory—all of which have threatened the state's and the Anglo population's control of the border region.

THE PACIFICATION OF THE
U.S.–MEXICO BORDER REGION, 1848–1918

The second half of the nineteenth century and the early twentieth century were particularly violent in the border region, as the political definitions that had been imposed upon the region by the Treaty of Guadalupe Hidalgo of 1848 and the Gadsden Purchase of 1853 had to be continually reinforced. Spanning seven decades, these efforts culminated in massive repression in response to a *mexicano* insurrection in South Texas. This long process can be viewed as an attempt on the part of U.S. officials as well as Anglo settlers and elites to pacify, or subdue, the Mexican American population residing in the border region. Much of the pacification process centered on land struggles, ultimately resulting in the widespread dispossession of Mexican Americans in the region. Mexican Americans lost their land to Anglos through a variety of measures, including theft, intimidation, swindles, dubious legal challenges and the burden of related court costs, taxes and other debts, as well as purchases.[18]

In addition to ongoing, low-level violence during the period, innumerable bloody conflicts erupted periodically in the border region, which were divided along ethnic or racial lines—Anglo, *mexicano,* and Native American—and crosscut with class issues as well.[19] There were also a number of invasions into northern Mexico by opportunistic attackers during this era, especially by Anglos intent on seizing Baja California.[20] One result of this continual conflict was the establishment of a series of U.S. Army forts along the border, some of which were later to become modern military bases.[21]

A particularly illustrative case of border conflict during the nineteenth century is the Cortina War (1859–1860) that took place in and around Brownsville, Texas. Following a precipitating violent dispute, conflict ensued that lasted for seven months. During much of this time the local rancher Juan Cortina and his forces controlled the Lower Rio Grande Valley and gained widespread support among the Texas Mexicans, who made up the overwhelming majority of the total population. Two proclamations made by Cortina emphasized three major grievances underlying the campaign: *mexicanos'* loss of land through legal manipulation and intimidation, the impunity with which Anglos killed *mexicanos,* and the arrogance of Anglo racism. Eventually U.S. Army troops, accompanied by Texas Rangers, defeated Cortina's forces and pacified the area. Cortina's defeat was followed by indiscriminate retaliation by Anglos, principally the Rangers, against *mexicanos* in the Valley—"a fit of bloody terrorism," according to Rosenbaum.[22]

This was by no means the only such confrontation to occur in the Lower Rio Grande Valley. The Valley remained an especially violent region of the border well into the twentieth century, due to a number of factors similar to those underlying the Cortina War. Moreover, for many years *mexicanos* on both sides of the Rio Grande shared a desire for reunion, since the river was a particularly artificial and disruptive boundary in this area. The Rio Grande Valley had not been a part of the colonial Mexican province of Tejas, but rather of the province of Nuevo

Santander. This latter province occupied a broad swath of land on both sides of the Rio Grande, stretching from the Gulf Coast to Laredo, while the southern border of the province of Tejas had been the Nueces River, some 100 miles north of the Rio Grande.[23] Furthermore, there was a long-standing dispute between Mexico and the Republic of Texas, as well as the United States, as to whether the demarcation of the southern Texas and U.S. boundary with Mexico was the Nueces River or the Rio Grande. This dispute was aggressively pursued by the United States and played a precipitating role in the U.S. war with Mexico during the mid-1840s.[24]

In spite of the violence that prevailed in much of South Texas during the nineteenth century, some accommodation did take place between the new Anglo elites (primarily a mercantilist group) and landowning Texas-Mexican upper-class families. By 1900, however, through legal and illegal coercive means, these Texas-Mexican families had been largely dispossessed of their land, except in a few border enclaves. They were replaced by Anglo elites such as the King family, whose enormous ranch covered more than 500,000 acres.[25] Texas law enforcement authorities' participation in extralegal, coercive acquisitions of Texas-Mexican land by Anglo ranchers was so notorious that among *mexicanos* in the Lower Rio Grande Valley "the Texas Rangers were known as *'los rinches de la Kineña'*—the King Ranch Rangers—to underscore the belief that they acted as King's strong-arm agents."[26]

The dispossession of Texas-Mexican landholders in the Lower Rio Grande Valley was not complete until the early twentieth century. This process was facilitated and enforced by increased violence against *mexicanos* by Anglo law enforcement officials and vigilantes. The 1904 establishment of a railroad link to Brownsville brought a large influx of Anglo settlers from the North and Midwest who bought up subdivided ranch land and introduced intensive irrigation in "one of the most phenomenal land movements in the history of the U.S."[27] Unlike many Anglo ranchers at that time, the remaining Texas-Mexican landholders were reluctant to sell their ranches. Consequently, they were displaced from the land through now familiar means—fraud, declining livestock markets, coercion, and legal battles.[28]

The net effect of this process of dispossession, in tandem with mass Anglo migration into the area, was to reduce most Texas Mexicans to the status of landless workers dependent for their livelihood on agricultural wage labor. Moreover, the new Anglo farmers were especially racist, more so than the older, more established Anglo ranchers and merchants. A volatile situation developed when a number of *mexicanos* were killed by

Anglos—including some 16 killed by Texas Rangers between 1907 and 1911—under what could only generously be described as clouded circumstances. In response to these events, a 1911 meeting in Laredo of some 400 Texas-Mexican leaders, known as the Congreso Mexicanista, denounced the lynchings and attacks on the Texas-Mexican population, called for an end to discrimination, and urged Texas Mexicans not to sell their land.[29]

The increasing strife in South Texas—coupled with nearby developments in northern Mexico during the Mexican Revolution (1910–1920)—led to the most extensive *mexicano* uprising against the Anglo occupation, and to an extreme instance of border militarization intended to quell the uprising. The political scope and origins of this rebellion are still not entirely clear. However, it does seem beyond dispute that from 1915 through mid-1916, Texas Mexicans in the Lower Rio Grande Valley took up arms against targets identified with Anglo domination. In groups numbering 25 to 100, Texas Mexicans and their allies from the other side of the border engaged in widespread raiding against Anglo ranches, farms, railroads, and other targets. These raids, which peaked between July and November 1915, stemmed from the irredentist, revolutionary program outlined in the Plan de San Diego (signed in San Diego, Texas). The plan proclaimed independence from "Yankee tyranny" and called for a rebellion by a "Liberating Army for Races and Peoples," to include Mexicans, Blacks, Japanese, and Indians. It proposed the creation of an independent republic to be made up of Texas, New Mexico, Colorado, Arizona, and California. The plan also called for every Anglo male over the age of 16 to be killed. Between 1,000 and 3,000 men reportedly signed the Plan de San Diego. Many came from the classes of the Texas-Mexican community that were most threatened by the rapidly expanding Anglo farm economy, and the majority of the guerrilla raids took place in the counties most affected by this new economy.[30]

The immediate governmental response was to send Texas Rangers and some 1,900 U.S. Army troops into the Valley to suppress the insurrection.[31] Meanwhile, some 30,000 people fled the Valley in fear, Anglos to the north and Texas Mexicans to the south across the border.[32] The Army troop and Ranger deployments—along with the actions of local Anglo law enforcement officials, posses, and vigilantes—led to savage repression of Texas Mexicans. Estimates of the number of Texas Mexicans killed vary widely, ranging from 300 to 5,000, while 62 Anglo civilians and 64 soldiers died.[33] The Texas Rangers were particularly vicious and indiscriminate. Walter Prescott Webb, the otherwise sympathetic historian of

the Rangers, described them as having carried out "an orgy of blood-
shed" and having imposed "a reign of terror" over Texas Mexicans.[34] Indeed, the commander of U.S. Army forces in the area referred to the
Rangers as "scoundrels."[35] Army troops apparently acted with much
more restraint, but were nonetheless complicit with the Rangers' and
vigilantes' harsher efforts.[36] In response to the savage repression inflicted
by Texas Ranger and Anglo vigilante forces, as well as the shifting political context in northern Mexico, the raids subsided by July of 1916.[37] Nevertheless, by August 1916 some 28,000 federalized National Guard and
active-duty Army troops were deployed for several months in the Lower
Rio Grande Valley. This deployment was part of a larger federal effort to
secure the entire border region in response to the overflow of the Mexican Revolution into various areas of the U.S. side of the border.[38]

Some of the military conflicts on the border were more directly related to the Mexican Revolution. For example, in 1911 the Mexican Liberal Party under the leadership of the Flores Magón brothers sought to
launch a socialist-anarchist revolution in Baja California. Predominantly
non-Mexican, the Magonista forces invaded Baja California from the U.S.
side. They briefly controlled the border from the Colorado River to the
Pacific, but were defeated by Francisco Madero's forces in mid-1911. In
1914, a Pancho Villa supporter recruited volunteers on the U.S. side of
the border in an effort to seize control of the Baja California governor-
ship, but lost in a bloodless coup to a Carranza follower. The most famous episode of border militarization by U.S. forces was triggered by a
military raid by Villa's forces on Columbus, New Mexico, in March 1916,
during which 18 U.S. citizens—as well as some 100 Villista raiders—were
killed. In response, the U.S. government sent a "punitive expeditionary
force" of some 20,000 Army troops under General "Blackjack" Pershing
into northern Mexico for a year. Further, over 100,000 National Guard
troops were deployed along the border from Yuma to Brownsville by
the fall of 1916.[39] Subsequently, from 1916 through 1919, several cross-
border raids in the West Texas Big Bend area were carried out by Mexicans associated with various factions of the Mexican Revolution. In two
especially brutal acts of reprisal, Texas Rangers (with U.S. Army complic-
ity, though not direct participation) executed 15 *mexicanos* taken from a
Texas village on the Rio Grande and four Mexicans taken prisoner during
a punitive raid in Mexico—all of whom were apparently unconnected to
the activities against which the Texas Rangers were retaliating.[40]

On the whole, it is clear that from its establishment in 1848 through
the Mexican Revolution, the U.S.–Mexico border was the site of conflict

as well as periodically intense, militarized efforts to pacify the region. *Mexicanos* did not quietly submit to Anglo domination, but rather contested the official definition of the border in a variety of ways (only the most obvious of which are discussed here), resisting Anglo control of the border region for some 70 years. Such open conflict and intense militarization did not occur after this period. This may have been in part due to the fearsome legacy of the pacification period. Events from that era made it clear that *mexicanos* on the U.S. side of the border occupied a subordinate position in the region and would suffer severe sanctions if they attempted to alter significantly the status quo. With this principle emphatically established, border militarization assumed relatively subtle forms in subsequent decades.

BORDER ENFORCEMENT AS LABOR CONTROL, 1918–1977

The modern era of border enforcement following the pacification of the region was defined by efforts to maintain control over the flow of Mexican immigrant workers into the United States, typically in ways that also significantly affected Mexican Americans. It was characterized by the application of what Cockcroft has termed the "revolving door" immigration policy of alternating periods of large-scale immigration and massive deportation. This practice was initiated during the 1920–1922 U.S. recession, when—after being recruited to work by the Cotton Growers Association during World War I—Mexican immigrant workers on cotton farms in the Southwest were scapegoated for allegedly causing unemployment among U.S. workers. As a result, a substantial number of them were deported (many of them returning shortly thereafter).[41] A key development accompanying this practice was the establishment in 1924 of a permanent border enforcement unit, the U.S. Border Patrol, which became the chief guardian of the "revolving door" and the main agent of the comparatively less severe forms of border militarization carried out during ensuing decades.

Large-scale Mexican immigration to the border region began during the first part of the twentieth century. From 1900 to 1930 approximately 685,000 Mexicans legally immigrated to the United States (60% of whom went to Texas). Most of this flow occurred during the 1920s, when over 487,000 Mexicans legally immigrated to the United States. Much of the migration flow was circular, involving frequent movement back and forth between Mexico and the United States, although many immigrants did eventually opt for permanent settlement in the United States. While there were many reasons for the growing influx of Mexicans (e.g., the Mexican Revolution), the need of southwestern employers for cheap labor and their agents' active labor recruiting practices in Mexico strongly contributed. The Southwest's economy was rapidly expanding with the onset of intensive irrigation agriculture and new growth in the mining and railroad sectors. In addition, changes in the immigration laws, which restricted the immigration of Asian and European laborers, helped create a labor shortage. Thus, cheap Mexican laborers became more essential to the region's development, and controlling them became an increasingly vital task.[42]

The Border Patrol was created by the Immigration Act of 1924, a law better known for setting restrictive quotas for Asian and European immigrants. The official mission of the Border Patrol was simply to exclude "illegal aliens," but its enforcement efforts underwent several notable shifts in the unit's early years. At first, the unit was quite small, and focused its resources on excluding Asian and European immigrants attempting to enter the United States from Mexico. Soon, however, and lasting until the repeal of Prohibition in 1933, the Border Patrol concentrated chiefly on stemming the flow of alcoholic beverages smuggled across the border. Following the end of Prohibition, the unit devoted the bulk of its efforts to immigration enforcement directed against Mexicans, though the force was constrained by a lack of resources.[43] These activities marked the beginning of the ongoing, regular use of a federal police force to enforce legal residence criteria as a means of formally separating, and thus better controlling, Mexican immigrants and Mexican Americans. Henceforth the Border Patrol served to regulate the flow of Mexican undocumented immigrants into the country.

The Border Patrol's relationship with employers of Mexican laborers in the Southwest was by no means always a harmonious one. Over time, however, the two parties developed a de facto working relationship, whereby the Border Patrol came to act basically as the gatekeeper of the "revolving door." While immigration enforcement was inconvenient at times for employers, it also gave them a powerful means of control and discipline to wield over Mexican undocumented immigrant laborers: the looming threat of deportation by the Border Patrol.[44]

At the time of its inception the Border Patrol had a definite and consciously constructed paramilitary character, evidenced in features ranging from the design of its uniforms to the INS commissioner's militaristic characterizations of his force's activities in his early annual reports.[45] This is perhaps not surprising, given that the aforementioned U.S. military activities along the border had only recently concluded.[46] Significantly, many of the original members of the Border Patrol in Texas were former Texas Rangers, a distinctly paramilitary force, which had recently been very active in the border region.[47] Given the Rangers' past and recent record of brutality and violence against people of Mexican origin, this did not bode well for their human rights.

At a more general level, the human rights problems posed by immigration enforcement efforts aimed at Mexican-origin people are graphically illustrated by the treatment of Mexican immigrant workers following the onset of the Great Depression in 1929. Mexican workers, with a growing reputation as labor organizers and agitators, proved to be useful scapegoats for the economic crisis. An estimated 500,000 to one million Mexicans—many of them children born in the United States and thus U.S. citizens—were either deported outright or intimidated into returning to Mexico.[48] The deportation and "repatriation" programs were conducted by federal and local authorities, and were directed at virtually all people of Mexican appearance. The parent agency of the Border Patrol, the Immigration and Naturalization Service, conducted numerous raids throughout the Southwest in the early 1930s, which resulted in some 80,000 deportations by 1935. Most of the effort, however, took the form of locally organized "repatriation drives" in which Mexican immigrants were "officially encouraged" to leave the United States by local authorities.[49] The Jim Crow segregation system prevailing in many areas proved especially useful in carrying out the "repatriation drives," which were accompanied by gross civil and human rights violations that included the seizure and theft of Mexican residents' property. The sheer demographic effect of these actions was immense: between 1930 and 1940 the Mexican-born population in Texas dropped 40%.[50] These actions clearly qualify as a blatant instance of state repression against Mexican-origin people, particularly those in the border region.[51]

Following the massive deportation and "repatriation" campaign against Mexicans during the 1930s, the INS underwent a major change. With the Roosevelt administration anxiously monitoring the development of World War II, immigration and border enforcement came to be considered more as national security issues. Consequently, in 1940, the INS was transferred from the Department of Labor to the Department of Justice.[52] Over time the INS came to take on the character of other Department of Justice agencies such as the Federal Bureau of Investigation (FBI), becoming more secretive, deceptive, and propagandistic.[53] Shortly thereafter, with the entrance of the United States into the war, the country experienced an urgent labor shortage. In response, the "revolving door" of U.S. immigration policy and enforcement took another turn. This time the U.S. government reached an official agreement with the Mexican government in 1942 to import Mexican agricultural laborers, thereby establishing the Bracero Program, which was maintained through 1964 by periodic renewals of the agreement by the two governments.[54]

During the 1950s the "revolving door" of U.S. immigration enforcement policy swung again, however, back to the mass deportation of Mexican immigrants. Named "Operation Wetback," this effort was carried out in 1954. It was the first large-scale, systematic implementation of military strategy and tactics by the INS against Mexican immigrant workers. Thus, this episode merits extensive examination for the purposes of this monograph.

The context for the operation was formed by the convergence of several factors, including an economic recession in the United States during 1953, a rapid rise in INS apprehensions of undocumented immigrants in previous years, and tense political negotiations between the U.S. and Mexican governments over a new *bracero* agreement. The *bracero* negotiations resulted in much tension at the border. For example, in early 1954 U.S. officials undermined the Mexican government's bargaining position by unilaterally offering legal status to Mexican agricultural workers crossing the border, while Mexican military troops were deployed to prevent their crossing.[55] Several months later the U.S. role was reversed entirely.

During 1953 Attorney General Herbert Brownell and top INS officials began to devote serious attention to undocumented immigration, which for various reasons had been increasing despite the possibility of legal immigration available through the Bracero Program. The number of INS apprehensions of undocumented Mexican immigrants had jumped from 182,000 in 1947 to over 850,000 by the end of 1953.[56] Meanwhile, Southern California agricultural interests had begun to complain about the situation, and the national press picked up the issue, presenting it as a worsening crisis. The Border Patrol meanwhile appeared to be overwhelmed and in disarray. Amid this growing anxiety, one immigration official described the situation in starkly militaristic terms as "the greatest peacetime invasion ever complacently suffered by another country under open, flagrant, contemptuous violations of its laws."[57]

It was against this alarmist background that plans for Operation Wetback were drawn up. Various elements of militarism are clearly identifiable in the planning stage of the operation. For example, Attorney General Brownell initially sought to use U.S. Army troops to conduct the massive roundup and to patrol the border. However, U.S. Army officials balked at the plan, on the grounds that it would disrupt their programs and require too many troops—one division alone to control the immigrant influx and more to seal off the border.[58] Brownell also reportedly advocated an even more extreme method—allegedly suggesting to a group of U.S. labor leaders that "one method of discouraging wetbacks would be to allow the border patrol to shoot some of them."[59]

Although Brownell was unable to summon U.S. Army troops, he did manage to appoint a recently retired U.S. Army man, Lieutenant General Joseph Swing, as commissioner of the INS in May 1954. Interestingly, Swing's lengthy military career included participation in General Pershing's "punitive expedition" into northern Mexico against Pancho Villa in 1916. He brought with him to the INS two more former Army generals, who introduced military terminology and strategy in the planning and implementation of the operation and established an INS intelligence service as well. The overall result was that the agency began to operate with the "precision, timing, and efficiency of a trained military or semimilitary body."[60] The Border Patrol had been a paramilitary organization since its formation, but these efforts took this characteristic to new extremes.

Two military principles guided the reorganization of the Border Patrol for Operation Wetback: flexibility of organization and mobility of forces. The basic plans for the reorganization were hatched by a high-ranking, experienced Border Patrol official. The centerpiece tactic for Operation Wetback was the "mobile task force concept," according to which a "special mobile force" of some 400 Border Patrol agents aided by 75 auxiliary personnel (altogether ranging up to 750 staff at times) was to be concentrated in designated sectors containing high concentrations of "illegal aliens." Their basic tactics involved conducting mass roundups in these areas and working in concentric, widening circles to push the "aliens" across the border. Other Border Patrol agents conducted "mop-up operations" with support from aircraft, which helped to search out undocumented immigrants and direct ground units to their location. The operation was implemented in one targeted Border Patrol sector at a time over the course of several months, moving from west to east along the border. State and local law enforcement agencies were also enlisted in this effort. Another key tactic of the INS was a carefully orchestrated media and publicity campaign to intimidate undocumented Mexican immigrants

into fleeing the United States on their own, as the INS did not have sufficient personnel to conduct a comprehensive border sweep. The most
crucial, long-lasting internal changes stemming from Operation Wetback
were the reorganization of the Border Patrol and the enhancement of the
force's autonomy within the INS.[61] Perhaps the most important principle
evident in the Border Patrol's leading role in Operation Wetback is that
undocumented immigrants were treated in terms analogous to that of an
"enemy" to be repulsed and driven out.

The INS simultaneously took steps to appease politically powerful agricultural interests that were dependent on Mexican immigrant labor. A
special liaison from the Department of Labor was assigned to assist the
INS in efforts to ensure that growers had an adequate supply of Mexican
immigrant laborers through the Bracero Program. Top INS officials met
regularly with growers in the affected areas. The INS promptly legalized
many of the apprehended immigrants at the border, especially in Texas,
in order to ensure an adequate, "legalized" labor supply. However, grower
support for Operation Wetback was mixed. California and Arizona growers were mostly tolerant if not supportive, while their Texas counterparts
were more divided in their reactions. Many in the Lower Rio Grande Valley were quite resentful of the INS, and Valley newspapers were inflammatory in their opposition to the operation.[62] Nonetheless, the INS efforts directed toward the growers illustrate the true purpose of Operation
Wetback, and of INS enforcement activities in general: to regulate and
shape the flow of Mexican immigrant labor—not to prevent it.[63]

It is important to point out that the Mexican government, despite its
clashes with U.S. authorities at the border just five months earlier, fully
approved of this roundup campaign and in fact actively collaborated in
it. The Mexican government helped to ship deported Mexican citizens
away from the immediate border region to the interior via train and
boat, so as to prevent immediate border recrossings.[64] This change in
posture is largely attributable to the fact that a new *bracero* agreement
had been reached prior to the initiation of Operation Wetback. The
Mexican government felt that immigrant workers would be better protected and provided for under the Bracero Program than they would be
as undocumented immigrants.[65]

The quantitative results of Operation Wetback were massive, though
their exact dimensions are the subject of debate. It is impossible to determine precisely the number of actual apprehensions effected by the
INS forces involved in the roundup; estimates range from 107,000 to
164,000.[66] In contrast, the INS claimed that, in total, some 1.3 million

undocumented persons had been deported or had fled on their own from the United States to Mexico, although this claim is regarded by researchers as an exaggeration based largely on rough estimates of those who voluntarily fled out of fear.[67] At any rate, hundreds of thousands of Mexican immigrants were forced to leave the country in the face of a massive, military-style roundup campaign.

On the whole, Operation Wetback forcefully illustrated once again that Mexicans were welcome in the United States only as long as their labor was needed, and then only so long as their arrival was arranged by means of state mechanisms. Moreover, Mexican Americans were also negatively affected, because the operation graphically reinforced the principle of their having to be prepared at all times to prove their U.S. citizenship or face deportation. Those who were unable to provide proof of their U.S. citizenship or legal-resident status would be potentially subject to arrest and deportation.[68] At the very least, Operation Wetback was an assault on the dignity of Mexican immigrants and of Mexican-origin people more generally. Yet again they were the victims of state repression, this time carried out in a new, starkly militaristic manner and implemented by a single federal police agency. However, the stifling character of the larger U.S. political climate in the wake of the anticommunist hysteria fomented by the McCarthy purges was not conducive to protests against repressive immigration enforcement measures.[69]

Subsequent years were calmer in the border region, in that INS apprehensions of undocumented immigrants declined sharply. The Bracero Program expanded markedly during the remainder of the 1950s. Upon the termination of the program in 1964, the INS did not resume an aggressive enforcement posture toward undocumented immigration. Rather, the agency adopted a much lower profile in the border region and entered a period of waning influence within the U.S. governing apparatus until the mid-1970s.[70]

Social conflict in the border region continued, however, taking on new forms with the emergence in force of the Chicano civil rights movement during the 1960s and its expansion in the early 1970s. In many regards the multifaceted Chicano movement can be plausibly interpreted as a new, direct attempt to overturn the internally colonized status of Mexican-origin people in the U.S. Southwest. Much of this activity was based on a Chicano cultural nationalism focused on the reclamation of rights (and lands) long denied to Mexican Americans by the larger Anglo-dominated society. Many of the movement's most important events occurred in the border region—e.g., the legendary electoral victory in Crystal City, Texas, and the various farmworker organizing efforts and strikes in the Lower Rio Grande Valley. Further, the Raza Unida Party was based largely on appeals to Chicano cultural nationalism and enjoyed considerable support in the border region. The party garnered for its candidate some 18% of the vote in southern and western Texas counties in the 1972 Texas gubernatorial elections.[71] Though the Chicano movement declined during the second half of the 1970s for a variety of reasons, it was seen as a threat by authorities, as is evident in the substantial police efforts to infiltrate and disrupt Chicano organizations in the border region.[72] The anxiety of many Anglo authorities about the separatist tendencies in the Chicano movement led some Anglo elites to fear the emergence of an "American Quebec" in the Southwest.[73]

Shortly after the Chicano movement's high point of influence came the economic downturns and the energy crises of the middle and late 1970s. These structural economic problems were in turn accompanied by the reemergence of the "illegal alien problem." By the mid-1970s, INS apprehensions of undocumented immigrants began to approach the levels that had preceded Operation Wetback, while once again a military man was appointed to head the INS, this time the ex-general Leonard Chapman. He played an aggressive role in shaping an INS media campaign promoting the "illegal alien problem" as a national crisis.[74] With the politically combustible mixture of an economic crisis and undocumented immigration further coalescing by the late 1970s, it appeared that conditions were ripe for another episode of scapegoating and harsh immigration enforcement against Mexican-origin people.

To sum up, during the modern era border-region immigration enforcement efforts served to subordinate and regulate the flow of Mexican immigrant workers. Moreover, Mexican Americans were also often adversely affected by these endeavors. While the enforcement tactics used against Mexican-origin people during the modern era were far less coercive than those of the previous era of border pacification, they were still periodically severe and even militarized on occasion, typically during economic downturns. The Border Patrol became the main border police force during the twentieth century and focused most of its efforts (after the Prohibition era) on immigration enforcement against people of Mexican origin. The unit's paramilitary character and its autonomy were greatly expanded by the massive Operation Wetback of 1954. Subsequently, however, the Border Patrol's stature—and that of the INS—waned. More recently, the Chicano movement fundamentally altered the balance of political power in the border region. Nonetheless, undocumented Mexican immigration emerged once again in the middle and late

1970s as a prominent political issue, suggesting the possibility of a new round of escalated immigration enforcement measures in the border region. However, before turning to a detailed examination of contemporary patterns of immigration enforcement in the border region, it is necessary first to present an overview of the military doctrine that is used in this study as a comparative framework to interpret contemporary immigration and drug enforcement efforts in the U.S.–Mexico border region.

Low-Intensity Conflict: "A War for All Seasons"

This section provides a broad and critical overview of low-intensity conflict (LIC) doctrine, a sophisticated and far-reaching theoretical framework constructed by the U.S. military-security establishment.[75] The purpose is to provide sufficient background to develop an ideal type of low-intensity conflict doctrine and its associated practices, which can then be used throughout this monograph as a basis of comparison for analyzing contemporary immigration and drug enforcement efforts in the U.S.–Mexico border region. Sources drawn upon here include official LIC documents, military press reports, and critical analyses of the doctrine, which together provide extensive details and a variety of perspectives on this new U.S. military-security framework. This discussion is framed by an underlying concern for the status of human rights.

The potential relevance of LIC doctrine to the analysis of immigration and drug enforcement efforts in the U.S.–Mexico border region is suggested by at least two previously noted trends. First, there is a lengthy history of periodically severe, militarized enforcement measures initiated by the state against Mexican-origin people in the border region. Second, since the latter 1970s, forceful if not outright militarized enforcement responses have been implicitly suggested as necessary in the many characterizations, by government officials and the media, of undocumented immigration and drug trafficking as potential or actual threats to U.S. "national security." Likewise, it should be noted that the same two issues are listed by a prominent former U.S. military official as part of the broader agenda of U.S. national security interests in Latin America for which he feels LIC doctrine is the best-suited approach.[76] In order to discern whether militarized border enforcement measures have in fact been pursued to address these issues, the most useful military framework to draw upon is LIC doctrine, given the unconventional, multifaceted, and relatively subtle forms of militarization that it advocates as well as the importance it places on controlling targeted civilian populations.

Low-intensity conflict doctrine emerged in the early 1980s during the Reagan administration. It was crafted primarily as a means to counter revolutionary insurgencies in the third world, especially in Central America. However, the origins of LIC doctrine date back at least to the Kennedy administration's formulation of counterinsurgency doctrine, if not to much earlier U.S. involvement in a host of so-called small wars.[77] This form of militarization fell out of favor during the 1970s following the Vietnam War and ran counter to the views of most people in the U.S. military establishment, who were focused instead on large-scale conventional and nuclear warfare between the two superpowers, the United States and the Soviet Union. Nonetheless, during the early and middle 1980s LIC doctrine was developed and frequently implemented by various portions of the U.S. military and intelligence communities (especially the Central Intelligence Agency). By the late 1980s and early 1990s it had become a relatively institutionalized component of both the doctrinal-theoretical apparatus and the formal command structure of the U.S. military-security establishment, though currently the doctrine is still undergoing further refinement.[78]

The term *low-intensity conflict* is derived from the Pentagon's abstract division of the "spectrum of conflict" into three levels: high, medium, and low. Guerrilla wars and other relatively limited conflicts involving irregular units are labeled "low-intensity conflict"—although the impact of such conflicts can be quite devastating and violent for local populations.[79] This type of conflict is labeled "low" because of its implications for U.S. forces—namely, the avoidance of the sustained deployment in battle of U.S. troops and the U.S. casualties that would ensue, particularly in distant third-world conflicts. Moreover, LIC-doctrine measures are ideally to be employed in a preemptive or preventive fashion, to forestall the development of outright armed conflict within the "host" country.[80]

While LIC doctrine was crafted primarily as a U.S. strategy to counter revolutionary insurgencies in the third world, low-intensity conflict is a much broader concept, spanning the vast continuum of strife "ranging from relative peace to conventional war."[81] The U.S. Army's official definition of low-intensity conflict is exceptionally broad:

> Low-intensity conflict is a limited politico-military struggle to achieve political, social, economic, or psychological objectives. It is often protracted and ranges from diplomatic, economic, and psycho-social pressures through terrorism and insurgency. Low-intensity conflict is generally confined to a geographic area and is often characterized by constraints on the weaponry, tactics, and level of violence.[82]

This expansive and ambiguous characterization of low-intensity conflict applies to a wide variety of U.S. military actions. These include the invasions of Grenada (1983) and Panama (1989), the bombing of Libya (1986), underwriting and providing a wide range of support and "advisers" for counterinsurgency warfare in El Salvador (1980–1992), a broad array of support for a counterrevolutionary insurgency in Nicaragua (1980–1990), virtually continuous military training exercises in Honduras throughout the 1980s, antidrug military operations in Bolivia (1986), humanitarian-aid effort turned combat mission in Somalia (1992–1993), and many more activities. Thus, low-intensity conflict is indeed a "war for all seasons."[83] One important outcome of this broad-ranging conceptualization of the field of conflict is that military forces have become increasingly involved in matters that are not ostensibly military in nature.[84]

The principal concern of LIC doctrine has been with countering revolution (especially in Central America during the 1980s),[85] followed by a concern for maintaining social control in other unstable settings. Within these areas, there are three general focal points of LIC doctrine: (1) an emphasis on the internal (rather than external) defense of a nation, (2) an emphasis on controlling targeted civilian populations rather than territory, and (3) the assumption by the military of police-like and other unconventional, typically nonmilitary roles, along with the adoption by the police of military characteristics. Most importantly, this overall approach has frequently had a profoundly negative impact on the status of human rights for people in those contexts in which LIC doctrine has been implemented. These points become evident in a more detailed examination of LIC mission areas.

On the basis of his detailed study of the Pentagon's LIC documents, Klare specifies six principal LIC "mission areas":

1. *Foreign internal defense:* Counterinsurgency and related actions to aid governments allied with the United States in their efforts to combat insurgent threats.
2. *Proinsurgency:* The sponsorship and support of anticommunist insurgencies against third-world governments considered hostile to U.S. security interests.
3. *Peacetime contingency operations:* Short-term, rapid military activities taken in support of U.S. policy, such as show-of-force operations, rescue missions, and punitive strikes.
4. *Terrorism counteraction:* Defensive and offensive measures ("antiterrorism" and "counterterrorism," respectively) taken by the armed forces to prevent and counter terrorism.

5. *Antidrug operations:* The use of U.S. military resources to curb the flow of illegal drugs into the United States and to attack and destroy sources of illegal drugs in foreign countries.

6. *Peacekeeping operations:* The use of U.S. military forces to police cease-fires or to establish a buffer zone between hostile armies.[86]

Four of these mission areas merit additional elaboration for the purposes of this monograph, because they contain operational characteristics, and in some cases mission content, potentially applicable to border enforcement efforts. They are foreign internal defense, antidrug operations, terrorism counteraction, and peacetime contingency operations. An overview of them will enable the construction of an ideal type of LIC doctrine that can be used comparatively to examine key aspects of contemporary immigration and drug enforcement practices and policies in the U.S.–Mexico border region.

FOREIGN INTERNAL DEFENSE (COUNTERINSURGENCY)

Foreign internal defense is the most well-developed component of low-intensity conflict doctrine and is largely made up of counterinsurgency efforts,[87] most of which were set forth in the 1960s in counterinsurgency doctrine.[88] Consequently, the present discussion draws heavily upon analyses of that doctrine, and uses the terms "counterinsurgency" and "foreign internal defense" interchangeably. This LIC mission area is especially focused on countering revolutionary insurgent movements. While this topic is not directly relevant to the U.S.–Mexico border region, a detailed examination of LIC doctrine's counterinsurgency guidelines will illustrate key general characteristics of the overall framework, which in turn will be applied later in analyzing border enforcement efforts.

Counterinsurgency doctrine was originally formulated in the early 1960s by the Kennedy administration as a rather panicked response to the growth and success of revolutionary guerrilla insurgencies around the world—especially the Cuban Revolution of 1959. The principal threat of these movements, as perceived by U.S. policymakers through their Cold War interpretive framework, was their role in the worldwide spread of communism.[89] Counterinsurgency doctrine was constructed to have a distinctly internal focus—meaning that military and security forces came to view the *enemy within* the nation (e.g., internal subversives) as a grave threat to "national security" (broadly defined)—rather than the more traditional military focus on defense against external threats (e.g., foreign armies).[90] As a result, domestic civilian populations rather than geographic territory became the contested ground, as it were.[91] This approach entailed the development of elaborate internal-security infrastructures to conduct surveillance and coercive strike operations. While theoretically designed to be used selectively, these measures often led to widespread repression and human rights abuses, including, in a disturbing number of cases, "death squads"—the ultimate means of securing social control.[92]

Counterinsurgency efforts placed a particular emphasis on the "professionalization" of third-world militaries, whereby U.S. military advisers instructed their third-world counterparts in not only military matters but also virtually all aspects of social, economic, and political life. These broad categories of interest were all viewed as being intimately tied to a country's "national security," particularly the potential for communist subversion. This "new professionalism" led third-world militaries to intervene with increasing frequency in domestic politics and social issues in the name of "national security." The outcome of such interventions was particularly devastating in Latin America, where by the late 1970s military forces throughout the region had overthrown their own civilian governments and assumed the reins of state power for extended periods.[93] Thus, one crucial consequence of the United States' promotion of counterinsurgency doctrine and related concepts was the increased militarization of societies where it was implemented—again, typically justified in the name of "national security," which was conceptualized in all-encompassing, totalizing terms. Indeed, expanded "national security" considerations were so crucial that elaborate, far-reaching politico-military doctrines of the concept were developed by the United States and many of its Latin American allies during the Cold War.[94] However, U.S. policies and actions were by no means the sole cause of these militarizations, though they unquestionably played an instrumental role.[95]

A critical feature of foreign internal-defense activities is the integration of police, paramilitary, and military forces in a unified effort. Police forces are viewed as particularly vital in internal-defense efforts, because they act as a "first line of defense," and in many cases are better equipped than the military to gather intelligence and handle low levels of violence and subversion.[96] Consequently, during the 1960s, U.S. training programs were devised for third-world police forces, with the larger political goal of stopping communism. These efforts entailed a "professionalization" of police forces through training in administrative practices, communications and intelligence operations, riot-control methods, and (ominously) interrogation techniques, among other topics. The primary

U.S. program carrying out this police-training role during the era of counterinsurgency doctrine, the Office of Public Safety, was phased out in 1974, amid numerous allegations that it was linked to actions of political repression and state terrorism, and even to the actual administration of torture.[97] However, the U.S. training of Latin American police forces was begun again during the mid-1980s, justified this time in terms of antiterrorism.[98]

In general, foreign internal-defense efforts have typically been characterized by a complex combination of coercive activities and innocuous or even apparently benign measures intended to establish control over targeted civilian populations. At the more innocuous end of the continuum, common U.S.-promoted tactics have included increasing local police and military capabilities through training, aid, and equipment upgrades; promoting development through economic assistance; urging social and political reforms; and bolstering noncommunist unions, youth groups, and political parties.[99] Moreover, military and paramilitary forces have typically been involved not only in internal-security matters but also in "nation-building," often by working closely with civilian development officials in "military-civic action." The latter entails assistance by the military in development projects designed to provide basic services (particularly high-visibility projects such as visits to villages by military health-care personnel and the construction of community water systems), in order to build support for the military among the local civilian population.[100] According to leading LIC officials in the Pentagon, these efforts "may include military forces assuming functions normally the responsibility of the local government."[101] It is the elaborate combination of political, economic, social, psychological, and military tactics that led U.S. Army Colonel John D. Waghelstein, a commander of the U.S. military mission in El Salvador during the 1980s, to declare that low-intensity conflict is "total war at the grass-roots level."[102]

Despite the many seemingly benign and relatively subtle measures called for in LIC doctrine, it is important to reemphasize that actual implementations of foreign internal-defense efforts have frequently been accompanied by widespread human rights violations carried out against civilians by military and security forces, often with instrumental U.S. assistance.[103] These abuses have typically stemmed from zealous campaigns to eliminate or "neutralize" suspected "subversives" within the society. While in theory such coercive measures are to be employed selectively against suspected subversives, the category of potential subversives has often been defined in practice to include broad sectors of the civilian population (e.g., the peasants of an entire region, labor-union members, university students and youth in general, and members of reformist opposition political parties). Sweeping "national security" interests have typically been invoked to justify widespread repressive measures. On the whole, it is the complex combination of apparently contradictory measures—some relatively subtle and seemingly benevolent, others harshly coercive and repressive—directed toward various (and sometimes even the same) sectors of the civilian population that distinguishes foreign internal-defense efforts.[104] While foreign internal defense is the most developed mission area, LIC doctrine is a much broader framework.

ANTIDRUG OPERATIONS, TERRORISM COUNTERACTION, PEACETIME CONTINGENCY OPERATIONS, AND DOMESTIC FACETS OF LIC DOCTRINE

Antidrug operations are the most directly relevant LIC mission area for the U.S.–Mexico border region during the contemporary period, as drug enforcement has come to the fore there. The use of the military in antidrug efforts in general was greatly expanded following a 1986 National Security Decision Directive signed by President Reagan, which designated illegal drug trafficking as a threat to U.S. national security. This measure authorized the Department of Defense to become involved in a wide range of antidrug activities.[105] Antidrug operations constituted a new mission area for the military, one that was very much a law enforcement activity in which the military had little specific background or expertise. It also entailed the establishment of a new form of ongoing military collaboration with civilian law enforcement agencies and security forces, both domestic and foreign, as antidrug operations typically involved working with such agencies. However, the categorization of antidrug operations as also a military responsibility has often met with resistance from the military itself, especially prior to the end of the Cold War in 1989—usually with the rationale that such involvement would have a detrimental impact on military preparedness and combat readiness. In general, many sectors of the U.S. military were reluctant to become involved in an activity that was explicitly one of law enforcement. Nonetheless, LIC antidrug operations have had great "growth potential," particularly in the post–Cold War era as the military has groped to find new missions.[106] Overall, antidrug operations have become one of the more dynamic components of LIC doctrine, though their urgency seems to be especially subject to shifts in larger social, political, and military contexts (i.e., the Persian Gulf War). In conclusion, it should also be noted that antidrug operations by U.S. allies in Latin America have involved widespread human rights abuses.[107]

The next LIC-doctrine mission area of interest here is terrorism counteraction. As noted previously, official characterizations of terrorist threats have on occasion referred to the U.S.–Mexico border region, which suggests that the area could be a site for related countermeasures. Terrorism counteraction is defined by the Army as including all measures for the prevention of and defense against terrorist activities, as well as operations to combat terrorist groups and governments tied to them. Thus this mission area encompasses defensive and offensive operations (i.e., "antiterrorism" and the much more broad-ranging realm of "counterterrorism," respectively). It was also inspired by a National Security Decision Directive from President Reagan (signed in 1984), and likewise is a relatively new area of responsibility for the military.[108] It should be noted that terrorism was viewed as a very broad concept by the Reagan administration; its official task force on the topic defined it as "the unlawful use or threat of violence against persons or property to further political or social objectives."[109] This same task force's profile of potential terrorists was similarly sweeping: "Fully 60 percent of the Third World's population is under 20 years of age; half are 15 or less. These population pressures create a volatile mixture of youthful aspirations that when coupled with economic and political frustrations help form a large pool of potential terrorists."[110] In a related vein, one military analyst, assessing possible terrorist threats in the United States, predicted the rise of extremist groups that would "feed on the anger and frustration of recent Central and South American immigrants who will not realize their own version of the American dream."[111] These views of terrorism have implications for the U.S.–Mexico border region, because it is where the United States adjoins the third world, and it is a crossing point for millions of immigrants.

Peacetime contingency operations make up the fourth and final LIC-doctrine mission area considered here. This category is exceptionally broad and has a strong political emphasis. It illustrates the extent to which LIC doctrine appears to have been constructed to address almost any topic with security implications, which would seem to include border enforcement. Activities included in this mission area include the suppression of civil disorders and the maintenance of order; show-of-force (e.g., mass troop deployments to intimidate opponents) and strike force operations, as well as other means of "projecting power" rapidly; and intelligence-gathering missions. These operations often involve an integration of efforts between military and civilian agencies.[112] Implicit in this strategy is the notion that much of the world is threatened by endemic violence, and that the U.S. military's role is to act as an enforcer of global order so as to protect U.S. interests—however broadly these may be defined.[113]

U.S. military training exercises abroad are an important part of peacetime contingency operations, although such exercises often involve more than just training. Military exercises allow for the total preparation of the conflict area prior to the onset of hostilities, the cultivation of the support of nearby allies, or even the prevention of actual hostilities in the region (via a show of force). For example, frequent U.S. military exercises involving a wide variety of forces, especially National Guard units, were a particularly strong component of LIC efforts in Central America during the 1980s.[114] Further, the Army conducted 300 training exercises in Latin America during just one year in the late 1980s.[115]

It is important to note that activities that would appear to fall within the category of peacetime contingency operations have also been considered to have domestic applications in the view of some prominent Pentagon-commissioned planners. Military training exercises in the United States have been recommended by a key LIC proponent (see discussion below). In addition, one influential and relatively early Pentagon-commissioned report on LIC doctrine proposes that one of the three basic roles for the U.S. Army in low-intensity conflict is "the federal exercise of police power within the United States."[116] The same report also states in its working definition of low-intensity conflict that "low-intensity operations are not confined to overseas but may be necessary within the United States in response to civil disorder and terrorism."[117] It goes on to present several LIC scenarios, including one entitled "A U.S. City in Revolt," complete with a description of an implementation of military contingency measures. It envisions an armed urban uprising, based in Los Angeles, led by "a combination of poor and minority activist elements," to which the White House responds by sending in "regular Army units to restore order, disarm dissidents, and close all border traffic."[118] Similar domestic applications were not a conspicuous part of subsequent Pentagon formulations of LIC doctrine (at least not in those available to the public). Nonetheless, this scenario supports the notion that low-intensity conflict may indeed have implications for domestic U.S. law enforcement efforts, particularly in light of the military's role in quelling the 1992 Los Angeles riots.

Beyond this drastic scenario, there are additional domestic aspects of LIC doctrine. One of the most important of these is a special focus on the U.S. political scene—principally in the form of psychological operations to justify new forms of intervention abroad to a reluctant public at home.[119] This concern was of special relevance during the 1980s in the U.S.–Mexico border region, which was one of the primary sites of potential contact between U.S. citizens and refugees fleeing LIC policies in Central America. Another more ominous domestic focus of LIC was called for by a prominent proponent of LIC doctrine who essentially recommended domestic LIC military excercises to desensitize the U.S. citizenry to this form of militarization of society. Specifically, in 1985, U.S. Army Colonel John Waghelstein proposed:

> I think we've also got to begin to do counterinsurgency training here in the U.S., not just on military reservations where it's been for the last few years, but out in the countryside . . . in civilian areas. . . . [I]t gets the populace familiar with this type of warfare. . . . We've got to recondition our populace again, so that a soldier practicing for a war, for this type of war, is seen as a regular and necessary thing.[120]

A third component of LIC doctrine with domestic implications is the provision of so-called humanitarian aid, often by private-sector U.S. organizations (e.g., churches, relief organizations, and businesses). This "aid provider" role may also be undertaken by military and security forces. Such measures can play an important role in winning support for LIC policies among the host-nation population as well as among the U.S. public.[121]

In addition to the various LIC mission areas and operational characteristics discussed thus far, it is important to devote brief attention to the forces, equipment, and hardware used in low-intensity conflict. These are more tangible elements of LIC doctrine, whose presence in border enforcement efforts would provide some evidence that some portions of the doctrine have been implemented. In general, the military forces featured in low-intensity conflict are either elite troops (including Special Operations and Ranger forces, light infantry divisions, and the Marine Corps) or decidedly non-elite, "weekend warrior" troops (i.e., National Guard and reserve units).[122] The equipment used by such forces in low-intensity conflict, as well as the equipment prescribed specifically for antiterrorism efforts (a LIC concern), includes the following:

• A variety of helicopters (e.g., AH-1S Cobra gunships, UH-60 Blackhawks for transport, and OH-58Cs for reconnaissance)

- Small, pilotless, remote-controlled airplanes, which contain a small TV camera and forward-looking infrared (FLIR) night-vision sensors
- Seismic, acoustic, magnetic, and infrared electronic sensors, most of which were originally developed for use in the Vietnam War, to detect vibration, sound, and heat
- Night-vision goggles and infrared weapons sights
- Closed-circuit television systems for surveillance purposes
- Day and night imaging enhancement systems to determine the nature of intrusions detected by sensors
- The construction of chain-link fences to increase the effectiveness of guards and intrusion sensors[123]

LIC SUMMARY

The information on LIC doctrine presented above spans the definition and origins of the doctrine, its mission categories and related practices, and its forces and equipment. The purpose of this broad-ranging discussion has been to develop a detailed overview that would make possible the construction of an ideal type of low-intensity conflict doctrine and associated practices, to operationalize, roughly, the term "militarization" for use in this monograph. The following specific characteristics, which are based on the above discussion, will serve in this study as a rough outline of an ideal type of low-intensity conflict:

- Military equipment and hardware associated with low-intensity conflict and antiterrorism efforts
- Coordination, collaboration, and integration of police, intelligence, paramilitary, and, military forces and their areas of responsibility— i.e., the police acting more like the military and vice versa
- Expanded intelligence and surveillance efforts, and expanded communication systems
- The use of Special Operations Forces, light infantry divisions, and Marine units, as well as National Guard and reserve forces
- An emphasis on training efforts for local forces
- Military and paramilitary training exercises outside of military bases
- Increased contact by military, paramilitary, and police forces with civilians in benevolent, public-service activities
- Psychological operations to influence political and social attitudes among civilian populations
- Incorporation of so-called humanitarian aid—particularly that provided by private organizations—into military and police-related projects

- Various other operational characteristics of the four LIC mission areas discussed previously: foreign internal defense (counterinsurgency), antidrug operations, peacetime contingency operations, and terrorism counteraction

In this monograph, these criteria will serve as the specific basis for the comparison of LIC doctrine with contemporary immigration and drug enforcement efforts in the U.S.–Mexico border region.

In conclusion, it is crucial to emphasize the contradiction between the sophisticated and relatively subtle forms of militarization called for by LIC doctrine and the often widespread human rights violations accompanying the doctrine's implementation. Even in its abstract form, LIC doctrine greatly extends the reach of military-security apparatuses throughout society, thereby facilitating the militarization of society down to the grassroots level, carried out in order to control targeted civilian populations. This framework thus represents a more totalizing and insidious form of militarization, one which combines innocuous and often seemingly benign measures with harshly coercive tactics that are theoretically to be applied selectively. In practice, the coercive tactics have often been zealously and broadly applied, resulting in widespread human rights abuses. This troubling outcome has been frequently repeated during the implementation of LIC-style militarizations in societies throughout Latin America and elsewhere by their own military and security forces, often with instrumental U.S. assistance. Such abuses have been most prominent in foreign internal-defense efforts, the most developed mission area of LIC doctrine. These measures have often been justified in the name of furthering "national security" interests. Thus, the broad-ranging field of activity proposed in LIC doctrine, which ideally emphasizes relatively subtle forms of militarization, has in practice often included escalated coercive activities that negatively affect the status of human rights.

Conclusion

Analyzing immigration and drug enforcement in the border region in terms of a military framework, as proposed in this study, is an admittedly unconventional and imprecise project. Yet militarization is by no means an entirely unknown or irrelevant issue in the U.S.–Mexico borderlands. There is ample historical precedent for the use of harsh as well as militarized law enforcement practices in dealing with Mexican-origin people in the region. During the twentieth century, such efforts have most frequently been carried out in response to the issue of immigration. Moreover, in the contemporary era undocumented immigration and illegal drug trafficking have often been portrayed in the media and by key governmental officials as potential or actual threats—concentrated in the U.S.–Mexico border region—to U.S. "national security." The implication of these portrayals is that vigorous law enforcement and even military measures are necessary policy responses to such security threats. Whether and to what extent such courses of action have actually been undertaken has thus far not been widely considered. The purpose of the present work is to broach this topic. The thesis of this monograph is that the U.S.–Mexico region has been gradually militarized from 1978 through 1992, as a consequence of the broad range of measures adopted by U.S. government agencies to address the issues of undocumented immigration and illegal drug trafficking.

The invocation of "national security" concerns in discussions of immigration and drug issues, as well as in related proposals for expanded border enforcement measures, suggests that a military framework may have some relevance in examining such efforts. LIC doctrine is the most applicable framework in this regard, given its call for a sophisticated combination of police and military activities to effect social control over targeted civilian populations. Further, it should be remembered that although LIC doctrine is geared primarily for third-world settings, it is not devoid of domestic implications for the United States. More importantly, the implementation of LIC doctrine has often been accompanied by widespread human rights violations, typically justified as necessary for defending "national security." Thus, the prospect of some degree of LIC-style militarization in the U.S.–Mexico border region is also worthy of consideration due to its ominous implications for the status of human rights in the borderlands.

Nonetheless, some observers will undoubtedly object to a militarization-oriented analysis of border enforcement efforts as being inappropriate or even hyperbolic. Yet if this approach were categorically excluded from consideration, we would be less likely to recognize or examine key dimensions of important and subtle shifts in contemporary immigration and drug enforcement activities in the borderlands. Such an oversight would be especially unfortunate, given that these current border enforcement endeavors have by and large not been closely examined by conventional researchers. New approaches and new studies would seem to be in order, if for no other reason than to try to shed some light on these often overlooked topics. Moreover, it is important to consider the possibility that the implementation of relatively subtle forms of militarization associated with LIC doctrine could readily facilitate the later adoption of more obvious and coercive forms of militarization, many of which are also encompassed by LIC doctrine. Such possibilities have, up to this point, not been considered for the U.S.–Mexico border region. At the very least, the increased emphasis on immigration and drug enforcement in the border region, together with the linking of these topics to "national security" concerns, suggests that related border enforcement efforts should be examined closely, and that at least some consideration of militarization issues be kept in mind. This is not to suggest, however, that all immigration and drug enforcement efforts in the border region are likely to have been militarized, but rather that it is worthwhile to examine them closely in order to discern any militaristic characteristics, as per the previously specified criteria.

While militarization is the key idea framing this monograph, it is important to note some of the limitations of its use here. First of all, the scope and specifications of LIC doctrine are still evolving, and remain subject to much debate. Thus, the present discussion of this doctrine is necessarily somewhat uncertain and imprecise. Second, other important dimensions of militarization having obvious relevance for the border region are not covered here, primarily due to limitations of space and to the author's lack of expertise in these subjects. For example, as mentioned previously, the use of military rhetoric and ideologies in border enforcement is not probed in this monograph, except to present occasional examples of it. Also, more obvious manifestations of militarization in the border region—such as the historical development and modern concentration there of U.S. military forces, bases, weapons ranges, and other related facilities—are not investigated. Nor is the role of the U.S. military during the nineteenth century as the first enforcer of the border covered in the present work. These and other significant dimensions of militarization in the border region have yet to be adequately examined by scholars, but also exceed the scope of this monograph.

A second, more general category of limitations of this study should also be acknowledged. Primary attention here is devoted to bureaucratic policies and practices, which are treated critically as potential sources of social problems rather than taken at face value as simply means of addressing such problems. This approach is guided by a concern for the status of human and civil rights in an era of bureaucratization as well as by an interest in furthering the principle of public accountability of bureaucratic power structures. (One inherent limitation of this approach, however, is the difficulty of "decoding" bureaucratic data with regard to issues they were not necessarily intended to illuminate.) Further, this study does not adequately attend to how individuals and groups interpret, respond to, or resist the initiatives of powerful institutions. (See appendix 4 for further elaboration of these issues.) A more immediate limitation of this study is that immigration and drug enforcement on the Mexican side of the border receives only scant attention. Unfortunately, these important topics could not be probed here because of limitations of space and a general lack of access to relevant sources, at least for this researcher. However, they certainly merit research and investigation. In addition, this study does not take into consideration the wide variation in social and physical conditions that exists between various portions of the border region, but rather takes a *more general* border-wide (on the U.S. side) perspective.

Nonetheless, it is hoped that the present work provides some new information on and analysis of immigration and drug enforcement in the U.S.–Mexico border region, as well as the broader topic of militarization, and that this will help to stimulate broader debate and further research on these and related topics. To that end, the remainder of this monograph is structured as follows. Chapters 2 and 3 focus on border-region immigration enforcement policies and practices of the Immigration and Naturalization Service during the 1978–1992 period, as well as on that agency's general evolution and growth during that era. Each devotes particular attention to the agency's Border Patrol and Detention and Deportation units, as well as the construction undertaken and equipment deployed in the border region. The multiagency, broad-ranging War on Drugs as it was pursued from 1981 to 1992 in the southwestern border region is examined in Chapter 4. Special emphasis is given to joint efforts involving the U.S. military and civilian law enforcement agencies (especially the INS). At the end of the discussion of each designated chronological period, usually at the end of the chapters, the immigration or drug enforcement efforts previously examined are compared with the framework of LIC doctrine outlined in this chapter. Chapter 5 presents a summation of the aspects of LIC militarization found in border-region immigration and drug enforcement activities during the 1978–1992 period, and concludes with a discussion of the broader implications of border militarization. A brief epilogue follows, discussing the general trends of immigration and drug enforcement efforts in 1993 and 1994. The theoretical concepts and methodological assumptions informing this study are discussed in appendix 4.

2

The Immigration and Naturalization Service during the Carter and Reagan Administrations, 1978–1988

The period from 1978 to 1988 included two presidential administrations—one from each major U.S. political party—and was an era in which the U.S. political scene became profoundly more conservative. Principal attention is devoted in this chapter to examining INS immigration enforcement efforts during this period. In doing so, the emphasis is placed on the agency's Border Patrol and Detention and Deportation units, which—aside from Inspections (located at official ports of entry)—are arguably the two INS programs that most squarely focus on and directly affect the U.S.–Mexico border region. They are also the primary components of the largest division within the INS, the Enforcement Division.[1] Moreover, their activities provide the most visible evidence of INS attempts to effect social control over undocumented immigrants and, more broadly, over those suspected of being such (i.e., chiefly Mexican Americans). This is especially relevant for the analysis pursued here, because maintaining social control over targeted civilian populations is the essence of low-intensity conflict doctrine, as is noted in chapter 1.

In general terms, the INS was expanded enormously between 1978 and 1988 (see appendix 1). Total INS funding provided by Congress jumped 185%—from $283.1 million in 1978 to $807.8 million in 1988.[2] The number of personnel positions authorized by Congress for the agency increased 53% between 1978 and 1988, rising from 10,071 to 15,453.[3] By 1988, the Enforcement Division's congressional funding was 76% more and its congressionally authorized staffing level slightly higher than the congressionally appropriated funding and staff levels for the entire INS had been in 1978.

It is important to consider briefly the larger U.S. socioeconomic and political context within which immigration issues gained prominence during this period. As noted previously, the sense of urgency related to the undocumented immigration "problem" intensified during the mid-

1970s—spurred on by the emphatic claims of INS representatives, especially Commissioner Leonard Chapman, a former military general. By the latter part of the decade, the issue had taken center stage politically. One indication of the issue's growing importance was President Carter's prominent unveiling of his immigration proposals early in his administration, in August 1977. The proposals included a call to double the size of the Border Patrol.[4] Yet this latter proposal seemed somewhat ironic, given Carter's appointment of Leonel Castillo as the first Mexican American in the institution's history to head the INS.[5] The proposed measures were put on hold in 1978, however, when Carter established a "blue-ribbon" commission to examine immigration issues: the Select Commission on Immigration and Refugee Policy. In the course of its deliberations and investigations, immigration issues were largely constructed in terms of border control and national security.[6] Indeed, the commission's final report framed immigration and refugee policy in terms of the "national interest"—which, though only vaguely defined, appears to be roughly analogous or at least directly related to the concept of national security—and its recommendations had a strong law enforcement emphasis.[7]

As the U.S. economy went into a severe recession during the late 1970s and early 1980s, and INS apprehensions in the U.S.–Mexico border region continued to increase in number, the notion of "regaining control of our borders" became more salient and politically expedient. The issue was portrayed in hysterical terms at times and, more generally, its promotion followed the timeworn U.S. political practice of scapegoating Mexican immigrants for U.S. economic crises.[8] This approach once again obscured the underlying causes of both the economic crisis and undocumented migration.

Probably the single event most important in crystallizing a crisis mentality regarding immigration issues and in framing subsequent debates over U.S. immigration policy was the 1980 Mariel Cuban boatlift. This boatlift brought some 125,000 refugees from Cuba to Miami in the spring of 1980.[9] It was presented with much drama in the U.S. media, particularly in television broadcasts, which showed what appeared to be an uncontrollable wave of immigrants pouring into the country during a very short time. Also during 1980, approximately 15,000 to 40,000 Haitian refugees arrived by boat in South Florida.[10] However, they were treated much more harshly by U.S. officials than were the Mariel refugees.[11] These mass international migrations with political overtones are significant by almost any standard. Yet politically inspired mass international migration was by no means without precedent during the same approximate period in U.S. history. For example, tens of thousands of refugees from Indochina (the so-called boat people) fled their homelands and were allowed to enter the United States following the end of the Vietnam War in 1975.

The Mariel boatlift, however, was seized upon by advocates of stricter immigration policy and used as an example of the type of crisis threatening the United States due to its "weak" immigration policy and "lax" border enforcement. Subsequently immigration issues rapidly gained political ascendancy and in 1986 reached a high point with the passage of the far-reaching Immigration Reform and Control Act (IRCA). Thus, the 1978–1988 decade is a crucial period for the examination of INS immigration enforcement activities and policies.

Before proceeding, a brief organizational overview is in order. This chapter, which is structured chronologically by presidential administration (Carter's and Reagan's, respectively), examines primarily immigration-related policies and practices of the INS in the U.S.–Mexico border region from 1978 through 1988. Similar INS activities under the Bush administration (1989–1992) are covered in the following chapter. At the conclusion of each chronological (presidential administration) section, INS activities are analyzed in relation to the framework of low-intensity conflict doctrine outlined in chapter 1.

The INS during the Carter Administration, 1978–1980

The growing political salience of immigration issues was accompanied by changes in INS enforcement efforts during the latter years of the Carter administration. These changes are important to briefly note, for they marked the initiation of a buildup process that was to accelerate under succeeding administrations. Emphasis was placed primarily on equipment upgrades and enhancements (see appendix 3), while personnel increases were more modest. Some aspects of these trends coincided with characteristics of low-intensity conflict doctrine (which had yet to be developed and was still known as counterinsurgency doctrine during this period), especially in the realm of equipment and hardware. These trends were consistent with the representation—increasingly frequent during this period—of undocumented immigration as a threat to national security. They occurred against the backdrop of an expansion in INS resources, which included a 24% increase in funds (to some $351.3

million) from 1978 to 1980, and an 8.7% increase in the total number of authorized staff positions (to 10,943) during the same period.[12]

EQUIPMENT AND CONSTRUCTION
INCREASES IN THE BORDER REGION

INS equipment enhancements from 1978 to 1980 included high-technology equipment as well as less sophisticated hardware for immigration enforcement. A graphic example of the latter are the sections of 10-foot-high chain-link fence (the so-called tortilla curtain) erected on the border in areas with high rates of undocumented crossings. These sections of fence were constructed as an upgrade and expansion of previous fences in portions of the El Paso, Chula Vista (San Diego), Yuma, and Tucson Border Patrol sectors.[13] Examples of more sophisticated equipment used in immigration enforcement are numerous. From 1978 through 1980 the Border Patrol employed two helicopters in its Chula Vista sector, and used small fixed-wing aircraft in all nine of its sectors along the U.S.–Mexico border.[14] Electronic intrusion-detection ground sensors and transmitters originally deployed at strategic locations during 1973 and 1974 were replaced and (apparently) upgraded in two Border Patrol sectors (Del Rio and Laredo) during 1979, and the same was scheduled for four others (Yuma, Marfa, El Paso, and McAllen) before 1981.[15] Closed-circuit television systems were installed during 1979 in five border-region detention facilities to improve internal and perimeter security.[16] Further, new construction was begun to expand the capacity of the Port Isabel, Texas, detention center.[17] In addition, research to evaluate the impact and effectiveness of various radar and infrared detection systems for the Border Patrol was initiated during this period. Some of these systems were apparently already in use to a limited extent, and the INS wanted to obtain more of them.[18] Overall, it appears that a number of substantial moves were made to maintain, increase, and upgrade INS immigration enforcement equipment in the border region.

DETENTION AND DEPORTATION TRENDS

Staffing levels for the Detention and Deportation program were not favored with the same type of support between 1978 and 1980 as was provided for technological hardware and fences. The number of Detention and Deportation staff remained virtually constant, although the funding level increased by 27% (see appendix 1). During the same period, the number of immigrants who were detained declined by 29%, to 243,087 people in 1980 (see appendix 2).[19] This is due in part to the fact that the Cuban Mariel refugees were not formally considered detainees in 1980 but rather refugees, although many were detained for varying periods in various facilities—including several U.S. military bases at which there was some detainee unrest over inadequate camp conditions and lack of due process—and were supervised by INS staff. Meanwhile, the average length of stay in detention was fairly constant, falling slightly from 2.7 days in 1979 to 2.4 days in 1980.[20]

The INS apparently operated four full-time detention centers—El Centro, California; Port Isabel and El Paso, Texas; and New York City—while other facilities were used on a temporary basis.[21] Approximately 60% of the detainees were held in INS facilities, while the remainder were held in state and local jails. The number of immigrant expulsions carried out by the INS during the 1978–1980 period, while still large in historical terms, fell 23%, to 736,474 (see appendix 2).[22] In addition to the staff and resources diverted to the Mariel boatlift, deportation and detention activities were further limited due to the fact that the INS scaled back its overall immigration enforcement operations during the 1980 census count (in order to allow for a more complete count of all residents of the United States, including undocumented immigrants).[23]

Despite the generally large numbers of people detained, the INS detention criteria for undocumented immigrants was relatively low-key in comparison to what would later become the norm during the Reagan administration. Specifically, INS Commissioner Leonel Castillo stated that the purpose of detaining undocumented immigrants was not to punish them, but rather to ensure that they would be available for deportation and expulsion proceedings, and also to care for their welfare.[24] Only those who were deemed a threat to public safety or likely to abscond were to be detained.

THE BORDER PATROL

The Border Patrol was expanded slightly in terms of personnel between 1978 and 1980, while its funding was increased less significantly. However, this unit also experienced a temporary decline in its traditional immigration enforcement activities due to various larger political factors. The number of Border Patrol positions authorized by Congress increased from 2,580 in 1978 to 2,694 in 1980 (a 13% increase). There was strong sentiment in Congress for a much greater expansion, but the Carter administration opted to delay significant increases in Border Patrol staff until the Select Commission on Immigration and Refugee Policy had presented its findings and recommendations. Meanwhile, Border Patrol congressional funding was expanded by 6% from 1979 to 1980, to some $82.6 million (see appendix 1).[25]

During the same period, the number of Border Patrol apprehensions of undocumented immigrants dropped 13% (see appendix 2), although the absolute number was still high in comparative historical terms. As was the case for the Detention and Deportation program, the Mariel refugees were not included in this count. Also, the decline in apprehensions was in large part due to the diversion of personnel and resources to handle the Mariel influx, as well as to the deliberate reduction of apprehension activity by the Border Patrol during the 1980 census count.[26] At the same time, Border Patrol enforcement efforts were no doubt enhanced somewhat by the expansion of INS intelligence activities when the agency joined INTERPOL in 1979, which enabled it to consult with law enforcement officials in 136 countries.[27] Another intelligence effort that had implications for the Border Patrol was the INS's participation in the multiagency El Paso Intelligence Center (EPIC), which was administered by the Drug Enforcement Agency (DEA). In addition, the INS intelligence unit maintained coordination and liaison relations with a variety of other federal agencies, including the FBI, CIA, Customs Service, Coast Guard, Secret Service, DEA, and the Department of Defense.[28] As the main enforcement arm of the INS, the Border Patrol was likely to have been a principal beneficiary of these various INS intelligence efforts.

Beyond the Mariel boatlift and the 1980 census, one particularly noteworthy political constraint on Border Patrol activities was the negative fallout from incidents of Border Patrol mistreatment of undocumented immigrants, which came to light in the national press.[29] An exchange that occurred during a 1980 congressional hearing is revealing. Acting INS Commissioner David Crosland was questioned about the recent convictions of two Border Patrol agents for civil rights violations against undocumented immigrants. The convictions came as a result of the discovery of an "organized brutality ring" made up of Border Patrol agents. Crosland responded: "We are not satisfied that this was an isolated incident and do not believe that this one case will serve as an adequate deterrent to others whose activities are less than professional."[30] It appears from this candid admission, as well as from other evidence, that violations of undocumented immigrants' civil rights by Border Patrol agents were indeed not "isolated incidents," but instead rather commonplace.[31]

The publicity surrounding those abuses damaged the political image of the Border Patrol, but not enough to stem the growing tide of restrictionist sentiment favoring an expansion of the unit.

THE LIC FRAMEWORK APPLIED TO INS POLICIES AND ACTIVITIES DURING THE CARTER ADMINISTRATION

On the whole, during the latter portion of the Carter administration the INS underwent significant qualitative changes that enhanced its immigration enforcement capacity in the U.S.–Mexico border region, while experiencing modest levels of growth in its enforcement resources— despite a worsening economy and mounting federal budget constraints. Several aspects of INS efforts during this period coincide with elements of the LIC framework, especially in the areas of technology and equipment. For example, electronic sensors, infrared radar, helicopters, closed-circuit television monitoring, and even fence barriers are prescribed LIC hardware. Also, the INS actions of joining INTERPOL, participating in the multiagency El Paso Intelligence Center, and maintaining intelligence liaison relations with a wide variety of federal security, police, and military agencies all fall within the realm of the LIC operational emphasis on expanding intelligence systems and increasing the level of integration and cooperation among intelligence, police, and paramilitary organizations. Furthermore, apart from the LIC framework, the use of military bases to hold and process Cuban refugees from the Mariel boatlift represents an instance of the militarization of immigration enforcement. At the very least, it seems clear that the use of military-related technology against civilian populations (undocumented immigrants in this case) in the course of immigration enforcement in the U.S.–Mexico border region was on the rise. Such moves are consistent with the fact that undocumented immigration was becoming a more politically salient issue, one often colored by national security concerns—e.g., the notion that "our borders are out of control"—particularly in the wake of the massive 1980 Mariel boatlift.

The INS during the Reagan Administration, 1981–1988

The expansion of the INS was taken to an unprecedented level during the Reagan administration, as the urgency surrounding immigration and "border security" topics became even greater during this period. The issue of undocumented immigration, in particular, galvanized the political sentiment for "regaining control of our borders," which climaxed in the passage of the Immigration Reform and Control Act of 1986, or IRCA. Moreover, the Reagan administration at times starkly framed the topic of undocumented immigration as a national security issue—e.g., invoking images of "tidal waves" of refugees and of terrorist infiltration across the U.S.–Mexico border. This alarmist approach was intimately related to Reagan's aggressive, interventionist foreign policy in Central America (see chapter 1). Following the passage of IRCA, "border security" concerns shifted to addressing the issue of illegal drug trafficking, although drug and immigration enforcement activities were frequently intermingled. Thus, during this era the issues of drugs and terrorism (both prominent in LIC doctrine), as well as fears of an uncontrollable flow of refugees, were key elements of the rhetorical political climate that helped to foster an enormous expansion of the INS.

The passage of IRCA was the principal political event of direct consequence for the INS during the Reagan administration, as the INS was charged with implementing the new law. Although a full discussion of the legislation and the many issues surrounding it is beyond the scope of this monograph, several key points bear mentioning. The primary intention of IRCA was to reduce drastically undocumented immigration into the United States. This goal was to be accomplished via a "carrot-and-stick" approach. The "stick" took the form of expanded enforcement efforts, principally sanctions against employers who hired undocumented immigrants as well as increased enforcement activity in the border region. The "carrot" consisted of extensive amnesty and legalization programs for undocumented immigrants, which some three million people (the vast majority of them Mexican) took advantage of. Much attention has been devoted elsewhere to the "carrot" aspects of IRCA as well as to the employer-sanctions portion of the "stick."[32] This monograph focuses on a largely neglected dimension of the "stick," namely, INS immigration enforcement efforts in the U.S.–Mexico border region.

The expansion of the INS during the Reagan administration is readily apparent at a general quantitative level. Congressional appropriations for the agency jumped 130% in funding and 41% in the number of staff positions authorized from the close of the Carter administration in 1980 through the end of the Reagan administration in 1988, arriving at $807.8 million and 15,453 staff posts (see appendix 1).[33] A large portion of these increases in resources went to the Enforcement Division, which garnered the equivalent of 60% of the new funds and 82% of the new staff positions allocated to the INS by Congress from 1982 through 1988.[34] In addition, congressional appropriations were supplemented substantially in 1987 and 1988 by funds from two newly imposed user fees, one for inspections and another for applications under the IRCA legalization program.[35] Collectively, these new fees generated $137.3 million and 1,534 staff positions in 1987 and $280.7 million and 2,831 staff posts in 1988.[36] These fees added to the INS's congressionally appropriated funding by the equivalent of 21% in 1987 and 35% in 1988, and to congressionally funded staff levels by some 10% in 1987 and 18% in 1988. Thus, the INS financed some of its high-profile, more service-oriented activities with user fees, while congressional support was largely devoted to the agency's enforcement efforts. In addition to these large-scale quantitative increases, the INS also implemented numerous, far-reaching qualitative innovations in its border enforcement efforts, which are detailed in this section.

EQUIPMENT AND CONSTRUCTION
INCREASES IN THE BORDER REGION

Enhancing the amount and quality of infrastructure was a primary focus of the INS expansion process throughout the Reagan administration (see appendix 3). During Reagan's second term (1984–1988), the introduction of new equipment was increasingly justified in terms of furthering the INS's drug enforcement efforts, though much of it also aided immigration enforcement activities. As noted above, drug and immigration enforcement efforts often coincided, such that much of the same equipment was used for both.

Some of the more notable new equipment introduced during the Reagan administration consisted of sophisticated high-tech air-support resources. Most importantly in this category, the number of helicopters increased from two placed in just one Border Patrol sector at the close of the Carter administration in 1980, to nine in five sectors by 1982, and to twenty-two in all nine border sectors by 1988.[37] Most of these were OH-6 spotter-observation helicopters on loan from or donated by the U.S. Army. However, they were used for more than observation and detection: for example, during 1981 they were also employed as a means of intimidating undocumented immigrants with aerial spotlights and loudspeakers, in order to deter them from crossing the border.[38] One particularly noteworthy portion of the expansion in the helicopter fleet was the 1988 acquisition of five new A-Star 350-B helicopters, each with a carrying capacity of seven people. These sophisticated helicopters were outfitted with "Nite Sun" searchlights and forward-looking infrared radar (FLIR), which had heat-sensing capabilities enabling nighttime surveillance and detection. They were intended for use in supporting "special operations, such as BORTAC [a particularly paramilitary special Border Patrol unit, discussed later], drug interdiction, and alien smuggling surveillance."[39] The helicopter fleet's total flight hours grew from 4,487 hours in 1982 to over 6,757 hours in 1983.[40] The INS also maintained a fixed-wing aircraft fleet, which grew from 28 to 46 planes between 1981 and 1988.[41] The combined total of flight hours for fixed-wing aircraft and helicopters exceeded 30,000 in 1986 for the third straight year.[42] Thus, by the end of the Reagan administration the INS had greatly expanded its air support resources, most of which were used to aid the Border Patrol.

Other types of sophisticated equipment, in addition to aircraft, were expanded, upgraded, or introduced. For example, various detection systems and hardware were substantially upgraded in quality and increased in quantity during the Reagan administration. Under the Carter administration the INS added only seven night-vision scopes to the 59 it already owned. In contrast, during the Reagan administration the INS ordered 278 new night-vision scopes (for a total of 344) and greatly increased its diversity and technological level by introducing night-vision goggles, large tripod-mounted "starlite" and infrared scopes, and vehicle-mounted infrared telescopes with remote-imaging capabilities.[43] In addition, the replacement and apparent upgrading of electronic intrusion-detection ground sensor systems, which was begun by the Carter administration in two Border Patrol sectors, was carried out in four more Border Patrol sectors by 1982 and was scheduled to be completed in three additional Border Patrol sectors by 1984.[44] Further, portions of six of the nine southwestern Border Patrol sectors were also either outfitted with or scheduled to soon have installed low-light-level television surveillance systems to detect nighttime undocumented crossings over key sections of the border.[45] Moreover, the INS continued a joint research project with the U.S. Air Force to develop a two-mile-long linewatch sensor system, while also working with the U.S. Army to develop new varieties of infrared night surveillance equipment.[46] In addition, communications equipment was markedly upgraded. For instance, microwave communications systems to be used in Texas and Southern California were developed jointly by the INS and the Federal Aviation Administration.[47] And the INS reportedly deployed a new intrusion-data collection-

and-processing system that also included automatic dispatching—Computer Assisted Detection and Reporting Enhancement (CADRE)—in all nine Border Patrol sectors by 1986.[48]

Construction activities were another major growth area for the INS during the Reagan administration, and they likewise reflected an emphasis on border enforcement. For example, some 22 Border Patrol stations and four traffic-inspection checkpoints in the border region were either constructed, scheduled and fully funded, or at least planned and awaiting action. Most of these projects involved rebuilding and expanding existing structures. In addition, two detention centers (at El Centro, California, and Port Isabel, Texas) were expanded, two new ones (at San Pedro, California, and Oakdale, Louisiana) were under construction, and a former prison (in Florence, Arizona) was outfitted as a third new detention center.[49] That so much construction took place in the southwest border region (and nearby) suggests that this was the agency's geographical focus for immigration enforcement.

Overall, the equipment and construction increases during the Reagan administration were substantial. It seems clear that the Border Patrol was the primary beneficiary of this largesse, for it was the main user of the helicopters, intrusion-detection and surveillance hardware, and many of the communications systems, as well as of the refurbished and new Border Patrol stations and traffic-inspection checkpoints. The Detention and Deportation program appears to have been the second principal beneficiary, as it received several new or expanded facilities. In contrast, equipment and construction for INS service-oriented programs were rarely mentioned during the Reagan years in the voluminous annual INS budget documents submitted to Congress, which seems especially curious given the massive, high-profile legalization programs mandated by IRCA. These trends in equipment provision and new construction reflect the agency's priorities, namely, enforcement over service.

DETENTION AND DEPORTATION TRENDS

A number of important changes took place in the policies and practices of the Detention and Deportation program, which in turn led to substantial growth in the program during the Reagan administration. The expansion is most evident in its budget and staff increases: from 1980 to 1988, congressional appropriations for the Detention and Deportation program's budget jumped approximately 191%, to $128.8 million, while the number of staff increased by 47%, for a total of 1,623 personnel (see appendix 1), with most of the latter increase occurring in a single year, 1986–1987.[50]

Undergirding this expansion was a historic change in INS detention policy enacted in the early part of the Reagan administration. Previously, from 1954 until July 1981, the INS followed a general policy of releasing undocumented immigrants while their immigration cases were pending, thereby avoiding "needless confinement," unless the immigrants were considered a threat to national security or likely to abscond.[51] In an insidious turn, however, detention came to be seen instead as a punitive means of deterring undocumented immigration, especially by people from countries allied with the United States who sought to apply for political asylum. The criteria for political asylum had just recently been broadened considerably under the 1980 Refugee Act, but the Reagan administration sought to restrict or even reverse this change. As Attorney General William French Smith remarked in July 1981, "Detention of aliens seeking asylum was necessary to discourage people like the Haitians from setting sail in the first place."[52] In a related vein, INS Commissioner Alan Nelson indicated that the INS had expanded its detention practices to now include long-term detention.[53]

This use of detention as punishment to deter unwanted immigration stands in stark contrast to the prior emphasis on using short-term detention to safeguard immigrants' well-being, as outlined by former INS Commissioner Leonel Castillo (noted previously). Under the Reagan administration, the detention of immigrants (especially political asylum applicants) seems to have been consciously crafted as a form of punishment. It is important to note here that undocumented immigration is a misdemeanor offense,[54] which makes the Reagan administration's harsh detention policy seem all the more onerous, especially considering that it was also punishing those who had already fled persecution elsewhere.

Most undocumented immigrants, however, were unaffected by this policy change, because the vast majority were Mexicans, who were typically returned promptly across the border, without formally being deported. Nonetheless, this fundamental shift in INS detention policy affected many immigrants. The use of detention as a punitive measure to deter Haitians from migrating and applying for political asylum set an ominous precedent for the subsequent treatment of Central American refugees by the INS during the Reagan administration.[55] Through the early and mid-1980s, Haitian and Central American refugees—who were fleeing repression carried out by military and security forces that were allied with right-wing, anticommunist governments supported by the Reagan administration in its Cold War geopolitical agenda—were the most notable targets of the new explicitly punitive INS detention policy.[56] This punitive detention policy was later applied even against children from these countries, for by 1984 the INS began holding "unaccompanied minors" in various districts along the border—a practice that sparked outcries by human and civil rights advocates but nevertheless continued through 1992.[57] The hard-line detention approach was further expanded in scope and applied to different groups following the passage of IRCA and various anti–drug-trafficking bills in the later 1980s, measures that charged the INS with apprehending and detaining "criminal aliens," especially drug offenders (see chapter 3).

These harsh and highly politicized detention policies were paralleled in the political asylum process. In 1988, the Los Angeles Federal District Court found that the INS had systematically coerced refugees from El Salvador (whose government was a key anticommunist U.S. ally in Central America) into not applying for political asylum.[58] In contrast, during 1987 Attorney General Meese had established procedures to give special consideration to political asylum applicants from Nicaragua (whose government the Reagan administration actively sought to overthrow).[59] Overall approval rates for asylum applicants from Central America reflected the Reagan administration's Cold War geopolitical biases. From 1984 through 1988, annual approval rates ranged from 2% to 4.5% for Salvadorans, from 0.3% to 5% for Guatemalans (whose government was also a U.S. ally), and from 8.5% to 84% for Nicaraguans (the higher figures coming after Meese's policy shift for Nicaraguan cases).[60]

A key development accompanying the shift on the part of U.S. authorities toward viewing detention primarily as a form of punishment was an increase in the number of detention facilities used by the INS. For example, the number of INS facilities went from five in 1982 (three on the Southwest border) with a 1,720-person total capacity, to eight by 1988 (four on the Southwest border), with a ninth on the way (also in the Southwest). This gave the INS a normal detention capacity in 1988 of at least 3,239 persons in its own facilities, and an emergency capacity of 8,239 persons.[61] In addition, the INS maintained an unspecified number of temporary detention holding areas (so-called service staging areas), and a temporary detention center at Fort Allen in Puerto Rico to hold Haitians.[62] Of special interest among the INS detention centers is the massive Oakdale, Louisiana, facility, which had a 1,000-bed base capacity and an extra 5,000-person emergency capacity. This was a joint detention center–prison shared by the Bureau of Prisons and the INS, which the INS hoped would free up fast-filling, crowded detention space in the Southwest. These plans were temporarily set back, however, by a 1987 uprising at the Oakdale facility of some 1,000 Mariel Cuban detainees (who were long-term prisoners with little prospect of being released), which rendered the prison unusable for a time.[63]

Further, the INS began novel programs to cut labor costs and to expand its detention capacity by contracting with private security companies to provide guards for INS detention centers as well as to run entire detention facilities—practices that raised the issue of the legality of giving private security guards formal authority over INS detainees who were public charges.[64] Seven private-contract detention facilities were under contract with the INS at various points during the mid-1980s, all in the Southwest, which gave the INS an additional detention capacity of 940 persons.[65] Significantly, the INS was also able in some instances to use volunteer-agency housing for detention purposes.[66] Also, in order to cut costs, the INS continued its long-standing and questionable practice of enlisting detainees to provide labor in the detention centers for virtually no pay ($1 a day).[67]

Thus by 1988 the combined detention capacity of the INS's detention centers and private-contract facilities appears to have been approximately 4,200 persons under normal conditions and 9,200 persons under emergency conditions at some 15 sites.[68] In addition, the INS continued its practice of using state and local jails to hold immigrant detainees. For example, over 900 jails were used in 1984, although this number declined to 600 by 1987. Overall, the percentage of INS detainees held in non-INS facilities rose from 37% in 1982 to 53% in 1985, before declining to 45% in 1988 (which was still higher than the 40% of the Carter years).[69] Meanwhile the total number of people detained annually fell approximately 65% during the 1981–1988 period, to 92,799 in 1988, but the average length of a detention stay climbed from 3.6 days to 15.2 days during the same period (see appendix 2).[70] It seems that these statistics include the long-term Mariel Cuban detainees.[71]

Although it is difficult to determine the meaning of these contradictory trends solely on the basis of aggregate data, some tentative interpretation is possible. The dramatic increase in the average length of a detention stay was consistent with the Reagan administration's repressive view of detention as a form of punishment, while the decrease in the number of detainees was not. The two trends were probably related, however, as those detained tied up detention space for longer periods of time, leaving less space available to detain others. Furthermore, the INS clearly lacked the resources to strictly enforce a repressive policy at all times in all border areas. Rather, the severity of INS detention practices varied widely across its various districts along the border, depending largely on the availability of detention space and immediate budget resources.[72] Another likely mitigating factor was that some 95% of those apprehended in the U.S.–Mexico border region were Mexicans, who could thus be quickly expelled.

On the whole, detention was a "growth industry" for the INS during the Reagan administration. The administration adopted a hard line on detention, establishing it as a form of punishment for non-Mexican undocumented immigrants and would-be applicants for political asylum. In implementing the administration's policy, the INS devoted ever increasing budget and staff resources to the detention and deportation process. The INS notably expanded its own detention facilities and broadened its supplemental places of detention beyond the regular use of state and local jails to include sites administered by private contractors and even charity organizations. These trends have a number of unsettling implications, particularly the use of jailing as a deterrent to political asylum applications and the evolution of an immigration agency into a quasi prison bureau. This is especially disturbing when it is recalled that undocumented immigration itself is a misdemeanor offense.[73]

THE BORDER PATROL

The Border Patrol also experienced enormous growth and numerous qualitative enhancements during the Reagan era, in addition to the previously noted acquisition of an array of sophisticated equipment. From 1980 through 1988 the number of congressionally appropriated Border Patrol staff positions increased some 90% and congressional funding for the unit jumped 149%, reaching 5,530 staff positions and $205.3 million by 1988 (see appendix 1).[74] The Border Patrol accounted for 27% of the INS funding increases and 58% of the INS staff increases appropriated by Congress during the Reagan administration. The 50% jump in authorized staff positions from 1986 to 1987 was the result of the 1986 passage of IRCA, which mandated that the Border Patrol's personnel level be increased by 50%.[75] As of 1988, approximately 85% of all congressionally authorized Border Patrol positions were assigned to sectors along the U.S.–Mexico border.[76] The unit's exceptional growth further enhanced its long-standing dominant claim on INS resources.

It is important to point out, however, that the number of Border Patrol positions appropriated by Congress and the number of Border Patrol positions actually filled varied considerably. For example, in the case of the congressionally authorized positions that were assigned to the border region, the percentage of staff posts actually filled fluctuated from 94% in 1985 to 102% in 1986 to 87% in 1990.[77] Even under ideal conditions, the hiring and training of a large number of new agents takes a significant amount of time. And the Border Patrol experienced less than ideal conditions in this regard. (See chapter 3 for further discussion of this topic.)

Another important point to keep in mind is that a substantial proportion of new Border Patrol agents were Latinos, particularly Mexican Americans. It seems clear that the employment of Latino agents has been a growing trend over the past fifteen years, at least. This development raises a number of thought-provoking issues regarding race and ethnic relations and the role of police agencies in shaping them, because most of those apprehended by the Border Patrol are Mexican immigrants and the Patrol also has long focused much of its enforcement efforts on Mexican American communities. Unfortunately, data on trends in the employment of Latino agents in the Border Patrol were not readily available.[78] Nonetheless, this is a vital issue, meriting in-depth investigation and analysis elsewhere.

One common quantitative indicator of Border Patrol activities is the number of apprehensions of undocumented immigrants. This number doubled from 1981 to 1986, peaking at 1.69 million before declining sharply between 1986 and 1988, falling by some 40%, to 969,214 (see appendix 2).[79] It is important to note that apprehension levels increased rapidly in the several years prior to the passage of IRCA in late 1986, during which time various bills to control immigration were being hotly debated in Congress. Then, as apprehension totals dropped substantially in 1987, the INS attributed the decline to the employer-sanctions provisions of IRCA, although it had hardly begun to enforce the sanctions by 1987.[80]

The meaning of these apprehension statistics is by no means clear. First of all, as many have noted previously, these statistics represent events, not people; that is, the same person may be apprehended numerous times, each of which counts as an apprehension. Second, thus far it has been impossible to determine whether apprehension figures vary over time due to actual changes in immigration flows, or due to other intervening factors such as changes in Border Patrol deployment strategies and enforcement priorities. Starting in 1987, the latter included a new responsibility for enforcing employer sanctions and a new emphasis on drug enforcement as well as apprehending "criminal aliens" (discussed in chapter 3).[81] Another factor to consider is that the legalization of large numbers of undocumented immigrants in the United States decreased the size of the resident immigrant population that was subject to apprehension by the Border Patrol.

The position adopted here is that, to a significant extent, INS apprehension statistics reflect INS enforcement priorities, which in turn are influenced by the prevailing political climate as well as the current list of INS enforcement responsibilities.[82] For example, the growing emphasis on drug enforcement activities may have led the Border Patrol to devote less attention to undocumented immigration. From 1981 through 1986, when immigration was a highly charged political issue, INS apprehensions appear to correlate closely with Border Patrol linewatch deployment hours (the actual amount of time spent by agents on the border). In contrast, the degree of correlation is quite inconsistent from 1987 through 1989,[83] a period when immigration issues were less prominent in national politics and when drug enforcement issues took on increasing importance for the Border Patrol. On the whole, however, questions about the changing rates and real meaning of INS apprehensions are politically contentious and are not likely to be resolved solely through the examination of aggregate statistical data. Also, such data does not allow for the investigation of regional differences in enforcement priorities along the border.

In addition to becoming substantially larger and broadening its enforcement responsibilities, the Border Patrol implemented a variety of qualitative changes during the Reagan administration. On a tactical level, several multifaceted patrolling techniques were added. First, in 1984, the Border Patrol reintroduced horse patrols in the southern region, along portions of the New Mexico and Texas stretch of the border. The horse patrols served at least two purposes: enforcement and public relations. With regard to the latter, it was hoped that Border Patrol agents could function as "ambassadors of good will while enhancing the image of the Border Patrol" through school and public appearances.[84] Second, in 1985 and 1986, the Border Patrol established ongoing joint foot patrols with police departments in the Laredo, El Paso, and San Diego areas. The general purpose of these foot patrols was to reduce the level of crime in border areas, and in San Diego they were specifically intended to halt the violent crimes that were being perpetrated against undocumented immigrants by a host of assailants.[85]

While crime in border areas—especially that committed against highly vulnerable undocumented immigrants—was and continues to be a serious problem, the implementation of the joint foot patrols raised several troubling issues. Most notably, the San Diego joint patrol unit was prominent in its reliance on the use of deadly force. From August 1986 through December 1989 this unit killed eight people and wounded four others, with many of these incidents taking place under questionable circumstances.[86] On a less severe level, it was reported that in El Paso the patrols often questioned people simply because of their ethnic or racial appearance.[87] On such occasions, the Border Patrol agent and the police officer on joint patrol would commonly pass the "suspect" back and forth between them, thereby effectively merging two jurisdictions: immigration and state law. For example, they might stop and arrest a person under suspicion of either shoplifting or having undocumented immigration status. These practices were rife with possibilities for harassment and civil and human rights abuses.

Qualitative changes in the Border Patrol took on a much more elite character in 1984 with the establishment of the Border Patrol Tactical Team (BORTAC). Initially made up of 45 officers, with plans for expansion to 100 officers, this force received special training in riot control, counterterrorism, and other paramilitary activities similar to the training provided to U.S. marshals and the FBI Special Weapons and Training (SWAT) teams. BORTAC officers were Border Patrol agents who were ordinarily stationed in different sectors around the country on regular Border Patrol duty, but who periodically trained together for special emergency situations.[88] The unit also had its own commander. One Border Patrol official characterized BORTAC as being "much like a *special forces team* for us" (emphasis added), stating that "they're utilized in situations such as riot control at different locations."[89] BORTAC members were placed on alert twice in 1984: once during the Olympics in Los Angeles, and once during the bridge-blocking protests at the Piedras Negras–Eagle Pass port of entry (over "irregularities" in state elections in Coahuila).[90] By 1987 BORTAC was taking part in drug enforcement and crop eradication efforts in the United States.[91]

Beyond various tactical changes, the Border Patrol also underwent a historic shift in strategic focus during the Reagan administration: whereas before 1986 it had been concerned almost exclusively with immigration enforcement, following the 1986 passage of IRCA it became increasingly preoccupied with drug enforcement.[92] (This shift in focus reportedly had already been under way in some areas for several years, however.)[93] The most significant push in this direction was the 1986 establishment of the Southwest Border Drug Task Force (later known as Operation Alliance), which was composed of various federal, state, and local agencies (see chapter 4). The Border Patrol was prominent in this task force because it was assigned the lead role in drug interdiction on land between border ports of entry.[94] Another sign of the Border Patrol's change in strategic priorities was that although it received little mention in the 1986 Anti–Drug Abuse Act, both it and the INS as a whole received substantial attention in the 1988 Anti–Drug Abuse Act, in the form of calls for increased funding, equipment, and staff in order to further aid the nation's drug enforcement efforts.[95]

As a result of this expanding enforcement focus, the Border Patrol's scope of legal jurisdiction was considerably broadened. As of 1987, Border Patrol agents were cross-designated (i.e., deputized) to enforce Title 21 of *U.S. Code* (by the Drug Enforcement Agency) and Title 19 of *U.S. Code* (by the Customs Service), covering drug and contraband smuggling, respectively. By 1988, some 2,800 Border Patrol agents were cross-designated to enforce these statutes.[96]

The expansion of the Border Patrol's responsibilities to include drug enforcement allowed for significant changes in its inventory of equipment. Most notably, the Patrol gained access to high-powered military-issue rifles such as semiautomatic M-14s and automatic/semiautomatic M-16s, which were said to be necessary to meet the growing dangers posed by drug enforcement activities.[97] These rifles were not carried by all agents at all times, but they were made available to those in settings deemed particularly dangerous. The drug enforcement efforts were to have other far-reaching implications for the Border Patrol, including its immigration enforcement activities, as the two activities would overlap in practice. (See chapters 3 and 4 for a more detailed discussion of these issues.)

In sum, during the Reagan administration the Border Patrol experienced unprecedented growth and underwent important qualitative changes that accentuated its paramilitary character and expanded its scope of enforcement. Much of this change resulted from the passage of IRCA in 1986, but the assignment of drug enforcement responsibilities to the Border Patrol also played a key role. These changes laid the foundation for further expansions in both the scope and the reach of the unit's efforts and authority.

THE ALIEN BORDER CONTROL COMMITTEE
AND IMMIGRATION EMERGENCY PLANS

The INS did more than tremendously expand its enforcement presence in the border region during the Reagan administration, however. It also participated in a multiagency task force charged with drawing up elaborate contingency plans for massive civilian control and roundup operations that included the border region both explicitly and implicitly. In 1987, in the middle of congressional hearings on legislation to compensate Japanese Americans and others who were unjustly imprisoned by the U.S. government during World War II, Congressman Norman Mineta of California revealed that similar contingency plans had been recently drawn up:

> I believe that it is vital to bring to the Subcommittee's attention that in recent months a Department of Justice task force has proposed as legal and appropriate the mass roundup and incarceration of certain nationalities for vague national security reasons. A camp has been identified in Louisiana, and rolls of barbed wire, cots, tents, et cetera, are all ready on the site, waiting for just such a roundup.[98]

Congressman Mineta then submitted copies of internal Justice Department documents from 1986 that appear to have been leaked to him, and that outlined some of the plans being formulated by that task force. The INS was a leading participant in the preparation of these plans, which included a few items specific to and with additional implications for immigration enforcement in the border region. These plans merit substantial attention, especially given their relevance to the topic of militarization.

The task force was named the Alien Border Control Committee (ABCC). Its purpose was to implement specific recommendations made by the Vice-President's Task Force on Terrorism (chaired by George Bush) regarding the control and removal of alien terrorists from the United States. The INS and its commissioner, Alan Nelson, were charged with heading the ABCC, which first met in September 1986. Other participants included the FBI, the CIA, the State Department, the Customs Service, U.S. Marshals, numerous Justice Department offices, and several other unidentifiable entities.[99] In reviewing the committee's plans, it is important to bear in mind that the Reagan administration applied the label "terrorist" quite broadly, and often in a highly politicized fashion.

The documents submitted by Congressman Mineta related to only one of the four ABCC subcommittees, namely the group charged with conducting a "review of contingency plans for removal of selected aliens from the U.S. and *sealing of the borders*" (emphasis added).[100] One of the submitted documents was a May 1986 report by the INS Investigations Division entitled "Alien Terrorists and Undesirables: A Contingency Plan," which served as a point of departure for the subcommittee's meetings.[101] This report called for the INS—along with other agencies—to exclude, apprehend, detain, prosecute, and deport members of targeted groups of nationalities to be later specified. (North African and Middle Eastern countries were used extensively as examples in the report—not surprising, given the Reagan administration's bombing of Libya in 1986.) Furthermore, the INS was to hold all apprehended aliens, charge them with "international terrorism," resist any judicial efforts to set bail, and, on the basis of national security, exclude the public from any hearings. Moreover, components of the Immigration and Nationality Act would be used to limit entry into and exit from the United States by both targeted aliens *and* U.S. citizens.[102] As the main enforcement arm of the INS, the Border Patrol was slated to play a prominent, if not very clearly specified, role in the execution of this part of the plan.[103] There was no specific mention in the INS report of either how entry and exit would be limited or how the borders would be sealed, both of which seem overwhelming tasks.

Plans for the detention of the population targeted for roundup, which was presumed to be less than 10,000 persons, were more fully delineated. They called for the Oakdale detention facility to be expanded to house up to 5,000 people in tents on an emergency basis, with just four weeks prior notice. Should the number of potential detainees exceed 1,000 persons, the Department of Defense would be asked to provide assistance with "facilities and logistics," under what was referred to as the South Florida Plan.[104] No explanation of the South Florida Plan was provided in the report or in the other leaked documents, however. Thus it is left to us to contemplate the type or extent of military assistance that would plausibly be provided in the realm of "facilities and logistics." At the very least, the use of military bases for detention purposes would seem likely, if not also the use of military transportation equipment and some personnel.

The ABCC continued its work beyond the initial steps in 1986, according to INS Commissioner Alan Nelson when he was directly questioned about the ABCC in a congressional hearing in March of 1987.[105] Also, at least one key element of the ABCC contingency plan was later pursued; Nelson reported during another 1987 congressional hearing that plans were under way to investigate the use of Pentagon facilities for alien detention—a tactic that the INS had considered periodically since at least 1982, however.[106] Unfortunately, detailed information on subsequent ABCC activities is not yet publicly available.

One particularly crucial detail not found in the initial INS report for the ABCC was: Who were the "undesirables" (alien or otherwise) designated to be rounded up along with the "alien terrorists"? Since the plan's title, "Alien Terrorists and Undesirables: A Contingency Plan," referred to both, they would appear to be distinct categories. The portion of the plan contained in the congressional hearing report referred only to "alien" groups. However, one is left to wonder whether some groups of U.S. legal residents and citizens might also have been included in the larger plan, especially those perceived as somehow being allied with or supportive of the designated "alien terrorists." On the basis of admittedly partial and circumstantial information from other sources, this seems at least somewhat plausible. For example, in Reagan's first term, the Federal Emergency Management Agency (FEMA) reportedly designed elaborate contingency plans for the imposition of martial law and the massive roundups of both foreign-born and native-born civilians in the United States in the event of widespread civil unrest and, moreover, reportedly held joint roundup exercises with the Department of Defense.[107] Also, several sources relate reports of plans to surveil, round up, and detain thousands of U.S. citizens and Central American refugees in the event that a direct U.S. military invasion of Nicaragua caused a flood of refugees across Mexico into the southwestern United States and provoked a widespread domestic public outcry against the invasion.[108] It should be recalled that bringing down the revolutionary Sandinista government of Nicaragua was a chief Cold War foreign-policy obsession of the Reagan administration. These plans shared some important similarities with the plan of the Alien Border Control Committee, but were apparently far more grandiose. Given the highly sensitive nature of such projects, however, it is unlikely that their details will ever be made fully public. Still, that such alarmist contingency plans, similar in type, if not scale, to the ABCC plan, were apparently formulated has disturbing implications for U.S. citizens and immigrants alike.

The information about the ABCC plan made public by Congressman Mineta in 1987 was not the first indication that the Reagan administration and the INS had devised severe contingency plans in response to their fears of "aliens" besieging the United States; there are a number of indications that such efforts had been afoot for years. For example, in 1982 Nelson reported to Congress on an "illegal alien contingency plan," to be employed in the event of a large influx of aliens, that included the use of military and former military facilities as detention facilities.[109] In a related and more far-fetched vein, Congressman Miller of Ohio suggested in 1983 that U.S. military forces could be effective in assisting the Border Patrol in guarding the border, and INS Commissioner Nelson responded affirmatively.[110]

Further evidence of a siege mentality within the Reagan administration in response to immigration issues is found in the Immigration Emergency Act proposed in 1982. This bill appears to be related to the "illegal alien contingency plan" Nelson referred to (noted above) and was written largely in response to the fallout from the Mariel Cuban boatlift of 1980. Specifically, this bill sought to give the president the power to declare an "immigration emergency" for a period of up to 120 days if the following three conditions, all quite vague, were met: (1) a "substantial number" of undocumented aliens had embarked or were about to embark for the United States, (2) INS resources and the procedures established by the Immigration and Nationality Act were deemed inadequate to respond to the expected number, and (3) the influx was thought to "endanger the welfare of the United States or any United States community."[111] The bill would have allowed the president to exempt actions undertaken to address an "immigration emergency" (especially those involving detention camps) from environmental restrictions. It also would have granted the government the authority to detain for an indeterminate period of time all "illegal aliens" who came into custody during the emergency period. In addition, the judiciary would have been precluded from ruling on executive branch decisions during this period, and the "full resources and expertise of the federal government would [have been] available to the President," including components of the Department of Defense.[112]

While this 1982 bill did not pass, its provisions reemerged later to become law as part of the 1986 Immigration Reform and Control Act (IRCA). Specifically, IRCA called for the appropriation of $35 million for the establishment of an "Immigration Emergency Fund" to be made available for border patrolling and other enforcement activities. It gave the president the authority to determine whether or not an emergency exists and stipulated that the president must certify that fact to the Senate and House judiciary committees.[113] This provision was made operational in 1990 with a congressional appropriation of $35 million for the fund; the criteria defining what would constitute an "immigration emergency" were the same as those in the 1982 proposal.[114]

This emergency fund and the contingency plans discussed above have obvious ramifications for the U.S.–Mexico border region. First of all, it is important to recall that throughout this period U.S. border-security efforts were focused on South Florida and the U.S.–Mexico border; thus these areas were most likely to be affected by an "immigration emergency" or "alien border control" plans. Furthermore, it is clear that any effort to implement such plans would likely lead to large-scale violations of basic human and civil rights of targeted civilian populations along the border and also probably within the interior of the United States as well. Other related potentialities relevant to the border region include the use of military bases as detention sites and the possible deployment of military personnel in some capacity on the border, probably to help seal off sections of the border. On the whole, the formulation of contingency plans for dealing with "immigration emergencies" and "alien terrorists and undesirables" indicates that immigration enforcement efforts were conceived of in broad and at times severe terms by Reagan administration officials, potentially involving the use of repressive police-state tactics in both the U.S.–Mexico border region and other areas.

THE LIC FRAMEWORK APPLIED TO INS POLICIES AND ACTIVITIES DURING THE REAGAN ADMINISTRATION

Many elements of INS activities and plans during the Reagan administration are consistent with the low-intensity conflict framework. Technological hardware is the most obvious area of similarity. Examples include the supplying of M-14 and M-16 military-issue rifles to the Border Patrol (under the rubric of drug enforcement), the greatly expanded use of helicopters (the number increasing from 2 to 22, almost all on loan from the U.S. Army), the introduction of an extensive array of sophisticated night-vision equipment, the expanded replacement and apparent upgrading of intrusion-detection electronic ground sensor systems to include seven additional Border Patrol sectors along the U.S.–Mexico border, the introduction of low-light-level television surveillance equipment along the border in parts of six Border Patrol sectors, and the introduction of airborne infrared radar. The joint development of a linewatch sensor system and new varieties of infrared night surveillance equipment by the INS, the U.S. Army, and the U.S. Air Force is also a clear instance of potential border militarization. It represents the development of technology explicitly for use by both the U.S. military and the civilian agency responsible for domestic border enforcement, that is, the INS.

At the level of strategy and tactics, there are also a number of similarities between INS practices during the Reagan administration and key operational characteristics of the LIC framework. Take the formation of the Border Patrol Tactical Team (BORTAC), the INS's own elite, special-forces team trained in riot control, counterterrorism, and other unspecified paramilitary activities. The use of such special forces is central to almost all LIC mission categories. In addition, the increased participation in joint task forces exemplified by the Border Patrol's joining the multiagency Southwest Border Drug Task Force (Operation Alliance) is similar to the LIC tactic of enhancing the integration and coordination of various police and military forces. (Note too that antidrug operations are an LIC mission area.) The integration-of-forces principle is also evident in the establishment of joint foot patrols by the INS and local police in several urban areas along the border. Moreover, the Border Patrol moved further toward becoming a broad-ranging national police force with its new additional enforcement responsibilities (e.g., employer sanctions) and its broadened formal legal authority (i.e., cross-designation, or deputization, granted by the DEA and the Customs Service) to enforce drug and contraband laws. And in a very different vein, the use of charity organizations' housing resources for INS detention purposes is consistent with the LIC tactic of incorporating nongovernmental organizations in the supplying of what is portrayed as "humanitarian aid," which is in fact linked to larger military-security efforts.

Perhaps the most vivid instance of overlap between INS strategy during the Reagan period and LIC doctrine can be found in the formation of various contingency plans for "immigration emergencies" and the roundup of "alien terrorists and undesirables." It is significant that the development of these plans seems to have been intimately related to the Reagan administration's application of LIC doctrine in Central America and other "trouble spots." The plans appear to represent the domestic counterparts of the LIC mission areas of foreign internal defense, terrorism counteraction, and peacetime contingency operations. In their emphases on internal defense and counterterrorism, as well as their goal of projecting power rapidly to head off civil unrest deemed to be a threat to national security, the contingency plans fit almost perfectly within those particular mission areas of the LIC framework. These plans call for sealing off the border (or portions of it), rounding up and detaining massive numbers of civilians, and using military facilities (and probably even personnel) in the border region. Also, a variety of police and intelligence agencies were involved in the planning process. Taken together, such measures are consistent with the LIC strategy of increasing the integration and coordination of police, paramilitary, and military forces. Furthermore, these contingency plans are an expression of the intent to exert social control over targeted civilian populations—which is the essence of LIC doctrine.

Other facets of the INS buildup during the Reagan administration also reflect this essential LIC goal of controlling targeted civilian populations, though they are less obviously related to specific LIC tactics and strategy. For example, the near doubling of congressionally authorized Border Patrol staff positions certainly enhanced the INS's capacity to exert social control over a specific population in the border region, that is, undocumented immigrants. Further, the deployment of additional sophisticated, military-related equipment, to be used mainly by the Border Patrol, seems likely to have reinforced the early-established paramilitary character of the unit. In addition, the much-expanded construction efforts in the border region provided the Border Patrol with more general support for their immigration enforcement efforts there, efforts that were focused on maintaining control of particular civilian populations. Moreover, the great increase in INS staff levels and detention space and the introduction of seven detention centers operated by private contractors in the Southwest provided the INS with additional infrastructure toward the same end. These increased detention efforts were fueled by the Reagan administration's historic shift in policy, whereby detention became a form of punishment to deter undocumented immigration as well as political asylum applications from people fleeing U.S.-allied countries. The joint foot patrols by INS and local police officials established in several border areas were also aimed at maintaining control over civilians. U.S. residents and citizens were more directly affected by this endeavor, as all those of Latino or "foreign" appearance became potential targets of enforcement. Moreover, the growing visibility of the green-clad INS personnel along the border made the increased presence of a federal police force more obvious to local residents.

At a more general level, it is evident that Reagan and other high-ranking administration officials considered the issue of undocumented immigration to be closely connected to the political and social unrest in Central America. In addition, they were apparently concerned about the prospect of similar unrest in Mexico, and the influx of Mexican refugees that might ensue. Thus it seems likely that some of the feared immigration "emergencies" were thought to involve a large increase in the number of Central American or Mexican immigrants—the "tidal wave" of "feet people" spoken of by Reagan in the early 1980s (see chapter 1). It was precisely in Central America and the Caribbean that the Reagan administration most aggressively implemented the newly developed LIC doctrine. Thus it is safe to conclude that undocumented immigration and low-intensity conflict doctrine were in all likelihood related issues for the Reagan administration. Moreover, the aforenoted contingency plans, with their profound implications for the border region, appear to have been linked to the Reagan administration's interventionist policies in Central America and the Caribbean. In addition, undocumented immigration was a hot political issue for most of the period, and it was often portrayed as a lingering potential threat to national security. Given such a political context, then, it is no surprise that many aspects of the expansion of INS immigration enforcement endeavors in the U.S.–Mexico border region were analogous to or consistent with various provisions of LIC doctrine. Nonetheless, it should be recalled that this adoption of more militaristic operational characteristics and equipment was in many ways merely a continuation and expansion of a process that began under the Carter administration.

3

The Immigration and Naturalization Service during the Bush Administration, 1989–1992

INS activities during the Bush administration were characterized by two general trends. First, immigration enforcement became more severe. The most graphic illustrations of this were the roundup and detention of thousands of Central American political asylum seekers in the Lower Rio Grande Valley during 1989 and 1990 and the construction of a thin steel wall along the border between San Diego and Tijuana. Second, more emphasis was placed on drug enforcement, and the agency's drug enforcement activities were increasingly intermixed with its immigration enforcement efforts. On the whole, the Bush administration was a period of relative prominence as well as some significant change for the INS.

In terms of overall resources, between the close of the Reagan administration and the end of the Bush administration, INS funding grew, while overall staffing levels dropped off. Congressionally appropriated staff positions for the agency dropped 23% between 1988 and 1992, falling to 11,869 job posts in 1992, while funding appropriations grew some 19% during the same period, reaching $961.3 million in 1992 (see appendix 1).[1] Once again, Congress privileged the Enforcement Division of the INS over the agency's service-related components, as the Enforcement Division's funding was increased 41% (although the division's number of appropriated staff positions was cut 10%). The vast majority of congressional allocations for the INS were increasingly concentrated in the Enforcement Division over the 1988–1992 period.[2] The Enforcement Division's share of all INS funds derived from Congress grew from 62% to 73%, and its proportion of congressionally appropriated INS staff posts increased from 69% to 80%.

In addition to congressional appropriations, fee-generated resources grew enormously and became increasingly strategic for the agency. The number of fees imposed for INS service-oriented activity expanded from two to four, with the addition of an examinations fee and a land border-crossing fee (the latter implemented on a very limited basis).[3] From 1988 through 1992 fee-generated funding jumped 73% and fee-program staffing shot up 80%, arriving at $484.9 million and 5,101 staff in 1992.[4] However, these particular resources were devoted almost entirely to more service-related units, such as inspections, adjudications and naturalization, and information and records management, while none were allocated to the Border Patrol. By 1992 fee resources supplemented congressional funding for the INS by 50% and congressionally appropriated staff positions by 43%, although in absolute terms, the 2,270 increase in user-financed staff from 1988 through 1992 was not nearly enough to offset the 3,584 cut in congressionally funded staff posts during the same period. The growing imposition of user fees during the Bush administration signaled a shift toward regressive financing of INS service-oriented activities by clients rather than by Congress. In addition, access to such massive fee-financed resources appears to have given the INS increased institutional autonomy, shielding it somewhat from the budgetary power held by Congress over federal agencies through its appropriations authority, and thereby possibly limiting a key means of subjecting the INS to some level of public accountability.[5] Clearly, the use of fee programs and resources to finance INS service-related efforts merits in-depth investigation, but this topic lies outside the focus of the present work, namely, the agency's immigration and drug enforcement efforts in the U.S.–Mexico border region.

At a more general level, during the Bush administration the INS appeared to struggle under the weight of having to administer the enormous and far-flung growth in overall resources coupled with its substantially broadened service and enforcement responsibilities. Much of the agency's dilemma appears to have stemmed from the implementation of the multifaceted, complicated components of IRCA and the huge expansion in accompanying resources. The INS became larger, more complex, and apparently more unwieldy as a result.[6] Further, the agency was charged with implementing key portions of the Immigration Act of 1990, which focused primarily on legal, documented immigration. This was the third major piece of immigration legislation affecting the INS since 1980, and the three collectively required a staggering amount of change by the INS in a relatively short period of time.[7] Added to these expanding immigration duties during the Bush administration were much-expanded INS drug enforcement efforts and a growing emphasis on apprehending and detaining "criminal aliens."

It is also important to highlight briefly several crucial events in the larger and fast-changing socioeconomic and political context that helped shape INS policy and practices during the Bush administration. The most notable of these was the end of the Cold War in late 1989, which profoundly reshaped international and domestic politics and economics. It created an immense vacuum in U.S. politics that came to be filled in part by the War on Drugs, in which the INS became a key actor. The Gulf War of 1991 against Iraq also filled, briefly and intensely, the political vacuum. Meanwhile, U.S. foreign policy in Latin America shifted away from Cold War geopolitical confrontation in Central America, as unrest there gradually began to wind down. (The exception to this trend was the U.S. invasion of Panama in 1989, ostensibly to remove General Manuel Noriega from power, an action justified by the Bush administration largely in terms of Noriega's drug trafficking ties.) Rather, the Bush administration more strongly emphasized expanding trade and economic integration with Mexico, which was in the midst of massive neoliberal economic reforms that were favorable for large-scale foreign and domestic investors. Economic concerns also came to dominate the domestic political scene, as the U.S. economy entered a sustained period of recession and large corporate layoffs in the latter part of 1990.

Overall, the INS survived quite well and even appeared to thrive in this fluid political and economic context. The agency remained more well funded and intact, in relative terms, than did many other U.S. military, police, or security agencies in this era of growing fiscal constraints. This can in part be attributed to the INS's enthusiastic participation in the politically salient War on Drugs, although this participation led to some serious practical problems when it was combined in the field with immigration enforcement efforts.

This chapter covers the same core topics as did the previous chapter. These are INS equipment and construction in the border region, the Detention and Deportation program, and the Border Patrol. In addition, attention is also devoted to human rights abuses by INS agents in the border region, the massive INS crackdown in 1989 and 1990 on Central American asylum seekers in the Lower Rio Grande Valley, and the collaboration of Mexican and U.S. authorities in immigration enforcement efforts. On the whole, INS enforcement activities in the U.S.–Mexico border region during the Bush administration appear to coincide with the provisions of low-intensity conflict doctrine to a substantially greater degree than do the same activities in previous administrations.

EQUIPMENT AND CONSTRUCTION
INCREASES IN THE BORDER REGION

The acquisition of equipment and the initiation of new construction projects was a strong focus for the INS under the Bush administration (see appendix 3). The planning and construction of more imposing border barriers in high-traffic areas was an especially prominent activity. Various elements of the U.S. military played instrumental roles in these efforts, while also providing additional general construction and maintenance support to the INS, especially the Border Patrol. The INS continued to expand its construction of various types of facilities and its deployment of sophisticated intrusion-detection equipment throughout the border region. Moreover, the number of helicopters at the disposal of the INS increased dramatically.[8]

The most controversial construction projects during the Bush administration were the efforts to upgrade various border barriers, termed the "Berlin Wall" approach by some observers. The major effort in this regard was the construction in 1991 of a 10-foot-high wall of thin corrugated steel along seven miles of the border from the ocean inland, between San Diego and Tijuana in the Chula Vista Border Patrol sector. (The wall was eventually expanded to 14 miles in length. See the epilogue.) The wall represented a significant escalation from merely maintaining or expanding the sections of chain-link fence built during the latter portion of the Carter administration and labeled the "tortilla curtain" by critics. The new thin wall consisted of welded-together panels of surplus steel, corrugated military-aircraft landing mat. The U.S. Navy Seabees (a construction unit) built the wall, while California National Guard units improved and expanded nearby back roads along the border to facilitate greater border access and surveillance by the Border Patrol.[9]

INS and military officials said the border wall and road projects were primarily aimed at reducing drug smuggling through the area, while the curbing of undocumented immigration was presented merely as a secondary goal.[10] However, the targeted area was the largest single crossing point for undocumented immigrants on the border, and had not previously been listed among the principal drug-smuggling sites, though some significant drug smuggling undoubtedly occurred there. It soon became clear that the main purpose of the wall was to deter undocumented immigration, or at least channel it to other areas. INS officials readily admitted that the wall itself would not stop people from crossing the border. Yet they viewed it as an effective means of halting the growing practice of "drive-throughs" in open border areas. Moreover, officials hoped it would funnel people away from urban areas, where they were able to easily blend in and avoid detection by INS authorities, and instead force them eastward into rougher terrain and more remote areas, thereby increasing the prospect that the Border Patrol could apprehend them.[11]

The funneling of the flow of immigrants and smugglers eastward appeared to be taking place to some extent by mid-1992, as undocumented border crossings were on the rise somewhat in the region immediately east of the wall—an area that had previously been a focal point for the military's antidrug activities.[12] While pushing undocumented immigrants into more remote areas to cross the border may have increased the likelihood of apprehending them, it may also have exposed them to greater dangers. They were exposed to harsher physical conditions in the desert and mountains and may have been more vulnerable to criminal assaults in isolated areas by the assailants that typically follow and prey upon undocumented immigrants, as well as more likely to encounter armed drug traffickers or even armed military units and law enforcement officials on antidrug patrols (who might mistake them for drug couriers). In addition, Border Patrol agents were less likely to be subject to public scrutiny of their immigrant apprehension activities in remote, isolated areas.

The wall project had political reverberations on both sides of the border. For example, many Mexican observers viewed the wall as an insult and bitterly noted the irony of constructing a prominent border wall at the same time that the Bush administration was seeking greater economic integration with Mexico.[13] On the U.S. side, the wall's construction seemed to vindicate the agenda of nativist groups, who in 1990 had called for the construction of a 12-mile-long "impenetrable barrier" on the border between Tijuana and San Diego.[14]

The wall appears to have been the culmination of a series of INS proposals to upgrade border barriers, directed mainly at the San Diego area. These proposals included earlier plans for the construction of a "drainage ditch," the placement of cement barriers every four feet, and extensive fence repair. The ditch plan, however, was dropped following a storm of controversy and expressions of outrage in the Mexican press and by U.S. critics, who viewed the project as a veiled effort to construct a border barrier.[15] (Similar outcries about the wall had little effect, however.) These proposed enhancements of border barriers were consistent with the provisions of the Immigration Act of 1990, which explicitly called for "the repair, maintenance, or construction on the United States border, in areas experiencing high levels of apprehensions of illegal aliens, of structures to deter illegal entry into the United States."[16] In addition, the steel-wall project appears to fall within the mandate of this law. Nonetheless, it was at first unclear whether the wall project would be expanded to other urban border areas outside of San Diego–Tijuana, though after 1992 it became clear that similar projects were slated to be implemented in key parts of various urban border zones in California, Arizona, and New Mexico (see the epilogue).

During the Bush administration, the INS began to call upon the military to assist in a variety of construction and maintenance tasks in other areas, in addition to the wall and road projects in the Chula Vista Border Patrol sector. Although this type of joint activity seemed relatively innocuous, it allowed the INS to develop an ongoing, working relationship with the National Guard and other elements of the military. This collaboration was implemented under the rubric of drug enforcement (covered in chapter 4), but it included a variety of construction and maintenance projects that also aided immigration enforcement. One version of this assistance was the cleaning up of several border areas by military units. For example, in early 1989 the National Guard and the Army cleaned out a ditch on the border near Nogales, Arizona, which apparently helped deter undocumented border crossings in the area.[17] Similarly, in the summer of 1990 the INS oversaw an Army engineering unit's work in clearing brush along the Rio Grande in an area behind downtown Laredo, which had been a popular site for illegal border crossings and smuggling activities. Local downtown merchants were reportedly delighted to have the area cleared out.[18] Moreover, the Texas National Guard provided the Border Patrol in the Laredo and McAllen sectors (as well as in other unidentified sectors) with ongoing labor support for the maintenance of various communications, electronics, and transportation equipment, in addition to carrying out some construction projects, including the refurbishing of two Border Patrol stations in the McAllen sector. However, the Guard was technically precluded from participating directly in immigration enforcement activities.[19]

General INS construction activity in the U.S.–Mexico border region continued apace during the Bush administration. Some 19 projects for the border region were completed, under construction, or at least drawn up and fully funded. These projects ranged from the expansion of four detention centers and nine Border Patrol stations to the new construction or expansion of six traffic inspection checkpoints.[20]

Meanwhile, the INS continued to indulge its penchant for sophisticated electronics equipment, with the vast majority of new acquisitions placed along the U.S.–Mexico border. Most notable in this area was the enormous expansion in the inventory of INS helicopters from 22 to 58 between 1988 and 1992. (In contrast, the number of fixed-wing aircraft declined slightly, from 46 to 43, during the same period.)[21] It is important to note, however, that helicopters are expensive to operate, and the extent to which the INS used its newly expanded fleet is unclear due to the absence of data on helicopter flight hours logged per year. At any rate, the INS planned to phase out fixed-wing aircraft and switch over completely to helicopters, and to obtain a new fleet of helicopters to replace its inventory of aging OH-6A military spotter-observation helicopters.[22] With the winding down of the Cold War, an unspecified number of additional military helicopters (as well as land vehicles and foodstuffs) were slated to be turned over to the INS by the Pentagon in 1992.[23]

Various types of intrusion-detection equipment were also expanded during the Bush administration, thus allowing the Border Patrol to cover a much greater area using far fewer agents.[24] For example, the INS expanded its inventory (to an unspecified degree) of night-vision scopes and airborne forward-looking infrared radar (FLIR) equipment as a part of an "intrusion-detection initiative." It installed low-light-level television systems in portions of additional unspecified Border Patrol sectors.[25] (Only three sectors had not obtained this system previously.) It also sought to acquire additional portable electronic intrusion-detection ground sensors.[26] Further, in conjunction with the U.S. Army, the INS completed the production of 15 "Improved Image-Enhancement Vehicles," which were said to provide a low-cost, automated mobile surveillance system.[27]

The INS also introduced what could be termed a "high light level" system in the same heavily trafficked portion of the Chula Vista Border Patrol sector where the wall was constructed. Powerful floodlights were placed along the Tijuana River to light up a dangerous, high-crime area where as many as 1,000 people used to gather, waiting to cross the border. The lights were intended to break up the large groups, deter criminal activity directed against migrants, and divert people to other crossing areas. In contrast to the wall project, this effort was well received because it made a very dangerous area safer.[28] However, again, if one of the effects was the diversion of migrants to more remote areas, this may also eventually have made them more vulnerable to criminal assaults and new dangers.

On the whole, INS construction and equipment-provision efforts appear to have proceeded at roughly the same rate of expansion as that occurring during the Reagan administration. However, there were several crucial qualitative differences. First, the construction of a solid steel 7-mile-long, 10-foot-high wall was a significant escalation over previous border barriers. Second, various elements of the military were brought in to carry out or assist in INS construction projects and maintenance-support operations. While apparently low-key, such collaborative efforts helped the INS establish an ongoing relationship with the military. Meanwhile, the INS continued its previous efforts to deploy more helicopters and additional electronic surveillance equipment in the border region.

DETENTION AND DEPORTATION TRENDS

The Detention and Deportation program remained a central INS effort during the Bush administration, although its focus shifted and diversified. Its operations were increasingly focused on detaining immigrants categorized as "criminal aliens," rather than principally on asylum seekers from Central America and Haiti—although this was not a smooth, linear trend. (See the discussion later in this chapter of the crackdown in the Lower Rio Grande Valley.) Detention space continued to expand overall, and in the border region in particular.

Congressionally appropriated funding for the Detention and Deportation program increased by 23% from 1988 through 1992, while appropriated staff positions declined by some 6% from 1988 through 1992, arriving at $158.8 million and 1,519 staff positions in 1992 (see appendix 1).[29] The divergence of funding and staffing trends suggests that the INS may have been increasingly contracting out for guard labor and detention facilities, or that the agency was spending a growing portion of its funds on administrative or overtime costs.[30] At any rate, the Detention and Deportation unit generally appeared to be a dynamic sector of the INS.

The total number of people detained fluctuated substantially between 1988 and 1992. From 1988 through 1990, the number of people detained by the INS jumped 13%, topping 104,000 in both 1989 and 1990. This number then dropped to 82,326 in 1992 (a decline of 22% from 1990 and 11% from 1988). Undoubtedly much of this fluctuation was due to the massive INS detention campaign against Central Americans in the Lower Rio Grande Valley during 1989 and 1990 (discussed later in this chapter). The lower 1992 detention total does not appear to include the approximately 30,000 Haitian refugees apprehended on the high seas by the U.S.

Coast Guard and Navy, and held in the U.S. naval base at Guantánamo Bay, Cuba. While the total number of immigrants in detention varied, the average length of stay in detention climbed steadily from 15.2 days in 1988 to 26.3 days in 1992 (see appendix 2).[31] This rapid increase was in part caused by the INS's new emphasis on detaining immigrants convicted of crimes (see discussion below), who typically remained in detention much longer than other categories of immigrants.[32]

INS detention space was increased significantly during the Bush administration. Two new INS detention centers were opened in 1991, one in San Pedro, California (with a 400-person capacity), and another in Aguadilla, Puerto Rico (with a 44-person capacity).[33] After this expansion, five of the nine INS detention centers and most of the normal INS detention capacity were in the southwestern border region, while a large (1,000-person capacity) tenth center run jointly by the INS and the Bureau of Prisons was relatively near in Oakdale, Louisiana.[34] The INS was also planning a more extensive expansion in the Southwest in the near future, including the addition of 575 spaces spread among three existing INS border-region detention centers, as well as the establishment, in conjunction with the Bureau of Prisons, of a new 1,000-bed private-contract detention center near San Diego.[35]

Detention space was spread among a wide mix of facilities. For example, a detailed study by the U.S. General Accounting Office (GAO) put total INS detention capacity in 1991 at 6,259 people, including 2,864 spaces at nine INS detention centers, 653 at five private-contract facilities, 110 at a local hospital, 832 at a Bureau of Prisons facility, and 1,800 at local jails and prisons under contract to the INS.[36] The INS had contracts with over 900 state and local jails to provide detention space.[37]

However, determining the total actual amount of detention space available to the INS during the period is an imprecise and complex matter. The total INS detention capacity of 6,259 reported by the GAO appears to be a substantial undercount. First of all, the above GAO listing of 653 spaces at five private-contract detention centers fails to take into account 200 additional spaces and two more private-contract detention facilities found elsewhere in the same GAO report.[38] Second, the INS did not appear to report to either the GAO or Congress its use of at least four private-contract "soft" detention facilities to hold families in South Texas between 1989 and 1991 during its mass detention campaign against Central Americans there. These facilities had a collective capacity under normal conditions of at least 300 persons, and up to 1,000 or more in emergency conditions.[39] Third, the GAO obviously did not count the

5,000-person emergency capacity at the Oakdale, Louisiana, INS detention center (jointly run with the Bureau of Prisons), although the GAO may have included part of the Oakdale facility's regular capacity in its listing of 832 spaces available to the INS at an unidentified Bureau of Prisons facility. Still, this is 168 spaces short of the previously noted 1,000-person regular capacity available at Oakdale.

On the basis of this critique, it is reasonable to estimate that the GAO report of total detention space available to the INS is low by at least 750 regular detention spaces and some 5,700 emergency detention spaces.[40] Thus, regular INS detention capacity at all facilities probably reached at least 7,000 spaces by 1991, and the emergency capacity likely exceeded 12,700. However, in order to compare these estimates with detention capacity estimates from the end of the Reagan administration (see chapter 2), it is necessary to remove the 1,800 local and state jail spaces included in the GAO total, as available jail space was not quantified in earlier documents. This adjustment leaves an estimated total INS regular detention capacity of approximately 5,200 persons and an emergency capacity of some 10,900.[41] These figures are an increase over the estimated 4,200 regular and 9,200 emergency detention spaces available to the INS at the close of the Reagan administration.

The INS was still far from meeting its total detention-space needs, however. Between 1988 and 1990 some 489,000 immigrants (an average of 163,000 per year) reportedly met INS detention criteria, but, as noted earlier, the maximum number of people detained in any one year during this period was 104,000. Consequently, the INS would have needed to expand its detention space by approximately 60%, given similar average length of detentions to those of 1992. In addition, the INS expected that by the second half of the 1990s nearly 500,000 people annually would likely meet INS criteria for detention, a threefold increase over annual averages from the 1988–1990 period.[42] Given the previous assumptions, the INS would have needed to expand its detention capacity nearly fivefold to accommodate the projected numbers of detainable immigrants.

The nationality makeup of the INS detention population during the latter portion of the Bush administration changed markedly, from being heavily Central American and Haitian to being much more Mexican (a nationality barely present in the detention population during the 1980s). Specifically, 1991 data from 13 detention centers (seven INS and six private-contract facilities) presented by the GAO show the following distribution of nationalities: 27% Mexican, 24% Central American, 11% Haitian, 5% Indian, 4% Chinese, and 29% "others" (from 87 nations).[43]

One INS detention official attributed the newly expanded presence of Mexicans in detention to the agency's growing enforcement emphasis on targeting "criminal aliens."[44]

This shift in enforcement toward focusing on "criminal aliens" is reflected in the breakdown of the deportation categories of the detainees. For example, the same GAO study found that by 1991 some 34% of detention space used by the INS was devoted to "criminal aliens," while 37% was taken up by those in the "deportable" category and 29% by those who were "excludable." Among the four border-region INS detention centers surveyed, over 70% of the populations of the El Centro, California, and Florence, Arizona, detention centers were criminal aliens, and 34% of the El Paso center's population fell in that category. The Port Isabel, Texas, detention center held very few criminal aliens in 1991 (although this had changed by mid-1992).[45] By 1992, according to INS Commissioner Gene McNary, 60% of the agency's detention space was devoted to criminal aliens.[46] Further, the 1,000-bed private-contract detention facility near San Diego, scheduled to open in 1993, was to be used mainly for criminal aliens.[47] The INS projected the need to detain some 60,000 criminal aliens annually starting in 1991.[48]

The increase in the detention of "criminal aliens" merits elaboration, for it constitutes a historic change in INS detention practices. Throughout the 1980s the INS detention program was focused primarily on the low-security, lengthy confinement of non-Mexican undocumented immigrants—mainly Central Americans and Haitians, many if not most of whom were striving to gain political asylum. The legal offense committed by most members of this population was that of illegal entry into the United States, which is a misdemeanor violation, as noted previously.[49] Yet, during the Bush administration, these immigrants were confined at the same detention centers with "criminal aliens" convicted of more serious offenses.[50] Thus, the INS was simultaneously carrying out two very distinct detention missions in a problematic manner. On the whole, however, it appears that the INS detention program was increasingly evolving toward being a long-term criminal-detention project.

Detaining and deporting "criminal aliens" appears to be, at first glance, a logical activity for the INS. It was mandated by recent immigration and antidrug legislation, which stressed that immigrants convicted of drug offenses, violent crimes, or "aggravated felonies" should be detained and deported upon completion of their criminal sentences.[51] The INS apparently focused most of its "criminal alien" enforcement effort on immigrants convicted of those offenses.[52] This would seem to have been a far more judicious and politically acceptable activity than detaining immigrants whose sole crime was crossing the border illegally in order to seek work or to apply for political asylum.

However, "criminal alien" is an imprecise term. This imprecision rendered related enforcement efforts more complex and potentially problematic than would have seemed likely based solely on surface appearances. Most notably, crimes of "moral turpitude" were among the offenses that could expose legal resident immigrants to the possibility of deportation.[53] This category was extremely ambiguous and amorphous, as it was subject to varying moral standards in different locales. Moreover, crimes of "moral turpitude" included both criminal and misdemeanor offenses.[54] Thus, in theory, legal resident immigrants could be subject to deportation for one or two misdemeanor convictions falling under the "moral turpitude" rubric (for one conviction if the misdemeanor was committed within the first five years after entry; for two, if the misdemeanors were committed any time after entry).

An idea of the breadth of the actual use of the "criminal alien" label can be gleaned from the firsthand reports of several immigration attorneys regarding INS detention practices. It appears that many, if not most, of the "criminal aliens" detained in South Texas and Southern California during 1989 and 1990, and facing deportation because of drug convictions, were principally users and small-time dealers, not major traffickers.[55] In addition to drug offenses, legal violations making immigrants eligible for the "criminal alien" category in the Los Angeles area during 1990 included theft and assorted property crimes, assault, and even driving while intoxicated; most of these offenses fell under the "moral turpitude" classification.[56] An even more expansive interpretation was offered by two INS officials in Texas, who were of the opinion that anyone entering the United States illegally could technically be considered a "criminal alien."[57]

It is important to note that the INS played an active role in developing this new focus on "criminal aliens." One indication of this is that INS officials initially justified this enforcement emphasis by citing one obscure sentence on the topic buried in the lengthy text of IRCA, which was a largely unnoticed amendment introduced late in the legislative process. Further, prior to IRCA, the INS had already targeted criminal aliens and designed a program to facilitate their deportation.[58] Thus, the criminal-alien enforcement emphasis is rooted in INS initiatives and discretionary power as much as it is in formal legal mandates.

While the INS set overall detention priorities, such as those targeting criminal aliens, the agency also delegated to its district directors considerable discretionary authority in their implementation.[59] This delegation led to inconsistent and questionable detention practices across the various INS districts over time, which was particularly problematic for Central Americans. For example, the Lower Rio Grande Valley was virtually a "detention zone" during much of the 1980s for Central Americans seeking political asylum, while the restrictiveness of INS detention practices in the nearby Laredo sector varied with availability of INS budgetary resources.[60] Moreover, administrative discretion led to grossly inconsistent bail bond rates for Central American political asylum seekers across the various INS districts in Texas during the latter 1980s and in 1990. This had the effect of controlling and channeling the flow of Central American refugees and immigrants, as well as of denying them fair treatment and due process under the law.[61]

While the INS generally had broad powers in determining immigrant detention policies and practices, two legal changes constrained its detention and deportation efforts against Salvadoran and Guatemalan refugees during the second half of the Bush administration. First, the Immigration Act of 1990 granted Salvadorans present in the United States by September 1990 eligibility for "Temporary Protected Status" for 18 months (later extended twice, each time for a year, though in different forms).[62] Second, an out-of-court settlement reached in 1991 provided that all Salvadorans and Guatemalans who had previously applied for and been denied political asylum (over 150,000 people) were to have their cases reevaluated by newly trained asylum officers. The settlement also sharply limited INS authority to detain those same refugees while their cases were pending.[63] Both of these measures provided relief for many Salvadorans and Guatemalans, and were two of the most visible positive outcomes of a series of lawsuits against the INS, extensive lobbying efforts, and the long-standing work of various nongovernmental organizations providing free basic legal services to refugees. Nevertheless, these two important legal victories did not provide relief for refugees from other countries who were similarly discriminated against by U.S. immigration authorities.[64] During the first half of the Bush administration, however, detention and deportation practices against Central American asylum seekers had taken a decidedly severe turn in the Lower Rio Grande Valley (see the discussion later in this chapter).

On the whole, INS detention and deportation efforts continued to expand under the Bush administration, as budgetary resources and detention capacity grew. However, the focus of these programs, with some notable exceptions, shifted away from Central American political asylum seekers (although Haitian political asylum seekers continued to be a primary target). Instead, the INS increasingly directed its attention to "criminal aliens"—mainly those convicted of drug offenses and violent crimes—and Mexican immigrants subsequently came to make up a significant share of the INS detention population. "Criminal aliens" seemed likely to remain the main target group in the immediate future as well, although it was unclear how broadly the term "criminal alien" would come to be defined. Technically, it could be applied against immigrants very widely, and it apparently was, at least on occasion. While various legal mandates influenced changes in the INS Detention and Deportation program during the Bush administration, INS officials also shaped those mandates, especially at the arguably most meaningful level—implementation.

THE BORDER PATROL

The Border Patrol underwent a number of significant developments during the Bush administration. These include sizable funding increases accompanied by a decline in authorized staff positions, a growing emphasis on drug enforcement activities and related public-relations initiatives, broadened general law enforcement authority, and tactical changes focused on special units. More importantly, the paramilitary character of the Border Patrol was further enhanced, largely as a result of an increased emphasis on drug enforcement activities. While the antidrug activities of the Border Patrol (and other forces) are covered in detail in the next chapter, some aspects of these activities merit attention here for their relation to immigration enforcement and to the overall drift of the Border Patrol as an institution.

The Border Patrol substantially increased its claim on INS resources derived from Congress during the Bush administration. However, the unit did not experience unilinear growth across the board, but rather was subjected to opposing trends in congressional funding and authorized staff levels. Following several years of tremendous growth after the passage of IRCA, congressionally appropriated staff levels for the Border Patrol declined 11% from 1988 through 1992, arriving at 4,948 positions. Interestingly, Congress, the Bush administration, and the INS all largely ignored provisions contained in drug and immigration legislation passed during this period that called for an increase of some 1,435 Border Patrol positions.[65] In contrast, congressional funding for the Border Patrol shot up 59% between 1988 and 1992, reaching some $325.8 million in 1992 (see appendix 1).[66] The 1988–1992 increases in Border Patrol funding amounted to the equivalent of 78% of the growth in congressional funding for the entire INS. Meanwhile, the Border Patrol's share of all congressionally allocated INS funds grew from 25.4% to 33.9% from 1988 through 1992, while the Border Patrol's proportion of all INS staff positions funded by Congress expanded from 35.8% to 41.7% during the same period. One outcome of the growth in the Border Patrol's congressionally allocated funds and the simultaneous cuts in its congressionally appropriated staff positions was that the average amount of funds per agent increased 77%, jumping from $37,125 in 1988 to $65,845 in 1992. This would seem to challenge the common claim that the Border Patrol lacked sufficient resources to fund its authorized staffing levels.[67]

An explanation for the sharply divergent trends in Border Patrol staffing (11% decrease) and funding (59% increase) levels was not offered by INS officials in either their budgets or their testimony to Congress during the Bush administration; nor is a straightforward justification otherwise obvious. However, perhaps some of the large funding increase was devoted to overtime personnel costs.[68] Other portions of the funding increase may have gone to the acquisition and upgrading of sophisticated, high-tech equipment for the Border Patrol during this period, although many of these items were not listed in program descriptions for the Border Patrol in the annual INS budgets submitted to Congress, but rather were often listed in the description of other units' activities in those documents. At present, based on publicly available information, it is impossible to specify where the increased monies went. This crucial issue of financial accountability clearly merits in-depth research.

A more perplexing issue is the discrepancy between the number of Border Patrol staff positions appropriated by Congress and the number of positions actually filled. While it is impossible to precisely determine the latter, there is clear evidence that it was typically much lower than the former. For example, the proportion of congressionally authorized Border Patrol positions slated for the Southwest border region that were actually filled appears to have ranged from 80% to 87% from 1988 through 1990.[69] The actual number of Border Patrol agents posted in the U.S.–Mexico border region during the latter portion of the Bush administration was reported at anywhere from 2,500 (by the press, in 1992) to 3,669 (by the GAO, in 1990), with the higher figures supported by more detailed information.[70] The GAO also reported that in 1990 some 84% of all Border Patrol agents were deployed in the nine Southwest Border Patrol sectors, virtually the same proportion as the INS reported in 1988.[71] On the basis of the GAO data, it seems likely that the actual number of

Border Patrol agents deployed in the region by 1992 was up slightly from the 1990 level to approximately 3,700 agents, as the number of congressionally appropriated Border Patrol positions had increased by 100 posts.[72] While this is far more than the 2,500 agents the press reported in the region in 1992, it is 11% fewer than the 4,156 agents one would expect if all congressionally appropriated Border Patrol positions (4,948) were filled and the standard 84% of those agents deployed in the U.S.–Mexico border region.

Several factors appear to account for much of the Border Patrol's inability to fill all of their congressionally authorized positions, apart from the commonly cited lack of funds. Most prominent is the relatively high annual attrition rate, an estimated 13%, which would have led to a turnover of over half of the entire unit every four years.[73] Second, time lags in recruiting and training were considerable, which left the Border Patrol scrambling to keep up with the enormous IRCA-mandated and appropriated expansion in authorized staffing levels after 1986.[74] In addition, the training process apparently weeded out a significant proportion of would-be agents, as approximately 23% of the agents who started in training from 1986 through 1991 had not completed training by the end of 1991. Significantly the apparent weed-out rate for the last two years of that period was 43%.[75] However, funding could hardly have been a problem (see the previous discussion of Border Patrol funding). Perhaps the INS leadership's difficulties in managing the recent enormous growth in funds and enforcement responsibilities adversely affected their ability to increase the size of the Border Patrol. Once again, the available information does not lend itself to arriving at precise and comprehensive explanations for apparent discrepancies in the patterns of Border Patrol funding and staffing.

To sum up this discussion of Border Patrol staffing levels and budget issues: (1) Congress did not authorize in its appropriations all of the increases in Border Patrol positions that had been mandated in recent drug and immigration legislation; (2) the Border Patrol could not fill all of the positions that Congress actually did authorize, leaving uncertain what the actual Border Patrol staffing levels were for each year; and (3) within the INS, the Border Patrol was far and away the main beneficiary of continued congressional funding increases for the agency during the Bush administration. These issues obviously merit much more thorough investigation.

Moving into the realm of Border Patrol activities, the unit's number of apprehensions of undocumented immigrants continued the post-IRCA decline through 1989, until rising once again, to top 1.1 million annually in the 1990–1992 period, reaching 1.199 million in 1992. This resulted in a 35% increase from 1989 to 1992 (see appendix 2).[76] One notable sub-category of the overall data on apprehensions was "other than Mexican" undocumented immigrants (or "OTMs," in INS lingo). The apprehension of OTMs increased from 1988 to 1990, but fluctuated greatly within that period. Apprehensions of this group—the vast majority of whom were Central American—increased 47% during the 1988–1989 period, rising from 40,936 to 60,162. Declining to 48,504 in 1990, OTM apprehensions were still 18% higher than in 1988.[77] Much of this increase during this period was undoubtedly related to the massive crackdown on Central Americans in the Lower Rio Grande Valley in 1989 and 1990 (see discussion later in this chapter).

Once again, it is debatable what the overall increase in apprehensions reveals. It should be noted that "criminal aliens" taken into INS custody were counted as apprehensions, even though such "apprehensions" most often entailed a mere transfer of inmates from federal, state, and local prisons to INS detention centers; these accounted for only a minuscule portion of the increase in apprehensions from 1989 to 1992.[78] In any case, the overall rise in apprehensions led to increased political pressure on the INS. Many observers saw this growth as evidence that IRCA had not caused the much-anticipated substantial, long-term decline in the flow of undocumented immigrants. However, INS Commissioner McNary countered that the growth in apprehensions in 1990 and 1991 was in part due to the increased deployment of Border Patrol staff and resources on the border. Moreover, McNary explicitly objected to the assumption that INS apprehensions data were a gauge for the un-documented immigration flows, and even said that the increase in the agency's apprehensions was evidence of a smaller undocumented immigration flow.[79] This explanation was contrary to the previously long-held INS position that Border Patrol apprehension levels were a relatively ac-curate barometer of undocumented immigration flows and that in-creased apprehensions signified a growing undocumented flow. Signifi-cantly, McNary now attributed changes in apprehensions to shifts in Border Patrol enforcement tactics and strategy, maintaining that more apprehensions signified less undocumented immigration. However, the proportion of Border Patrol staff time spent on border-control activities declined from 71% to 60% between 1986 and 1990, while the actual amount of time spent on such efforts increased only 2% during the same period.[80] (The increase in the actual number of agents from 1986 to 1990 offset the declining portion of agent time devoted to border-control measures.) This would suggest that the 24% increase in apprehensions from 1989 to 1990 was not the result of increased border enforcement efforts. The stagnation in the overall level of attention devoted to border-control activities can in part be attributed to the Border Patrol's growing involvement in a variety of non–border enforcement responsibilities during the Bush administration. Most prominent among these were the enforcement in the border region of the employer sanctions mandated by IRCA and the apprehension and removal of criminal aliens,[81] both of which had begun at the end of the Reagan administration. The criminal-alien sphere was emphasized in a special new enforcement project centered in the border region, the Border Patrol Criminal Alien Program (BORCAP).[82] In addition, over the years the Border Patrol had placed some agents within the interior United States, hundreds of miles from the border, although INS Commissioner McNary pledged in 1991 to redeploy most Border Patrol agents from the interior to areas within 100 to 150 miles of the border.[83]

More important for the present purposes, the Border Patrol's growing emphasis on drug enforcement appears to have altered the qualitative character of border enforcement efforts during the Bush administration. There were undoubtedly important differences across the various Border Patrol sectors.[84] However, in 1989 the INS began to claim (and continued to do so thereafter) that the Border Patrol had primary responsibility among federal agencies for drug interdiction between official ports of entry along the U.S.–Mexico border.[85] The Office of National Drug Control Policy formalized and reinforced this role for the Border Patrol in 1991.[86] While a similar move in this direction had been made at the end of the Reagan administration, there was now an expanding emphasis on drug enforcement for the Border Patrol, which suggests that the unit may not have been as strongly focused on immigration enforcement as it had been previously. Although immigration and drug enforcement were not strictly separated in practice, they were given different priorities within different Border Patrol sectors, and the growing overall prominence of antidrug efforts may have diverted some of the Border Patrol's expanded, though still finite, resources from its previous overwhelming focus on immigration enforcement. In any case, it is clear that on the whole, the Border Patrol's antidrug activities were substantially escalated during the Bush administration.

The Border Patrol's legal jurisdiction was broadened considerably during the Bush administration, to include more than just drug and immigration enforcement. The Border Patrol's legal jurisdiction was augmented greatly by the Immigration Act of 1990, which granted INS officers general arrest authority under U.S. law. However, this increased arrest authority was made contingent upon the publication of final INS regulations regarding the use of force, the training of officers in arrest and enforcement standards, and the establishment of an expedited internal-review process for violations of INS enforcement standards.[87] This expansion of legal authority was a logical extension of the cross-designation status (i.e., deputization) that had been previously extended to the Border Patrol so that it could enforce drug- and contraband-smuggling laws (see chapter 2).

The expansion of Border Patrol arrest authority had also spread by 1991 to the state level in New Mexico and Arizona, where state governments had each granted Border Patrol agents peace officer status.[88] Three similar measures, at least one of which was filed at the request of Border Patrol officials, were introduced during 1991 in the Texas legislature by South Texas state congressional members. However, all such measures failed to make it out of committee, in part due to the organized and vociferous opposition of Texas civil and human rights advocates.[89] Nonetheless, the broad extension of the Border Patrol's legal authority—under federal law as well as in two border states—had far-reaching implications for the future shape and direction of this force.

This expansion of the Border Patrol's legal jurisdiction was accompanied by several tactical shifts in the unit. One important qualitative change that was in place by at least 1990, if not somewhat earlier, was the establishment of an "Emergency Response Team" for each Border Patrol sector. These teams were described by one Border Patrol official as somewhat less elite versions of the Border Patrol Tactical Team (BORTAC), a special unit developed in 1984 (see chapter 2). Each sector's team was composed of a select group of Border Patrol agents from within the sector, who were specially trained to deal with a variety of emergency situations, including riots.[90] Thus, the "special forces" approach symbolized at the borderwide level by BORTAC was implemented at the local, sector level along the entire U.S.–Mexico border.

The Border Patrol's growing expertise in handling emergency situations and in riot control was called upon during the 1992 Los Angeles riots, in late April and early May. Prominent among the 1,000-member task force of federal law enforcement officers dispatched to Los Angeles to help quell the riots (along with thousands of National Guard and active-duty U.S. military troops) were 400 Border Patrol agents, who were deployed in Latino immigrant neighborhoods. Some 1,044 undocumented immigrants were arrested (accounting for about 10% of all arrests during the uprising), all of whom were subject to deportation, regardless of whether or not they had committed any riot-related offense.[91] At least 700 were expelled from the United States within the first two weeks after the uprising, most of whom were never formally charged with riot-related offenses. These proceedings aroused allegations of widespread denial of due process to the arrested immigrants.[92] It is unclear which Border Patrol agents made up the 400-agent contingent, but it would seem logical that this group included members of BORTAC and the sector-level Emergency Response Teams, as these units had been specifically trained in riot control. It was also reported that "special border patrol units" were part of the federal task force deployed in Los Angeles and that some Border Patrol agents had been brought in from as far away as Arizona and Texas.[93]

In contrast to these harsh efforts, the Border Patrol also initiated several programs that fall into the broad category of "public relations." The most broadly based of these programs was the Border Patrol's large-scale drug-education program for schools, which was centered around its new dog inspection teams. By the early 1990s, the dog-team antidrug program reached approximately one million youths per year. This program was also heavily advertised on posters and billboards in the border region. While playing an instrumental role in the public-relations effort, the canine teams (dog plus trainer) had been established in the late 1980s ostensibly to detect smuggled immigrants and drugs. The canine units were based primarily at traffic inspection checkpoints; there were 71 canine teams in existence in early 1990 and double that number in 1991.[94]

Border Patrol public-relations efforts were furthered by the unit's sponsorship of Explorer Scout groups, in which agents worked with youths 15 to 21 years old. This project also served as a recruiting mechanism for the Border Patrol. The scouts received their own uniforms with a Border Patrol badge and occasionally even accompanied agents on patrol to do linewatch, although more frequently they helped around the office in communication and clerical support work.[95] This program was begun in the Laredo sector, where the Border Patrol also sponsored a soccer league and was generally very visible in the community. Once again, drug enforcement concerns were featured prominently in these high-visibility public-relations efforts.[96]

These public-relations activities undoubtedly helped gain community support for the Border Patrol and the INS in general, thereby increasing public acceptance of the Border Patrol's and the INS's less glamorous and sometimes more controversial endeavors. The drug issue was crucial in the process of fortifying the political legitimacy of the Border Patrol and the INS, as this politically popular issue replaced immigration as the primary topic of public concern in many border areas during the Bush administration. As one former Border Patrol agent observed, there was not much public-relations value or glamour in apprehending "illegal aliens," but there was plenty in making drug busts and apprehending drug traffickers.[97]

On the whole, it seems that the Border Patrol was strengthened in a number of regards during the Bush administration. While congressionally authorized staffing levels declined, the actual number of agents posted in the region apparently increased, though this number still fell significantly short of authorized staffing levels. At any rate, the unit undoubtedly benefited from greatly expanded financial resources. Further, the Border Patrol faced increased and diversified enforcement responsibilities and was also granted much broader legal jurisdiction, which ranged far beyond immigration and drug matters to cover all federal laws and even state laws in some cases. Meanwhile, the Border Patrol broadened its expertise by establishing additional units trained in riot-control tactics. At the same time the force engaged in expanded public-relations efforts to enhance its public image, mainly by promoting the antidrug activities. Drug enforcement became a much more central concern for the Border Patrol during the Bush administration than was previously the case, rivaling immigration enforcement in importance in some areas. Drug and immigration enforcement activities were not intermixed without problems, however. Some of these problems are outlined in the next section.

HUMAN RIGHTS VIOLATIONS
AND OTHER ABUSES OF AUTHORITY

During the Bush administration there were growing signs of civil and human rights violations as well as other abusive practices by Border Patrol and other INS agents. It is important to point out that the Border Patrol and the INS were by no means the sole source of rights violations in the border region, as a host of social actors from both sides of the border committed abuses against undocumented immigrants and border residents (e.g., other U.S. and Mexican police, thieves, assailants, and unscrupulous employers). However, rights abuses are especially egregious in the case of border-area police agencies (of which the INS was the largest), given that the duty to protect civil and human rights is part of their overall law enforcement mission.[98] While this contradiction between police behavior and duty was greater on the Mexican side of the border, the present discussion is limited to the U.S. side, and principally to the INS.

Abusive behavior by INS agents, and especially the Border Patrol, was by no means a new phenomenon, having been documented through the recent past.[99] More generally, the infliction of some measure of indignity on individuals suspected of being undocumented immigrants seemed to be a common part of the immigration law enforcement process.[100] People in the border region were routinely subjected to multiple kinds of scrutiny that was conducted by a variety of federal agencies, including ongoing public surveillance, stops at checkpoints, searches, and questioning about their activities and immigration status. The potential for rights violations and abuses of authority loomed ever present in these law enforcement activities, which were carried out on a far greater scale in the U.S.–Mexico border region than typically is the case elsewhere in the United States.[101]

However, during the Bush administration a fairly systematic pattern of increased rights abuses on the part of Border Patrol and other INS agents emerged more plainly from a diverse and much-expanded body of evidence. This information was reported by human rights groups, the press, congressional committees, the Mexican government, Mexican academic researchers, and even the U.S. Department of Justice. Recorded offenses included beatings, shootings and inappropriate use of firearms, sexual assault, destruction of property, denial of due process, verbal abuse and harassment, inappropriate and illegal searches, substandard detention conditions, and reckless high-speed chases.[102] The seriousness of these abuses led the prominent human rights organization Americas Watch to characterize INS abuses thusly: "The human rights abuses reported here are similar in kind and severity to those about which we have reported in many other countries [i.e., Latin American and Caribbean nations]."[103] However, the frequency of severe abuses appeared to be far lower than in the more troubled Latin American contexts.

A variety of sources indicate the existence of the aforementioned wide range of abusive practices by border law enforcement agencies on the U.S. side. The most systematic documentation of rights abuses in the U.S.–Mexico border region was conducted by the Immigration Law Enforcement Monitoring Project of the American Friends Service Committee. During the 1989–1991 period the project documented 971 offenses committed by members of various border police agencies against residents and immigrants in four border areas (San Diego, southern Arizona, El Paso, and the Lower Rio Grande Valley). Border Patrol staff accounted for 49.8% of the total number of abuses recorded, and other INS personnel accounted for 26.2%, resulting in a cumulative INS share of 76%. Approximately half of the victims were undocumented immigrants, while the remainder were (in order of frequency) legal residents, U.S. citizens, and documented visitors. The victims' ethnic or national backgrounds fell overwhelmingly in the diverse Latino category—principally Mexican and, to a lesser degree, Central American and Mexican American.[104] Official government statistics, as well as data gathered by human rights activists, also indicate a significant and growing number of INS abuses: the number of civil rights cases against the INS that were referred to the Civil Rights Division of the U.S. Department of Justice increased 57% in just two years, jumping from 178 in 1989 to 280 in 1991.[105] Further—in a survey conducted by Mexican researchers of undocumented immigrants waiting to cross the border—when asked in an open-ended question to cite the greatest risk they faced on the U.S. side when crossing the border illegally, immigrants' most frequent response was "physical abuse by INS personnel."[106] A similar 1991 survey (also conducted by Mexican academics) of undocumented immigrants who had been apprehended found that 5.9% of the respondents reported being subjected to abusive practices by the Border Patrol—only slightly fewer than the 6.2% who reported being assaulted by other social actors, such as criminal assailants.[107]

Yet the cases brought to light through these sources undoubtedly represent only a small portion of the total number of such abuses that occurred in the border region, because there was no mechanism in place to ensure a thorough tally and investigation of reports of rights abuses by border region law enforcement authorities. Furthermore, undocumented immigrants, in particular, are a highly vulnerable population, fearful of deportation and with little opportunity to report abuses, especially because of their justified fear that legal authorities cooperate with the INS, exposing them to even greater risk of deportation.[108] It seems that individuals who did try to file formal complaints reporting abusive behavior by INS agents were typically stonewalled, or their grievances were conveniently lost in a bureaucratic shuffle. All of this resulted in a very poor record for the INS in recognizing the existence of abusive practices by its agents and the policies that enable those practices, let alone in disciplining abusive agents.[109] The agency's sense of impunity was facilitated by the lack of INS and Border Patrol accountability, as no adequate external review mechanism existed to investigate charges of abuse or to allow civilian input. Thus the low complaint rate frequently cited by Border Patrol officials as evidence of the absence of abusive behavior by their agents appears to have resulted in large part from deeply flawed monitoring methodologies and policies.[110]

The frequency of abuses is a difficult issue to accurately assess, but several general points are worth noting. While it is impossible to determine precisely the total number of rights abuses by border law enforcement agents, it is important to reiterate that the level of such abuse did not appear to approach that found in more militarized, strife-torn settings in Latin America during the 1980s. Still, the level of abuse certainly seems to have been significant, and especially disturbing for a nation often presented to the rest of the world as a paragon of freedom and democracy. Further, the record of abusive practices by the INS and other border law enforcement agencies that have been documented suggests the existence of a systemic pattern of such activities in those organizations, especially in the INS.

The War on Drugs appears to have exacerbated the potential for human and civil rights abuses by law enforcement agencies in the border region, especially the Border Patrol. Their antidrug activities lent a greater sense of "paramilitary readiness" to border enforcement efforts in general, including immigration enforcement.[111] In the midst of such activities, uncertainty and anxiety about the level of danger present in various enforcement encounters emerged as a crucial problem for Border Patrol agents. Agents were less likely to know what sort of response to expect during enforcement encounters, especially in the increasingly frequent instances in which drug and immigration enforcement responsibilities overlapped. As one INS official put it, "They might stop a truck, open the back, and find a stack of cocaine with a smuggler bearing a machine gun, or they might find 15 suffocating Salvadorans without food or water for five days."[112]

This uncertainty and anxiety were problematic for the status of civil and human rights in the border region, because it implied that Border Patrol agents were increasingly on edge and disposed to approach a wider variety of enforcement encounters as being potentially hostile. This approach seems to have made confrontational encounters with undocumented immigrants more likely, at least until drug trafficking concerns were put to rest. Greater levels of anxiety and potential for confrontation would plausibly have increased the likelihood of abusive behavior and rights violations by the Border Patrol. (Police officers of virtually all types are more likely to use force and to overreact in situations that are either openly confrontational or perceived as potentially hostile, or in which they sense any threat to their authority.)[113] This sort of scenario would heighten the potential for human and civil rights abuses and was especially relevant for regions where drug traffickers and undocumented immigrants traversed adjacent, or even the very same, border crossing areas—such as was the case in the Brownsville, Laredo, and El Paso, Texas, and Douglas and Nogales, Arizona, areas (among other locales).[114] Suggestive of such a dilemma was one Border Patrol agent's terming of an area through which both immigrants and drugs were smuggled as a "danger zone . . . a war zone, if you will."[115]

The potential for civil and human rights abuses was further expanded due to the problematic enforcement assumptions held by some Border Patrol agents, which stemmed from their growing emphasis on antidrug activities. For example, it was reported during 1990 that in Southern Arizona "seasoned agents say when a suspect runs from agents along the border, it is likely he is a drug smuggler."[116] To equate running away with being guilty of drug trafficking had ominous implications for undocumented immigrants, in that those who fled apprehension attempts were likely to be considered "drug runners" and therefore dangerous. An even more problematic practice among leading INS officials in Washington, D.C., was the new tendency to closely associate the categories of "illegal alien" and "drug trafficker."[117] This practice had particularly dangerous ramifications, for undocumented immigrants were more likely to experience harsh treatment if authorities were predisposed to consider them to be associated with the "enemy" in the War on Drugs.

The grave danger of these drug enforcement–inspired assumptions is tragically illustrated by two Border Patrol shootings that occurred in Southern Arizona during 1992. The first took place on March 18 near Nogales, when a Border Patrol agent opened fire with an M-16 rifle on a group of some 25 to 30 undocumented immigrants on foot, whom he had mistaken for drug couriers. One immigrant was wounded.[118] Significantly, this incident became publicly known only months later during the court trial centering on a second, deadly shooting by the same Border Patrol agent.

On June 12 the Border Patrol agent, Michael Elmer, killed an unarmed Mexican man, shooting him in the back twice with an AR-15 rifle as he fled toward the border. The victim was 26-year-old Darío Miranda Valenzuela of Nogales, Sonora. The shooting occurred at dusk during a drug enforcement stakeout seven miles west of Nogales, Arizona, near the border in a rugged canyon that was known as a frequent drug-trafficking site. Agent Elmer attempted to cover up the shooting by dragging the still-living Miranda some 50 yards out of sight, in order to return later to bury him. His partner came upon him during this process, and Elmer allegedly threatened him with the same rifle in an attempt to secure his silence about the incident. However, 15 hours later the partner reported the shooting, and Elmer was arrested and charged with first-degree murder, the first such charge formally filed against a Border Patrol agent in living memory.[119]

Agent Elmer's explanation was that he "freaked out" during the pursuit of two suspected drug-trafficking "scouts." He had heard gunshots nearby, was then warned via radio that a suspect was headed his way, and shortly after saw a man in camouflage pants run toward and then past him. The scene was rife with confusion and panic, evidently somewhat self-inflicted by the agents, as the shots that spooked Elmer apparently came not from the smuggling suspects but from his own partner, who had fired numerous warning shots at the suspects.[120] According to the second suspected drug scout, who escaped the scene, he and Miranda were unarmed (and no firearms were found on Miranda afterward). However, the Border Patrol agents had opened fire without warning and continued to fire as he and Miranda fled, with one agent yelling in Spanish, "I'm going to kill you!"[121] It is not entirely clear whether Miranda was crossing the border as an undocumented immigrant to seek work or as a scout for drug smugglers, as allegations of both purposes were offered by conflicting parties.[122] Regardless, it is clear that he was unarmed and presented no immediate threat to the agent who shot him in the back as he fled.

Nonetheless, in December 1992 the trial jury found Elmer not guilty of all charges, believing that he acted in self-defense in a tense border-area "war zone." The defense successfully portrayed Elmer as a "law officer on the front line of our nation's war on drugs," who shot Miranda because he feared for his life.[123] Elmer's lawyer had maintained that the shooting was legally justified because Miranda continued to run away after agents had ordered him to stop.[124] Further, he had initially claimed, "With this war on drugs, this is a military border and these agents were on patrol in what is a war zone."[125] Following the trial, the jury foreman also asserted that the border area was "absolutely" a war zone and that Border Patrol agents "are without question putting their lives on the line . . . protecting our borders."[126] Thus, the most extreme implications of the term War on Drugs were seized upon and made explicit to legitimize the shooting in the back of an unarmed Mexican man by a Border Patrol agent.

Border human rights activists were appalled by the verdict of not guilty and saw it as evidence of a disturbing climate of impunity for Border Patrol shootings of undocumented Mexican immigrants, justified by the War on Drugs.[127] The verdict established broad parameters of tolerance for the use of excessive force by the Border Patrol in its antidrug activities—as well as for deadly mistakes committed by its agents—all of which suggests that the unit had effectively been granted additional sweeping discretionary power in conducting this new "war." This certainly boded very poorly for those undocumented immigrants caught in the crossfire of expanding drug trafficking and antidrug efforts in the border region, as their human and civil rights, if they were considered at all, were apparently to be viewed as acceptable casualties in the War on Drugs.

The Elmer trial also revealed evidence of routine violations of the Border Patrol's firearms policies, which in turn increased the potential for accidents and abuses. Agents testified that they regularly ignored regulations prohibiting warning shots, and often fired such warnings when they encountered suspected "mules" (i.e., drug couriers) in order to scare them into dropping their load.[128] Further, agents ignored rules requiring them to report any weapons firings, and instead covered up their firings by simply replacing their spent ammunition. More grievously, agents failed to report the earlier shooting incident, in March of 1992 (discussed previously), in which an undocumented immigrant was shot by a Border Patrol agent and shortly thereafter was simply returned to the border.[129]

Thus, the 90 reported Border Patrol shooting incidents in 1990 were probably a substantial undercount. (Records of those shootings indicate that five civilians were killed and six were wounded, as were two agents).[130] Of course, such Border Patrol shootings were by no means unprecedented. Along the California-Mexico border (mainly in the San Diego–Tijuana area), agents from the Border Patrol and the joint Border Patrol–San Diego police unit shot 38 people between 1986 and 1990, killing 20. Many of these shootings appear to have occurred under quite dubious circumstances.[131] (Border Patrol shootings in the San Diego area apparently subsided in the first half of 1991.)[132] Granted, the border area near San Diego was especially hectic and dangerous, as it was the site of numerous criminal assaults, shootings, and even acts of racist vigilantism against undocumented immigrants. However, members of the Border Patrol and its joint patrol with the San Diego police frequently appear to have used very questionable judgment, too often employing excessive force on debatable grounds. Rather than reducing the conflicts in this tense setting, they seem to have repeatedly contributed to an escalating spiral of violence. Their violent record in border enforcement near San Diego stands in stark contrast to that of a newly established elite Mexican police unit in Tijuana, Grupo Beta, which was highly effective in de-escalating and reducing border crime and conflict without using deadly force (see discussion later in this chapter).

Overall, the unprecedented body of wide-ranging evidence covering an array of civil and human rights abuses committed by INS personnel during the Bush administration indicates a substantial, and apparently increasing, level of abuse in the border region. The evidence is especially significant, because cases of abuse were typically rendered less than readily accessible to detection due to the often difficult and complicated circumstances facing victims. The pattern, extent, and types of abuse revealed in these divergent sources suggests that abuse was not an isolated problem but rather a systemic one. This may have been related to the growing emphasis on drug enforcement during this period and the more coercive approach it entailed, which made for a volatile mix with immigration enforcement. María Jiménez, director of the Immigration Law Enforcement Monitoring Project of the American Friends Service Committee, offers a more broadly based explanation: that INS agents were assigned a "mission impossible." She states:

> National policy makers have decided to treat the complex socio-economic problems of international migration and illicit drug traffic as domestic police problems. The result is that enforcement authorities on the U.S.–Mexico border have had placed on their shoulders responsibility for dealing with: our nation's policy to curtail domestic drug consumption, the human exodus from wars in Central America, and the movement of people resulting from the growing debt crisis and capital flight in Mexico and the rest of Latin America. Casting such massive social and political phenomena into problems of border control is a recipe for disaster and is grossly unfair to immigration officials, particularly Border Patrol agents.[133]

One case in particular graphically illustrates some of the pitfalls of casting complex international phenomena as a domestic "border-control problem" and merits closer examination.

THE LOWER RIO GRANDE
VALLEY CRACKDOWN, 1989–1990

The Lower Rio Grande Valley in South Texas during 1989 and 1990 was the site of a large-scale immigration enforcement crackdown on thousands of refugees from Central America, most of whom were applying for political asylum. This was the most massive immigration enforcement effort since Operation Wetback in 1954, although it was more selective and more geographically specific. INS activities in this case are especially illustrative of the contemporary emergency-contingency capacities of the Border Patrol and the INS as a whole. This effort involved a variety of measures, including the deployment of select intelligence assets and a large mobile task force of the Border Patrol, the mass detention of thousands of political asylum applicants, a strong public-relations effort, and intimate cooperation between the INS and U.S. government intelligence agencies. The description offered here focuses primarily on INS enforcement strategy and tactics employed in the crackdown.

Before proceeding, however, it is important to summarize surrounding events. In February 1989, the INS implemented a policy of detaining all persons who applied for political asylum in the Lower Rio Grande Valley, as an explicit means of deterring the flow of refugees from Central America. This tactic was consistent with overall INS detention policy in the 1980s, but it was the last step in the reversal of a previous and landmark change. From mid-May through mid-December of 1988, the INS had allowed asylum seekers in the Lower Rio Grande Valley to travel to other areas of the country to pursue their claims. This short-lived loosening of restrictive procedures resulted in a tremendous increase in Central Americans applying for asylum in the Valley, effectively funneling the flow of refugees from Central America through this remote area of the border. In response, the INS first restricted asylum applicants to the Valley and thereby left thousands of refugees stranded and homeless, overwhelming the area's already limited social services. Following a series of legal challenges to this policy, the INS brought in a large task force of extra Border Patrol agents (along with a variety of support personnel) to round up, detain, and deport the thousands of Central American refugees languishing in the Valley. INS leadership justified this crackdown by claiming that most asylum applicants were filing "frivolous claims" and abusing the asylum process. Civil rights violations by the INS were reportedly widespread during the campaign—especially denials of due process and severely overcrowded conditions of detention. These harsh, exceptional measures were implemented most forcefully during the first half of 1989, and were emphasized again during the winter of 1990, albeit on a smaller scale.[134]

The specific INS strategy and tactics for this massive and severe immigration enforcement effort are clearly laid out in a February 16, 1989, internal INS document that is entitled "Enhancement Plan for the Southern Border."[135] The plan was predicated on a three-pronged strategy: (1) the aggressive enforcement of immigration laws and detention for violators, (2) a thorough and expedited adjudication of asylum claims, and (3) "a media campaign aimed toward public understanding and acceptance of the difference between claims [for political asylum] made from a third country and those made after entry [into the United States] without inspection."[136] The centerpiece was the introduction of an additional 250 Border Patrol agents to the Valley, the bulk of whom were to be deployed alongside local Border Patrol agents (normally numbering some 375) in a large mobile task force charged with the responsibility of apprehending undocumented immigrants. In addition, 96 agents were to be used as security guards at various detention facilities.[137]

Detention plans included contracting with the Red Cross to establish a "soft" detention center for families, women, and children on federal property in Brownsville. Further, the nearby INS Port Isabel detention center was to be expanded with temporary accommodations (tents), while other INS detention centers in the region as well as locally managed private facilities were also to be used. Given the massive influx of INS personnel and the nature of the operation, the report noted one especially far-reaching possible outcome: "It is likely that the containment area will effectively be a 'Federal Reservation' and as such, responsibility for criminal and civil law enforcement rests with the Service."[138]

Of particular interest are the various intelligence-gathering activities outlined in the INS plan. One effort listed under this heading was a mass public-relations campaign for the larger enforcement operation. This was intended to generate positive public sentiment locally, and also to intimidate and deter Central Americans on their way to the United States. Another, far less conspicuous intelligence activity outlined was the deployment of 10 INS agents in Mexico and Guatemala to gather information about changes in the migration flows from Central America. Their purpose was to determine the impact of the enforcement operation and the surrounding publicity on the flow of refugees from Central America, in order to make any necessary adjustments in the deployment of the Border Patrol mobile task force and antismuggling resources in South

Texas.[139] Moreover, INS intelligence activities were to involve substantial collaboration with other federal intelligence agencies. This sensitive issue merits special attention, especially because the INS plan was quite explicit on the matter:

> The INS Intelligence Program will continue on-going liaison with other government agencies, particularly CIA [Central Intelligence Agency], DIA [Defense Intelligence Agency], and the Department of State to monitor changes in those conditions in source countries which most heavily impact on emigration. . . . The information provided by these agencies will be analyzed in conjunction with statements provided by the aliens during debriefings. Information collected by the INS will be shared with these agencies so that they have a complete picture of the situation as it emerges.[140]

It is important to note that such information sharing between the INS and federal intelligence agencies was particularly dangerous for refugees applying for political asylum, because U.S. intelligence agencies also collaborated with their counterparts in Central American nations. Most of the latter had an especially onerous record of systematic human rights abuses and were often directly tied to the persecution that many asylum seekers were fleeing. Thus, the sharing of information from refugee debriefings could have endangered those refugees and their family, friends, and associates in Central America. Moreover, this sort of information sharing is entirely contrary to the confidentiality guaranteed to political asylum applicants regarding the details of their case. In addition, it is significant that collaboration between the INS and various U.S. intelligence institutions was apparently not unique to this episode, as the quotation indicates that the INS Intelligence Program *will continue ongoing liaison* with the CIA, DIA, etc. In the absence of additional information, however, it is impossible at present to determine the full content and range of this collaboration.

The implementation of the INS plan to crack down on Central American political asylum seekers resulted in the detention of thousands of men, women, and children in the Valley for months at a time. They were held at various locations within a web of at least six different INS and private-contract detention facilities in the Valley—including among the latter a so-called soft detention center for apprehended families, run by the American Red Cross.[141] Many who gave up on appealing their asylum cases as a result of detention were deported. Most asylum claims (including virtually all of those filed by non-Nicaraguans) were denied at hastily held, often ill-prepared initial adjudication hearings. Those who chose to appeal these initial rulings faced a lengthy detention in grossly over-crowded facilities; consequently, most accepted deportation.[142]

Following the brunt of the crackdown on Central American asylum seekers, the Lower Rio Grande Valley was the site of continuing, notable INS enforcement incidents. The most outstanding of these was an un-precedented INS raid in September 1990 on an internationally renowned refugee shelter run by the Catholic Church, Casa Romero in Brownsville, ostensibly conducted to locate possible Iraqi and (subcontinental) Indian "terrorists." Pre–Gulf War hysteria appears to have played a major role in the incident.[143]

The 1989–1990 INS crackdown on Central American refugees in the Valley was the most severe and intense, though selective, INS immigration enforcement campaign since Operation Wetback in 1954. This case provides illustrations of sophisticated INS contingency capacities that could probably be adapted to other border areas and focused on other categories of immigrants, should the need to do so arise. Moreover, it appears that the agency has the ability to alter the geographical concentration of refugee flows, such that these flows are directed into relatively contained areas. The Lower Rio Grande Valley crackdown is especially significant because it illustrates not only the capacity of the INS to employ draconian immigration enforcement tactics against carefully targeted immigrant populations and to sever any supportive relationships between the targeted and local populations, but also its ability to do so in a way that allows border business, traffic, and life to continue as usual for most of the local residents. The "problem" in this case was conveniently swept away to remote and inconspicuous detention centers.[144]

U.S.–MEXICAN COLLABORATION
IN IMMIGRATION ENFORCEMENT

There are a number of indications of increasing collaboration between U.S. and Mexican officials in immigration enforcement during the Bush and Salinas administrations. Collaborative immigration efforts appear to have been focused on Central Americans traveling through Mexico as well as on the apprehension of criminal suspects near the border, with very little attention being given to the politically sensitive issue of undocumented Mexican immigration. This cooperative binational rela-tionship was further expanded via joint drug enforcement activities (see chapter 4).

The expanded working relationship between U.S. and Mexican officials was most visible in efforts to apprehend Central American immigrants and refugees. Evidence of this surfaced during the above-noted INS crackdown in the Lower Rio Grande Valley, when the INS dispatched intelligence agents to Mexico to assess the migration patterns of Central Americans in that country. At the same time, the INS District Office in Mexico City was slated to continue its liaison activities with the new director of the Mexican Immigration Service to address the issue of third-country migrants traveling through Mexico en route to the United States.[145] In addition, the U.S. State Department contacted the Mexican government in 1989 regarding the need to reduce the flow of Central Americans through Mexico.[146] More concretely, during the 1989–1990 period and afterward, INS officials provided training to their counterparts in the Mexican Office of Immigration Services, as well as to Mexican federal police agents and customs officials. The INS also regularly exchanged information with these agencies and expanded its overall cooperation and collaboration with them on immigration enforcement matters.[147]

Meanwhile, during roughly the same time period, Mexican authorities implemented a much more restrictive approach in dealing with third-country nationals en route to the United States. Mexican apprehensions and deportations of undocumented immigrants (overwhelmingly Central American) jumped from 14,000 in 1988, to 85,000 in 1989, to an estimated 160,000 in 1990.[148] In mid-1993 it was revealed that the United States Congress had, at least for recent years, appropriated $350,000 per year to pay Mexico for costs incurred in deporting from Mexico third-country nationals headed toward the United States.[149] These efforts were primarily focused on the Guatemalan border in the southern state of Chiapas and in the areas south of Mexico City, although the northern border region also received additional scrutiny.[150]

It is important to note that immigration and drug enforcement in Mexico overlapped at times, as law enforcement officials posted at controversial drug-interdiction checkpoints in 1989 and 1990 also carried out immigration enforcement against Central Americans.[151] The Salinas administration dropped the controversial antidrug checkpoints in mid-1990, but rights abuses continued to occur in other law enforcement settings. Many of the Mexican police and security forces participating in these various immigration and drug enforcement efforts—especially the Mexican federal police and its elite antidrug unit—were associated with recurrent human rights abuses of all types.[152]

There were also indications of less objectionable forms of collaboration between U.S. and Mexican immigration authorities, particularly in the realm of the apprehension of criminal suspects. One form of collaboration was developed following several highly publicized and controversial shootings of unarmed and undocumented Mexican immigrants in 1989 and 1990 by the Border Patrol, when the Salinas and Bush administrations established a high-level binational working group. This working group was to address issues related to Mexican immigration to the United States and border enforcement efforts, in order to facilitate binational cooperation (where possible) and regular communication on these sensitive matters.

The leading initiative in constructive border enforcement and binational collaboration was the formation of the Grupo Beta police force in Tijuana, a highly innovative, elite group of some 40 agents led by a former psychology professor. Grupo Beta was formed in 1990 by the Mexican government for the express purpose of reducing the level of violence in the heavily trafficked Tijuana border area by protecting immigrants from the numerous violent criminals active in the area as well as from corrupt Mexican police who routinely extorted bribes from immigrants. The Mexican government was intent on reducing appearances of instability and disorder on the Mexican side of the border, as it sought closer economic ties with the United States. Grupo Beta was remarkably successful in its mission and also established a close working relationship with U.S. Border Patrol officials and the Border Crime Intervention Unit (a joint project of the San Diego Police and the Border Patrol), particularly with respect to the apprehension of criminal suspects. The elite force even received training and equipment from its U.S. counterparts. However, in strong contrast to those U.S. forces, Grupo Beta officers had not shot anyone as of mid-1992, and they received high marks from human rights officials in the area. The unit's success prompted Mexican officials to consider establishing similar forces in other border cities, such as Ciudad Juárez and Matamoros.[153]

Nonetheless, Grupo Beta members walked a fine line between conducting general law enforcement in a unique border context and not violating a specific Mexican law that prohibits interference with the emigration of Mexican citizens. This line was apparently blurred in early 1992 when INS officials pressured Mexican immigration authorities and Grupo Beta into stopping a dangerous and especially visible new form of undocumented immigration: groups of people rushing, en masse, through border ports of entry positioned on freeways, running directly up traffic lanes, dodging oncoming vehicles. Efforts by Mexican authorities to halt this practice were justified by Mexican officials on the grounds of pedestrian and driver safety.[154]

While Grupo Beta activities appear to have been constructive on the whole, there are also indications of more questionable, though less direct, collaborative efforts between Mexican and U.S. officials in the border region. For example, in March 1992 the Matamoros police implemented a mounted horse patrol along several miles of the Rio Grande near the international bridge, ostensibly to cut down on crime in the area. However, Border Patrol agents posted nearby noted that shortly after the unit's formation the flow of undocumented immigration through adjacent areas on the U.S. side was noticeably reduced. Moreover, the Matamoros police patrolling the river area on horseback and the Border Patrol also appeared to collaborate, at least on occasion, in the apprehension of undocumented immigrants who were not "criminal aliens" but were nonetheless deemed troublesome by authorities.[155]

Another measure implemented in Matamoros appears to have had as one of its purposes the reduction of undocumented immigration along a visible stretch of the river border. In July 1992 work was completed on a well-lit, 10-foot-high wall and fence structure stretching about one mile along the top of a levee adjacent to the Rio Grande. The wall covers an area between two international bridges, immediately opposite downtown Brownsville, which had previously been a popular crossing point for local, undocumented young men.[156]

The origins of the Matamoros horse patrol and wall are unclear, but both served, at least in part, to deter undocumented immigration by local Mexican citizens in an area that was particularly visible to U.S. and Mexican authorities. These measures may have been justified in terms of public safety, as the affected crossing areas were sites of frequent robberies and assaults. However, one likely effect of both measures was to force the relocation of this activity (i.e., undocumented crossings and crimes committed by those who prey upon crossers) to more remote, less visible areas, which could well have made undocumented crossings even more dangerous.

On the whole, collaboration between Mexican and U.S. officials on immigration and various border enforcement issues appears to have increased noticeably during the Salinas and Bush administrations. These activities were previously viewed with far less enthusiasm in official circles in Mexico. However, in the 1989–1992 period several initiatives emerged and were advanced considerably, most notably immigration enforcement against third-country nationals in Mexico, as well as more low-key collaboration between select police authorities on both sides of the border. The outcome and future direction of the various Mexican immigration and border enforcement measures remain to be seen. Nonetheless, joint U.S.–Mexican endeavors in these areas are likely to be a salient issue in the future, as the two countries undergo greater economic integration and establish closer political ties.

THE LIC FRAMEWORK APPLIED TO INS POLICIES
AND ACTIVITIES DURING THE BUSH ADMINISTRATION

Many facets of INS border enforcement efforts during the Bush administration described in this chapter coincide with the low-intensity conflict (LIC) framework as it was outlined in chapter 1. To begin with, much of the equipment introduced by and construction carried out for the INS in the border region from 1988 through 1992 is characteristic of that recommended in LIC doctrine. One of the more obvious developments in this regard was the introduction of 36 new helicopters. Also falling under this rubric is the expanded deployment of sophisticated intrusion-detection equipment such as low-level-light television, infrared radar, night scopes, and portable electronic ground sensors, as well as the production of 15 "improved image-enhancement" vehicles. Most prominent was the construction of seven miles of a corrugated steel wall on the border between San Diego and Tijuana. This measure appears to be similar in kind to, but also to exceed, the use of fences as an antiterrorism measure, which falls under the LIC mission category of terrorism counteraction. Further, the new wall as well as the expanded traffic checkpoints, INS detention centers, and Border Patrol stations in the Southwest during the Bush administration are all arguably related to low-intensity conflict doctrine: these efforts enhanced the agency's social-control capacity over targeted civilian populations (in this case undocumented immigrants, drug traffickers, and those suspected of being either one), which is the essence of low-intensity conflict doctrine.

The use of National Guard and various other U.S. military troops to assist the INS in a variety of construction projects and other ongoing support operations in the U.S.–Mexico border region more clearly fits the LIC framework. The military's support was formally justified under the pretext of drug enforcement, but it also aided the INS's immigration enforcement efforts in the border region. The most prominent case of this military support was the construction of the new border wall near

San Diego. Military support also took other, less obvious forms, including aid in communications, electronics, and transportation maintenance, as well as additional construction efforts. At least one of the construction efforts (brush clearing near downtown Laredo) was akin to the "military-civic action" component of low-intensity conflict, whereby military forces are involved in local public-service provision, construction projects, and development efforts. In addition, the military's support for the INS facilitated some degree of integration and coordination among distinct police and military forces, which is a particularly central tactic in the LIC framework. These joint activities enabled various elements of the INS and the military establishment to develop working relationships under low-key circumstances. That the INS took the lead role in these endeavors is also consistent with LIC provisions, which favor the use of police forces in visible roles—backed up by support from military elements—in the handling of many security matters.

INS detention and deportation practices and policies during the first half of the Bush administration also have some LIC-related implications, principally at the broader level of enhancing the agency's social-control capacity over targeted civilian populations. Most notable was the shift in emphasis to "criminal aliens" from the previous focus on political asylum seekers, especially those from Central America and Haiti. While this change may appear at first glance to have been a reasonable approach, it was made problematic by the ambiguous nature of the definition of the term "criminal alien." INS officials focused their efforts mainly on immigrants convicted of drug offenses and violent crimes. However, the term "criminal alien" can legally be applied much more broadly. It appears that all "aliens"—even legal residents—can be potentially subject to deportation if they have two or more relatively minor brushes with the law (i.e., misdemeanors that fall within the amorphous "moral turpitude" category). Such deportation apparently occurred at least on occasion during this period. The broad parameters of the definition of the term "criminal alien" had particularly serious implications for those vast segments of the immigrant population in the United States (and especially in the Southwest) who are not citizens, such as most Mexican immigrants. The social-control power over select groups of civilians technically afforded by these "criminal alien" enforcement measures is quite consistent with the targeted social-control objective of low-intensity conflict. This same capacity was enhanced by the continued expansion of detention space available to the INS throughout the Southwest, including the opening of a new detention center in Southern California.

Many of the changes experienced by the Border Patrol during the Bush administration also overlap substantially with various aspects of LIC strategy and tactics. First of all, this unit was the primary recipient and utilizer of the plethora of newly deployed LIC-related equipment noted previously. Second, the Border Patrol was increasingly involved in drug interdiction, which is a key part of the LIC mission area of antidrug operations. Third, the range of its legal authority was expanded considerably with the granting to INS officers of general arrest authority under federal law and of state law enforcement authority in two border states. This gave the Border Patrol formal enforcement authority similar to that of the broad-ranging national police forces found in LIC contexts of the third world. This expansion of authority was accompanied by the growth of the unit's list of primary enforcement responsibilities to include not only drug interdiction, but also criminal alien apprehension and the enforcement of employer sanctions in the border region. Thus, the way was opened for the transformation of the Border Patrol into a formal national and even state-level police force, should such become politically expedient. However, it seems clear that regardless of how broad its formal authority, the Border Patrol has long focused and will likely continue to focus most of its attention on Latino, especially Mexican-origin, peoples and communities in the border region. Another development characteristic of the LIC framework was the implementation of the "special forces" concept on the local level through the formation of Emergency Response Teams in each Border Patrol sector. Meanwhile, the Border Patrol's increased public-relations efforts in school drug-education programs and the Explorer Scout program resemble the LIC emphasis on increasing benevolent contact between security forces and civilians.

The most graphic illustration of the implementation of the LIC framework in the border region during the Bush administration was the 1989–1990 INS crackdown on Central American refugees in the Lower Rio Grande Valley. This campaign was in part an extension of LIC policies implemented in Central America by the Reagan and Bush administrations and their allies during the 1980s, which were fundamental in creating the social, political, and economic conditions that many of the Central Americans were fleeing. The Valley crackdown appears to have been the forceful imposition of a "last line of defense" by policymakers in their attempt to control Central America and to keep some of the politically damaging fallout (e.g., large flows of refugees) from reaching the U.S. public. Further, the selective nature of the enforcement campaign—i.e., its focus on political asylum seekers from Central America—raises a troubling potentiality (and lesson). It indicates that the INS has the ca-pacity to target specific groups within a particular border area for the ad-ministration of harsh enforcement measures, and can do so in a manner that is minimally disruptive to the surrounding populace.

The specific INS strategy and tactics used in the crackdown campaign fit the LIC framework almost perfectly. For example, the INS media cam-paign to simultaneously generate local public support for and immigrant fear of the crackdown activities has all the markings of an LIC psycho-logical operation designed to influence civilian populations. The large-scale, short-term deployment of Border Patrol agents in a mobile task force resembles the temporary-show-of-force aspect of the category of LIC doctrine of peacetime contingency operations. (The tactic of using mobile task forces also hearkened back to Operation Wetback in 1954.) Further, the elaborate intelligence efforts and interagency collaboration set out in the operation plan are entirely consistent with LIC doctrine's emphasis on such measures. Moreover, the enlisting of private agen-cies—particularly the Red Cross—by the INS to aid in its enforcement campaign by providing "soft" detention facilities is similar to the LIC tac-tic of portraying security operations as a form of "humanitarian aid" and seeking to incorporate the participation of private-sector aid organiza-tions in such endeavors. The entire mass roundup, detention, and depor-tation campaign against Central Americans in the Valley is clearly a stark example of social-control measures taken against a specifically targeted civilian population—a practice that is quite consistent with the overall emphasis of the LIC paradigm.

In a related vein, aspects of expanded collaboration between U.S. and Mexican authorities in immigration matters also concur with several characteristics of the LIC framework. At a general level, the accelerated Mexican campaign to prevent the transit of Central Americans through Mexico can easily be viewed as an extension of the United States' imple-mentation of low-intensity conflict doctrine in Central America; it cre-ated additional "lines of defense" between the region and the United States. The U.S. government even paid the Mexican government for its assistance on this issue. More specifically, the use of U.S. police and secu-rity forces to train their Mexican counterparts is very similar to the "U.S. trainer-adviser" and "host-nation–force trainee" roles commonly con-tained in LIC efforts. Further, the expansion of ongoing communication and coordination between U.S. and Mexican police and security forces in the border region is an example of the force integration characteristic of low-intensity conflict, though raised to a binational level.

Perhaps the most consequential and disturbing instance of coincidence between INS border enforcement efforts and LIC practices lies in the realm of human and civil rights abuses. Such violations have frequently accompanied the implementation of LIC doctrine, as well as other militarization efforts, by U.S. forces and their allies in Latin America and elsewhere in the third world. While the level of rights abuses committed by members of various border-region U.S. law enforcement agencies did not reach the level often found in LIC contexts, the corpus of evidence of rights violations by personnel from those agencies (the vast majority coming from the Border Patrol and other INS units) does suggest that such abuses were not isolated incidents, but rather constituted an organizational pattern, and a systemic, institutional problem within the Border Patrol and the INS. The Border Patrol's prominent participation in border antidrug operations while also carrying out immigration enforcement responsibilities appears to have contributed to the unit's propensity for committing rights violations during the Bush administration. The fact that most of the abuses perpetrated by Border Patrol agents and other INS officers were apparently directed against members of a highly vulnerable civilian population—undocumented immigrants—is especially problematic and disturbing.

Overall, during the Bush administration, INS policies and activities in the U.S.–Mexico border region overlapped to an unprecedented degree with LIC equipment and operational characteristics. The paramilitary nature of the cumulative buildup of INS equipment, forces, and other resources, in conjunction with ever expanding law enforcement responsibilities and authority, became increasingly evident. Effects of this paramilitary expansion on civilians in the border region also emerged more clearly—in the form of human and civil rights abuses carried out by INS enforcement personnel. However, the evolution of INS immigration and general enforcement efforts make up only part of the overview of southwestern border enforcement measures. The multifaceted War on Drugs brought about a more explicit militarization of the U.S.–Mexico border region.

4

The War on Drugs in the U.S.–Mexico Border Region, 1981–1992

The Reagan and Bush administrations (1981–1988, 1989–1992) waged a highly publicized antidrug effort, which they termed the War on Drugs, to limit the flow of illegal drugs into the United States. While such efforts are not unique in U.S. history, particularly in the U.S.–Mexico border region, this most recent version was characterized by a sustained sense of urgency.[1] The political momentum propelling the issue seemed almost limitless at times, although the clamor appeared to have subsided somewhat by 1992.[2] The political escalation of the issue had reached a new level in 1986, when President Reagan signed a secret directive that formally designated illegal drug trafficking as a "significant threat to national security" and authorized the Pentagon to engage in a much broader range of antidrug activities.[3] This campaign involved a wide range of government agencies and was conducted both domestically and abroad, especially in Latin America.

The interpretation offered here is that the sum of the antidrug activities pursued in the U.S.–Mexico border region from 1981 through 1992 clearly amounts to border militarization.[4] This is in no small part due to the fact that the military was involved in a variety of forms of antidrug activities in the border region from the outset, and subsequently saw its role expanded in scope and depth. Moreover, it should be recalled that antidrug operations are a specific mission area of low-intensity conflict doctrine (see chapter 1). Consequently, antidrug efforts in the border region qualify, virtually by definition, as a form of militarization. More importantly, civilian police and military agencies shared this mission and actively worked together in carrying it out, increasing their collaboration over time. Thus, the War on Drugs evokes the issue of border militarization much more directly than do the immigration enforcement efforts previously examined in this monograph. The key difference is that in previous chapters militarization was used as an analogy (i.e., the INS adopted various characteristics that resembled those of LIC doctrine), whereas in this chapter militarization takes on a much more literal sense (i.e., the direct and indirect involvement of military forces in particular domestic law enforcement matters). Despite these differences, it is important to point out that immigration and drug enforcement efforts often overlapped to varying degrees, which suggests that the differing forms of militarization could affect both realms of law enforcement.

Overall funding for antidrug efforts in general increased rapidly in the late 1980s and early 1990s, with the overwhelming share being devoted to punitive law enforcement activities aimed at reducing drug supplies. Specifically, the federal government spent some $21 billion on counternarcotics efforts from 1981 to 1989, of which $16 billion (76%) was dedicated to drug law enforcement endeavors to reduce drug supplies, including $7 billion (33% of total spending) for the interdiction of drugs being smuggled into the United States. In comparison, the same approximate funding (over $20 billion) was requested for the following two-year period alone ($9.48 billion in fiscal year 1990 and $10.63 billion in fiscal year 1991), with a slightly smaller proportion dedicated to drug law enforcement activities (71%) and a reduced share of the total funding devoted to interdiction efforts (22%). It appears that the vast majority of these funds were to be focused on domestic antidrug activities, as only 6% of the funding was specifically devoted to "international initiatives," while 64% was targeted for interdiction and criminal-justice efforts, mostly the latter.[5] The U.S.–Mexico border region was one of the focal points for drug enforcement activities, and various federal law enforcement agencies devoted some $441 million to such endeavors in 1991 and were slated to spend $541 million there in 1992.[6] On the whole, these figures suggest that the War on Drugs gave comparatively little emphasis to demand-reduction measures such as education and treatment. Punitive law enforcement measures were clearly the preferred approach.

The U.S.–Mexico border region was one of the primary sites for stepped-up antidrug efforts from the early 1980s onward, as drug trafficking in the area reportedly expanded markedly. One indication of the region's prominence in this campaign is that apparently nowhere else on the "domestic front" of the nebulous War on Drugs did the activities of civilian law enforcement agencies and the military become so deeply intertwined and complementary over such a sustained period of time. The effective integration of military and civilian forces took many forms and included the extensive sharing of equipment, the joint deployment of personnel, and collaborative strategizing. This process was in large part made possible by a series of changes to long-standing, general U.S.

legal prohibitions against the use (except in rare instances) of active-duty military forces in domestic law enforcement activities.

Before proceeding, it is important to note that many of the antidrug efforts in the border region from 1981 through 1992 appear to be at odds with the available information on the nature of drug-flow patterns. Antidrug activities were largely focused on areas between official border ports of entry and relied heavily on general patrolling and even clandestine observation operations. Yet the Drug Enforcement Agency (DEA) reportedly estimated during the same period that 85% of illegal drugs entering the United States were hidden in legitimate means of transportation,[7] which use official ports of entry (land, air, or sea) to enter the country. Moreover, it was reported in 1990 that the DEA also estimated that the bulk of the cocaine, virtually all the heroine, and half of the marijuana smuggled into the United States came through official land ports of entry in vehicles and their cargo or in people's personal possession.[8] Thus, there was an apparent spatial discrepancy between key locational focal points of border-region drug enforcement efforts (i.e., territory in between land ports of entry) and the sites of the suspected principal drug-flow routes (i.e., official land ports of entry). This contradiction, as well as the issue of active collaboration between civilian and military forces, suggests that border-region antidrug activities merit careful and critical examination.

One obstacle to such scrutiny, however, is the difficulty in obtaining detailed, reliable information on this sensitive topic, especially when it is apparent that the government has withheld information on this issue in (i.e., censored) publicly available government documents.[9] No doubt this is in part due to the formal designation of drug trafficking as a "national security" issue, as well as the military's own predilection for secrecy. Nonetheless, it is possible to gain some degree of understanding of antidrug efforts in the border region from available information, though such materials should be used with care and viewed comparatively. Investigating this topic is a necessarily inexact process. (See appendix 4 for a discussion of related methodological issues.)

The primary purpose of this chapter is to determine which aspects of low-intensity conflict doctrine were present in drug enforcement activities in the U.S.–Mexico border region from 1981 through 1992. Its secondary purpose is to discern some of the implications of these antidrug activities for immigration enforcement and more broadly for the status of civil and human rights in the borderlands. Relevant materials are presented in chronological order along issue-substantive (rather than presidential-administration) time lines, with 1986 being taken as the temporal dividing point, as it is the year in which drug trafficking was formally designated as a national security issue. Primary attention is devoted to the 1986–1992 period, because drug enforcement efforts in the border region expanded markedly during this period. The larger project embarked upon here is to examine antidrug efforts in the border region during the contemporary period using an admittedly unconventional framework, with the intention of shedding new light on those activities and stimulating fuller consideration of their potential impact on residents and immigrants in the borderlands.

Antidrug Activities, 1981–1985

The period 1981–1985 marked the start-up phase of this most recent version of the War on Drugs. During this time crucial legal changes were enacted, elaborate plans were prepared, and a host of activities were initiated. These efforts paved the way for the much larger buildup of drug enforcement measures in subsequent years. A crucial starting point in opening the domestic "front" of the War on Drugs was the legal changes that in effect altered the Posse Comitatus statute, changes that were included in the Defense Authorization Act of 1982 (passed in late 1981).[10] Originally established in 1879, the Posse Comitatus statute made the use of "any part of the Army or Air Force as a posse comitatus" (i.e., deputized by civilian law enforcement officials to assist in putting down any type of civil disorder or to otherwise carry out the law) a felony, "except in cases of and under circumstances expressly authorized by the Constitution or an act of Congress."[11] Thus this provision largely prohibited deputizing active-duty military personnel to assist in domestic law enforcement activities, except in extreme and rare instances.[12] However, the Defense Authorization Act of 1982 effectively loosened these restrictions by literally adding a new chapter to U.S. law regarding the use of the military, entitled "Military Cooperation with Civilian Law Enforcement Officials."[13] Most important, military personnel were now explicitly allowed to *assist* (not just support) civilian law enforcement agencies in newly specified ways—by operating and maintaining military equipment loaned to federal law enforcement agencies. However, military personnel were only allowed to operate or maintain military equipment on loan to civilian law enforcement agencies to the extent that it was "used for monitoring and communicating the movement of air and sea traffic."[14] In addition, military personnel were still forbidden to participate directly in the interdiction and stopping of vessels and vehicles, and to search, seize, or arrest individuals.[15]

While keeping this crucial prohibition in place, the 1982 Department of Defense (DOD) Authorization Act also contained a number of additional significant relaxations of the Posse Comitatus statute. Specifically, the secretary of defense was allowed to make any military base or research facility available "to any federal, state or local civilian law enforcement official for law enforcement purposes."[16] Further, the military was allowed to share with federal, state, and local law enforcement officials any information collected during the normal course of military operations that could be relevant to a violation of any federal or state law within those officials' jurisdiction.[17] In addition, military personnel were allowed to train federal, state, and local police officials to operate and maintain any military equipment loaned to them, "and to provide *expert advice* relevant to the purposes of this chapter" (emphasis added), which apparently was drug enforcement, though the chapter title was much broader in nature, as noted previously.[18] The latter provision, in particular, assumes that the military had expertise in drug and other types of civilian law enforcement, areas in which the institution had little if any background.

It is especially important to note that the forms of military cooperation with civilian police outlined in the 1982 DOD Authorization Act seemed to be available for much more than drug enforcement. The only form of military assistance that was specifically restricted to law enforcement agencies with certain types of jurisdiction was the previously noted provision of military personnel to maintain and operate loaned military equipment. This sort of aid was limited to agencies with jurisdiction to enforce *drug, customs, and immigration laws.*[19] Nowhere did the provisions of the 1982 act limit the various forms of military assistance described solely to drug enforcement matters; rather, the far more broadranging term "law enforcement" was most often used. Such guidelines appear to have allowed the U.S. military to become involved at least indirectly in various types of civilian law enforcement—most notably, immigration enforcement.

It should be noted, however, that the National Guard, which is ordinarily under the control of state governors, is not covered by Posse Comitatus restrictions, except in the relatively rare cases in which the president formally places it under federal authority.[20] This has allowed state governors to make free use of the National Guard in domestic law enforcement throughout the twentieth century, to contain labor strikes, racial or ethnic strife, student protests, and other types of civil unrest.[21] Furthermore, neither the U.S. Navy nor the Marine Corps is technically covered by Posse Comitatus restrictions, although DOD regulations restrict those forces in a similar manner.[22]

The impact of the 1982 DOD Authorization Act in altering the Posse Comitatus statute, however, should not be underestimated. Assistant Secretary of Defense Lawrence Korb later noted, "When the law was changed in 1981, we were basically repealing 100 years of American history."[23] The restricted use of the military in domestic law enforcement activities was and largely remains a hallmark of U.S. society and its democratic ideals. It has helped distinguish the United States from many other nations, particularly those whose military forces periodically committed extensive civil and human rights violations in the process of engaging in domestic law enforcement activities—such as those countries in which the United States had promoted counterinsurgency and LIC doctrine, among many others. The initial relaxation of Posse Comitatus restrictions on U.S. military involvement in domestic law enforcement laid the formal groundwork for the military to be enlisted in the War on Drugs. More far-reaching changes were to follow.

Before proceeding, the term "interdiction" should be defined, since interdiction was one of the principal objectives of the U.S. government's antidrug effort, particularly the portion in which the military participated. According to the military's coordinator for drug enforcement policy and support during the Bush administration, Stephen M. Duncan, interdiction has several phases, including detection, identification of possible drug traffickers, interception, tracking and monitoring, apprehension, search, seizure, and arrest. In practice, these phases often overlap.[24]

The first instance of major military involvement in drug-interdiction efforts was the South Florida Task Force on Organized Crime, formed in 1982 and headed by Vice President Bush. This task force was to serve as a model for future antidrug efforts along the U.S.–Mexico border (and elsewhere) that would involve a wide variety of forces. The assortment of military support used in the South Florida project was extensive. A partial list includes E-2B, E-2C, and P-3 radar and surveillance aircraft and UH-1N helicopters, as well as hydrofoil, frigate, and destroyer sea vessels, for the Navy; AWACS (or E-3) radar aircraft and aerostat radar balloons for the Air Force; and UH-1H, Cobra, and Blackhawk helicopters, as well as OV-1 Mohawk tracker aircraft, for the Army.[25] Among the many participating law enforcement agencies was the U.S. Coast Guard. However, during the same period the U.S. Coast Guard was also carrying out a campaign to interdict Haitian immigrants in coastal waters off South Florida and elsewhere in the Caribbean sea. This overlap of immigration and antidrug efforts in the same region (or at least adjacent areas) by some of the same participating agencies was later repeated on the U.S.–Mexico border.

This South Florida Task Force model was extended to the borderlands in March 1983, when President Reagan created the National Narcotics Border Interdiction System (NNBIS). The NNBIS was also headed by Bush. Its mission was to act as an "interface" between the Department of Defense and the civilian law enforcement community in order to coordinate resources for drug-interdiction efforts. The NNBIS began operating in June 1983 by establishing five regional centers, including two in the greater border region—one in El Paso, and one in Long Beach, California. The participating federal agencies included the Department of Justice Criminal Division, Army, Air Force, Navy, FBI, Customs Service, Drug Enforcement Agency, INS, Federal Aviation Administration, CIA, and Bureau of Alcohol, Tobacco, and Firearms, along with various other representatives from the State, Treasury, and Defense departments.[26]

The Southwest contained a large pool of military resources for the NNBIS to establish a collaborative relationship with, as there were over 25 military bases in the region, approximately half of which were in California.[27] The NNBIS coordinated numerous evaluations for civilian law enforcement agencies of military resources in the region, including Army air cavalry (helicopter) training operations in West Texas, Army and Marine radar systems, and Air Force ground radar installations in southern New Mexico. Southwestern NNBIS officials also met with representatives from all major Air Force bases in the border region, as well as with representatives of the National Guard in New Mexico, Texas, and Arizona to discuss the use of training flights to support police antidrug efforts and other military resources that could possibly be made available to local law enforcement officials. In addition, NNBIS officials requested the loan of night-vision goggles for Customs Service officials from Fort Sam Houston and Fort Bliss in Texas and Fort Huachuca in Arizona. In its first year (1983–1984) the NNBIS established contact with representatives from 16 major Army bases located near U.S. borders and 33 National Guard commanders in border and maritime states to establish communication between them and civilian law enforcement officials.[28]

Spurred on by such initial collaborative efforts, the military increasingly began to make its training and equipment-operation plans with an eye toward border surveillance. For example, advanced land reconnaissance training for the Green Berets (i.e., U.S. Army Special Forces) and U.S. Army Ranger units was being evaluated by military officials for desert sites, apparently along the southwestern border, as a means of gathering information for drug-interdiction efforts. Further, the Air Force saw its new "Over-the-Horizon Backscatter" radar as a potential means of providing low-level radar detection for the entire U.S.–Mexico border. One ambitious National Guard official went so far as to draw up an $800-million plan to provide state-of-the-art air support (including airborne radar, tracking, and chase capacities) for drug-interdiction efforts in four states, two of which were Texas and California.[29]

There are relatively few details available regarding actual Pentagon assistance in antidrug efforts in the Southwest during the period 1981–1985, though disclosures made in congressional hearings on the topic suggest that some efforts were initiated. For example, the Army conducted surveillance operations in Texas using OV-1 Mohawk aircraft equipped with infrared radar.[30] Meanwhile, in the Southern California desert, Air Force and Marine Corps personnel, aircraft, and radar equipment were brought in to aid a special joint drug-interdiction operation that involved a range of federal and local police agencies.[31] In addition, during the 1983–1985 period the U.S. Army Intelligence School at Fort Huachuca, Arizona, initiated two frequently conducted border surveillance operations. The first was Operation Groundhog, an oft-repeated one-week training exercise for ground-surveillance radar operators that was conducted in a purportedly stressful environment along the border near Yuma, Arizona. In its first year, this operation "reported 1,083 targets which resulted in the apprehension of 372 illegal aliens by the Border Patrol."[32] It appears, then, that this border surveillance operation was not focused solely on aiding antidrug efforts, but included immigration enforcement as well. The second operation run by the U.S. Army Intelligence School at Fort Huachuca was Operation Hawkeye, which consisted of ongoing OV-1 Mohawk aerial surveillance training flights along the border between Douglas and Nogales, Arizona (59 missions were conducted in 1984 and 72 in 1985); the information gathered was passed on to the U.S. Customs Service.[33] Further, in 1983 Army air-defense artillery units from Fort Bliss (El Paso), Texas, conducted two high-visibility training exercises on the border in support of Customs Service anti–drug smuggling operations.[34] Moreover, Army units participating in other non–border-focused military training exercises in the border region (e.g., the massive 1985 Desert Star Training Exercise) were instructed to report any border-crossing information they gathered to the NNBIS.[35]

On the whole, during the early 1980s the military was called on to take a new and expanding role in antidrug efforts in the border region, one which centered on providing high-tech equipment and conducting surveillance operations and training exercises. The Defense Department was apparently slated to become extra "eyes and ears" for civilian agencies engaged in drug enforcement activities and, at least on occasion, in playing this role it also aided immigration enforcement efforts on the border. However, much of the collaboration and support was still on paper and had not yet actually taken place. Indeed, a 1985 evaluation of NNBIS "interface" activities found that they had yet to show significant evidence of having established better relations or greater coordination between civilian law enforcement agencies and the military.[36] Apparently, official antidrug rhetoric was far ahead of practice.

THE LIC FRAMEWORK APPLIED TO
BORDER-REGION ANTIDRUG ACTIVITIES, 1981–1985

It is important to recall that antidrug operations are a specific mission area of low-intensity conflict doctrine. In addition, antidrug activities along the U.S.–Mexico border from 1981 to 1985 manifested other more specific elements of LIC doctrine. Although much activity was still in the planning stages, the die was apparently cast. The most important coincidence with LIC doctrine during this period was the military's new domestic law enforcement focus made possible by the amendment in 1981 of the long-standing Posse Comitatus statute, which technically allowed the military to assist not only in civilian drug enforcement efforts but also more broadly, if indirectly, in other types of law enforcement—most notably immigration—within the United States. Furthermore, the formation of the NNBIS, with its military-civilian law enforcement agency "interface" mission, exemplified the LIC characteristic of coordinating and integrating police, intelligence, paramilitary, and military actions. The heavy emphasis on surveillance and the participation of forces from a border-area Army intelligence school were also examples of this LIC characteristic. In addition, they manifested another element of LIC doctrine—the expansion of intelligence operations, as surveillance efforts are a key component of such activities. Moreover, they were instances in which the military was positioned directly on the border to aid drug enforcement efforts.

The preparation and initiation of military training exercises in support of civilian drug enforcement efforts was quite similar to the LIC emphasis on exercises and maneuvers by military forces, especially in "problematic" areas. Further, the high-tech radar and night-vision equipment used in these endeavors were LIC-related hardware. Finally, both the plans to make extensive use of National Guard air support in Texas and California and the possibility of conducting U.S. Army Special Forces and Ranger training exercises in the border region reflected the emphasis in LIC doctrine on the use of reserve and elite forces. This flurry of military antidrug activity, planning, and equipment loans suggests that the military as an institution was beginning to implement the far-reaching changes in the Posse Comitatus statute affected by the 1982 DOD Authorization Act. Thus there are a number of indications of the use of LIC doctrine–related equipment and force operational characteristics to support drug enforcement efforts in the border region during this period, particularly by the military itself. Future activities expanded the process greatly.

The War on Drugs along the U.S.–Mexico Border, 1986–1992

The War on Drugs expanded in dramatic fashion in the U.S.–Mexico border region during the 1986–1992 period, as the issue acquired greater political momentum and official attention focused increasingly on the border region. This expansion was linked to the apparent rise in illegal drug trafficking in the region, which was due in part to the disruption caused by earlier drug-interdiction efforts in South Florida. By 1990 the newly formulated National Drug Control Strategy called for drug-interdiction efforts to be focused specifically on the southwestern border, and for the Defense Department to play a larger role in border anti-drug efforts.[37] Once again, law enforcement supply-reduction initiatives were the main priority of antidrug activities, rather than more service-oriented demand-reduction measures (e.g., education and treatment). Also in 1990 a 150-mile-wide swath of territory running the length of the border was designated as a "High-Intensity Drug-Trafficking Area" (HIDTA), one of five such sites in the nation (the other four sites were cities).[38] An extra $50 million were devoted to increasing drug-interdiction and related law enforcement efforts in these five areas. On the whole, there was a large-scale expansion of law enforcement and military resources devoted to antidrug efforts in the U.S.–Mexico border region. Not surprisingly, these efforts greatly expanded the use of LIC-doctrine tactics in the borderlands.

OPERATION ALLIANCE

The most fully developed joint venture between the military and civilian law enforcement agencies in border drug enforcement during this period was the dubiously named Operation Alliance. This project was set up by Vice President George Bush and Attorney General Edwin Meese in August of 1986, the same year that President Reagan formally designated drug trafficking as a national security threat.[39] It was an ongoing effort to interdict drugs along the border, based on the coordination of local, state, and federal law enforcement agencies, with the military playing a support role.[40] Basically, Operation Alliance was a more serious attempt to accomplish what the NNBIS had set out to do. Between 1986 and 1992 it was *the* primary coordinating body for collaborative drug enforcement efforts in the border region, and as such was involved in some fashion with virtually all of the activities outlined in this chapter (with the exception of changes in U.S. law). Its joint-command structure included senior officers from the Customs Service, Coast Guard, DEA, FBI, and INS–Border Patrol, as well as representatives from various law enforcement agencies in each of the four border states.[41] Further, the interagency U.S. Southwest Border Intelligence Task Force was established by the DEA as part of Operation Alliance, in order to provide "strategic assessment of all aspects of drug traffic from Mexico to the United States."[42]

The Department of Defense's support for Operation Alliance in its initial stages apparently took fairly low-key forms, including the provision of aerial surveillance and extensive loans of such resources as night-vision equipment and portable ground radar.[43] Subsequently, DOD personnel participated in joint training exercises with civilian law enforcement agencies and under the aegis of the HIDTA program, which in the U.S.–Mexico border region were coordinated by Operation Alliance.

It is important to note, however, that Operation Alliance's scope apparently extended well beyond drug enforcement. According to the program's senior tactical coordinator, James Bowen, "Operation Alliance was established to interdict the flow of drugs, weapons, *aliens,* currency, and other contraband across the southwest border" (emphasis added).[44] Of particular interest here is the acknowledgment that the mission of Operation Alliance included immigration enforcement, at least to some degree. This view that drug and immigration enforcement activities overlapped in the border region was also apparently shared by a senior official with the Office of National Drug Control Policy.[45] Such an overlap raised the prospect that many nonimmigration authorities such as local police, DEA and Customs Service agents, and even military personnel might become involved at least indirectly in immigration enforcement—something for which most of them were wholly unqualified. This possibility raised some unpleasant implications for the status of civil and human rights in the region: it would have likely increased the chances for mistakes and abuses.

The extensive use of cross-designation (deputization) to broaden the authority of law enforcement agents from various agencies involved in Operation Alliance also raised some ominous possibilities (see chapter 3 for a related discussion of the use of cross-designation). The Customs Service granted not only all Border Patrol agents but also some 600 local and state law enforcement officials in the border area, the authority to enforce contraband laws (Title 19, *U.S. Code*). Similarly, the DEA granted drug enforcement authority to all Border Patrol and Customs Service agents in the border region (Title 21, *U.S. Code*).[46] A senior Customs official maintained that this practice "enables those agencies to conduct warrantless border searches which are valuable in the border communities and inland areas vulnerable to air smuggling."[47] It is not clear how widely this authority extended,[48] but such an expansion of police power did not bode well for the civil rights of either border residents or immigrants passing through the area. Indeed, it seemed to further the border area's reputation as a "deconstitutionalized zone."[49]

In more concrete terms, Operation Alliance apparently facilitated the expanded deployment of resources for border-region law enforcement activities. For instance, Operation Alliance officials claimed that the project coordinated the operation of 90 aircraft from civilian federal agencies deployed on the border 16 hours per day, 7 days per week.[50] Further, in order to enhance communications coordination between the various law enforcement agencies involved, the Customs Service loaned 512 voice-privacy radios to state and local enforcement agencies and operated a "secure voice-radio network."[51]

DOD equipment support provided to Operation Alliance was extensive. It included such advanced aircraft as two E-2C radar planes, four Blackhawk helicopters, two high-speed interceptors (unspecified), six aerostat balloons outfitted with radar (placed along the length of the border), one C-12 aircraft outfitted with sophisticated radar, one P-3 radar plane, and an unspecified number of large, high-tech AWACS radar planes.[52] Further, in 1989, the Customs Service requested the loan of twenty UH-1H (Huey) helicopters from the Department of Defense, in order to support "ground interdiction missions" in the U.S.–Mexico border region.[53] National Guard forces also supplied a great deal of support to Operation Alliance, including equipment such as forward-looking infrared radar (FLIR) and side-looking airborne radar (SLAR, especially useful for monitoring activities across the border). Other support included flying photo reconnaissance missions, making available satellite and secure voice-radio communications, conducting "covert intelligence gathering and surveillance operations" with the Border Patrol, and providing "specialized training."[54] Overall, DOD resources provided to Operation Alliance appeared to be quite extensive and included a plethora of sophisticated equipment.

Additional resource allocations for Operation Alliance came from civilian agencies. This included the establishment of two aviation support facilities in Texas as well as a Southwest Border Tactical Operations Center in Houston to coordinate the drug-interdiction efforts of federal, state, and local agencies. Further, approximately 1,500 new federal law enforcement officers from various agencies were newly deployed along the border during the 1986–1987 period (this number apparently included the additional Border Patrol personnel noted in chapters 2 and 3). Periodically, interagency task forces of about 75 federal agents conducted "mobile corridor operations" in which they were sent to a specific section of the border to enhance enforcement efforts for two to three weeks at a time.[55]

The development and integration of organizational infrastructure was also a key effort for Operation Alliance. For example, at the local level, border-area officials claimed to have established 18 Border Alliance groups and nine anti–air smuggling groups (all of which were joint task forces in different locations along the border).[56] These organization-building activities appear to have intensified in 1990, as Operation Alliance led an elaborate and unprecedented effort among several hundred officials from federal, state, and local law enforcement agencies, as well as representatives from the regular military and the National Guard, to formulate a borderwide drug enforcement strategy.[57] Specific details of the plan are unavailable, but it was revealed that the plan generally emphasized intelligence activities, the creation of "multi-agency rapid-response teams at and between ports of entry," and the expansion of military support for drug law enforcement efforts in the region.[58] In addition, a new organizational entity, the Border Interdiction Committee, was slated to be established in 1990 in order to further facilitate interagency policy coordination. This group was to have representatives from at least ten federal agencies, including the National Security Council, INS, FBI, DEA,

Customs Service, Federal Aviation Administration, and Coast Guard, and the departments of Defense, Justice, and State.[59] While undoubtedly fraught with practical difficulties, the myriad organizational efforts appeared to be aimed at creating an unprecedented degree of integration and coordination among a wide variety of distinct institutional forces, from the local to the national level.

Despite the ambitious nature of Operation Alliance, there were indications that it had yet to make a significant impact on the ground. For example, a 1988 congressional report found that in practice Operation Alliance was beset with problems and far less effective than officials typically claimed.[60] These more critical findings were also supported by the comments of several Customs Service agents from South Texas who were interviewed in 1990. Their perspective deserves detailed examination, because it is rarely considered in "official" publications. Specifically, the agents reported that Operation Alliance, the NNBIS (which was officially terminated by the Antidrug Act of 1988), and the numerous elaborate coordination efforts had not significantly improved their ability to carry out their duties in the field. They were especially critical of the propensity of such operations to acquire high-tech surveillance hardware (singling out the aerostat radar balloons in particular), which they emphatically stated was no substitute for the additional staff urgently needed to follow up the numerous drug-trafficking leads already identified in the border region. Moreover, they considered interagency task force work to be extremely labor-intensive and laden with bureaucratic requirements. However, they reported that ongoing interagency collaboration in day-to-day enforcement activity was good, especially between the Customs Service and the INS. All things considered, they appeared to be quite overwhelmed and frustrated by the enormity of their task and by what they viewed as the misdirected and overblown program efforts and pronouncements emanating from Washington.[61] A 1992 investigative press report reinforces some of the critical comments of these Customs Service agents. The report found that the six costly and much heralded aerostat radar balloons on the southwest border were often inoperable and down for repairs, and that there was no evidence that they had contributed to a single drug bust or arrest along the border in the previous year.[62] Thus it would seem ill-advised to take at face value the claims of program effectiveness made by high-ranking drug enforcement officials in formal hearings and reports (especially those made for funding purposes).

Regardless of its actual effectiveness, Operation Alliance certainly increased the scope and degree of collaboration between a wide variety of governmental entities (ranging from the Department of Defense to local police), and greatly expanded the amount of resources and equipment deployed (however misguidedly) along the U.S.–Mexico border. Though the project faced many practical difficulties, its leading officials seem to have had rather grandiose aspirations of achieving something akin to "total force integration." Moreover, it is important to keep in mind that the purview of Operation Alliance extended beyond antidrug efforts to include immigration and other areas of law enforcement in the border region. On the whole, it appears that this particular law enforcement project provided much of the organizational infrastructure for border-area law enforcement between 1986 and 1992, as it presided over the coordination and implementation of a growing drug enforcement effort there. Most important for the present purposes, it facilitated ongoing relations between elements of the U.S. military and civilian law enforcement agencies in the border region.

FURTHER LEGAL CHANGES
EXPANDING THE ROLE OF THE MILITARY

A host of new legislative measures during the 1986–1992 period served to further loosen the Posse Comitatus statute's restrictions regulating the participation of U.S. military personnel in domestic law enforcement.[63] These changes deserve considerable attention, because they allowed a much expanded use of U.S. military forces in domestic law enforcement efforts (primarily antidrug activities), especially in the U.S.–Mexico border region. The first relevant measure during this period was the Defense Authorization Act for fiscal year 1989, passed in late 1988. This law revised and expanded the previous changes in the 1982 DOD Authorization Act, which had effectively relaxed Posse Comitatus restrictions by substantially broadening the guidelines for allowable military assistance to domestic civilian police agencies.[64] Once again, many of these provisions technically applied not only to drug enforcement efforts, but rather to law enforcement in general. And also as in the 1982 act, one of the most direct forms of explicitly allowed military assistance available to civilian law enforcement agencies (i.e., soldiers operating loaned military equipment for civilian police in the latter's operations) was specifically available to police agencies with the authority to enforce *drug, immigration, and contraband laws.*[65]

Beyond this important point of continuity, the 1989 DOD Authorization Act contained a number of significant revisions that further broadened the scope of military support allowed for various types of law enforcement at home and abroad. Among the more important were the following. Military personnel could not only now operate and maintain military equipment on loan to the various types of federal law enforcement agencies noted above, they could also do the same for state, local, and even foreign police agencies that were involved in the enforcement of similar laws.[66] Further, military personnel were allowed to operate military equipment not just to monitor and communicate the movement of air and sea traffic (as the 1982 act had allowed), but now also to conduct aerial reconnaissance missions, intercept vessels and aircraft outside of the United States (for communications purposes), and pursue them into the United States.[67] On a somewhat less intense level, the military was also now strongly called upon to take into account the information needs of civilian police agencies in the planning and execution of military training exercises and operations.[68] On the whole, it seems that the military was allowed to become much more involved in interdiction and other law enforcement activities.

Despite this broadening of permissible military support for civilian law enforcement, military personnel were still prohibited from directly participating in searches, seizures, arrests, or other similar activities.[69] Nonetheless, the clamor surrounding the 1989 DOD Authorization Act for greater military participation in drug enforcement suggested that this crucial prohibition would eventually be lifted. Indeed, William Taylor of the Center for Strategic and International Studies—by no means a liberal organization—posited that the "question will no longer be *whether* the Federal military and National Guard will be involved in searches and seizures, but *how* and to what extent they will be employed" (Taylor's emphasis).[70]

Several other sections of the DOD Authorization Act for 1989 were directed specifically toward drug enforcement efforts. For example, the Department of Defense was designated the "lead agency" for the detection and monitoring of the aerial and maritime transport of illegal drugs into the United States. Furthermore, it directed the secretary of defense to integrate the various U.S. command, control, communications, and intelligence assets (C^3I) that were dedicated to drug interdiction into an effective communications network.[71] The law also called for enhancing the National Guard's role in drug interdiction and related enforcement efforts, mostly by providing new funds for National Guard troops' participation in drug interdiction and enforcement operations as well as for the operation and maintenance of National Guard equipment and facilities used in such operations.[72] In addition, it provided $300 million for DOD drug-interdiction efforts (including $40 million for the National Guard's antidrug activities).[73]

It is important to note here that in the process of crafting this legislation during 1988 Congress made a number of unsuccessful attempts to expand the military's domestic drug enforcement role much more drastically, a trend that was opposed by both Pentagon and INS officials. Most notably, both houses initially passed recommendations calling for the military to be authorized to make drug-related arrests. Also, the House sought to require the military to seal U.S. borders to all drug traffic. Both of these measures were later dropped. Pentagon officials opposed these efforts because they felt that the added responsibilities would interfere with their traditional duties, and they also opposed the use of military forces in civilian police activities.[74] That such extreme measures were seriously considered was an ominous sign, though probably due partly to the fact that 1988 was a national election year and tough "law and order" posturing on drug issues was quite politically popular. Interestingly, INS Commissioner Alan Nelson went on record in mid-1988 as being "strongly opposed" to any efforts to deploy military troops along the U.S.–Mexico border to interdict drugs or to aid in immigration enforcement (although he was willing to support low-key forms of military assistance), characterizing proposals for such military involvement as unworkable and simplistic.[75]

The Defense Authorization Act for fiscal years 1990 and 1991 (passed in late 1989) pulled the military farther into the domestic front of the War on Drugs, effectively relaxing the Posse Comitatus restrictions even more. It specifically mandated that the military conduct training exercises "to the maximum extent practicable" in drug-interdiction areas, defined as land or sea areas in which drug smuggling into the United States occurred or was believed to have occurred.[76] This definition clearly implicated the U.S.–Mexico border region. In addition, the military was allowed to transfer surplus military supplies, including small arms and ammunition, to federal and state agencies for their use in counterdrug activities.[77] Moreover, the 1990–1991 act called for some $450 million of the overall 1990 budget of the Department of Defense to be devoted to drug-interdiction and counterdrug activities (including $70 million for the National Guard's counterdrug efforts).[78] This was a 50% increase over the previous year (and a 75% increase for the National Guard specifically). By this time, the military had dropped many of its previous reservations and was becoming much more enthusiastic about participating in the War on Drugs, both in the United States and abroad, due to the end of the Cold War and the increased importance attributed to the drug issue by the Bush administration.[79]

Subsequently, the Defense Authorization Act for fiscal year 1991, passed in 1990, reiterated many of the provisions of the previous act, but also expanded upon them considerably. Once again, this broadening of military support for domestic drug enforcement efforts effectively further loosened the restrictions imposed by the Posse Comitatus statute.[80] The 1991 act formally permitted the military to provide "counterdrug-related training" to law enforcement personnel of federal, state, and local governments as well as those of foreign governments.[81] It also allowed for a host of additional military support activities for counterdrug efforts, including the establishment of antidrug bases of operations and training facilities within and outside the United States; the carrying out of aerial and ground reconnaissance patrols *outside, at, or near the borders of the United States;* the construction of roads and fences and the installation of lighting on U.S. borders; the transporting of personnel, supplies, and equipment within or outside the United States to facilitate counterdrug activities; the establishment of command, control, communications, and computer networks for the "improved integration" of law enforcement, military, and National Guard activities; and the conducting of not only military training exercises, but also military operations (apparently both within the United States and abroad) to aid civilian law enforcement agencies.[82] In addition, the 1991 act authorized $1.08 billion to pay for the military's drug interdiction and counterdrug activities (a jump of 140% over the previous year's funding for such activities), out of which $105.5 million was to go to the National Guard.[83] Significantly, direct military participation in search, seizure, and arrest activities remained formally proscribed, as the 1991 and 1990–1991 acts contained no amendments on these crucial matters. Nonetheless, virtually all other forms of assistance and participation were formally allowed, thus giving the military enormous leeway in their involvement in domestic drug enforcement activities, especially in border regions, and particularly the southern border. The Defense authorization acts for fiscal years 1992 and 1993 basically called for the continuation of this trend, though they devoted far less attention to drug enforcement issues.[84]

The most outstanding of these various legal changes to expand the military's role in domestic drug enforcement efforts were the provisions allowing (1) military ground and aerial reconnaissance activities at or near U.S. borders, (2) military operations within the United States to aid civilian law enforcement agencies, and (3) ill-defined training for a wide variety of U.S. and foreign law-enforcement personnel. Consistent with the second provision, active-duty military forces were granted authority in 1990 to provide a variety of operational support to drug enforcement efforts within the United States, including actively participating in marijuana-eradication efforts on federal lands and other activities such as administrative and logistical support, air and ground transport, and reconnaissance of marijuana gardens.[85] In addition, ground and aerial reconnaissance efforts in border regions clearly seem to qualify as military operations occurring within the United States. However, the military was still prohibited from entering private lands without permission, though efforts were under way to remove this prohibition as well. Senator DeConcini of Arizona (Democrat) played a leading role in the attempts to increase military authority in drug enforcement efforts in the border region. An aide from his staff characterized the problems inherent in this process in the following manner: "We have to come up with something that won't make everybody think we're trying to create a military state along the southwestern border. It's a fine line."[86]

This framing of the issue clearly points to a potential threat to civil and human rights in the border region, a threat tied to a larger issue underlying the expanded military role allowed in drug enforcement: Namely, when does military "aid" or "support" to civilian law enforcement officials become de facto military law enforcement activity? Although important, the military's lack of formal authority to participate directly in stops, searches, seizures, and arrests may at some point be rendered largely symbolic by the ever growing list of allowable military activities in domestic drug enforcement. Given the wide leeway provided to the military regarding their involvement in domestic drug enforcement, the actual outcome may largely depend upon the enthusiasm of leading military officials (which in this period was by no means overwhelming) as well as on future political pressures. At any rate, the effective relaxations of the Posse Comitatus statute that were passed in 1988, 1989, and 1990 opened the door much wider to the military's participation in domestic law enforcement, especially in the U.S.–Mexico border region.

It is important to reiterate that these various de facto relaxations of the Posse Comitatus statute apparently allowed the military to participate in law enforcement matters beyond the realm of drug enforcement. For example, in referring to the changes in the Posse Comitatus statute that allow the use of military personnel to operate and maintain military equipment on loan to civilian law enforcement agencies, a report from the House Government Operations Committee stated: "Such use of military personnel is authorized only for specific operations and only with respect to criminal violations of certain federal laws, chiefly *drug and immigration laws*" (emphasis added).[87] Thus it appeared legal for the military to become involved, at least indirectly, in immigration enforcement efforts.

A hypothetical example from a leading military official in the Pentagon's antidrug efforts more concretely illustrates how the weakening of Posse Comitatus restrictions might be translated into practice. U.S. Army Lieutenant General Thomas Kelly, director of operations for the Joint Chiefs of Staff, stated: "Number one, if you've got a detection and monitoring airplane that happens to be a Blackhawk helicopter that also has cops on board, then it also conceivably could be a pursuit and apprehension asset, which is a combat multiplier."[88] Thus, while military personnel were prohibited from directly conducting stops, searches, and seizures, and from making arrests, they apparently could nonetheless participate in pursuit and apprehension activities as long as law enforcement personnel were present to make the actual arrest. This further obscured the line beyond which military participation in domestic law enforcement efforts became illegal. Such activities seemed to reduce the prohibitions against direct participation to legal technicalities that could be largely circumvented in practice. Moreover, General Kelly's comments were made prior to the 1990 and 1991 legal changes that allowed many additional forms of military involvement in the antidrug activities of civilian police forces.

A more important issue surrounding military involvement in domestic drug enforcement is the questionable disposition, if not ability, of military forces to respect legal procedures of due process, and human rights in general. The comments of General Kelly proved insightful once again, as they illustrated the potential pitfalls of this vexing dilemma with a rather graphic, if also confusing, analogy. He stated:

> We're learning to work with law enforcement agencies, and there's difficulties in doing that and it's a *cultural difficulty on our part*. When you deal with police officers, they think in terms of going to court and we don't. We're sort of like the special operations soldier who is taught to clear a room by *killing the bad guys* and not touch the hostages, a regular old infantry soldier just flips a grenade through the door. We're sort of like the infantry soldier right now and we've got to learn to work better with them.[89] (emphasis added)

It is unclear whether General Kelly saw military involvement in police agencies' antidrug efforts as being analogous to the activities of the special-operations soldier or regular infantry soldier. Regardless, neither approach indicated any consideration to due process or human rights. Such "cultural difficulties" are part of what makes the expanded use of the military in drug interdiction so potentially dangerous. The military is trained (quite proficiently) to kill, and generally not to make the careful distinctions between "bad guys" and "good guys" (nor to follow the due-process guidelines) that are necessary in carrying out law enforcement activities.[90] This sort of difficulty makes it clear that the flurry of legal maneuvers relaxing the Posse Comitatus restrictions on the military's involvement in domestic law enforcement had far-reaching and troubling implications. Consequently, subsequent developments emerging from these legal changes merit careful scrutiny and full public debate, rather than being left to the policy-analysis "experts" or to the discretion of military and law enforcement officials.

DOMESTIC MILITARY ACTIVITY
IN SUPPORT OF THE WAR ON DRUGS

In recent years the military has been compelled, partly as a result of its newly mandated "lead agency" status, to report on its efforts to support drug enforcement activities within the United States. This section provides a general overview of some fairly obvious types of military support, while later sections provide more detailed information on the most militaristic forms of support, that of joint operations between the military and civilian law enforcement agencies, and the military's border-area antidrug task force. In addition to the more obvious forms of military support for the War on Drugs that are examined here, it is important to recall that military assistance also took more low-key forms, such as administrative, construction, maintenance, and communications aid. Not surprisingly, military support for domestic drug enforcement activity appeared to increased substantially between 1986 and 1992, with most of it focused on the U.S.–Mexico border region.

The most obvious indicator of the increase in DOD drug enforcement activity was the growth in DOD funds dedicated specifically to antidrug activities. Funding for DOD antidrug programs jumped from $438.8 million in 1989 to an estimated $1.08 billion in 1991, with slightly larger amounts requested for each of the following two years. These figures included funds for both domestic and international programs; and although no breakdown was provided, the Andean region of South America and the U.S.–Mexico border region were the key geographical focal points for the military's antidrug efforts.[91] While the overall amount of funding was a minuscule portion—less than 1%—of the Pentagon's total annual budget, it was a substantial amount of funding for what was essentially expanded military participation in law enforcement efforts.

A crucial turning point in the expansion of DOD participation in drug enforcement activities was the secretary of defense's designation in September 1989 of the drug fight as a "high-priority national security mission" for the Department of Defense. This move caught many in the Pentagon off guard, as the designation was traditionally used sparingly, and had far-reaching implications for Pentagon operations.[92] Its application indicated that the Department of Defense was to take a central role in the War on Drugs. As a result, Pentagon officials reported that subsequent military support to civilian law enforcement agencies expanded significantly and took myriad forms in the U.S.–Mexico border region. These included conducting small-unit and long-range reconnaissance patrols in hard-to-cover areas; providing, deploying, and monitoring electronic ground sensors; providing intelligence support; clearing brush and improving roads along the border; training law enforcement personnel in intelligence analysis and survival skills; providing air transport of law enforcement personnel in interdiction and eradication efforts; staffing listening and observation posts; using remotely piloted reconnaissance aircraft; staging military exercises in suspected drug trafficking zones; conducting radar and imaging missions; providing operational planning assistance; and providing DOD personnel to develop data bases as well as mapping and reconnaissance folders for Border Patrol sectors.[93]

National Guard troops figured most prominently in the provision of DOD support to border-region law enforcement personnel. These troops included not only regular "weekend warriors," but also elite elements of the National Guard, including Special Forces and military intelligence units, Long-Range Reconnaissance Patrols, and other specialized units.[94] As part of the previously cited funding for DOD drug enforcement activities, Congress specifically appropriated funds to the National Guard for domestic drug enforcement efforts. National Guard funds grew from $40 million in 1989, to $110 million in 1990 ($70 million for antidrug activities, $40 million for support equipment), to an estimated $163.3 million in 1991—thus making up approximately 10%–15% of total DOD antidrug funding.[95] The four southwestern border states fared very well in this funding; collectively they received $21.8 million of the $70 million designated for National Guard antidrug activities in 1990.[96] (As noted above, the other $40 million of the Guard's $110-million total for 1990 went for support equipment.) However, the much-expanded drug enforcement role for border-state National Guard units not only brought them increased federal funding (and political prestige), it also provided new opportunities for corruption: An official internal investigation reportedly found that the former head of the Texas National Guard's antinarcotics task force was implicated in cross-border drug trafficking during his tenure in the late 1980s and early 1990s.[97]

One particularly visible and noteworthy National Guard antidrug program involved the regular deployment of troops at official ports of entry along the southwest border. Starting in 1988, National Guard personnel aided the Customs Service by working as cargo inspectors at major land ports of entry, focusing primarily on truck cargo inspection. The initial program involving 100 troops was deemed a success, and was expanded as National Guard troops were regularly deployed at major land ports of entry along the length of the border.[98] Although they were not directly involved in making arrests, their participation in vehicle inspections did appear to violate the spirit if not the letter of the search prohibitions contained in the Posse Comitatus statute. As previously noted, however, unless the National Guard was under federal control, it was not formally covered by Posse Comitatus.

The latter point raises the issue of how the amendments to the Posse Comitatus statute were interpreted in the field. Leading military officials professed to be quite sensitive to the limits of their police power and to the potential for creating scenes reminiscent of totalitarian police states.[99] They apparently were often not certain about what was or was not permitted under the host of new legal provisions that effectively relaxed the Posse Comitatus statute, as they reportedly sought opinions from Pentagon lawyers for virtually all military antidrug operations planned for the border region.[100] This process was rather tedious and lengthy, often frustrating the border-area law enforcement agencies that were requesting DOD assistance. It led some local police officials in Arizona to call for the decision-making locus for military involvement in specific police-led antidrug operations to be moved from Washington to border-area military bases, as local base commanders were reportedly more willing to authorize assistance.[101] However, other law enforcement officials reportedly feared that the loosening of Posse Comitatus restrictions might turn the Department of Defense into a "super law enforcement agency" that would infringe on their turf—although DOD representatives had pledged to support law enforcement agencies, not to convert the Pentagon into one.[102]

Thus the military responded to de facto relaxations of Posse Comitatus restrictions on an experimental, case-by-case basis, with actual limits being defined in practice. It may take years for the military to adjust to the effective changes in Posse Comitatus, which had stood for over a century as a stable framework largely prohibiting military participation in domestic law enforcement. However, it is clear that the new legal changes that effectively revised the Posse Comitatus statute granted the military a great deal of discretionary power in this area.

Another issue that raised crucial questions of interpretation and implementation was the Department of Defense's designation in the Defense Authorization Act for fiscal year 1989 as the "lead agency" for detecting and monitoring aerial and maritime drug smuggling into the United States. Initially, Pentagon officials were uncertain about the meaning of this designation—with reason, it appears.[103] This uncertainty stems in part from the fact that detection and monitoring are two early phases in the overall interdiction process, which, as previously noted, also includes the phases of interception, apprehension, search, seizure, and arrest, all of which often overlap.[104] A House Government Operations Committee report was more clear in assessing the probable outcome of the "lead agency" designation, concluding that the "DOD is likely to become the *de facto* lead agency for all interdiction."[105] This was another issue that had yet to be determined in practice, though again there appeared to be ample opportunity for the Department of Defense to exercise substantial authority should it choose to do so.

On the whole, general military support for domestic drug enforcement efforts clearly expanded, in depth and breadth, from 1986 through 1992. The U.S.–Mexico border region was a primary (though by no means exclusive) focal point for the Pentagon's domestic antidrug activity. While much of the shape and the actual extent of these endeavors remained to be determined in practice, it seems nonetheless that the military was an up-and-coming actor in borderlands drug enforcement. These developments merit closer examination, due not only to civil and human rights concerns, but also to the increased possibilities for corruption within military institutions.

PENTAGON–CIVILIAN LAW AGENCY
JOINT TRAINING EXERCISES AND OPERATIONS

One type of military involvement in border-region drug enforcement efforts worthy of special attention is the joint training exercises and operations of the military and civilian law enforcement agencies. These military–civilian police training exercises and operations in the border region were a relatively new area of activity for the Pentagon, at least in the contemporary historical period. Such activities appear to have expanded significantly after 1988. They clearly illustrate the growing articulation between the military and civilian law enforcement agencies in the border region. Furthermore, they represent one of the most obvious forms of militarization on the U.S.–Mexico border. These joint efforts were usually coordinated or facilitated by Operation Alliance (discussed previously) and the military's own border-area drug task force (see next section), and they frequently involved the National Guard and the Border Patrol.

One of the most far-reaching implications of the joint training exercises was voiced by a Marine Corps spokesperson, who in 1990 noted: "You can perform an actual operation and at the same time, a training scenario is going on. Part of the training is conducting missions as you would normally run them."[106] Such an approach raises the following question: How and when do training exercises become actual operations? As the above quotation suggests, the difference appeared to be subtle indeed. Similarly, Lieutenant General George Stotser, commander of Joint Task Force 6 (discussed in the next section), noted that military training exercises in support of civilian law enforcement agencies offer "unique real-world training to a variety of military units."[107] Moreover, as was discussed previously, the effective changes to the Posse Comitatus statute contained in the various DOD authorization acts did not limit the military to mere training exercises, but also authorized them to conduct actual operations to support the drug enforcement efforts of civilian law enforcement agencies.

Specific information on joint exercises and operations was not forthcoming from military and law enforcement officials, however, as they regarded these efforts as highly sensitive and preferred to keep the details shrouded in secrecy. Details typically came to light as a result of grave mishaps during the exercises and through investigative journalism. Consequently, relatively little is known about these joint operations. Nonetheless, available information on several cases of such activities in California, Arizona, and Texas illustrate a number of key points and the potential dangers inherent in these efforts.

Joint training exercises and operations between 1988 and 1992 appear to have often consisted of covert reconnaissance operations. For purposes of clarity, it should be noted that reconnaissance is defined by the Department of Defense as "a mission undertaken to obtain, by visual observation or other detection methods, information about the activities and resources of an enemy or potential enemy."[108] Reconnaissance ground-patrol operations in the borderlands most frequently involved the quiet deployment of National Guard troops and Border Patrol agents into areas thought to be high-traffic drug-smuggling sites, and the collection of intelligence on suspicious movements in the area via small-unit patrolling and surveillance activities. During 1989, such joint National Guard–Border Patrol observation exercises were carried out in (or at least slated for) Texas, New Mexico, and California, while in Arizona the U.S. Marines teamed up with the Border Patrol.[109] The senior tactical coordinator of Operation Alliance noted in 1989 that the National Guard had been "extremely active" in collaborative antidrug efforts over the past year in the border region and further stated, "They have participated with the Border Patrol in conducting *covert intelligence-gathering and surveillance operations*" (emphasis added).[110]

Joint antidrug operations between the military and civilian law enforcement agencies in the border region appeared to begin in earnest with "Operation Border Ranger" in October 1988. This effort involved National Guard personnel and local sheriff's deputies in the California-Mexico border area east of San Diego. Officials characterized it as a "combat operation" that involved heavily armed "police 'commandos'" who were "to attack drug traffickers and seize their illicit shipments."[111] Intended to be a secret operation, it became publicly known because a California National Guard helicopter crashed in Imperial County. The crash resulted in the death of eight people on board, including five local law enforcement personnel and three National Guard members.[112]

Undeterred, National Guard officials reinitiated a less aggressive version of the project in an expanded form in mid-1989 as "Operation Border Ranger II," which was a secret operation that officials said was conducted for purposes of "observation," though they disclosed few details. This effort provided additional "eyes and ears" for the Border Patrol, Customs Service, and local law enforcement agencies over a one-month period, and employed an unstipulated portion of the 400 National Guard troops involved in a variety of antidrug activities throughout California at that time (there was also unspecified participation by the Army and Marine Corps). Part of the operation involved the clandestine deployment of National Guard troops armed with M-16 rifles and clad in camouflage uniforms at observation posts in the desert along the border. Most important, their mission exceeded drug enforcement to include immigration enforcement, as troops passed on information regarding unauthorized border crossers in general to the INS and other enforcement authorities.[113] (The inclusion of immigration enforcement concerns in this operation contradicted the guidelines of a California National Guard antidrug operation proposed just eight months earlier. This proposal had explicitly stated that guard units would not be deployed against undocumented immigrants.)[114] A spokesperson for the California National Guard described the troops' observation mission in even broader terms, stating, "If the individual [guardsperson] in the field observes *something that could possibly be of an illegal nature,* the information would be passed along to the appropriate law enforcement agency" (emphasis added).[115] These efforts led to the arrest of several hundred undocumented immigrants. This same operation was scheduled again for 1990 on a much-expanded basis, as the California National Guard planned to use greatly increased federal military appropriations for such activities to fund "its most wide-ranging effort ever to interdict illegal drugs being smuggled across the U.S.–Mexico border."[116] It is unclear whether this effort also included incidental immigration enforcement, but it seemed likely to do so, given the previous operation.

Given that the enforcement concerns of Operation Border Ranger II included not only drug trafficking, but also undocumented immigration and anything "that could possibly be of an illegal nature," an obvious question is: How could troops who were unqualified to deal with broad-ranging civilian law enforcement matters make such crucial legal distinctions in the field? This situation was fraught with problematic issues regarding the assurance of civil and human rights.

A Texas case offers an example of the more elite joint antidrug operations that were undertaken in the border region. Two clandestine reconnaissance patrolling operations (dubbed Operation Unity) of Border Patrol agents and National Guard troops took place in Big Bend National Park in the fall of 1988 and spring of 1989 for one week and two weeks, respectively, as a pilot project to assess the feasibility of such operations. (This part of West Texas has long been a popular drug- and contraband-smuggling area.) The participating Border Patrol agents and National Guard troops were armed with M-16 rifles. Reportedly, a former member of Delta Force—a supersecret, elite, antiterrorist unit of the U.S. military—provided training to National Guard personnel in infiltration techniques. The National Guard participants were handpicked from an Airborne Ranger unit, while the Border Patrol agents came from the elite BORTAC force. Following the initial operations in Big Bend, future operations by the two forces were under consideration for other areas along the border.[117] That elite units from both the National Guard and the

Border Patrol were used in this clandestine operation suggests that a high priority was placed on these efforts and that they were viewed as sensitive activities. (However, such concerns were undermined by the fact that the Texas National Guard's antidrug task force was led during this period by an officer who was reportedly involved in cross-border drug trafficking during his tenure.)[118]

While the Big Bend operations were apparently conducted in a remote and lightly populated area, it may be that similar activities could be expanded to more densely populated areas in the future, because much drug smuggling also takes place in such locations, and not just in remote areas such as Big Bend. Indeed, the effectiveness of military surveillance activities in support of antidrug operations was questioned in a 1988 Rand Corporation study, which noted that surveillance efforts were not likely to be effective if smugglers could blend in with regular traffic (and the local population), especially in more densely populated areas.[119] Significantly, the senior tactical coordinator of Operation Alliance identified the Brownsville, Laredo, and El Paso areas in Texas and the Tucson, Nogales, and Douglas areas in Arizona as the main locales for smuggling on the border.[120] Several of these locations are relatively densely populated, especially Brownsville and El Paso. Thus it is plausible that the joint Border Patrol–National Guard patrols and covert intelligence-gathering efforts could be expanded to those areas, which would increase the probability of such patrols having contact with or observing ordinary border-area residents in addition to the sought-after drug smugglers.

There are several indications that these joint training exercises and operations increased in frequency during the late 1980s and early 1990s—which is no surprise, given the legal changes that occurred during the same period and the strong political momentum behind the issue. For example, in 1990 the INS reported on several DOD-INS joint training operations along the U.S.–Mexico border, in which the military provided Border Patrol agents with "training pertaining to small-unit tactics, patrolling, map reading, land navigation, and other areas of expertise," while the Border Patrol provided military personnel with "training in tracking, countertracking, and other skills."[121] Moreover, in discussing military support for civilian law enforcement agencies during 1990 and early 1991, military officials made passing references to similar "cross-trainings" between Border Patrol and military personnel, as well as references to military staffing of listening and observation posts on the border in support of the Border Patrol (apparently similar to or including the previously discussed exercises in California and Texas).[122] Meanwhile, plans were made in the fall of 1990 for DOD electronic sensor surveillance training exercises in the McAllen, Texas, area to aid the Border Patrol.[123] Furthermore, in September 1990 U.S. Marines and agents from a dozen civilian law enforcement agencies in Arizona (including the Border Patrol) conducted the largest antidrug operation in the state's history, involving some 400 military and law enforcement personnel and covering the entire Arizona-Mexico border.[124]

Joint operations and training exercises in the border region reached a new qualitative level in 1989 with the introduction of active-duty military troops into such activities. Prior to the September 1990 operation involving U.S. Marines (as well as National Guard and reserve forces) discussed above, in October 1989 it was reported that the Marines had recently agreed to join the Border Patrol in conducting training and surveillance operations along the border, primarily in California and Arizona. The joint training and operations were to involve no more than 50 Marines temporarily assigned to the INS at any one time, and was to stress nighttime ground reconnaissance and other observation activities.[125] Shortly thereafter, this led to one of the most serious confrontations on the border up to this point.

A 50-member platoon of Marines was training Border Patrol agents in the Tucson-Nogales, Arizona, area in military surveillance and intelligence techniques, while also serving as reconnaissance backup for the Border Patrol. In the course of the training they conducted an exercise turned joint operation that was kept secret from local authorities and in which a small group of Marines accompanying a Border Patrol officer on patrol became engaged in a brief firefight with drug smugglers northwest of Nogales on December 13, 1989. The joint Border Patrol–Marine unit came upon several suspected smugglers on horseback during a nighttime patrol. The smugglers fled after being ordered to halt, and the Marines shot up a flare to illuminate the night sky. The smugglers then fired upon the Marines, who themselves then fired their M-16s on the order of the lone Border Patrol agent accompanying them. These were the first reported shots fired by active-duty military personnel on the border in drug enforcement activity. The flare started a fire that burned 300 acres of federal forest land (which is the principal reason the incident became publicly known). This episode escalated the level of confrontation on the border between smugglers and law enforcement officials and was a dramatic departure from past practices, although subsequently the military purposefully sought to avoid such armed clashes.[126] This example clearly illustrates how the dividing line between joint training exercises and actual police-military operations could vanish in some instances along the border.

Several other joint exercises and operations carried out in Texas and Arizona illustrate the overlapping of drug and immigration enforcement roles undertaken in these activities. One of these took place in early 1990, when a small U.S. Marine unit working in collaboration with the Border Patrol deployed and operated a drone (a small, remotely piloted aircraft), equipped with high-tech observational equipment, for a 3-week period along an 80-mile stretch of the border west of Laredo, Texas. The information provided by the Marine drone helped the Border Patrol capture 1,009 pounds of marijuana *and* 372 undocumented immigrants (double the number usually caught in that area). The exercise was so successful that the INS considered expanding it to other sectors.[127]

A second case, from Arizona, is perhaps more illustrative of the intermingling of immigration and drug enforcement in the course of joint training exercises. In August 1992, some 250 Marines from the Second Reconnaissance Battalion (based in Camp Lejeune, North Carolina) were deployed to Fort Huachuca, Arizona. However, at least part of their training maneuvers were conducted off-base, in and around nearby border towns (Naco and Douglas, Arizona). Their primary mission was to conduct reconnaissance training, which included patrolling, staffing observation posts, and other activities. Their secondary mission was to support a small number of Border Patrol agents (fewer than 20 at the first site) based in Naco and Douglas, Arizona, "in intercepting drug shipments and stanching the flow of illegal immigrants." The troops were under orders "to report any suspicious activity" observed during their training to the local Border Patrol.[128]

These joint training exercises and operations raise a troubling issue: Would the military become at least indirectly involved in immigration enforcement activities on an ongoing basis, via its participation in the War on Drugs? As the above examples demonstrate, this possibility appeared to be a recurring theme in practice. Further, as noted previously, since 1989 the California National Guard also focused some attention on undocumented immigration during its drug enforcement observation exercises on the border. Reports from the Tucson area have also confirmed this practice. First of all, some officials conceded that many of the new sensors and much of the other equipment ostensibly introduced for drug enforcement were used primarily to apprehend undocumented immigrants.[129] Moreover, an INS official from Tucson acknowledged that in practice the joint military–Border Patrol operations in the area tended to cover both drug and immigration enforcement, on the grounds that Mexican nationals (documented and undocumented) were prominently involved in the drug trade.[130] This conflation of the categories of "drug trafficker" and "undocumented immigrant," as noted previously, would seem to have greatly increased the potential for gross human rights violations, such as occurred in the shooting to death of an unarmed, undocumented immigrant and alleged drug scout by the Border Patrol in June 1992 near Nogales, Arizona (see chapter 3). In turn, military participation in the increasingly intermingled realms of drug and immigration enforcement would seem to have increased the potential for eventual military involvement in human rights violations in the borderlands.

The expansion in the scope of border-region joint operations and training exercises conducted by the military and civilian law enforcement agencies to exceed drug enforcement and include, to at least some extent, immigration and broader law enforcement matters raises a number of provoking questions. How militarized would law enforcement in the borderlands become if such trends were continued? Was the precedent now established for the use of military forces to address other vexing law enforcement problems in the future (especially as political leaders customarily sought seemingly straightforward, "get tough," punitive solutions to what are often complex social problems)? Most importantly, how would the status of human rights in the border region be affected by the military's at least indirect participation in immigration enforcement, or by any further militarization of law enforcement in the area? These issues merit careful consideration by policymakers as well as open public debate—processes that had yet to emerge by 1992 from the long political shadow cast by the War on Drugs on the larger political scene.

JOINT TASK FORCE 6 (JTF-6)

A more specialized and prominent manifestation of military involvement in domestic drug enforcement meriting special attention is Joint Task Force 6 (JTF-6), set up in November 1989 at Fort Bliss Army Base in El Paso. JTF-6 marked the formal establishment of ongoing participation by active-duty U.S. military forces in antidrug efforts on the U.S.–Mexico border. As such, it was the most prominent indication that the military had put aside many of its previous qualms about such active involvement in drug enforcement matters within the United States. JTF-6 grew out of President Bush's National Drug Control Strategy, which was unveiled in September 1989.[131] Interestingly, JTF-6's geographical area of operation includes not only a 50-mile-wide corridor running the length of the U.S.–Mexico border, but also nonborder areas such as the entire Texas gulf coast, Houston, and Los Angeles.[132]

In general, military joint task forces are organized for special missions and draw from more than one branch of the armed forces. JTF-6's mission was to "serve as a planning and coordinating headquarters to provide support from the Defense Department to federal, state, and local law enforcement agencies."[133] Among the activities initially outlined for JTF-6 were "aerial reconnaissance and surveillance training, transportation assistance, ground radar monitoring, training, and general engineering support."[134] This list expanded in practice to include virtually all of those military activities outlined in previous sections, as JTF-6 played the main role in providing and coordinating these efforts with Operation Alliance. In characterizing the relationship between JTF-6 and law enforcement agencies, Lieutenant General George Stotser, the commander of JTF-6, stated: "Joint Task Force 6's relationship with law enforcement, in my view, is one of *total integration*" (emphasis added).[135] Yet this budding "integration" at least initially caused some concern among civilian law enforcement officials, who were worried that JTF-6 would infringe on their operations and lead the military to become overly involved in domestic drug enforcement matters.[136]

The actual number of military personnel formally assigned to JTF-6 was quite small, reportedly ranging from approximately 60 to 120, as no operational troops were permanently assigned to the task force. Rather, JTF-6 was run by a small group of essentially military administrators, while operational troops were brought in on an ad hoc, rotating basis from various military bases and National Guard units to conduct specific operations and exercises. These activities were planned, arranged, and coordinated by JTF-6 personnel, working in close association with Operation Alliance and the civilian law enforcement officials requesting military support.[137] This behind-the-scenes organizing role allowed JTF-6 to maintain a low profile. As one official put it, "We're not in the business of advertising we're here."[138]

Nonetheless, JTF-6 was quite busy conducting a wide variety of missions in support of antidrug efforts in the border region from 1990 through 1992. These missions, totaling 775 in all, fell into three broad categories: operational, general support, and engineering (see table 1).[139] The principal beneficiary of JTF-6's efforts was the Border Patrol, as the majority of the missions were carried out for it.[140] The operational category is the largest of JTF-6's three mission categories, with 384

Table 1. Number of JTF-6 Missions Completed, by Fiscal Year and Type, 1990–1993

Mission Type	1990	1991	1992	1993
Operations				
Listening & observational posts	5	35	57	67
Electronic-sensor deployment	4	12	9	8
Ground patrols	0	18	35	30
Terrain-denial support activities	0	9	8	11
Aerial reconnaissance & transport	0	48	86	67
Other	0	13	45	79
Subtotal	9	135	240	262
Engineering				
Road construction & upgrades	1	6	7	26
Range construction	0	4	7	10
Helipad or taxiway construction	0	3	6	4
Fence construction	0	2	5	4
Building & facility construction	0	1	7	5
Engineering assessments	1	3	11	5
Subtotal	2	19	43	54
General support				
Training	5	45	74	66
Intelligence	4	17	37	59
Transport (personnel & equipment)	0	18	13	8
Photo interpretation	2	33	46	22
Translation	0	0	7	8
Canine training or support	0	7	7	6
Other	10	2	0	0
Subtotal	21	122	184	169
Total	32	276	467	485

Source: U.S. Army, Corps of Engineers 1994: 4-2.

operational missions (50% of the total number of missions) conducted between 1990 and 1992. While there is relatively little information available on this category of activities, they appear to be the most obviously militaristic ones conducted by JTF-6. Most of them involved the actual deployment of military troops in the border region. It seems that the vast majority of the operational missions were focused on observation and surveillance, involved relatively small contingents of troops (from 10 to 120), and lasted up to one month. The less-frequently conducted "terrain denial" operations were distinguished by the large scale on which they were conducted, however, for they involved anywhere from 60 to 900 troops, divided into 45-member ground patrol units. The principal purpose of these missions was to prevent the entry of drug traffickers into the country (i.e., to literally deny drug traffickers access to specific areas), although other illegal activities were also to be detected and reported to authorities.[141] While few details on these "terrain denial" operations are available, they appear to have involved a sort of saturation deployment of a number of ground patrol units in a show of force within a fixed geographical area where "significant illegal actions" are suspected to occur. The large-scale presence of military troops is apparently supposed to act as a deterrent to illegal activity. For example, the previously discussed reconnaissance training by 250 Marines near Naco, Arizona, in August 1992 seems to have been a "terrain denial" operation.

In contrast, the other two JTF-6 mission categories comprised more low-key antidrug support activities. Of these two, the broad-ranging general-support category had the greatest number of missions, with 327 (42% of the total) carried out between 1990 and 1992. Interestingly, the two most significant and numerous activities (excluding photo interpretation) in this category were intelligence and training efforts, which would seem to be the most militaristic of any in this category. While almost nothing is detailed about intelligence efforts, it was reported that training activities consisted of the dispatching of mobile training teams of two to five soldiers to instruct law enforcement officials.[142] The third JTF-6 missions category is engineering, which contained 64 missions (8% of the total) that were conducted from 1990 through 1992. The most notable of these were construction efforts, which included (through 1993) some 30 miles of new roads, approximately 800 miles of upgraded roads, 11 new helicopter landing pads, and about 30 miles of repaired and new fencing (most of it wall-like, consisting of solid steel matting).[143] Thus, although JTF-6 attempted to maintain a low profile, clearly it was very active in the early 1990s.

Unfortunately, publicly available information does not allow for the precise determination of either the types or number of troops typically placed by JTF-6 on the border at any one time. In part, this undoubtedly stems from the fact that JTF-6 has had very few staff permanently assigned to it, but has rather supervised troops that are brought in on a rotating basis for specific missions. Moreover, obtaining such specific information is impeded by the unit's low profile and its involvement in the obviously security-laden matters of drug enforcement.

Nonetheless, it is possible to gain some understanding of the types and number of troops JTF-6 involved in border antidrug efforts at any one time. For example, in early 1991 a JTF-6 official stated that there could be up to 10 or more military support operations taking place along the border at any one time, each operation typically involving no more than 50 troops.[144] However, in late August 1992, a JTF-6 spokesperson reported that 62 joint exercises were occurring at that point in the four border states, which evidently meant within JTF-6's geographical area of activity (i.e., within 50 miles of the border and the Texas gulf coast).[145] Thus, a conservative estimate would be that some 500 troops could have been deployed in antidrug operations in the border region at any one time, and a high estimate would put the figure at some 3,000 troops. Meanwhile, the types of troops deployed in JTF-6 efforts appear to have varied widely. Initial deployments were evenly divided between Marine and Army units. Among the latter, JTF-6 appears to have favored the use of such specialized forces as Army Rangers, Green Berets (i.e., Special Forces), and paratroopers.[146] And of course, as noted previously, border-state National Guard troops also played a prominent role.

It is important to note that, according to a JTF-6 spokesperson, the "rules of engagement" under which these troops operated during the operations granted them permission to "shoot to kill" if they or other personnel they were backing up were endangered.[147] Thus, while the Pentagon was not anxious for military personnel to become involved in deadly firefights on the border, these guidelines did not appear to limit that possibility in a serious way.

Military involvement in domestic drug enforcement efforts was organizationally expanded in 1990 when another antidrug command center was established on the border, in Tucson, Arizona. The Arizona Interagency Interdiction Operation was set up at Davis-Monthan Air Force Base, in what officials declared was "a ground breaking development in joint law enforcement–military operations." It included representatives from nearly a dozen federal and state law enforcement agencies (including the Border Patrol and Customs Service), as well as the military.[148] Similarly, a proposal was also made to locate Operation Alliance headquarters next to JTF-6 headquarters at Fort Bliss,[149] which in fact was subsequently carried out. These joint command centralization efforts centered at border military bases clearly increased the formal integration of military, paramilitary, and police forces.

The establishment of JTF-6 and its coordinating role in working with local, state, and federal law enforcement agencies in antidrug efforts raised some fairly ominous possibilities. If nothing else, it signaled that the military was expanding its participation in particular domestic law enforcement efforts. This participation was ostensibly focused on, but apparently not limited to, drug issues. Given their unprecedented nature in the United States during the contemporary historical period, these activities have undoubtedly been fraught with difficulties in coordination and organization. Nonetheless, the prospect of ongoing military involvement and collaboration in domestic law enforcement compares in principle to institutional patterns in Latin America and other regions of the world where the U.S. military has long promoted the doctrines of counterinsurgency and low-intensity conflict. And as noted in chapter 1, the result of such practices abroad has often been widespread human rights violations. At any rate, in the immediate term it is clear that JTF-6 brought the military to a new, increased level of involvement in the domestic arena of the "drug war," and may have helped open the way toward even greater military involvement in domestic law enforcement in the future in the border region—and perhaps beyond. Any moves in this direction would merit public debate and thoughtful consideration, rather than a reflex turn toward ever more strident law enforcement measures.

U.S.–MEXICAN COLLABORATION IN DRUG ENFORCEMENT

While it is well beyond the scope of this monograph to address fully the issue of collaboration between U.S. and Mexican forces in drug enforcement efforts, it is nonetheless important to note its existence and expansion in the late 1980s and early 1990s, as several aspects have particular relevance for the U.S.–Mexico border region. Such binational antidrug collaboration has a relatively lengthy past, emerging on a significant scale in the 1970s in the form of U.S. assistance for Mexican crop-eradication programs, which were largely carried out by the Mexican military.[150] Such collaboration expanded markedly after the installation of the Salinas administration in 1988, as President Salinas termed drug trafficking a "national security issue," and in doing so moved to help alleviate a major source of contention in U.S.–Mexico relations during the 1980s.[151] This clearly fit within Salinas's overall efforts to improve binational relations in his quest for a free trade agreement. However, U.S. antidrug efforts on the U.S. side in the border region may have been instrumental in pressuring Mexican officials to agree to greater bilateral cooperation against drug trafficking in the border region.[152] In any case, U.S. antidrug and military aid to Mexico jumped dramatically in the late 1980s and early 1990s, as moves toward economic integration were apparently to be accompanied by increased security and military linkages.[153] The increase in such aid was a significant departure from Mexico's postrevolutionary tradition of fierce independence from large-scale U.S. influence among its military and security forces.

The manifestation of U.S.–Mexican collaboration most relevant to the border region was the development of Mexico's Northern Border Response Force (NBRF). Formed in 1990, this unit was a rapid-response team made up of agents from the notorious Mexican Federal Judicial Police, whose forces had been widely cited for human rights abuses (as noted previously). The NBRF had six helicopter bases in border cities, and another five in northern Mexico within 200 miles of the border. The unit's objective was to apprehend drug traffickers and break up their networks in northern Mexico as they landed at airstrips before attempting to cross the border. The United States was instrumental in establishing, supplying, and training this force. A U.S. military counternarcotics team based at the American Embassy worked closely with the unit, providing operational planning assistance and sharing drug-trafficking intelligence information. Meanwhile, "advisers" from the U.S. Drug Enforcement Agency worked more closely with the unit on an ongoing operational basis. More generally, the United States supplied the at least occasional use of a P-3 radar plane and 21 helicopters to Mexican drug-interdiction forces (including nine UH-IH helicopters specifically for the NBRF).[154] U.S. military officials glowingly cited the NBRF as a model for future U.S.–Mexican antidrug collaboration.[155]

Several additional manifestations of U.S.–Mexico collaboration on antidrug efforts had implications for the border region. These involved a closer integration of forces. For instance, Mexican military officials met with their counterparts in the California National Guard to exchange information on crop-eradication efforts. These meetings were planned to continue and possibly to be expanded to include National Guard units in other states.[156] In another instance of reciprocity, similar to the posting of U.S. DEA agents in Mexico, Mexican officials requested (and subsequently obtained) permission to post Federal Judicial Police in Mexican consulates in high drug-trafficking and drug-consumption areas in the

United States, including the border region.[157] More recently, in a new turn of events, the Texas Department of Public Safety (i.e., Texas state police) initiated in 1992 a training program for Mexican police from the border region. The purpose of this program was to develop closer working relations between Texan and Mexican border-area police forces, especially in drug-trafficking and car-theft cases. Interestingly, the program was in part arranged by the Texas Department of Commerce, in an effort to enhance Texas's relations with Mexico.[158] These efforts suggest that drug enforcement collaboration between the United States and Mexico was expanding and becoming more reciprocal in nature.

On the whole, joint U.S.–Mexico collaboration in antidrug efforts seems to have grown substantially in recent years, with the common border area being a focal point of attention and activity. Most importantly, this collaboration helped establish vital links between the two nations' security and military forces. It also raised troubling issues, given that Mexican police and security forces had a dismal human rights record—especially the Federal Judicial Police and its antidrug forces. These developments obviously merit much further investigation and discussion elsewhere.

THE LIC FRAMEWORK APPLIED TO
BORDER-REGION ANTIDRUG ACTIVITIES, 1986–1992

Developments in the War on Drugs during the period 1986–1992 appear to represent the implementation of LIC operational characteristics to an unprecedented degree in the U.S.–Mexico border region. This is perhaps to be expected, given that antidrug operations are a specific mission area of LIC doctrine. Still, the extent to which other LIC characteristics emerged in the borderlands between 1986 and 1992 is exceptional. No other group of activities in any time period examined in the present work so clearly illustrates the applicability of the LIC framework to the U.S.–Mexico border region.

The major drug enforcement program of this period, Operation Alliance, exemplifies a number of specific LIC characteristics. The very nature of the project's thrust to bring together and coordinate—in effect, integrate—the drug enforcement activities of law enforcement agencies from all levels of government, with the military playing a supporting role, is a fundamental LIC characteristic. Operation Alliance especially evidenced this characteristic in its effort in 1990 to formulate a border-wide drug enforcement strategy, as this process sought to coordinate and integrate, to an unprecedented extent, a morass of police and military forces in the border region. (The moving of Operation Alliance headquarters to a new location next to Joint Task Force 6 at Fort Bliss promoted further integration of forces and seemed likely to blur even more the line between the law enforcement agencies and the military.) LIC doctrine emphasizes such force integration, as well as the use of police forces as the "first line of defense," with the military playing a less conspicuous advisory and support role, which is precisely what Operation Alliance strove for. In addition, the program's emphasis on upgrading and expanding high-tech military equipment (e.g., helicopters, sensors, etc.) is quite characteristic of LIC doctrine as well, though some of the new equipment (e.g., aerostat radar balloons and over-the-horizon backscatter radar) exceeded the scale and level of sophistication of equipment typical for low-intensity conflict. Nonetheless, such equipment was intended for surveillance purposes, which is generally consistent with the LIC framework.

Operation Alliance's emphases on training and intelligence activities are also common to low-intensity conflict doctrine. In addition, the expanded authority of various types of border police agents to conduct warrantless searches in the border region, which resulted from the program's extensive use of cross-designation of disparate law enforcement authority, facilitates a larger LIC objective: achieving greater social control over targeted civilian populations. The same end is furthered by the program's involvement in other areas of law enforcement besides antidrug activities—most notably, immigration enforcement. Also, the somewhat tactically decentralized nature of Operation Alliance evidenced in its establishment of 27 local Border Alliance groups seems to be a step in the direction toward the LIC characteristic of bringing war efforts to the grassroots level. On the whole, though its projects faced numerous obstacles in practice, Operation Alliance nonetheless appears to have greatly furthered the de facto implementation of key aspects of LIC doctrine in the U.S.–Mexico border region, principally in facilitating ongoing relations between the military establishment and civilian law enforcement agencies in the borderlands.

The host of legal changes contained in the Defense authorization acts for fiscal years 1989, 1990, and 1991 further increased the Pentagon's involvement in domestic antidrug activities, and opened the way to further implementation of LIC doctrine in the borderlands. The effective relaxation of the Posse Comitatus statute afforded by these acts brought the U.S. military establishment much closer to domestic law enforcement functions, as did the formal designation of the Defense Department as the "lead agency" in drug-interdiction efforts—though military forces were (and remain) still formally prohibited from participating directly in searches, arrests, and seizures. Most outstanding are the legal changes allowing military reconnaissance activities at or near the border, the conducting of other military operations within the United States, and military training of civilian law enforcement personnel. Also noteworthy is the legal provision that mandated that the military conduct training exercises "to the maximum extent practicable" in border drug trafficking areas. Moreover, the military was again allowed to maintain and operate its equipment for civilian police agencies with authority to enforce not only drug laws, but also immigration and customs laws. Further, many other forms of less direct military support were allowed for police agencies of all types. Taken together, such measures would seem to have provided the means for erasing the crucial distinction in our society between domestic police efforts and military operations, or even to render largely symbolic the long-standing formal prohibitions on the military from carrying out arrests, seizures, and searches.

It appears that the overall goal of these legal changes was to integrate military and civilian forces in a common law enforcement mission. These changes opened the door to increased loans of military equipment and personnel, as well as the provision of military training and the conduct of military operations—all to support civilian law enforcement agencies in the border region and elsewhere. Such activities exemplify a central tactic of LIC doctrine in which U.S. military "advisers" attempt to "professionalize" local forces through training and equipment assistance. More important, the use of actual military operations to support the antidrug efforts of civilian law enforcement agencies clearly brought the military into the realm of "internal security" matters, which is a central focus of LIC strategy. The fact that such facets of low-intensity conflict are elsewhere frequently accompanied by widespread human rights violations suggests that such moves merit extensive public scrutiny and debate.

The de facto implementation of the LIC framework in the border region is more evident in the actual domestic military activities undertaken in support of drug enforcement. One example of this is the routine use of National Guard personnel in customs inspections at border crossings. This is an obvious instance of direct, ongoing military involvement in domestic law enforcement—i.e., in the search phase of the search, seizure, and arrest process. However, the seriousness of this example pales in comparison to other activities.

The development and expansion of joint training exercises and operations between the military and civilian law enforcement agencies (most notably between the National Guard as well as the Marine Corps and the Border Patrol) are the most important instances of the implementation of LIC doctrine in the border region. First of all, the joint operations and exercises increased the integration of civilian police and military forces. Second, their emphasis on training, as well as the types of training provided (e.g., covert reconnaissance patrols, intelligence gathering, and small-unit tactics), are quite characteristic of LIC doctrine. Moreover, the use of training exercises as a means of conducting actual special operations—of whatever variety—is a classic LIC tactic. The resulting difficulty in differentiating *real* military operations from *training* exercises is by no means unique to the War on Drugs effort in the border region. It is also common in more obviously conflictive LIC settings such as Central America in the 1980s, where U.S. military "advisers" became embroiled in firefights with opposition forces in the course of their "training duties" and "exercises" with local military forces.

The actual military operations carried out in support of civilian law enforcement efforts made ample use of the types of forces characteristic of LIC activities: elite military units and National Guard troops. The technology used in these efforts is also characteristic of low-intensity conflict, particularly the pilotless aircraft and electronic sensors. Most important, the fact that these joint operations focused not only on drug enforcement but also on undocumented immigration—and more generally on "something that could possibly be of an illegal nature"—appeared to open the door to greater military participation in a much broader spectrum of domestic law enforcement efforts. It is important to note that much of the shape and reach of these efforts remains to be determined in practice, as military officials experiment with their newly broadened discretionary authority to become key actors in domestic law enforcement. All of this highlights the overarching characteristic that is so vital to the LIC framework, which is the use of the military and its resources to control targeted groups of civilians. If such use continues to develop in the U.S.–Mexico border region, the question becomes, Where will military involvement in border law enforcement lead, and how will these developments affect the surrounding society? At a minimum, present trends do not bode well for the status of the civil and human rights of border residents or undocumented immigrants passing through the area. Indeed, the "cultural difficulties" faced by the traditional military establishment in adapting to its new domestic drug enforcement role (i.e., altering an approach centered on killing or neutralizing "the enemy" to allow for making complex legal distinctions) suggest the potential for grave problems for the "targets" of their enforcement efforts.

The Pentagon's establishment of Joint Task Force 6 to aid in drug-interdiction efforts on the border takes the integration of military and civilian law enforcement forces to a new level. It brings the military yet another step closer to assuming a central partnership role in domestic law enforcement responsibility in the U.S.–Mexico border region. The scale and scope of JTF-6 activity is indeed impressive. The task force conducted some 775 missions from 1990 to 1992 in support of border-region antidrug efforts; fully half of these missions were of the more obviously militaristic variety, consisting of operational missions as well as training and intelligence activities. More specifically, JTF-6's emphasis on conducting small-unit operations, training civilian law enforcement officials, and providing military hardware for domestic law enforcement are all key elements of LIC strategy. Further, the small number of troops permanently assigned to JTF-6, accompanied by the frequent temporary rotations of numerous active-duty military and National Guard personnel through the region, are very similar to LIC practices elsewhere—e.g., Central America during the 1980s. JTF-6 clearly represents a more advanced, institutionalized phase of the military's involvement in the domestic side of the War on Drugs. As such, it increased the likelihood of the military's involvement in domestic law enforcement encounters with civilians in the borderlands, not only with drug traffickers but also with other persons who might have been considered "suspect," for whatever reason.

The growing trend of U.S.–Mexico collaboration in drug enforcement endeavors, particularly in Mexico's northern border region, also suggests the implementation of elements of the LIC framework. As in other LIC settings, U.S. "advisers" and strategists were actively working with host-nation forces to provide training, equipment, and financial support. Thus, the integration of military and security forces was taken to a binational level.

Overall, it seems that the War on Drugs advanced to an unprecedented level the implementation of LIC doctrine in the U.S.–Mexico border region. In general, throughout the various antidrug efforts surveyed here, it appears that the military was trying to play a low-key support role for law enforcement agencies. As noted previously, this itself is an LIC tactic, however. Indeed, when low-intensity conflict is done right, it is a relatively subtle form of militarization that integrates various military, police, and security forces. However, the achievement in practice of this ideal type is by no means a given. Indeed, it is important to again point out that the actual implementation of LIC doctrine in other settings (e.g., Central America) has often been accompanied by widespread and systematic human rights violations. This fact should give us pause with respect to the effective adaptation of LIC doctrine characteristics in the U.S.–Mexico border region.

5

Conclusion

In drawing conclusions, it is important first to recall and address briefly the larger question underlying this unconventional study: Why should militarization be used as a framework through which to view and interpret contemporary drug and immigration enforcement efforts along the U.S.–Mexico border? The most straightforward answer is that low-intensity conflict (LIC) and similar forms of militarization tend to eventually lead to human rights violations on a widespread and systematic basis. This scenario has been played out repeatedly in Latin America and other parts of the third world, with U.S. security and military officials frequently facilitating, if not actually carrying out, these efforts. While the U.S.–Mexico border region is quite distinct from those settings in many crucial regards, any preliminary evidence of similar military-security patterns in the region ought nonetheless to be carefully scrutinized.

One noteworthy criticism of using a militarization-centered framework is that it is inappropriate in the absence of manifestations of military confrontation, or at least fairly conventional and obvious military activities. But it is precisely those forms of militarization that are unconventional and broad-ranging, and that address issues that have traditionally been largely outside the purview of the military, that are featured prominently in contemporary U.S. military doctrine and national security concerns, especially with respect to the third world. The U.S.–Mexico border is the United States' most immediate point of contact with the third world. Thus, the LIC framework should not be excluded a priori as inapplicable to an analysis of immigration and drug enforcement in the border region. Rather, its applicability is an open empirical question, one that this monograph has attempted to address, at least in part.

Militarization has been viewed in this study as a dynamic phenomenon stretching across the broad continuum of measures contained in low-intensity conflict doctrine, many of which are sophisticated and fairly subtle. This continuum ranges from the relatively innocuous use of military surveillance equipment by police agencies all the way up to the more obvious, large-scale deployment of military forces to maintain security and stability. The larger objective of LIC doctrine is to effect social control over targeted civilian populations by drawing selectively from this vast continuum of tactics to address any threat to stability (from a broad range of security concerns) in a manner that theoretically is more judicious and appropriate than are heavy-handed, less discriminate, conventional military approaches.

If the definition of militarization were limited to the severe end of the continuum, we would be left much less well equipped to recognize, let alone evaluate or debate, the general drift of contemporary immigration and drug enforcement efforts in the border region. The expansive and insidious nature of low-intensity conflict doctrine can readily lend itself to a "slippery slope" or "creeping" dynamic of militarization, whereby preliminary LIC doctrine measures can open the way to the adoption of more problematic and repressive measures.[1] Such a course of events is not an axiomatic, necessary outcome in the case of the U.S.–Mexico border region. Nonetheless, this possibility ought to be carefully considered, and any evidence of emerging militarization in the border region should be closely examined. The seriousness of the potential negative impact of border militarization on the status of human and civil rights in the region makes it imperative that we consider, study, and debate the issue.

The militarization focus of this study, however, was not adopted to suggest that all border-area immigration and drug enforcement efforts are expressions of various facets of militarization. Rather, the aim has been to note the features of those efforts that resemble or replicate specific characteristics of a particularly troubling U.S. military doctrine. The goal in using this unconventional approach has been to bring out issues that have typically gone unexamined or unquestioned in investigating and formulating U.S. immigration and drug enforcement policies and practices for the U.S.–Mexico border region.

The first objective of the remainder of this chapter, then, is to summarize the general applicability of LIC doctrine to immigration and drug enforcement policies and practices in the U.S.–Mexico border region from 1978 through 1992. The second is to draw out some of the theoretical implications of border militarization, and then to consider briefly the North American Free Trade Agreement and the 1992 Los Angeles riots with these implications in mind. It is important to stress that the conclusions offered here are not proposed as definitive explanations of the issues discussed in this monograph. Rather, they are intended to provide a distinct, systematic, and hopefully plausible interpretation of contemporary trends in immigration and drug enforcement policies and practices in the U.S.–Mexico border region, in order to stimulate further research and debate on these topics.

LIC Doctrine and Immigration and Drug Enforcement in the Border Region

Overall, it seems clear that immigration and drug enforcement efforts in the U.S.–Mexico border region during the 1978–1992 period coincided to a significant extent with the precepts of LIC doctrine.[2] (See table 2 for some of the key points of overlap between LIC doctrine and immigration and drug enforcement efforts in the border region.) The militarization of the border generally occurred in an uninterrupted and ever increasing fashion during this time, which spanned three different U.S. presidential administrations from the two major U.S. political parties. It reached a high point under the Bush administration, mainly via the expansion of the War on Drugs. However, the implementation of important characteristics of LIC doctrine in the U.S.–Mexico border region does not appear to have been a conscious, calculated project on the part of either policymakers or border-area law enforcement officials. Rather, it seems to have occurred in a largely piecemeal fashion, cumulatively resulting in the de facto militarization of the U.S.–Mexico border. This outcome is not entirely illogical, however, given that many policymakers periodically, if not consistently, portrayed undocumented immigration and illicit drug trafficking principally as security issues—indeed, drug trafficking was formally elevated to the status of "national security threat." Consequently, enforcement efforts in the U.S.–Mexico border region were expanded and additional resources set in place to further pursue a punitive, coercive, and largely unilateral approach in addressing undocumented immigration and illicit drug trafficking—complex issues that were intimately related to much larger international social, political, and economic phenomena.

Much of the process of border militarization was centered in the INS. Congressionally appropriated funding for the agency expanded 240% in unadjusted dollars from 1978 through 1992. Most of the new funding was directed to the agency's Enforcement Division, whose funding and authorized staffing levels were increased some 153% and 44%, respectively, during the 1982–1992 period alone. INS immigration enforcement

Table 2. Selected LIC Equipment and Operational Characteristics
Present in Immigration and Drug Enforcement in the U.S.–Mexico
Border Region, 1978–1992

LIC Equipment	INS Equipment in the Border Region
Helicopters	Increased from 2 in 1980 to 58 in 1992 (most from military)
Night-vision equipment	335 night-vision scopes by the mid-1980s, & numerous subsequent expansions Extensive loans of various types of night-vision equipment from the military Infrared radar in several helicopters Low-light-level television surveillance systems (in portions of 6 out of 9 southwest Border Patrol sectors)
Electronic intrusion-detection ground sensors	1,221 replaced & upgraded by 1984, & numerous subsequent expansions (in all 9 southwest Border Patrol sectors)

LIC Operational Characteristics	Border-Region Enforcement Examples
Coordination & integration of distinct forces (especially police with military)	Alien Border Control Committee: a multiagency federal task force that designed contingency plans in the mid-1980s for the mass roundup of targeted aliens & for sealing the border Loosening of legal restrictions on the use of the U.S. military in domestic law enforcement, thereby allowing joint military-police efforts (mainly antidrug) Operation Alliance: a joint antidrug effort (established in 1986) of federal & state law enforcement agencies (LEAs), with military support Joint Task Force 6 (JTF-6): a military antidrug unit established in late 1989 to support LEAs in the U.S.–Mexico border region (JTF-6 conducted 775 missions of various types from 1990 to 1992)

Continued on facing page

Table 2 (continued)

LIC Operational Characteristics	Border-Region Enforcement Examples
Military training of local forces	Reconnaissance, intelligence gathering, & small-unit tactics training provided by the military to border-region LEAs
Military training exercises outside military bases	Various types of training exercises conducted by military units in border region to support LEAs, primarily in drug enforcement (e.g., JTF-6 conducted 384 operational missions, 1990–1992, though not all were outside bases)
Emphasis on intelligence efforts	Deployment of INS field agents in Mexico & Central America to gather intelligence information on undocumented immigration flows Sharing of immigration intelligence information among the INS, CIA, DIA, & State Department Formation of the Southwest Border Intelligence Task Force (focused on drug enforcement)

efforts dating back to the late 1970s played a key role in the militarization of the border, as immigration issues took on a greater sense of political urgency between then and 1986. Subsequently, the militarization of immigration enforcement was furthered principally through its being interwoven with the rapidly ascending issue of drug enforcement, which was addressed in a decidedly more militaristic manner.

For present purposes, U.S. immigration and drug enforcement efforts in the U.S.–Mexico border region are considered with regard to three general dimensions of LIC doctrine: equipment, operational characteristics (i.e., tactics and strategy), and the overall social control essence of this framework. Turning now to the first of these dimensions, it is clear that LIC-related hardware is well represented among the equipment used by the INS in the border region from 1978 through 1992. The most obvious points of coincidence—the greatly expanded use of helicopters (from 2 to 58), night-vision equipment, infrared radar, and electronic intrusion-detection sensors—are detailed in table 2. In addition, one of the most visible LIC-related projects was the expansion of border barriers. During the late 1970s the INS built 10-foot-high chain-link fences in portions of four Border Patrol sectors that were frequented by undocumented border crossers. In 1991 and 1992, the fence between San Diego and Tijuana was rebuilt and expanded by U.S. military construction units as a thin steel wall stretching seven miles inland from the ocean. Additional LIC-related and other military equipment (not detailed in table 2) that was introduced in the border region during the 1978–1992 period included M-16 rifles for the Border Patrol, six aerostat radar balloons capable of covering the length of the border, closed-circuit television-surveillance systems in four border-region INS detention centers, and 15 "improved image-enhancement" automated land surveillance vehicles. Further, a host of additional LIC-related communications and surveillance equipment, as well as aircraft, were loaned to civilian police or deployed by the military, via its participation in border-area drug enforcement efforts.

The second and more significant dimension of the militarization framework utilized in the present monograph is that of the operational characteristics of low-intensity conflict. (Table 2 outlines the most important developments in border-region drug and immigration enforcement efforts that corresponded to these characteristics.) Expanded antidrug operations (itself a mission category of LIC doctrine) in the border region from the late 1980s onward fueled many of the most obvious implementations of LIC operational characteristics. These involved the deployment of U.S. military forces in a wide variety of roles to support border-area law enforcement agencies—that is, the military began to take on police roles. This was facilitated by a series of legal maneuvers that effectively altered the long-standing Posse Comitatus statute, which had largely prohibited the use of the U.S. military in domestic law enforcement. While principally intended to allow military support for drug enforcement efforts, many of the legal changes were more general in nature. In addition, one key provision specifically allowed the military to operate and maintain equipment it had lent to civilian police agencies that had jurisdiction to enforce *drug, customs, or immigration laws.* These legal changes greatly enhanced the prospects for the coordination and collaboration between military and civilian police forces, a key operational characteristic of LIC doctrine. The Pentagon was not initially eager to become directly involved in domestic drug enforcement, and the legal changes left intact the prohibitions against military personnel's direct participation in stops, searches, and arrests of civilians. Nonetheless, these changes facilitated, and in some cases specifically mandated, a wide variety of military activities to support the antidrug efforts of border-region law enforcement agencies. The activities ranged from loaning a wide variety of equipment to border-area police agencies, to providing these agencies with construction support as well as communications, electronics, and transportation maintenance, to conducting various joint operations and training exercises with them.

One key initiative that institutionalized ongoing military assistance to civilian police was the establishment in late 1989 of Joint Task Force 6, which was set up at Fort Bliss in El Paso by the Pentagon to coordinate the military's expanding support for the antidrug efforts of border-region police agencies. JTF-6 enabled greater coordination and integration of military and police forces, which, as noted previously, was a prominent operational characteristic of LIC doctrine. JTF-6 was quite active from 1990 through 1992, as it conducted 775 operational, engineering, and general support missions to aid border law enforcement agencies' antidrug efforts. The most obviously militaristic of these efforts were the numerous deployments of ground and air troops to monitor and patrol the border, usually in conjunction with the Border Patrol and typically in remote areas. Such activities account for approximately one half of all JTF-6 missions conducted from 1990 through 1992.

However, it is crucial to point out that in practice the military's support was not limited solely to drug enforcement endeavors. At least some of the various joint operations and training exercises featuring Border Patrol agents working with National Guard and Marine troops stressed immigration and other broader law enforcement concerns as secondary emphases. Further, many of the additional military support operations (e.g., the construction of the border wall in San Diego) substantially aided immigration enforcement efforts. Thus, military troops were at least indirectly involved in immigration and other broader law enforcement concerns in the border region. This development (which was a spillover effect of sorts) illustrates the "slippery slope" or "creeping" dynamic of LIC doctrine–style militarization.

The militarization of the border was also heightened via the adoption of LIC doctrine operational characteristics by the INS and its Border Patrol unit—that is, the police taking on military characteristics. For example, the Border Patrol formed several elite "special forces," namely, the paramilitary Border Patrol Tactical Team and Emergency Response Teams. On the less severe end of the continuum, the Border Patrol also implemented the LIC tactic of increasing the amount of benevolent contact between security forces and civilians, through its extensive drug-education program in public schools and its sponsorship of Explorer

Scout youth groups. These efforts bolstered the public image of the Border Patrol in new ways. However, the single border-region police action that combined the greatest number of LIC operational characteristics was the INS's massive operation to round up and detain thousands of Central American asylum seekers in the Lower Rio Grande Valley during 1989 and 1990. Among the LIC qualities manifested in this INS campaign were the stark exertion of social control over a specifically targeted civilian population, emphases on intelligence gathering and on quasi-psychological operations, the sharing of intelligence information with various U.S. intelligence agencies, and the enlistment of a private relief agency (the Red Cross) to offer "humanitarian assistance" as a part of a larger security operation.

The coordination and integration of various types of forces was of central importance to LIC doctrine, and there were several significant cases, besides those previously noted, that illustrate such coordination in border-area immigration and drug enforcement efforts. Consider, for example, the increased collaboration between U.S. and Mexican military and police forces in antidrug and immigration enforcement (the latter involving police forces and directed against third-country, non-Mexican nationals). The most prominent instance of the force integration characteristic of low-intensity conflict is the effort of Operation Alliance from 1986 through 1992. Its very mission was to coordinate the antidrug efforts of a wide variety of federal, state, and local law enforcement agencies along the entire U.S.–Mexico border while calling on the military to provide support. Interestingly, this operation also included immigration enforcement in its concerns. In addition, one of the most ominous instances of force integration was the Alien Border Control Committee, a multiagency federal task force created in 1986 and headed by the INS that created an elaborate contingency plan to round up and deport thousands of "alien terrorists and undesirables" and to supposedly seal the border. The U.S. military was to be called upon to provide various types of support (e.g., detention facilities and transportation). This project greatly resembles those outlined in the LIC mission areas of peacetime contingency operations and counterterrorism activities. Force integration was also much less drastically exemplified in the joint foot patrols of local police and Border Patrol agents established in several urban areas along the border. All of these cases furthered, to widely varying degrees, the militarization of the U.S.–Mexico border.

The third dimension of border militarization considered here (and not covered in table 2) is the essence of low-intensity conflict: the maintenance of social control over targeted civilian populations. The previously outlined LIC-related equipment and examples employing various LIC operational characteristics were used toward this end. The targeted populations were principally undocumented immigrants, smugglers of drugs and immigrants, and persons suspected of belonging to either of these categories (with most of the suspects, in the eyes of the INS and its Border Patrol unit, being Mexican Americans and Mexican immigrants).

Several other features of border-region enforcement, particularly as practiced by the INS, also provide evidence of this third dimension of border militarization. The expansion of and shifts in INS detention efforts are examples of the principle of targeted social control. Throughout the 1980s, INS detention endeavors were used to punish and deter Central American and Caribbean refugees, especially those wishing to apply for political asylum. In the 1990s they were used increasingly against the ambiguously defined population of "criminal aliens," which was mainly interpreted to mean immigrants who had been convicted of drug offenses or violent crimes. However, this politically expedient label could technically be (and has been at least on occasion) applied much more broadly to include even some misdemeanor offenders. (This provides authorities with an option to employ this convenient label as a means of social control over many immigrants throughout the greater border region, and elsewhere.) Furthermore, in order to detain at least a portion of the targeted populations, the INS greatly expanded its detention capacity, most of which was concentrated in the Southwest, from 1978 through 1992.

The ability to effect social control over targeted civilian groups in the border region was also enhanced by expansions in Border Patrol resources and enforcement authority. The number of Border Patrol agent positions authorized by Congress grew by 92% from 1978 through 1992, while congressional funding for the unit jumped 317% (in unadjusted dollars). Meanwhile, the unit's enforcement jurisdiction was greatly expanded, as the unit was first formally deputized in the late 1980s to enforce drug- and contraband-smuggling laws, and then in 1990 was granted general arrest authority under federal law (and also under state law in New Mexico and Arizona).

Despite this broadened jurisdiction, the primary target populations for the enforcement efforts of the Border Patrol have remained undocumented immigrants in the Southwest, smugglers of immigrants and drugs, and persons suspected of being smugglers or immigrants. In practice this meant that both Mexican immigrants and Mexican Americans continued to bear the brunt of the Border Patrol's law enforcement efforts. Thus, a growing federal police force with greatly expanded legal authority was largely devoted to overseeing and controlling people of Mexican origin. There is a certain continuity between this trend and that of border-region law enforcement and military efforts in earlier historical periods.

Finally, there is substantial evidence, from the late 1980s onward, of extensive human and civil rights violations as well as other abuses of authority in the border region. On the U.S. side of the border, recorded abuses were overwhelmingly committed by the Border Patrol and other INS personnel, to the extent that there was an organizational pattern of rights violations and abuses of authority. The broad range of existing evidence suggests that abusive behavior and rights violations were systemic problems in this institution, especially in its main enforcement arm, the Border Patrol. The primary victims were Mexican and Central American immigrants (particularly the undocumented), as well as Mexican Americans in the border region. It is significant that these violations occurred during a period when the paramilitary character of the Border Patrol was markedly enhanced by its expanded drug enforcement responsibilities and activities, which were increasingly intermixed with its immigration enforcement activities.

In summary, key aspects of drug and immigration enforcement efforts in the border region from 1978 through 1992 were either analogous to or direct expressions of one of three dimensions of LIC doctrine: equipment, operational characteristics, or the general essence of the framework. Viewed as a whole, these developments provide compelling evidence that the U.S.–Mexico border was gradually militarized in a manner consistent with the LIC framework. While this outcome appears to have been unintentional, it nonetheless has significant and problematic implications.

Implications of the Militarization of the U.S.–Mexico Border

The potentially far-reaching implications of the militarization of the U.S.–Mexico border have not been widely considered, as the phenomenon of border militarization has gone largely unrecognized.[3] The present discussion, then, is necessarily speculative in outlining several general interpretations of the broader implications of the militarization of the border. In addition, brief consideration is given here to contemporary border-region immigration and drug enforcement efforts in relation to the recently passed North American Free Trade Agreement and the 1992 Los Angeles riots. The purpose of this discussion is neither to construct definitive explanations nor to offer precise predictions of future trends, but rather to stimulate further investigation, consideration, and debate of contemporary border enforcement efforts.

Before proceeding, however, it is important to outline the several key theoretical propositions that inform the interpretations offered here. The first set of propositions is focused on the topic of repression, which is by no means an unknown phenomenon in "advanced" industrialized and even democratic societies, though it often occurs in an insidious fashion. In such societies, the use of highly developed technology is vitally important in the construction of elaborate military-security apparatuses and in the enactment of often subtle yet also repressive social-control measures, while the designation of an "enemy" is crucial to justifications of these actions. Further, repression may be carried out in a preventive fashion against people perceived to be potential threats, particularly members of "marginalized" groups, who authorities may fear will form or support opposition movements seeking large-scale social change. Moreover, in general, large-scale bureaucratic organizations tend to undermine the human rights of the "truly disadvantaged" members of society and to periodically repress intellectual and political dissidents that advocate on their behalf.

The second set of theoretical propositions informing the interpretations presented in this discussion center on economic issues. The relocation of production processes from high-wage to low-wage areas of the world has been instrumental in the renewal of labor control and discipline both in the United States and abroad, and has resulted in higher levels of corporate profits as well as class polarization. In addition, the world economy has become increasingly integrated through the greatly expanded mobility of capital, goods, and services. This in turn has diminished the relevance of nation-state boundaries for most economic factors, though far less so in the case of labor. Within the United States, immigrant workers have provided low-cost, flexible labor in the restructured economy. However, many immigrant workers in the United States and other "core nations" are rendered more economically exploitable and politically vulnerable by immigration enforcement efforts initiated at nation-state boundaries, efforts that help to criminalize those workers. Also, the enforcement of national political boundaries, which formally reinforces the separation of first- and third-world nations, is crucial to the designation of profitable investment sites in the global "periphery." (See appendix 4 for a more detailed treatment of these topics.)

Based on the above theoretical propositions, four general interpretations of the implications of the militarization of the U.S.–Mexico border are elaborated here.[4] The first is that the militarization of the border carried out by U.S. agencies served to reinforce not only the political separation between Mexico and the United States but also the asymmetrical power relationship between the two countries. This trend in U.S. immigration and drug enforcement in the southwest border region may have aided in the designation of Mexico as a profitable site for U.S.-based foreign investment. In general, the U.S.–Mexico border is unique as a vast site of international power stratification, in that it is the longest, if not the only, land boundary separating a first-world nation from a third-world nation.[5] The militarization of the U.S.–Mexico border undoubtedly helped to maintain and reinforce the importance of the border as a point of separation and power stratification between the United States and Mexico[6] (or rather Mexican citizens, if not the Mexican government). This is illustrated by the fact that the militarized border-region immigration and drug enforcement efforts were largely directed against Mexican immigrants and smugglers, and people suspected of belonging to either of these groups (which for the Border Patrol meant Mexican American and Mexican nationals).

Meanwhile, during the same approximate period Mexico became an increasingly important site for U.S.-based foreign investment. The northern Mexican border region in particular was the site of tremendous expansion in the maquiladora sector after 1982.[7] Despite its growing diversity, this sector maintained its largely enclave-like character, and was based largely on low-cost labor (as measured on a global scale) and a less stringent regulatory climate with respect to working conditions and environmental issues.[8] More generally, U.S.-based foreign investment in Mexico expanded markedly, especially after 1988, with the Salinas administration's aggressive implementation of neoliberal economic policies.[9] In addition, Mexico's continued servicing of its massive foreign debt during its profound economic crisis (1982–1988) led to a substantial transfer of wealth out of the country, especially to U.S.-based financial institutions.[10]

Thus, during the 1980s and into the early 1990s there was a positive correlation between an expansion in U.S. investments in and wealth extracted from Mexico, and the increasing militarization of the U.S.–Mexico border by U.S. law enforcement and military agencies. Clearly, it is not possible here to advance beyond the theoretical realm the proposition that there was some sort of relationship between the two phenomena. Nonetheless, the positive correlation between them is a cause for concern and suggests that the topic merits further investigation and theoretical consideration, particularly in light of the North American Free Trade Agreement (a topic addressed later in this chapter).

The second general interpretation of the militarization of the U.S.–Mexico border offered here is that border militarization may well have helped shape (and, to a much lesser extent, limit) the flow of undocumented immigrants into the United States from Mexico as well as from points farther south. And in doing so it served to divide workers both within the United States and internationally. A substantial portion of border-militarization efforts were directly as well as indirectly (via drug enforcement) focused on undocumented immigration. These efforts served to reinforce the criminal status—or at least the nonlegal status— of undocumented immigrants, who were arguably becoming an increasingly vital sector of the U.S. working class. The process of intimidating undocumented immigrants into remaining legally "underground" began at the border and made them more economically exploitable and "flexible." Consequently, their "illegal" status was an obstacle to the development of labor solidarity between immigrant and native-born workers in the United States. The legalization programs of IRCA offered some potential relief from extreme subordination for many undocumented immigrants, although how much relief is still unclear. However, it appears that immigrants who were ineligible for these programs were pushed further underground.[11]

In addition, the buildup of border-region immigration and even overlapping drug enforcement efforts may have served to intimidate and discourage some would-be undocumented immigrants. In effect, this would have constituted a form of "disciplining" workers by encouraging them to remain in their home countries, where wages were low (at least on a global scale) and general labor rights were more restricted.[12] Such an outcome would have been advantageous to both domestic and international investors in Mexico, to the extent that it helped to maintain a surplus of labor and thereby keep wages down.[13] Further, the availability of a lucrative low-wage production site so near the massive U.S. market enabled multinational corporations to continue to pit workers in both countries against each other.

The third interpretation of the militarization of the U.S.–Mexico border proposed here is that it was in part a logical extension of an aggressive U.S. foreign policy toward Central America during the 1980s.[14] The border operated as a last line of defense, as it were, against a politically inexpedient side effect of U.S. interventionism: the increased flow of refugees and immigrants from Central America to the United States. Though this was a small subcategory of the overall immigration flow across the southwest border, its members were singled out as primary targets in the U.S.–Mexico border region for the Reagan administration's punitive detention policies, which were instituted to discourage political-refugee flows. The Bush administration oversaw a major escalation of the effort to discourage political refugees during the 1989–1990 INS crackdown in South Texas against Central Americans applying for political asylum. It is proposed here that these harsh immigration enforcement efforts were tied to the Reagan and Bush administrations' foreign policies toward Central America, which were generally focused on enforcing U.S. domination of that region.[15] Thus, the much-expanded migration of Central Americans to the United States may well have been viewed as a menace to U.S. foreign-policy objectives, especially given that many Central Americans were fleeing the military, political, or economic policies promoted by the United States and its allies in the region. Harsh, selective immigration enforcement along the southwestern border was designed to help discourage such migration to the United States, and also likely helped to intimidate many of the undocumented Central Americans who had made it past the border into maintaining a low profile once they were in the United States. One lesson to draw from these efforts is that harsh immigration enforcement measures can readily be applied in a selective fashion and could theoretically be directed against other immigrant groups in the border region, should authorities come to perceive those groups as a threat or serious political problem for whatever reason.

The fourth interpretation of the implications of the militarization of the U.S.–Mexico border offered here is that it helped U.S. authorities establish greater control over an area that was unquestionably growing in strategic importance, but was also potentially vulnerable to various forms of instability.[16] In general, during recent decades the binational border region developed from a remote area of limited significance to one of the most rapidly growing and industrializing regions in the western hemisphere.[17] This growth was in large part led by the maquiladora industrialization program in Mexico's northern border region, which was overwhelmingly dominated by U.S.-owned firms and their subsidiaries. Economic growth on the U.S side of the border was in turn increasingly tied to growth on the Mexican side, through the provision of goods and services to the maquiladora sector, the provision of international financial and business services, and retail sales to Mexican consumers.[18] In addition, various portions of the border region continued to be centers of intensive agricultural production. Also, nearby Southern California was one of the most economically vibrant areas of the United States until undergoing a severe recession in the early 1990s.

Along with the growth in the U.S.–Mexico border region there were also numerous signs that the region could be vulnerable to instability. Most notably, while enormous profits were generated in the area through a variety of economic activities, much of the region's population was marginalized and poor. Such socioeconomic conditions do not automatically make for instability, of course, but neither are they conducive to the overall well-being and long-term stability of the region. Although the border was a dividing line between first- and third-world nations, social infrastructure (e.g., education, housing, water services, and environmental cleanup and protection) on both sides of the border was notoriously lacking.[19] On the Mexican side, the vast working-class population in the northern border cities received public services that were noticeably inferior to services received by their counterparts in the major interior cities of Mexico, despite the general economic dynamism and relatively higher income level of the northern cities.[20] Furthermore, for most people in this group, their relatively superior income was insufficient to meet their basic consumption and housing needs.[21] Meanwhile, although communities on the U.S. side of the border were far wealthier than Mexican border cities, poverty (as per the U.S. definition) was nonetheless extensive, and particularly concentrated among the Mexican-origin population. For example, the Lower Rio Grande Valley of Texas, which is overwhelmingly Mexican American, has consistently had some of the highest rates of poverty in the United States.[22] Further, in El Paso the poverty rate among people of Mexican origin—who make up the vast majority of the city's overall population—jumped from 29% to 43% during the 1979–1989 period.[23] Even in wealthy San Diego County, the main border community of San Ysidro, overwhelmingly Mexican American, suffers a very high rate of poverty.[24]

There were also various political and social tensions in the U.S.–Mexico border region. The Mexican side of the border was the site of periodic local electoral protests, and even consumer protests, that affected the cross-border flow of commerce.[25] More generally, the long-taken-for-granted stability of Mexico and, relatedly, the security of the United States' southern flank were viewed as having been threatened by Mexico's severe economic crisis of 1982 to 1988 and its hotly contested

1988 presidential elections, which were marred by widespread fraud.[26] Meanwhile, on the U.S. side of the border, in wealthy San Diego County, tensions flared from the late 1980s onward, as various forms of hostility and abuse perpetrated by Anglos against Latino (mainly Mexican) immigrants increased markedly.[27] These latter events appeared to be disturbingly consistent with the long history of abuse and periodic repression experienced by Mexican-origin peoples in the border region. On the whole, these diverse political and social tensions, as well as the sharp economic contrasts, suggest that the border region was perhaps vulnerable to various forms of instability.

Thus, the militarization of the U.S.–Mexico border can be interpreted as a means of securing an area that was increasingly strategic economically, yet also potentially vulnerable to instability. This militarization was directed toward long-subordinated or "marginalized" groups, as immigration and drug enforcement efforts on the U.S. side of the border were focused principally on the Mexican-origin population (broadly defined to include Mexican commuters and immigrants as well as Mexican Americans). Among the notable features of these efforts were a heavy emphasis on surveillance activities involving the use of advanced military technology; the growing presence of law enforcement and military personnel; the greatly expanded legal authority of the Border Patrol; and the ongoing stops (especially at checkpoints), requests for identification from persons of "foreign appearance," searches, and deportations. These activities all helped to contain the Mexican-origin population in the border region. The cumulative effect of such efforts can be interpreted as "preventive repression," enacted to restrain the principal subordinate groups in an economically strategic and polarized area, to impede the development of critical ideologies and social movements among subordinate groups in a crucial region that was vulnerable to instability. In addition, if in the future U.S. authorities decide to implement more widespread and severe security measures in the region, the previous process of border militarization will likely play an instrumental role—for it will have enabled extensive practice in, and a more thorough preparation of, the target area, as well as facilitated the development of a highly collaborative relationship between police and military forces, which to a limited but growing extent is binational in character.

The construction of an "enemy," or at least the designation of a looming threat, was central to the implementation of the militarization of the border. In the contemporary period, undocumented immigration was characterized as a potential threat to U.S. "national security" and illegal drug trafficking was described as an actual threat, which implied that undocumented immigrants and drug traffickers were both "the enemy," either potentially or in fact. Given that related enforcement efforts in the border region were aimed primarily at Mexican-origin peoples, the process appears to have some continuity with the hostile practices of earlier periods that were focused on the same general population in the border region.

To summarize the discussion thus far, four interpretations of the implications of the militarization of the U.S.–Mexico border by U.S. agencies have been presented. First, the militarization of the border served to reinforce the political separation and stratification of power between the United States and Mexico during a period of increased U.S. investment in and economic integration with Mexico. A related proposition is that the process of separation and stratification helped the designation of Mexico as a profitable investment site for internationally mobile investment capital. Second, the militarization of the border helped to "discipline" undocumented immigrant workers coming into the United States by effectively reinforcing their "illegal" status, and hence their economic subordination. Third, the militarization of the U.S.–Mexico border was, in part, an extension of aggressive U.S. foreign policies toward Central America, in that Central American refugees and immigrants were singled out and subjected to especially punitive immigration enforcement measures. Fourth, border militarization served as a means to further secure a region that was increasingly strategic economically and also potentially vulnerable to instability. Beyond these admittedly unconventional interpretations of the general implications of the militarization of contemporary drug and immigration enforcement efforts in the border region, it is important also to consider briefly the implications of border militarization for several specific issues.

THE NORTH AMERICAN FREE TRADE AGREEMENT (NAFTA)

The passage of the North American Free Trade Agreement, with its creation of a new international politico-economic institutional framework, opens up a number of issues regarding border enforcement. This discussion will only consider these issues as they may relate to immigration enforcement in the U.S.–Mexico border region.[28] While NAFTA generated more interest in the U.S.–Mexico border region, and it renewed interest in the links between economic development strategies and undocumented immigration flows, border-region immigration enforcement issues were largely overlooked in the flurry of debates that took place prior to the passage of the accord.[29] Thus, several obvious questions regarding immigration enforcement have yet to be adequately considered. Most importantly, what will become of border militarization, as previously implemented by U.S. agencies? In the much anticipated era of greatly expanded economic integration afforded by the implementation of NAFTA, will border militarization wither away, will it be maintained or augmented, or will it assume new forms?

At first glance, the militarization of the border and other restrictive border enforcement measures would appear to flatly contradict moves by the United States, Mexico, and Canada toward economic integration, and the accompanying development of close political ties between the three countries. However, it is important to recall that in the several years prior to the passage of NAFTA, U.S.–Mexico economic integration was already proceeding rapidly and relatively smoothly, while at the same time the overall level of border militarization carried out by U.S. institutions also increased markedly. This suggests that border militarization and economic integration are not necessarily mutually exclusive developments.[30]

Based on the previously discussed implications of the militarization of the U.S.–Mexico border, there are a number of indications that stringent, if not militarized, immigration enforcement measures in the border region may well remain of central importance, and hence merit additional investigation. It is important to note at the outset, however, that as NAFTA has yet to be fully implemented, the present discussion of the possible relationship between the accord and border-area immigration enforcement efforts is necessarily tentative and highly speculative. Nonetheless, such discussion is offered here with the intention of proposing relevant topics for future research and stimulating broader consideration of related issues.

NAFTA was constructed, in part, to consolidate and institutionalize the neoliberal economic-reform agenda in Mexico—particularly the sweeping economic changes implemented by the Salinas administration—thereby reinforcing Mexico's status as a lucrative investment site for internationally mobile capital.[31] Border militarization efforts prior to NAFTA may have helped to reinforce the designation of Mexico as a profitable investment site by accentuating the political separation and stratification of power between the United States and Mexico. Consequently, it may be worthwhile to examine whether border-area immigration enforcement efforts in the NAFTA period play such a role.

Another previous interpretation that may be worth investigating in the NAFTA era is whether the militarization of the U.S.–Mexico border serves to further secure an increasingly strategic area that has periodically been potentially vulnerable to instability stemming from a wide variety of sources. There are several indications that this sort of interpretation may be worth keeping in mind when examining future border enforcement efforts. It is important to point out that NAFTA has security implications for Mexico and the United States. Among these are that officials in both countries viewed the institutionalization and expansion of economic integration as the best means of ensuring the economic and political stability of Mexico, and thereby further securing the southern flank of the United States.[32] In this regard, perhaps no area is of greater immediate importance for the maintenance of mutual security than the common border region, as it is the geographical point of contact for the integration of the two nations' economies. The expanded flow of trade across the border and the increased investment in the region's infrastructure and productive economic resources that are envisioned under NAFTA would seem to necessarily require a secure and stable borderlands. In a related vein, there are several possible scenarios in which border-area security measures would be escalated sharply to contain Mexican immigration—in response to political instability in Mexico or economic decline in the United States, or both.[33] Consequently, it would seem useful to investigate what role, if any, border-region immigration enforcement efforts in either Mexico or the United States play in reinforcing the security and stability of the border region, as the process of economic integration accelerates under NAFTA, and as the political system in Mexico faces increasing calls for democratic reforms.

The interpretation of the militarization of the border as having helped to "discipline" labor by shaping and perhaps limiting the flow of undocumented workers into the United States may also be relevant to the study of border-region immigration enforcement efforts under NAFTA. To make this case, it is necessary to examine the accord on a more general level. NAFTA seems to be focused on institutionalizing the international mobility of goods, capital, and services. However, it almost entirely ignores the issue of the international mobility of labor, as U.S. officials rebuffed Mexican efforts to raise this issue in any meaningful way during the treaty negotiations.[34] Indeed, the few brief immigration provisions in the accord allow the international mobility of members of only a few, relatively elite labor categories, primarily business professionals.[35] This would seem to facilitate the development of cross-national alliances and collaborations among various types of professionals and elites, while the vast majority of workers would remain confined to their respective nation-states, except for undocumented immigrants. Thus NAFTA appears likely to render nation-state distinctions less relevant for elites, some professionals, and much of the overall economic activity in the United States, Mexico, and Canada. In contrast, national cleavages between non-elite workers in the three nations will apparently remain in place, and thereby probably continue to represent a significant obstacle to the development of international labor solidarity. Hence it seems especially important to monitor the extent to which border-region immigration enforcement efforts maintain, strengthen, or lessen such cleavages, for example, by limiting or reinforcing the penalization of unauthorized international labor mobility.

Possible relationships between NAFTA and future trends in undocumented immigration from Mexico to the United States were widely speculated about prior to the passage of NAFTA. Most notably, one of the key arguments made in favor of the accord was that it would eventually lead to reduced levels of undocumented immigration by providing expanded opportunities for Mexican workers and increased prospects for developing the Mexican economy.[36] However, there was some concern that undocumented immigration would perhaps increase, at least in the short term, primarily due to the restructuring of the rural economy.[37]

Of greater importance than immigration flows per se is the issue of whether NAFTA will substantially improve opportunities as well as the living and working conditions for Mexican workers. This outcome is by no means guaranteed, and there are ample reasons to question whether these conditions will significantly improve. First, recent trends in the dynamic maquiladora sector are not encouraging with regard to its ability to play a key role in helping to establish a more integrated, broad-based economy built on export-oriented industrialization. As noted previously, despite explosive growth as well as the expanded adoption of leading-edge production and organizational practices during recent years, the maquiladora sector has largely remained an economic enclave with few linkages to the rest of the Mexican economy, and it has continued to rely heavily on low-cost labor. In addition, the establishment of the sort of restrictive labor discipline that has been crucial to the successful development of export-oriented industrialization programs in East Asian nations is thought to be necessary in Mexico if it is to achieve comparable success as it strives to follow a somewhat similar economic model under

NAFTA.[38] Further, it seems likely that NAFTA will cause some degree of economic restructuring and dislocation, producing various "winners" and "losers" in the Mexican economy, which will probably lead to less than universally positive outcomes for Mexican workers.[39] Such prospects do not point to an economic development ripe with expanded opportunities and improved living and working conditions for broad sectors of the Mexican population under NAFTA. Rather they imply some degree of hardship (in the short term, at any rate) and even subjugation to further labor discipline, and thus quite possibly at least a temporary increase in incentives to emigrate to the United States. Therefore, it would seem advisable to carefully investigate border-region immigration enforcement efforts under NAFTA taking into consideration what roles, if any, they may play in disciplining labor—whether by discouraging Mexican workers from attempting undocumented immigration, by intimidating those who do cross illegally into staying "underground," or by some other means.

In summation, my purpose in raising various critical points with regard to NAFTA and their possible implications for immigration enforcement has not been to imply that a continuation of the previous trend of increasingly militarized immigration enforcement efforts in the U.S.–Mexico border region is a necessary outcome in the coming period; indeed, I most decidedly hope that such trends will be reversed. Rather, the point of this exercise has been to suggest that border-region immigration enforcement efforts under NAFTA will merit close monitoring and investigation, and to identify potential research issues. More generally, my intention in this discussion has been to stimulate broader debate on and consideration of the possible relationships between border-region immigration enforcement practices and the politico-economic context that will become institutionalized under NAFTA.

THE LOS ANGELES RIOTS OF 1992

By way of conclusion, a brief overview of the 1992 Los Angeles riots illustrates, as an extreme case, several general points regarding the dangers of militarized law enforcement efforts, which may be relevant to the U.S.–Mexico border region. In addition, reflecting on this landmark event brings us full circle back to the introduction of this monograph wherein it was noted that LIC theorists had, in the early 1980s, constructed a scenario of an insurrection in Los Angeles requiring a military response and the sealing of the nearby border. The present discussion necessarily treats the 1992 riots in oversimplified terms. In general, members of poverty-stricken African American communities and recently established Latino (principally Mexican and Central American) immigrant communities rose up not only to protest the glaring miscarriage of justice in a notorious case of the vicious beating of a black man by white police officers—they were also apparently responding to broader, more complex racial conflicts and to growing economic deprivation.[40] While the origins and nature of the actual riots were far more complicated than anticipated in the previously constructed LIC scenario, the government's response bore a striking resemblance to that outlined in LIC documents, as thousands of military troops were dispatched to quell an urban riot for the first time since the late 1960s.[41]

In addition, some 400 Border Patrol agents were part of a contingent of 1,000 federal law enforcement agents sent to Los Angeles to help restore order. The Border Patrol agents were deployed alongside local police in Latino immigrant barrios located in and near the riot zone; some 1,000 undocumented immigrants were arrested, to be turned over to the INS for deportation despite the fact that most were never formally charged with any riot-related criminal offense.[42] (See chapter 3 for more details on the Border Patrol's involvement in quelling the riots.) The border was not closed during the riots nor was it directly affected by riot-response measures (in contrast to the scenario envisioned by LIC theorists in their hypothetical discussion of a Los Angeles insurrection). However, some of the main immigration enforcement resources in the border region were brought to Los Angeles to help subdue Latino immigrant communities. This tactic seems readily replicable elsewhere if deemed necessary, particularly given the now broad-ranging formal legal authority and expanded tactical capacity of the Border Patrol.

It is especially important to consider the context of pre-riot Los Angeles in comparison with the border region. During the 1980s and early 1990s Los Angeles had become a hub for global economic activity, but broad sectors of the African American and newly established Latino immigrant communities were relegated to poverty and marginalization. Meanwhile, the Los Angeles police force became increasingly militarized, and focused its harshest efforts on African American and, to a lesser extent, Latino youth in its response to the increased drug trafficking and related violence by youth gangs among these and other groups. The police committed a substantial number of abuses in these efforts, and tensions escalated between the police force and the minority youth targeted by its social-control efforts. Abusive, militarized police efforts thus played a central contributing role in the creation of a volatile context that was ripe for the precipitating event.[43]

At a very general level, pre-riot Los Angeles appears in hindsight to have some similarities with the border region. For example, in both places, economic activity became increasingly globalized while a substantial portion of the principal minority groups were left in poverty or otherwise marginalized, resulting in an economic polarization that fell somewhat along racial and ethnic lines. In addition, militarized law enforcement efforts that focused largely on the principal subordinated minority groups were common in both contexts. Drug-related social problems, in particular, were treated primarily as law enforcement issues, to the point of militarization.

Perhaps the most important general lesson for the border region (and elsewhere) to be gleaned from the Los Angeles case is the abysmal failure and disastrous consequences of addressing difficult and complex social problems—like illegal drug use and distribution—largely with heavy-handed "law and order" and even militaristic social-control measures. This one-dimensional, punitive approach seems especially ill-fated when coercive law enforcement efforts are vigorously focused on youth in subordinated, marginalized minority communities that are set within economically and socially polarized contexts. In the Los Angeles case, a primary emphasis on strong-arm police measures in dealing with "troublesome" minority youth, in the midst of spiraling economic and racial polarization, neither resulted in greater security nor established social control, but rather helped to further aggravate the situation to the point of provoking a riot.

In the U.S.–Mexico border region from 1978 through 1992, militarized drug and immigration enforcement measures were also apparently largely ineffective in achieving their ostensible goals, as the flows of illegal drugs and undocumented immigrants continued, for the most part, at high levels. However, while these measures were accompanied by an organizational pattern of police abuses of civilians, they did not provoke social unrest among the main minority groups targeted by them. Nonetheless, they do seem to have the potential to make relations between various racial and ethnic groups and even social classes more tense, in part because some of these groups are targeted by those measures, while others are not and may benefit at least indirectly from them.

A shift in emphasis from the heavy reliance on punitive procedures toward a more broad-based and in-depth approach that attempts to address some of the larger underlying issues could certainly help to avert such disastrous outcomes. Clearly, policy initiatives directed toward members of subordinated groups in economically and socially polarized contexts should include strong emphases on providing greater economic opportunities and broader avenues for meaningful political participation, as well as increased access to basic social resources such as education, housing, and water services. In the case of the U.S.–Mexico border region, the NAFTA debate provided new opportunities for these types of policy issues to be broached. However, the effect of the new policy initiatives forged during this debate for people on both sides of the border remains to be seen, and should be closely monitored. In practice, economic- and social-justice issues have rarely ranked high on the agendas of large-scale governmental or economic organizations. Rather, for such issues to be adequately addressed, members of subordinated groups and their allies must exert ongoing and mutifaceted pressure on these large-scale organizations and their elites, as well as participate in the formulation and implementation of policies theoretically designed to address their needs.

To sum up, it seems clear that during the contemporary period, in the course of addressing the issues of undocumented immigration and illicit drug trafficking, U.S. agencies gradually (though apparently unintentionally) militarized the U.S.–Mexico border in a manner consistent with the precepts of low-intensity conflict doctrine. This development has a number of disturbing implications for the human and civil rights of residents and immigrants in the border region. Evidence of serious human rights abuses by border-area police agencies has already been detailed in human rights reports during recent years. The threat to human and civil rights posed by increasingly militarized law enforcement initiatives in the southwestern border area has broader implications for the region as a whole, and for both Mexico and the United States. A militarized approach to immigration and drug issues, in particular, leads down an ill-fated path, and consequently warrants ample scrutiny. The numerous issues surrounding the militarization of immigration and drug enforcement efforts in the U.S.–Mexico border region deserve broader theoretical consideration and critical reflection, additional in-depth research and investigation, and full-fledged public discussion and debate. Such issues are too important to be left to the discretion of bureaucratic and policy-making elites, or to be defined by jingoistic demagogues, who scapegoat vulnerable groups. In addressing these difficult and complex issues, special endeavors should be made to avoid sacrificing the rights and well-being of subordinated minority groups for the real or supposed benefit of the majority or more privileged groups, because to do otherwise is not only fundamentally unjust, it is also ultimately a menace to the rights and well-being of us all.

Epilogue

Since 1992 immigration enforcement has taken on a renewed sense of urgency, while the War on Drugs has slipped further down the political agenda. With the passage and implementation of the North American Free Trade Agreement, the barriers to cross-border flows of trade and investment have been greatly lowered. The increasing economic integration between Mexico and the United States, however, has also been accompanied by a renewed U.S. emphasis on immigration enforcement in the border region and beyond. The political furor over undocumented immigration, especially in recession-ravaged California, has reached its highest point in recent history. The strongest formal expression of this hostility is California's recent landslide passage of Proposition 187, which would deny virtually all publicly funded social services to undocumented immigrants and would obligate social-service providers to aid INS immigration enforcement efforts. In general, undocumented immigration has been increasingly framed first and foremost as a crime issue to be resolved with ever more punitive measures.[1] The Clinton administration has largely acquiesced to the growing sentiment in favor of a crackdown on undocumented immigration, but has thus far opposed the most draconian proposals, including California's Proposition 187. Still, the administration and virtually all of the major participants in recent political debates on immigration have shared the assumption that immigration enforcement in the U.S.–Mexico border region should be greatly expanded. The main immigration debate has been largely focused on how to best carry out such enforcement, particularly whether or not to involve the military directly or to instead rely upon expanded, more aggressively deployed, militarized INS Border Patrol.

As the federal agency formally charged with carrying out immigration enforcement efforts in the border region (as well as significant continuing drug enforcement activities), the INS has continued to receive increased congressional appropriations.[2] This largesse has been bestowed upon the agency in an era of fiscal austerity marked by cuts in many other federal programs (including even the military) and despite recurring evidence of gross mismanagement throughout the INS and abusive behavior by agents.[3] However, there is now at least a much better chance that these problems will be addressed, as Doris Meissner, the new INS commissioner appointed by President Clinton is a noted, evenhanded immigration scholar as well as an experienced administrator. But her ability to effect significant reforms in the agency may be limited by the strong pressure to expand its immigration enforcement efforts.

INS immigration enforcement in the U.S.–Mexico border region indeed has been escalated sharply, as the Border Patrol has launched high-profile blockade-style operations to deter undocumented border crossings in several mostly urban high-traffic locations on the border. This approach is a marked departure from the previous emphasis on apprehending undocumented crossers once they were in the country. The first of these new operations began in El Paso in late September of 1993 (Operation Blockade, later renamed Operation Hold-the-Line), while another (Operation Gatekeeper) was launched approximately a year later in San Diego, and a similar effort (Operation Guardian) is scheduled for the near future in Southern Arizona.[4] While each operation has been adapted to the particular setting of its implementation, they have generally relied on a strong show of force directly on or near the border to deter would-be undocumented border crossers. These shows of force have typically included highly concentrated deployments of hundreds of Border Patrol agents, periodic aggressive helicopter patrols buzzing the border, the use of elaborate night-vision and electronic surveillance equipment, and the reinforcement of physical barriers on the border. Most notable among the barriers are a series of thin steel walls that have been constructed or proposed to be built by the U.S. military on the border in or near eight urban centers from San Diego east to El Paso (at least five walls have been built already). These range in length from 1.3 miles for the wall proposed to be built just west of El Paso to 14 miles for the wall near San Diego (expanded from the 7 miles built in 1991 and 1992). In addition, a prominent U.S. military research institution has drawn up for the INS much more elaborate proposals for the construction of triple-layer wall and fence barriers at numerous key locations along the border.[5]

The blockades and barriers have had a mixture of impacts on undocumented immigration in the targeted areas. The blockade operations have indeed led over time to dramatic reductions in Border Patrol apprehensions and undocumented border crossings in the areas in which they have been implemented, particularly in El Paso. It seems clear that these operations have been much more successful than previous efforts in bringing a semblance of order to previously chaotic urban crossing areas, and they have generally been quite popular among residents in the affected U.S. communities,[6] including many Mexican Americans in El Paso.[7] However (or relatedly), the operations have also raised nationalist tensions on both sides of the border.[8] Further, the blockade maneuvers and new border walls have not halted undocumented immigration by any means, but rather have made the crossing process more difficult, costly, and risky by diverting undocumented crossers to less fortified border areas, many of which are more remote and potentially dangerous. In El Paso, while some categories of undocumented border crossers (namely, older women, small-scale street vendors, and juveniles coming over to "hang out") have been largely "weeded out," much of the local undocumented labor migration has continued, though more discreetly and in different patterns. In addition, the deterrent effect of the El Paso blockade on undocumented border crossing has apparently declined the longer the operation has continued.[9] It is still too soon to tell if the San Diego and Arizona blockades will follow suit. However, thus far the San Diego operation does appear to be pushing undocumented crossers eastward into more remote and rugged areas and causing them to try more desperate and dangerous tactics to cross the border.[10]

More importantly, the immediate human rights impact of the blockades and barriers has also been mixed. In El Paso, the previous crescendo of allegations of abusive behavior by Border Patrol agents in that sector has fallen off dramatically.[11] This stems in large part from the fact that agents have generally had far less direct contact in enforcement encounters with either undocumented immigrants or Mexican American residents mistakenly suspected of being undocumented immigrants. However, reports of various abuses of authority at official ports of entry by Customs and INS inspectors have continued to mount.[12] In contrast, the San Diego blockade has led to a dramatic increase in reports of human rights abuses committed by Border Patrol agents against undocumented immigrants attempting to cross through the area.[13] Meanwhile, in Arizona the construction of a steel wall along the border in Nogales has incurred a human toll: numerous injuries have been reported among persons attempting to scale the new wall, and there has been an increase in violent assaults against immigrants who have been diverted underground, to the dangerous cross-border sewer-tunnel system.[14] While there are many possible reasons for the differing impacts of the various blockades and barriers on the status of human rights along the border, it is clear that the much touted "deterrence strategy" of increasing border blockades and barriers is not necessarily a less abusive or more humane approach across the board.

In general terms, the militarization of border enforcement efforts has continued since 1992, though with some changes. The current border enforcement policy is characterized by efforts to continually expand the Border Patrol, to focus the unit on blockade-style operations to repel undocumented immigration in and near urban areas along the border, and to outfit it with ever more sophisticated technology and equipment.[15] Much of the equipment and technology obtained is military in nature, as are many features of the blockade-style operations, which, for example, resemble the "terrain denial" exercises conducted by military units in remote border areas to deny entry to drug traffickers (see chapter 4). In addition, the INS has consulted with the Pentagon's Center for Low-Intensity Conflict to devise the most effective deployment of Border Patrol agents and surveillance equipment to enhance immigration enforcement efforts on the California-Mexico border.[16]

There have even been several moves in Congress (thus far unsuccessful) to open the way for the formal, open use of U.S. military forces to support the Border Patrol in immigration enforcement—a clear step beyond the ongoing collaborative drug enforcement efforts.[17] Proponents of these measures have tended to envision the military formally playing a "support" role similar to their role in border antidrug efforts, rather than being directly involved in border-region immigration enforcement. However, as detailed previously, the military's antidrug efforts in the border region have included not only low-key types of support (e.g., engineering and construction, equipment provision and maintenance, etc.), but also more obviously militaristic activities, such as border surveillance and patrolling activities. Further, the latter activities have sometimes led to at least indirect military involvement in immigration enforcement, while the former often aided immigration enforcement as much as drug enforcement (e.g., wall construction). These military antidrug efforts in the border region continued through 1993 and 1994, although at a somewhat reduced level in the second year, and were scheduled to proceed in 1995.[18] The key issue appears to be whether or not military activities in the border region will become formally focused on immigration enforcement. California Governor Pete Wilson clearly tried to push the California National Guard in this direction in late April of 1994.[19] However, so far the military and the INS and Border Patrol have shown little enthusiasm for such open, formally designated military involvement in border immigration enforcement activities.[20]

The approach currently being pursued seems to involve a much expanded and more militarized Border Patrol, as well as the construction of more elaborate border barriers by the military. Any meaningful consideration of measures to shift the focus of the immigration debate away from border enforcement and other punitive actions toward a more broad-based, socially constructive approach is apparently far removed from the political agenda for the time being, particularly with the rightward shift in the U.S. Congress in the wake of the 1994 midterm elections.[21] Meanwhile, the increasingly fluid economic and political conditions in Mexico may spur expanded undocumented immigration and in turn heighten the clamor in the United States for more stringent border enforcement. However, shifting conditions in Mexico may also eventually serve to illustrate the limitations of myopically treating undocumented immigration as a law enforcement problem to be resolved through ever increasing border enforcement and other punitive measures, and to open up new possibilities for more satisfactorily addressing the larger political and economic processes (in both countries) fueling undocumented immigration.

Appendices

Congressional Appropriations for INS Funding and Staff, 1978–1992
(funding in millions of unadjusted dollars)

	1978	1979	1980	1981	1982
Border Patrol					
Staff	2,580	2,801	2,915	2,872	2,890
Funding	78.1	65.5	82.6	85.6	98.7
Detention & Deportation					
Staff	1,112	1,095	1,106	1,105	1,027
Funding	34.9	39.2	44.3	48.4	70.7
Enforcement Total[a]					
Staff	*	*	*	*	6,630
Funding	*	*	*	*	277.7
INS Total					
Staff	10,071	10,997	10,943	10,886	10,604
Funding	283.1	303.7	351.3	370.1	441.5

	1983	1984	1985	1986	1987
Border Patrol					
Staff	2,865	2,857	3,695	3,693	5,541
Funding	110.1	114.1	141.9	150.9	194.6
Detention & Deportation					
Staff	1,040	1,044	1,152	1,180	1,644
Funding	65.8	69.0	75.6	82.4	91.7
Enforcement Total[a]					
Staff	6,586	6,677	7,723	7,796	10,635
Funding	293.8	307.8	351.6	365.8	415.5
INS Total					
Staff	10,483	10,601	11,649	11,694	15,453
Funding	492.5	507.4	580.0	574.3	651.1

Continued on facing page

Appendix 1 (continued)

	1988	1989	1990	1991	1992
Border Patrol					
Staff	5,530	5,485	4,848	4,929	4,948
Funding	205.3	246.4	261.1	295.5	325.8
Detention &					
Deportation					
Staff	1,623	1,611	1,534	1,510	1,519
Funding	128.8	155.3	149.2	147.2	158.8
Enforcement Total[a]					
Staff	10,604	10,610	9,466	9,480	9,511
Funding	497.2	580.3	598.7	641.5	701.7
INS Total					
Staff	15,453	15,293	12,388	12,221	11,869
Funding	807.8	821.0	844.6	891.3	961.3

Source: House Committee on Appropriations 1978–1993.

Note: Figures include only congressional appropriations allotted to the INS, and do not include staff and budget financed by a series of user and application fees implemented since 1986 to pay for immigration services. Total resources provided by user and application fees ranged from $137.3 million and 1,534 staff in 1987 to $484.9 million and 5,101 staff in 1992. None of these resources were devoted to the Border Patrol; the vast majority were split among the following units: inspections, adjudications and naturalization, and information and records management.

a. The enforcement total includes the following INS units: Border Patrol, Detention and Deportation, Investigations, Antismuggling, and Inspections.

* No data is available on this category in INS budget documents submitted to Congress for this year.

INS Undocumented Immigrant Apprehensions, Detentions, and Expulsions, 1978–1992

	Number of Apprehensions	Number of Detentions	Number of Detainees in INS Facilities	Average Length of Detention[a]	Number of Expulsions[b]
1978	870,646	340,297	211,750	*	1,003,886
1979	888,729	316,391	204,079	2.7	992,033
1980	759,420	243,047	147,730	2.4	736,474
1981	825,290	268,581	*	3.6	837,011
1982	819,919	229,135	144,555	4.6	823,731
1983	1,105,670	233,885	149,072	4.6	1,122,192
1984	1,138,566	169,070	81,144	7.3	1,012,720
1985	1,262,435	145,989	68,691	10.1	1,069,680
1986	1,692,544	137,332	75,114	10.5	1,614,519
1987	1,158,030	82,660	48,335	15	1,118,176
1988	969,214	92,799	51,527	15.2	939,853
1989	891,147	104,639	74,925	22.5	861,169
1990	1,103,353	104,889	51,222	22.9	1,054,225
1991	1,132,933	87,169	50,706	25.3	1,014,655
1992	1,199,587	82,326	46,589	26.3	1,112,281

Source: House Committee on Appropriations 1979–1993.

a. In days.

b. Combined total of deportations, voluntary departures, and exclusions.

* No data is available for this year in INS budget documents.

Partial List of INS Equipment and Construction in the U.S.–Mexico Border Region, 1978–1992

	1978–80	1981–88	1989–92
Helicopters	2 (1 sector)	22 (all 9 sectors)	58
Fixed-wing aircraft	unspecified	46	43
10-foot-high border fence	parts of 3 sectors	—	extensive repairs
New 10-foot-high solid steel border wall	—	—	7 miles done (between San Diego & Tijuana)[a]
Electronic intrusion-detection ground sensors (no. of sectors upgraded)	2	7[b]	unspecified expansion
New closed-circuit TV systems	4 detention centers	unspecified	unspecified
Miscellaneous research	infrared radar	2-mile linewatch sensor	15 image-enhancement surveillance vehicles
Night-vision scopes:			
Ordered	7	240	unspec. expans.
Total	66	335	unspec. expans.
Low-light-level TV (no. of sectors in which installed)	0	6	unspecified expansion
Airborne infrared radar	research on effectiveness	at least 5 (in helicopters)	unspecified expansion
Border Patrol stations (newly constructed or expanded)	—	23	9
Traffic inspection check-points (newly constructed or expanded)	*	4	6
New microwave communications systems	—	Texas & California	—

Sources: House Committee on Appropriations 1979–1993. House Committee on the Judiciary 1982, 1983b, 1985. *INS Reporter* 1989 (summer). Kamen 1992. McDonnell 1991b.

Note: This is only a partial listing of new INS equipment (most of it military-related) and construction. The INS does not divulge complete information on these matters.

a. Seven more miles are planned for the San Diego–Tijuana wall, while additional border walls are planned for at least five other communities in California, Arizona, and New Mexico.

b. All nine border-region sectors have been upgraded since 1978.

* No data is available.

Theoretical and Methodological Considerations

This section briefly outlines some of the key theoretical and method-ological positions that guided the conceptualization of the overall re-search problem and the investigation carried out for this monograph. This study broached an admittedly unconventional research topic, mili-tarization of the U.S.–Mexico border region in the contemporary period. Unfortunately, there are no overarching theoretical or methodological frameworks that specifically address this topic or, more generally, the enforcement of borders between highly developed and less developed nations. Consequently, a variety of theoretical materials and discussions of research methods were drawn upon in an eclectic fashion for this project. In addition to delineating some of the most salient theoretical and methodological issues for the present study, it is hoped that this dis-cussion also offers some concepts that would aid in the future construc-tion of theoretical models and research designs that specifically and more adequately address the issue of border enforcement in the contemporary era. Such issues certainly merit much additional consideration, because bureaucratized social-control processes (of which border militarization is but one rather stark form) are critical features of many societies, and their importance seems to be growing in the increasingly interconnected global scene.

Before proceeding, I should point out that the division of the present discussion into theoretical and methodological issues is not meant to im-ply that such matters are strictly separable. Rather, they are very much interrelated, as many theoretical premises are implicit in the methods discussion and vice versa.[1] However, theory and methods are somewhat artificially separated here for purposes of organization and clarity, al-though it is hoped that their intersection becomes evident in the course of the discussion.

THEORETICAL CONSIDERATIONS

The unorthodox interpretations offered in this monograph of contempo-rary trends in immigration and drug enforcement efforts in the U.S.–

Mexico border region and of their implications for the larger U.S. society are informed by particular theoretical positions on several subjects. The primary theoretical focus concerns the nature of repression in so-called advanced industrial societies, especially those with liberal-democratic political systems. A key subtopic within this focus is the effect of bureaucracy on the status of human rights. The secondary theoretical area of interest here is actually two related topics: the contemporary world economy and international migration.

Repression in "advanced industrial society" is not a topic frequently addressed by social theorists. Historical experience has shown, however, that repression does exist to varying degrees in such settings,[2] which suggests that the issue requires some theoretical explanation. Marcuse provides a useful point of departure at a highly abstract level. He views "advanced industrial society" as tending to be inherently repressive, largely because it has organized powerful technological apparatuses in ways that enable increasing levels of social control and the containment of qualitative social change—that is, large-scale, fundamental change in institutions and especially in production and distribution processes. One of the principal means of accomplishing this containment of qualitative social change is the use of technology to manipulate and channel individuals' needs and aspirations toward ends that reinforce the existing order of society. Such measures are central to the creation of a social environment that effectively precludes the emergence of threatening oppositional forces from among subordinated classes and groups. These relatively subtle, yet powerful, means of effecting social control are also accompanied by more coercive means, such as the loss of employment, police authority, the criminal-justice system, and the military.[3]

Marcuse proposes that social control in "advanced industrial society" is furthered through the construction of an "Enemy" both "from within as well as without." This process involves the creation of a foreign policy of containment (of the "Communist threat," for example) as an extension of the previously noted domestic policy of the containment of qualitative social change. In addition, the maintenance of a permanent "Enemy" is instrumental in the establishment of a "defense society." This not only stimulates economic growth through the buildup of the "defense" sector, it also more profoundly limits (in the interest of "national security," for example) possibilities for qualitative social change.[4]

Oppenheimer and Canning take a similar, though more direct, approach in pointing to the importance of an "enemy" to the emergence of authoritarian national security state apparatuses in both the third and first worlds: "Where communism is not an issue . . . other foes can always be found or, for that matter, invented."[5] Oppenheimer and Canning delineate several less abstract, key indicators of the existence of a national security state apparatus in first-world contexts, including an increased integration of the social-welfare and criminal-justice apparatuses; a central or centralizing national police force that includes both a domestic intelligence branch and a large-scale capacity for demonstration control and counterinsurgency activities; and the integration of this force with national police forces in other nations in the region via information exchange, training, and special assistance on projects. They cite the West German Border Guard and its transformation into a national tactical police unit used to contain political demonstrations as an example of a police force with a central role in the national security state apparatus.[6] This example suggests that among federal police forces, border police units may be especially adaptable to taking on missions far beyond their ostensible purview, including a special role in the containment of domestic social change.[7]

It is not necessary for an actual opposition movement to exist and threaten the control of dominant groups or the state for state security apparatuses to be directed toward enacting repressive measures. Rather, it is only necessary for authorities to perceive a potential threat of this type. Marcuse argued that this sort of preventive political repression, which he termed "preventative counter-revolution," was being carried out in the early 1970s. He saw it expressed in the increasing implementation of counterinsurgency measures both at home (against militant Black and Chicano activists and the student antiwar movement) and abroad (e.g., Vietnam) by the far-flung U.S. military-security apparatus. Marcuse explained this development thus: "Counterinsurgency is not only to prevent the revolution, it is also to counteract the aggravating contradictions of the capitalist system today."[8] These contradictions included the growth of what is currently often referred to as an underclass—that is, subordinated racial and ethnic minority groups with limited opportunities, the under- and unemployed, and those otherwise located at the margins of the mainstream economy.[9] Similarly, Oppenheimer and Canning stress that the existence of a growing proportion of "marginalized" peoples in a society (i.e., those who are impoverished, disadvantageously integrated into the economic and social system, or excluded from it altogether) obliges the state to step up its social-control and security measures. They link the growth of the "marginalized" population in first-world nations to their decline as powerful societies and their movement toward crisis—

most immediately, a state fiscal crisis that causes decreased social-welfare spending at a time when social-welfare needs are on the rise.[10] Thus, Marcuse, like Oppenheimer and Canning, views the social contradictions, polarizations, and crises associated with capitalist development as fueling the growth of state military security apparatuses and state repression to ensure social control and prevent the formation of threatening opposition movements.

In contrast, Sjoberg and Vaughan focus on bureaucracy, in both the private and public sectors, as the key to explaining much of the adverse treatment (including repression) of subordinate groups and dissidents in society. They propose that bureaucracies generally undermine the human rights of disadvantaged members of society as well as of intellectual and political dissidents. More specifically, they maintain that bureaucratic power structures in both the public and private sectors tend to treat these groups in accordance with a process they term "social triage": the "truly disadvantaged" (i.e., members of the most economically, politically, and socially subordinated groups) are sacrificed by large-scale organizations in the private and public sectors in the name of bureaucratic efficiency. Adequately addressing the needs of the truly disadvantaged would entail high economic costs and require a restructuring of the bureaucratic system in the economy and government, as well as substantial "sacrifices" by the elites who oversee this system. It is thus "inefficient" to economically assist and meet the needs of the truly disadvantaged. What's more, bureaucratic power structures periodically repress political and intellectual dissidents who advocate for the disadvantaged or challenge the structural relations that fuel the social triage process.[11] Consequently, the policies and practices of large-scale, bureaucratic organizations, at least as they have generally been constructed thus far, tend to undermine the protection and advancement of the human rights and dignity of subordinate groups and dissident members of society.

While the theoretical conceptualizations outlined above provide various explanations for repression in "advanced" industrial or bureaucratized societies, they do not address the apparent contradiction of repression existing in societies with liberal-democratic political systems. In this regard, Wolfe's critical examination of classical liberal political theory is especially useful. The essence of his argument is that classical liberalism is highly ambiguous with respect to the issue of repression. This ambiguity stems from the fundamental contradiction in classical liberalism's promotion of the ideals of political liberty and equality on the one hand, while advocating the principles of private property and capitalism—the chief mechanisms of economic inequality—on the other hand. Wolfe stresses economic factors in accounting for repression, arguing that the ultimate cause of repression lies in the existence of a society stratified by class.[12] He further proposes that repression in liberal-democratic societies (particularly the United States) has a class-biased character in that states tend to repress powerless groups in confrontations and to support powerful groups.[13]

More specifically, Wolfe maintains that Locke's famous defense of the right to rebel was directed to the emerging bourgeoisie, and that for Locke this right was negated if it came into conflict with property rights. When property rights were threatened "illegitimately" (i.e., outside the law), Locke saw the use of repressive measures to protect those rights as quite justified. Of course, members of the bourgeoisie were leading actors in establishing the new liberal-democratic legal frameworks. Thus, Wolfe proposes that freedom in Locke's framework meant freedom within the emerging capitalist order of his day—which was indeed a revolutionary break with feudal monarchy—and that the use of repression to preserve that emerging order was considered more than acceptable.[14] Hence Wolfe concludes that *"repression is an integral part of the theory of liberalism"* (Wolfe's emphasis).[15]

In addition to these theoretical explanations for repression in "advanced" and liberal societies, specific conceptualizations of the contemporary world economy and of international migration have strongly informed the analysis proposed in this monograph. The first of these is the work of Reich. He argues that the increasing globalization of the economy is rendering the category of the nation-state economically irrelevant, so that eventually there will no longer be "national economies." Capital, technology, information, and goods are all increasingly internationally mobile (often within a single, dispersed corporate apparatus), while labor has remained largely nation-state bound. In the case of the United States, this has led to increasing economic and social polarization, as many U.S. workers have lost ground in being played off against lower-paid laborers in developing nations, while top U.S. managers, analysts, and other corporate actors have benefited from working more closely with their counterparts throughout the world.[16] These developments suggest that the basic capitalist class structure is becoming further generalized on a global level.

The geographical mobility of capital, goods, and services is also a principal feature of Harvey's analysis of the fundamental changes in the contemporary world economy, in which he stresses the renewed prominence of the control of labor. In particular, Harvey highlights the importance of the geographical mobility of capitalist production processes. He proposes that this mobility, the "spatial fix," is a key feature of the new corporate strategy of "flexible accumulation," which is designed to increase profit levels through the lowering of wages for labor while also increasing labor's productivity. A central means of exerting such renewed labor control and discipline has been corporations' relocation of their production processes from higher-wage areas of first-world nations to lower-wage regions of the globe, such as third-world nations. Through worker displacement, this geographical shift of production has generated additional surplus first-world labor, which is then made available and more disposed to accept lowered wages and deteriorated working conditions.[17] A logical extension of Harvey's argument is that the imposition of greater labor "flexibility" and control would be furthered by (or even imply the necessity of) the use of more obviously coercive "disciplinary" measures,[18] including those entailed in border-area immigration enforcement efforts against undocumented international labor migrants.

In this regard, Sassen also offers several propositions on the political-economic implications of national border enforcement that are especially relevant to this monograph. On the one hand, the enforcement of national boundaries helps maintain the designation of certain nations as a part of the "periphery" where international capital can be more profitably invested (due to the prevalence of lower wages, more expansive labor discipline measures, less stringent regulatory processes, tax breaks, etc.). On the other hand, border enforcement aids the further use of low-cost labor in core nations such as the United States by assigning "criminal" status to an important and growing sector of the working class in those countries (i.e., undocumented immigrant workers) and thereby rendering those workers more politically vulnerable and economically exploitable.[19] Thus, the international mobility of labor often faces significant obstacles and sanctions,[20] which appear especially stark in comparison to the unfettered international mobility increasingly afforded to capital, goods, and services.

Within the United States, it appears that since the early 1980s low-cost immigrant labor has continued to play a vital role in the domestic economy, although its focuses of activity have shifted. Sassen demonstrates that in the restructured and more class-polarized U.S. economy that emerged from the severe recession of the early 1980s, there was a greater demand for low-cost immigrant labor in a variety of expanding economic activities based in major urban centers. These areas of activity include advanced services, downgraded manufacturing (including, ironically, some high-tech electronics production), and the growing informal sector—all of which fit within the new corporate strategy of "flexible accumulation" of profits.[21] Hence immigrant labor seems to have been particularly well suited for the burgeoning sectors of the U.S. economy that offered low wages and demanded great "flexibility" on the part of labor.

The growth of the international migration of labor to the United States is closely, somewhat reciprocally, tied to the increasing global mobility of U.S.-based capital, according to Sassen's framework. She proposes that U.S. foreign investment in specific third-world nations has been a significant factor fueling emigration from those countries to the United States during the contemporary period. More specifically, Sassen maintains that foreign investment tends to disrupt and restructure third-world economies by stimulating the expansion of large-scale commercial agriculture (which displaces peasants) and the recruitment of young women into the wage-labor force for export-oriented manufacturing assembly (which makes for a more competitive labor market overall). Another key factor influencing international migration is the U.S. government's cultivation of close political or military relations with specific third-world nations. In conjunction with U.S.-based foreign investment, these relationships establish linkages between those nations and the United States. Sassen argues that these linkages have in turn become migration-inducing factors, a development made possible by comparatively liberal (relative to other first-world nations) U.S. immigration policies since 1965.[22] In support of her unorthodox theory, she notes that many of the countries that have sent the most immigrants to the United States in recent decades have been the sites of substantial U.S.-based foreign investment or are nations with whom the United States has had strong political or military ties, or both. These nations, which are overwhelmingly located in Asia and Latin America, include Mexico, South Korea, the Dominican Republic, the Philippines, Vietnam, and Taiwan.[23]

METHODOLOGICAL CONSIDERATIONS

Given the unconventional analysis proposed in this monograph, it is important to outline the general methods, the sources of information, and the related theoretical premises employed in conducting the research for the work. The general methodological framework used here was the case study method, which Orum, Feagin, and Sjoberg define as "an in-depth, multi-faceted investigation, using qualitative research methods, of a single social phenomenon."[24] The case study method is particularly advantageous in enabling one to "deal with the reality behind appearances, with contradictions and the dialectical nature of social life, as well as a whole that is more than the sum of its parts."[25] More specifically, it is also the most useful method for investigating many vital features of powerful bureaucracies that are not otherwise readily discernible, such as bureaucratic secrecy, organizational deviance, and relations between these complex organizations and disadvantaged populations.[26] The methodological capacity to address the challenging concerns outlined above was by no means fully utilized in the research conducted for this study. Nonetheless, it was particularly helpful in gaining a greater understanding of the complex research issues of interest here, which are largely centered in bureaucratic polices and practices, and also in constructing a critical analysis of those practices and policies.

Of central importance to this study is a primary goal proposed for the case study method: to contribute to the extension and refinement of public debate in a democratic social order.[27] This goal stands in sharp contrast to the more often stressed objective of predicting specific outcomes. Specifically, this monograph aims to stimulate greater public consideration of and debate about as well as further research on immigration and drug enforcement policies and practices in the U.S.–Mexico border region during the contemporary period. Such attention is in order, as these efforts have gone largely unquestioned in many quarters and have been the subject of relatively little extensive, in-depth examination.

The main research focus of this monograph is on various bureaucracies—principally the U.S. Immigration and Naturalization Service (INS). This focus is grounded on the aforementioned theoretical position that the centralization of power in large-scale bureaucracies tends to undermine the human rights of members of disadvantaged, subordinated groups (such as ethnic and racial minorities) and of political and intellectual dissidents who serve as advocates for those groups. Consequently, a premise guiding the research conducted for this study is that the policies and practices of powerful bureaucracies deserve substantial critical attention. This assumption has a number of limitations, however, the most important being that it largely excludes the supposed "objects" of bureaucratic control and how they relate to and perhaps resist or alter such control. Unfortunately, it was possible only to suggest and initially probe the complex relationships between the bureaucratic power structures examined here and the various individuals and groups affected by them. This crucial topic exceeds the scope of this monograph and by and large has yet to be specifically addressed by academic researchers.

An important methodological principle used in this project is the conceptualization of the relationship between qualitative and quantitative change. The term "quantitative change" is used here not to refer to perceived shifts and trends in the data that are derived from sophisticated statistical procedures, but rather to refer simply to descriptive figures that indicate some variation in degree. In contrast, "qualitative change" is used in this study to indicate a shift in the presence or absence of particular qualities or phenomena—that is, it implies a more absolute distinction. The presupposition here is that these two distinct concepts are related, in that substantial levels of quantitative change can in some instances result in qualitative change. This conceptualization is drawn from Marx (and Cleaver's interpretation), who examined the hard-fought, ultimately successful struggle waged by the English working class during the early and middle nineteenth century to shorten the workday, which was eventually reduced from 15 or more hours to 8 to 10 hours—a substantial quantitative change. This in turn led to improved working conditions and consolidated a significant level of working-class political power—a significant qualitative change.[28] Hence, this work uses quantitative information with an interest in its qualitative implications. However, this is not to suggest that all qualitative change can be reduced to quantitative variations or that differences of degree always lead to qualitative transformations, but rather to propose that the two forms of change are intimately related in some cases.

Beyond the general methodological approach and assumptions outlined thus far, a number of guidelines were used regarding sources of information and the nature of the data they provide. As noted in chapter 1, the main sources examined for this project were publicly available government documents, especially congressional hearing testimony and congressional reports related to immigration and drug enforcement efforts in the U.S.–Mexico border region from 1978 to 1992. While complete coverage of all the relevant documents on these topics was not possible, close and sustained attention was devoted to this category of materials.[29] A broad range of other sources of information were also drawn upon, including mainstream and alternative press reports, military journals and selected documents, critical analyses of U.S. military doctrines and practices in Latin America, a limited number of INS documents, reports from human rights groups, interviews with (and in some cases limited field observation of) 15 federal border law enforcement officials in South Texas, and interviews with 12 human rights advocates.[30] The interviews were conducted during 1990 and 1992.

These sources were used with an investigative strategy that required poring over volumes of written bureaucratic records. The premise underlying this strategy was that bureaucracies typically do not readily lend themselves to outside investigation, but they do generate large numbers of documents, some of which are publicly accessible. This process entailed first becoming thoroughly familiar with both the "official positions" of the various bureaucracies (especially the INS) and the related government documents, and then comparing various stated positions and documents to each other and to other sources. The objective was to discover inconsistencies and contradictions, as well as similarities, in content, which—when viewed comparatively—were likely to provide greater insight into particular bureaucratic practices and policies.[31] Information gleaned from documents and other sources on two seemingly unrelated topics (domestic law enforcement policies and military doctrine) was compared in order to determine (1) if there were any basic similarities in organizational strategy and tactics, and (2) if there were any linkages between the two institutional realms with respect to the border region.

One possible advantage in researching immigration and drug enforcement topics was that their political saliency in recent years had resulted in a proliferation of related congressional hearings and reports. However, it was evident in conducting the research for this study that vital information is also deliberately withheld from public view, especially regarding the U.S. military's support of drug enforcement efforts (see chapter 4 for citations of examples of this). Nonetheless, the process of congressional oversight of federal agencies does generally bring to public light a great deal more information than would otherwise be the case. Yet as the instances of withholding of information suggest, the nature of the congressional oversight process places limits on the scope of that information. The primary limitation of the congressional oversight process, Aberbach argues, is that it is carried out within an "advocacy environment," wherein congressional committee members generally support the basic goals of the programs and agencies under review.[32] These shared assumptions shape and limit the scope of the information brought to public light through the congressional oversight process, typically ensuring that it is not overly indicting or fundamentally critical of the agency and programs under review. This is not to imply that nothing can be learned from this information, but rather that it must be treated with caution.

Hence, it is important to note the assumptions about bureaucratic data that guided their use in this project. The principal assumption is that the "official position" is only one representation of reality, and that it is therefore most advisable to consult various interpretations and representations of that reality.[33] Further, the "official" data provided by bureaucratic power structures typically neglect the concerns of the most disadvantaged, subordinated groups in society.[34] In addition, bureaucratic data are typically gathered for explicitly political and administrative purposes, many of which are related to aspects of institutional self-interest, such as justifying budget increases, expanding authority, and maintaining social control.[35] Thus, it was assumed in conducting the research for this study that publicly available bureaucratic data are a form of self-reporting, and as such are intended to present a favorable portrayal of an agency's activities and are unlikely to disclose politically inexpedient material or to directly address the concerns of subordinated groups over whom the agencies exercise authority.

Consequently, the bureaucratic information drawn upon here was not taken strictly at face value.[36] Rather, it was viewed comparatively in light of other sources and other bureaucratic cases. Specifically, the policies and practices that were officially reported by the INS (especially to Congress) were compared with military guidelines, critical evaluations of those military guidelines, human rights data, press reports, and other material. These procedures were necessarily unwieldy and inexact, because in large part they entailed attempting to decode bureaucratic data for information they were not necessarily intended to reveal. Consequently, it was essential to compare such data with that from a variety of other sources, although it was impossible in most instances to make precise comparisons. Despite these limitations, I decided that a comparative, critical approach built upon specific interpretive assumptions was preferable to simply accepting, without question, the information generated by powerful bureaucratic organizations and assuming that the data would speak for itself. The aforementioned theoretical and methodological assumptions were therefore crucial in interpreting the data from the various sources.

Nonetheless, the heavy reliance on government documents placed other far-reaching limitations on this project. First, these documents tend to treat the border region in overly general terms and typically do not take into account the great physical and social variations that exist between various portions of the border region (e.g., the vast, remote Big Bend area of West Texas versus the urban sprawl of San Diego and Tijuana). Second, and more importantly, such records offer, at best, only a glimpse into actual practices "in the field," as it were. This shortcoming was offset in part by conducting qualitative interviews during 1990 and 1992 with 15 federal law enforcement officials in South Texas and 12 human rights activists from the border region more generally. In using information here from the interviews with law enforcement officials, I chose to keep their identities anonymous in order to help protect them from any potential retribution. I was also able to tour four very distinct border-region detention centers used by the INS in South Texas and, on several occasions, to observe at first hand Border Patrol enforcement activities in the same general area. While helpful, these interviews and field observations afforded an incomplete view of actual border enforcement practices "in the field." (Unfortunately, due to a lack of resources, it was not possible for me to conduct additional interviews and make firsthand observations in other parts of the border region, outside of South Texas.) Consequently, this monograph tends to focus on top officials' portrayals of immigration and drug enforcement policies and practices for an admittedly overly generalized "border region," with an attempt being made to determine the extent to which those policies and practices overlap with the guidelines and practices associated with a specific U.S. military doctrine.

It is hoped, however, that this initial effort will provoke further investigation on these and related topics. Several general issues stand out as potential research topics, due to their importance and the current lack of knowledge about them. These issues all fall within the general theme of the relationship between bureaucratic power structures and the various individuals and groups affected by them. They are: (1) the various bureaucratic processes that shape immigration and drug enforcement practices on the day-to-day level, as they are actually carried out "in the field"; (2) the multifaceted impact of these processes and practices on surrounding communities, especially on members of subordinated groups; (3) the various reactions (especially resistance) to these bureaucratic processes and practices on the part of affected groups and communities as well as members of the bureaucracies themselves; and (4) the impact of these community, group, and bureaucracy members' various reactions on the bureaucracies charged with carrying out those activities.

In addition, further investigation efforts on these topics would do well to take an explicitly binational focus and draw on sources from both sides of the border, particularly given current trends in binational economic integration and the establishment of additional, closer political ties between the United States and Mexico. The pioneering work of investigative journalists and human rights activists in the region may serve as a useful point of departure in conducting in-depth academic research on these vital and often overlooked issues.

Notes

1. INTRODUCTION

1. See, for example, Acuña 1988 (especially chapters 1–5), Martínez 1988, Griswold del Castillo 1990. Thanks are due to Barbara Hines for bringing the third source to my attention.

2. See "Losing Control of the Borders" 1983, Chaze 1983, Russel 1985. (Thanks are due to Jana Walters for bringing two of these articles to my attention.) Fernández and Pedroza (1982) and Walters (1990) found that major U.S. newspapers and magazines during the 1970s and through the mid-1980s relied heavily on INS sources for their characterizations of the issue of undocumented immigration. Characterizations depicting undocumented immigration as a quasi–national security problem have become prominent again in the mid-1990s, as the issue has returned with a vengeance, especially in recession-ravaged California.

3. Quote from Reagan's speech reported in the *Washington Post* on June 21, 1983, as cited by Gómez 1984: 219. While hyperbolic, such claims were entirely consistent with the Reagan administration's extreme preoccupation with maintaining U.S. control over Central America, and its aggressive interpretation of U.S. national security interests in Latin America. For a virtual blueprint of the Reagan administration's Latin America policies, see Committee of Santa Fe 1980. The analysis and recommendations offered in this report were adopted almost to the letter by the Reagan administration.

4. H. Eugene Douglas, quoted in Sanders 1987: 209. Military officials were also apparently concerned to some degree with the issue, as is evident in a paper by a former Army staff strategist for Latin America and politico-military desk officer for Mexico, Lieutenant Colonel Richard T. Schaden: "The Strategic Implications of Immigration from Mexico and Central America: A Think Piece" (ca. mid-1980s).

5. Regarding Reagan's designation of drug trafficking as a national security issue, see Klare 1988: 72. Bush devoted his first nationally televised speech to this issue. See "Now It's Bush's War" 1989.

6. Johnson 1988.

7. House Select Committee on Narcotics Abuse and Control 1991b: 90. This quote comes from Warren Reece, coordinator of the Southwest Border High-Intensity Drug-Trafficking Area Program and director of Operation Alliance. The latter is an elaborate borderwide drug enforcement effort established in 1986. It is made up of various border law enforcement agencies, with the military providing a wide range of support.

8. For example, see the statement of Governor Mark White of Texas in House Select Committee on Narcotics Abuse and Control 1986: 6, 97–99. (I thank Ken Todd for his assistance in locating this citation.) See also Senate Committee on Appropriations 1986, Morley 1991.

9. As quoted by Kamen 1990.

10. In his overview, Barnet states that "the new element of 'low-intensity conflict' strategy is the extension of the military's domain over what used to be the functions of the police" (1988: 207). The latter, reciprocal part of the general principle defining low-intensity conflict—that the police assume a more military character—is based on my own review of the expansive literature on LIC doctrine and on an examination of specific cases of LIC-style militarization in Latin America.

11. Militarization and human rights concerns are also very relevant with regard to immigration and drug enforcement efforts on the Mexican side of the border (indeed, more so). This study, however, touches on them only briefly, an admittedly serious shortcoming. But Mexico's drug and immigration enforcement efforts exceeded the scope of this monograph. Devoting sufficient attention to those activities would have greatly extended an already lengthy research process and added considerable expense, as the bulk of the Mexican sources on these topics were not readily available. Regardless, these topics obviously merit in-depth research and debate by scholars, journalists, and the public, both within Mexico and abroad.

12. Sandoval (1991a, 1991b), Ramos (1991, 1995), Williams and Coronado (1994), Barry, Browne, and Sims (1994), Bean et al. (1994), Fried (1994), and, to a lesser extent, Bagley (1992) explore various aspects of contemporary immigration or drug enforcement efforts in the U.S.–Mexico border region. In addition, Bustamante (1990, 1992b) offers a provocative analysis of possible scenarios for future immigration enforcement in the border region, and Calavita (1989) briefly discusses border militarization as an option for future U.S. immigration policy that has been proposed by ultra-restrictionist groups. Several of these works are especially relevant to the present study. Sandoval's work is especially germane because he explicitly frames and examines the issue of border militarization, although his investigations differ from the present one in that they place greater emphasis on the analysis of the larger political and economic contexts of this phenomenon. Ramos's close examination of U.S. drug enforcement in the border region, including the involvement of military forces, is also very pertinent. While his work focuses on the contradictions and conflicts

among various bureaucratic actors, the present study is more concerned with the coordination and collaboration among various agencies. The work of Williams and Coronado is relevant, as they examine contemporary immigration and drug enforcement trends in the border region, referring to the thrust of these trends as the "hardening" of the borderlands, rather than militarization. Further, Barry, Browne, and Sims provide a fine overview of immigration and drug issues as they were played out in the border region, which they frame with a detailed examination of the principal economic-development strategy being pursued in the borderlands. In a different vein, Bagley addresses the topic of the militarization of drug enforcement in a critical manner, but he devotes only limited attention to the U.S.–Mexico border region. Finally, two recent studies (Bean et al. 1994, Fried 1994) on a new (September 1993), high-profile Border Patrol immigration enforcement effort in El Paso (Operation Blockade, renamed Operation Hold-the-Line) are some of the first works to examine in depth a specific contemporary immigration enforcement project in the border region. Relatedly, see also Vila 1994b (239–258) for an innovative analysis of the relationship between Operation Blockade and social-identity construction among border residents. Unfortunately, this important project falls outside the period covered in this study, and hence their investigations are discussed only briefly here (see epilogue). It is hoped that the present study, which is informed by the work of all these authors, will supplement their efforts.

13. In-depth research on INS border and immigration enforcement efforts during earlier periods are provided in the landmark works Calavita 1992, García 1980, and Langham 1984, and in portions of Perkins 1978 and Samora 1971. Calavita's work is especially significant for providing a state-centered, institutional analysis of immigration enforcement in the border region from the Bracero Program period up through the mid-1970s, while García's and Langham's important studies focus exclusively on the extraordinary INS mass-deportation campaign of 1954, Operation Wetback. In comparison, similar coverage of the INS's border-region immigration enforcement during the current period is sparse. While various important features of contemporary INS enforcement efforts are examined by Juffras (1991), Harwood (1986), and Morris (1985), only Harwood devotes a significant amount of attention (one chapter) to the agency's immigration enforcement in the border region, and he does not cover events beyond the early 1980s. Two notable recent exceptions to this trend are the previously mentioned detailed examinations of the Border Patrol's new (September 1993) immigration enforcement operation in El Paso, Texas (Bean et al. 1994, Fried 1994).

14. I am especially grateful for David Montejano's critical comments and suggestions in this section (as well as in other areas of this monograph).

15. Most of the sources drawn upon here tend to place Mexican-origin people at the center of analysis and to adopt a point of view that is sympathetic to their concerns, in contrast to the more common point of view favoring the

state or dominant groups. For a brief discussion of top-down–bottom-up perspectives as a general methodological issue in research, see Sjoberg et al. 1991: 35–36. For a detailed treatment of the same topic specifically with respect to research on race, ethnicity, and gender issues, see Williams and Sjoberg 1993.

16. Barrera 1979: 39. Also, not all Chicanos belonged to the same class, but they were (and remain) disproportionately concentrated in the lower classes (Barrera 1979: 103). Further, internal colonization has varied over time; during the contemporary period it has been far less harsh (Barrera 1979: 220).

17. Barrera 1979: 63. Álvarez 1985: 43, as cited by McLemore 1994: 246–247.

18. See Griswold del Castillo 1990 (chapters 5 and 6); Montejano 1987: 51–74, 106–117.

19. For an overview of these conflicts throughout the border region, see Martínez 1988: 81–95. For a more detailed discussion of many such confrontations throughout New Mexico and Texas, see Rosenbaum 1981 and De León 1983, respectively. Most frequently, *mexicanos* suffered the brunt of Anglo coercive force. Much less has been written on similar events in Arizona or on general Chicano history in that state. The two extensive historical documents reproduced in *The Mexican Experience in Arizona* (1976) provide some details, however. In addition, Heyman (1991) offers a richly detailed account, spanning a century (1886–1986), of several *mexicano* families who lived and worked on both sides of the Sonora-Arizona border.

20. Martínez 1988: 38–46. The most notorious was an 1853 invasion led by the infamous William Walker, who temporarily established the Republic of Lower California. After being driven from Baja California, Walker invaded Central America and in 1855 declared himself president of Nicaragua. He was killed shortly thereafter in Honduras.

21. See Hammond Incorporated 1989: U-30. Fort Bliss in El Paso and Fort Huachuca in southeastern Arizona are two of the early border forts that today are modern military bases.

22. Rosenbaum 1981: 43. The principal actor, Juan Cortina, was from a respected border-area family with large landholdings, and had fought against U.S. forces in the Mexican War. The original dispute involved his shooting an Anglo marshal in Brownsville for beating a *vaquero* who worked on the Cortina family ranch. Note that Mexican Americans outnumbered Anglos in the Valley by an estimated 12,000 to 300 at the time.

23. Rosenbaum 1981: 33–39. Paredes 1958: 7–15. I thank Michael Stone for suggesting that I consult the work of Paredes for this section.

24. Griswold del Castillo 1990: 8–14.

25. Montejano 1987. See chapters 2 and 3 for an extensive discussion of this process of dispossession.

26. Montejano 1987: 52. For a detailed overview of the Texas Rangers' repressive and especially violent treatment of *mexicanos* in the Lower Rio Grande Valley, see Paredes 1958: 20–32.

27. Montejano 1987: 107–108.

28. Montejano 1987: 110–117.

29. Montejano 1987: 113–116. Rosenbaum 1981: 49–50. For more detailed treatments of the Congreso Mexicanista and the diverse constituency this body claimed to represent, see, respectively, Limón 1974, Young 1994. For details of the especially famous and illustrative case of Texas law enforcement injustice during this period, the case of Gregorio Cortez, see Paredes 1958: 55–107.

30. Montejano 1987: 117–125. Rosenbaum 1981: 50–52. Acuña 1988: 162. See also Sandos 1992: 79–100; Samponaro and Vanderwood 1992: 73–98. The origins and key actors of the uprising have been the subject of considerable debate. For example, mainstream interpretations such as those of Rosenbaum and Samponaro and Vanderwood—like the accounts of Anglo authorities of the time—maintain that the uprising was the product of Mexican revolutionary factions seeking to pressure the U.S. government. In contrast, Montejano and Sandos attribute the uprising to local contextual factors and local actors. Sandos's detailed study draws out the indigenous anarchist character of the uprising.

31. Rosenbaum 1981: 51. Sandos 1992: 86, 90, 107. Samponaro and Vanderwood 1992: 99.

32. Montejano 1987: 122.

33. Webb 1965: 476, 478. Montejano 1987: 124. The figure for the American casualties appears to include all those incurred on the U.S. side along the entire length of the Texas and New Mexico border with Mexico from 1910 to 1919. For additional overviews of the violence inflicted during this period by both sides, see Sandos 1992: 87–110; Samponaro and Vanderwood 1992: 75–80. The massive retaliation against the population of Texas Mexicans in the Lower Rio Grande Valley, a small geographic area, is comparable in degree and nature to some of the most extreme cases of repression in Latin America during the first half of the twentieth century. One of the most infamous of these cases is the 1932 *matanza* (massacre) in El Salvador, where out of a total national population of one million, an estimated 10,000 to 30,000 peasants were killed (see Anderson 1971; Pearce 1986: 81–86; McClintock 1985a: 99–116). In light of the Valley's total population during this period (which was perhaps 100,000), the repression there is comparable in proportion to that in the Salvadoran case, if the higher estimates of the number of people killed are accepted.

34. Webb 1965: 478.

35. Rosenbaum 1981: 51.

36. Sandos 1992: 97, 106.

37. Montejano 1987: 118.

38. Samponaro and Vanderwood 1992: 99–100.

39. Martínez 1988: 47–49. Monticone 1981: 77. Milner 1979: 48, 51–54. Also, by way of comparison, it is telling that the killing of 18 U.S. citizens (most if not all of whom were Anglo) at the hands of Villa's forces is so widely known

in popular U.S. history, while the Texas Rangers' severe and much more wide-spread repression of Mexican Americans in South Texas and West Texas during the same period is generally unrecognized.

40. See Justice 1992.

41. Cockcroft 1986: 56–57. These initial deportations served to undercut the increase in labor organizing among Mexican immigrants. The organizers were allied with the radical Industrial Workers of the World (IWW), which was si-multaneously under attack from the federal government.

42. Barrera 1979: 64–74. Montejano 1987: 179–182.

43. García 1980: 107–108. Perkins 1978: 89–97. The Border Patrol was not the first immigration enforcement force in the border region. Perkins reports that the U.S. Immigration Service carried out extensive efforts dating back to 1908 to prevent Chinese immigrants from entering the United States through Mexico (1978: 7–24). Prior to that time the Customs Service had carried out this role. These efforts grew out of a series of laws excluding Chinese immi-grants, the first of which was passed in 1882. In contrast, Mexicans were offi-cially allowed to cross the border unimpeded until the passage of the Literacy Act in 1917, which required that immigrants pass a literacy test in some lan-guage (i.e., Spanish or English) in order to enter the United States. Even then, however, Mexicans were still readily able to make undocumented border cross-ings away from official ports of entry (Perkins 1978: 54–55).

44. Cockcroft 1986: 57–60. Barrera 1979: 126–128. See also Samora 1971: 48–51.

45. Perkins 1978: 91–93. Samora 1971: 51.

46. Justice (1992) notes that there was a substantial U.S. Army presence on the border in West Texas following World War I, which even included airplanes to conduct surveillance and facilitate communications in the rugged, mountain-ous border area. The last (and brief) punitive expedition into Mexico by the U.S. Army and Texas Rangers occurred in August of 1919.

47. Smithers Photography Collection, Harry Ransom Humanities Research Center, University of Texas, Austin. I thank Gilberto Cárdenas for bringing this source to my attention. Some years ago he uncovered the Texas Ranger–Border Patrol link in this rich and unique collection of photos, which includes material on early Border Patrol units in Texas.

48. Acuña 1988: 202–203. Cockcroft 1986: 59–61. One of the most notable examples of Mexican immigrants' increasing labor agitation (in the face of mass deportation) during the Great Depression was the formation of the 10,000-member Confederation of Mexican Peasants and Workers in California in 1934, shortly after a successful strike against strawberry growers in Los Angeles County.

49. Barrera 1979: 105–106. Acuña 1988: 203–204.

50. Barrera 1979: 105–106. Acuña 1988: 203–205. Also, on segregation prac-tices see Montejano 1987, especially chapters 8 and 9.

51. While "state repression" is admittedly a highly charged characterization, it is appropriate because various agents of the state systematically conducted a campaign of intimidation and coercion against Mexican immigrants that also affected Mexican Americans (especially immigrants' children born in the United States), all in the name of an explicit state policy of repatriation. However, the use of the term "state repression" here is not intended to refer to the extreme measures associated with it—e.g., death-squad assassination campaigns, torture, and the notorious "disappearances" carried out against civilians by state-related security and military forces. For an in-depth examination of such extreme activities in Central America and the United States' role in their development, see McClintock 1985a, 1985b. I thank David Spener for his discussion of and help in clarifying these concepts.

52. García 1980: 108.

53. Cárdenas 1979: 82–83.

54. Among the volumes written on the workings of the Bracero Program, Calavita's 1992 landmark work is the most recent, and arguably the most in-depth and theoretically innovative, study.

55. García 1980: 83–84.

56. Barrera 1979: 123.

57. Quote from an article by Willard Kelly that appeared in an INS publication, as cited by García 1980: 126. Kelly was the assistant commissioner of the INS. See Langham 1984: 86–88.

58. García 1980: 169, 171.

59. García 1980: 172. Quote from a May 12, 1954, telegram from William P. Allen, publisher of the *Laredo Times*, to President Eisenhower. This comment was reportedly made by Brownell to a group of labor leaders, who in turn told Allen. Brownell was said to have made the comment in order to elicit the support of U.S. labor leaders in the event that such shootings occurred and became publicly known. The event at which these alleged comments were made took place less than one month before the beginning of Operation Wetback.

60. García 1980: 173. Quote from a 1953 Texas Federation of Labor report, *Down in the Valley*. See also Langham 1984: 138–139.

61. García 1980: 173–178, 188. Langham 1984: 146, 151, 166–167.

62. García 1980: 179, 185, 197, 206–209, 220. Langham 1984: 162–163, 173. Langham notes that the three main Valley newspapers were owned by the Freedom House chain based in Orange County, California. According to 1990 reports from Valley human rights activists working with Proyecto Libertad in Harlingen, Texas, this chain was still owned by the same company, and its leadership was Libertarian. The latter point, were it also the case in the early 1950s, would explain much of their opposition to Operation Wetback.

63. Admittedly, this generalization is an oversimplification. For a distinct and more theoretically informed as well as nuanced interpretation of the INS, see Calavita 1992: 179–182.

64. García 1980: 175–176, 184, 201, 220.
65. García 1980: 73–74, 139.
66. Langham 1984: 175. García 1980: 228.
67. García 1980: 227–228. Langham 1984: 175. In contrast, Langham estimates that approximately 200,000 persons either fled or were deported.
68. García 1980: 230–231.
69. García 1980: 230–231. Langham 1984: 130–134. Cockcroft 1986: 73–74.
70. See Calavita 1992: 141–166.
71. Montejano 1987: 289–292. Acuña 1988: 307–362, 366–371. See Foley 1988 for a richly detailed case study of the effects of Raza Unida on one South Texas community. On the Chicano movement more broadly, see Muñoz 1989, Gómez-Quiñones 1990, García 1974.
72. Jamail 1981: 86. Acuña 1988: 350–352, 400–401.
73. Barrera 1979: 128. Acuña 1988: 374–375.
74. Barrera 1979: 123. On the growing villainization of Mexican undocumented immigrants, see Acuña 1988: 372–374. On General Chapman, see Cárdenas 1979: 83.
75. I am especially grateful to J. E. Morell, among others, for generously sharing her research materials on this topic. Further, Morell offered numerous critical insights in reviewing early drafts of this section, as well as other portions of this monograph.
76. Woerner 1991: 58, 60–61. The author is a retired U.S. Army general, and former commander in chief of the U.S. Southern Command in Panama (during part of the 1980s).
77. See Maechling 1988. For a more historical perspective on low-intensity conflict, see House Committee on the Armed Services 1990b. Klare and Kornbluh also trace the origins of LIC doctrine back to U.S. low-level wars conducted in third-world countries throughout much of the twentieth century (1988: 9–10).
78. While LIC doctrine evolved during the early and middle 1980s, it seems to have been accorded formal institutional status by the latter portion of the decade. In early 1987, President Reagan signed into law legislation to reorganize the military-security apparatus in order to address LIC concerns, through the establishment of the following: the Unified Command for Special Operations Forces; the position of Assistant Secretary of Defense for Special Operations and Low-Intensity Conflict; the position of Deputy Assistant to the President for Low-Intensity Conflict; and the Board for Low-Intensity Conflict of the National Security Council. The secretary of defense and joint chiefs of staff strongly opposed these measures and were slow to implement them (Thompson 1989: 12–15). Reagan also signed a National Security Decision Directive in June 1987 authorizing the development and implementation of a unified national strategy for low-intensity conflict (Klare and Kornbluh 1988: 6). By December 1989 the Army and Air Force had completed a three-year project to develop LIC doctrine and incorporate it into their field-training manuals (Hunt 1991: 51).

In 1991 the Army established a Proponencies Directorate to be responsible for the army-wide dissemination and integration of LIC doctrine (see sidebar, "Low-Intensity Conflict Proponencies Directorate" 1991). Moreover, between 1988 and 1991 *Military Review,* the theoretical monthly journal of the Army's Command and General Staff College, devoted seven entire issues to low-intensity conflict (in addition to numerous articles published previously). An example is the June 1991 issue, entitled "Low-Intensity Conflict: Gearing for the Long Haul."

To some extent, this flurry of activity represents a post–Cold War search for new missions by the U.S. armed forces in order to avert cutbacks. Further, the doctrine is still being refined in the wake of the end of the Cold War, as its relevance has increased with the eruption of a wide variety of local and regional conflicts around the world that had been long repressed or rechanneled by the previous bipolar East-West geopolitical order. See Taw and Leicht 1992, House Committee on the Armed Services 1993.

79. Klare and Kornbluh 1988: 6–7. The middle area of the Pentagon's "spectrum of conflict" refers to regional wars fought with modern weapons (e.g., the Iran-Iraq war of the 1980s and the Persian Gulf War of 1991), while the high end of the spectrum refers to both full-scale, global, conventional wars (e.g., World War II) and nuclear wars.

80. Miles 1986: 29. Woerner makes a similar point (1991: 62), as does Struthers (1990: 108); see also U.S. Army 1986: 13.

81. Klare 1988: 54. On the scope of low-intensity conflict, Klare quotes articles by U.S. military officers that appeared in various military journals. There has been considerable debate within the military on how broad the scope of low-intensity conflict is, and how broad it should be.

82. U.S. Army 1986: 2. See also Klare 1988: 53.

83. This point is made by Klare and Kornbluh, who provide a similarly broad-ranging definition of U.S. LIC operations (1988: 7).

84. Taw and Leicht 1992: 6–7. The Pentagon reportedly foresees an expanded role for the military in ostensibly nonmilitary operations. The U.S. Army has devoted increasing attention since the end of the Cold War to its involvement in "military operations short of war" (also termed "military operations other than war") and to "non-combat operations" as a part of its peacetime mission. Taw and Leicht note that this peacetime mission is the subject of considerable debate. They report that "conventional purists" fear that such a mission would adversely affect the military's combat readiness, while "anti-interventionists" fear that this mission "borders on colonialism" and would not benefit either the United States or the host nation.

85. Klare and Kornbluh 1988: 7.

86. Klare 1988: 55–56. Some ambiguity surrounds the designation of anti-drug operations and proinsurgency as LIC mission areas. For example, a key U.S. Army training pamphlet (U.S. Army 1986) on low-intensity conflict

excludes them, but lists the other four mission categories outlined by Klare. However, later reports on low-intensity conflict by military sources include antidrug operations as a key LIC activity. (See "Low-Intensity Conflict Proponencies Directorate" 1991; Hunt 1991: 55; Dixon 1987: 10.) Moreover, proinsurgency was obviously one goal of low-intensity conflict, as evidenced by the Reagan administration's support for counterrevolutionary forces around the world (e.g., in Nicaragua, Angola, and Afghanistan). On the support of such insurgencies as a part of LIC doctrine, see Foreign Service Institute 1988.

87. U.S. Army 1986: 13–15.

88. Barry (1986: 5–10) provides an excellent overview of the close relationship between counterinsurgency and LIC doctrines.

89. A crucial premise underlying counterinsurgency doctrine was that local insurgencies and indigenous radical political movements were directed or duped by outside communist forces (as in Moscow and Peking). See Maechling 1988: 21–25. Maechling served as director of internal defense in politico-military affairs for the State Department and as staff director of the National Security Council's cabinet-level group for counterinsurgency during the Kennedy and Johnson administrations.

90. Stepan 1976: 245–246. McClintock 1985a: 29–32. See also Maechling 1988: 30–31. Stepan discusses "internal security and national development" rather than counterinsurgency per se. However, both elements of his phrase are commonly invoked as themes in counterinsurgency doctrine literature.

91. Bacevich et al. 1988: 14, 40. All four authors are lieutenant colonels in the U.S. Army with extensive experience in counterinsurgency efforts.

92. For exceptionally well-documented case studies of foreign internal-defense activities in which U.S. intelligence and military agencies played major roles in the development of extensive internal-security networks that carried out gross human rights violations against civilian populations, see McClintock 1985a on El Salvador, McClintock 1985b on Guatemala, Valentine 1992 on Vietnam. For a more general overview of similar reorganizations of the military-security apparatuses in the Southern Cone countries of Latin America that likewise had onerous effects on human rights, see Fagen 1992. On the specific case of Brazil, see Moreira Alves 1985. In the Southern Cone, U.S. agencies and advisers played far less prominent, though still instrumental, roles than they did in Central America and Vietnam.

93. Stepan 1976: 247. Maechling 1988: 30–31. See also Fagen 1992. Many Latin American nations suffered military takeovers followed by extended periods of military rule, or at least tight military control of politics. These include Brazil, Chile, Uruguay, Argentina, Bolivia, Ecuador, Peru, Guatemala, El Salvador, Nicaragua, and Paraguay, among others. By the late 1970s, at least 15 Latin American and Caribbean countries were under military rule or tight military control of politics (Schoultz 1981: 250). Graduates of U.S. military training programs (especially the School of the Americas, established in 1946 in the Panama

Canal Zone) were particularly prominent actors in these military coups. See Barry and Preusch 1986: 87–90. For official information on the School of the Americas, see Escuela de las Américas 1978. By 1978 the school had trained some 35,311 officers and enlisted personnel from 20 Latin American nations. By 1993, some 56,000 Latin American soldiers had been trained at the school. For more recent and critical discussions of the School of the Americas (relocated during the early 1980s to Fort Benning, Georgia), see Imerman 1993, Waller 1993.

94. For a critical overview of the development and broad use of the concept of national security by U.S. policymakers, see Landau 1988. For an overview of the use of national security doctrine in Brazil, Argentina, Uruguay, and Chile to reorganize military and security forces to carry out widespread repression, see Fagen 1992. Struthers provides an overview of foreign (principally U.S.) influences on the construction and adoption of internally focused national security doctrines in Latin America during the Cold War era (1990: 161–170). For detailed discussions of the national security doctrine developed by the Brazilian War College, which was decidedly influenced by U.S. military and intelligence institutions, and was itself influential throughout the rest of Latin America, see Moreira Alves 1985; Comblin 1976; Archdiocese of São Paulo 1986: 60–67.

95. It is important to point out that specific constellations of political, economic, and social factors in "host nations" were central to the militarization of Latin American societies. Nonetheless, the myopic vision of communist subversion promoted by the U.S. military-security apparatus throughout the region was often readily adapted to local conflicts and contexts. I thank Beth Sims (of the Resource Center in Albuquerque) for her discussion and clarification of these issues.

96. Klare 1988: 57–58. McClintock 1985a: 54–57.

97. Maechling 1988: 33. Also, Fason (1989) examines the Office of Public Safety (OPS) in detail, as does McClintock 1985a: 54–72. The OPS, a unit of the Agency for International Development (which is attached to the Department of State), headed the principal U.S. program for police training. However, the Department of Defense also participated in the program in some countries. The OPS was initially headed (in 1962) by a former administrator of a CIA undercover program. At its peak the OPS was active in 40 countries. For a detailed case study of OPS activities and its ties to training in torture methods in Uruguay, see Langguth 1978. I thank Bill Fason for sharing his detailed study of the OPS.

98. Miles 1986: 40–41. Barry and Preusch 1986: 90.

99. Maechling 1988: 28.

100. Barry 1986: 41–58. Klare 1988: 59. Maechling 1988: 30. Barnes 1988. Fishel and Cowan 1988. Of these sources, Barry provides an excellent, detailed overview of military activities in conducting civic-action programs. Underlying

these efforts there seems to be the assumption that the military should act as a development agency of sorts, a role for which that institution is typically ill suited. The last two sources are articles by military officers, and they stress that the military's "civil affairs" and "civil-military operations" (categories of activities that are closely related to "military-civic action") are crucial means to the end of garnering civilian support for and establishing the legitimacy of host-nation governments allied with the United States.

101. U.S. Special Operations Command 1993: 8. This characterization is listed under the area of "civil affairs," which is closely related to military-civic action.

102. Waghelstein 1985: 42. The author views low-intensity conflict as primarily consisting of counterinsurgency activities.

103. Numerous cases of gross human rights abuses committed by forces allied with and trained by U.S. military and security forces have been reported around the world. For an overview of the alleged as well as documented linkages between U.S. military aid and human rights violations in Latin America in the 1960s and 1970s, see Schoultz 1981: 230–266. On the Operation Phoenix assassination program implemented in South Vietnam, see Maechling 1988: 43–44; Valentine 1992. See also McClintock 1985a on El Salvador and McClintock 1985b on Guatemala.

For additional detailed examples of abuses committed by military and security forces allied with the United States in their internal-security and counterinsurgency activities, see the following: For Guatemala, see Falla 1994; Amnesty International 1987; Americas Watch 1982, 1990b. For El Salvador, see United Nations Commission on the Truth for El Salvador 1993, Americas Watch 1991a, Amnesty International 1988, Americas Watch and American Civil Liberties Union 1982. For Brazil, see Archdiocese of São Paulo 1986, and for Argentina, see *Nunca Más* 1986. Many additional sources are available for these as well as other countries in Latin America.

One especially noteworthy illustration of this overall trend is the exceptionally brutal and well-documented record of massacres and other human rights violations committed by the Salvadoran army's elite (and recently disbanded) Atlacatl battalion, with whom U.S. advisers had a long and close relationship. See Congress Arms Control and Foreign Policy Caucus 1990, House Speaker's Special Task Force on El Salvador 1990, Doggett 1993 (especially pages 45–48, 221–231, 329–334), Danner 1993. I thank Charlotte McCann and Cindy Noblitt of the Documentation Exchange in Austin for providing detailed knowledge and invaluable assistance in my research on this issue.

104. McClintock argues that there is a fundamental contradiction and flaw in counterinsurgency's combination of reformist and apparently benign measures with coercive activities that often lead to human rights abuses (1985a: 49–50). I would counter that this combination of contradictory tactics may have a particular logic; it appears to be analogous to the "good cop–bad cop" strategy

in law enforcement, in which different police agents alternate between benevo-lent and coercive roles in encounters with criminal suspects, in order to confuse, manipulate, and better control and extract information from them.

105. Klare 1988: 72. Bagley 1992: 131–132.

106. Klare 1988: 71–73. By 1993, "counterdrug" efforts were listed as one of six "collateral activities" for U.S. Special Operations Forces. See U.S. Special Op-erations Command 1993: 7. Also see the July 1990 issue of *Military Review*, which is devoted entirely to the military's role in the War on Drugs. The articles display a mix of trepidation and enthusiasm regarding the military's involve-ment in antidrug operations.

107. Smith 1992: 14.

108. Klare 1988: 69–70. The text of this directive has never been made pub-lic, but it is known that terrorism was identified as a national security threat, and it is clear that the Reagan administration viewed the issue as a long-term struggle. See also Hunt 1991, "Low-Intensity Conflict Proponencies Director-ate" 1991.

109. U.S. Cabinet-Level Task Force on Terrorism 1987: 5. Of note, Vice Presi-dent Bush was the chairperson of this task force. For the similarly broad defini-tion used by the Army, see also Klare 1988: 69.

110. U.S. Cabinet-Level Task Force on Terrorism 1987: 5.

111. Sloan 1987: 6.

112. Klare 1988: 66–68. U.S Army 1986: 15–17. Hunt 1991: 55.

113. Klare 1988: 67.

114. Miles 1986: 29–30. For examples of some 16 U.S. military exercises in Central America during the mid-1980s, see Barry 1986: 57–58. These efforts all had civic-action and "humanitarian aid" components, and were often con-ducted in conjunction with host-nation forces. For a general discussion by two military officers of the role of military training exercises in providing "humani-tarian and civic assistance" to civilian populations, see Fishel and Cowan 1988: 47–48.

115. Woerner 1991: 65.

116. Robert H. Kupperman and Associates 1983: 22–23. The other two roles proposed for the Army in LIC are counterinsurgency and what appears to be equivalent to proinsurgency activities.

117. Robert H. Kupperman and Associates 1983: 21.

118. Robert H. Kupperman and Associates 1983: 25–26. The authors present a scenario of a successful movement centered in Los Angeles and active throughout the Southwest. Given that Mexican-origin people are the principal minority group in the region, this scenario appears to be a veiled reference to an uprising led by Chicano activists. By way of comparison, the other LIC sce-narios presented by Robert H. Kupperman and Associates are "A Caribbean In-tervention," "A Covert African Campaign," and a host of security crises in the Middle East (1983: 26–29).

119. Klare and Kornbluh 1988: 14. Miles 1986: 40. The Pentagon and the Reagan administration were deeply concerned with the "Vietnam syndrome"— that is, the public's reluctance to support costly, sustained U.S. interventions in the third world. For a detailed example of the Reagan administration's efforts to overcome this reluctance, see Kornbluh 1988. Kornbluh discusses an operation run by the National Security Council—in conjunction with State Department, Pentagon, and CIA officials—to manipulate the media and lobby southern congressmen for their support for U.S. aid for the contra war in Nicaragua, which was the Reagan administration's most prominent LIC proinsurgency project.

120. From Waghelstein's speech to the American Enterprise Institute, Washington, D.C., 16 January 1985, as quoted by Miles 1986: 43–44.

121. Miles 1986: 43. Barry 1986: 34–37. Taw and Leicht 1992: 40–41. U.S. Special Operations Command 1993: 32–33. Much humanitarian aid served military purposes, as in the case of U.S. humanitarian aid to the Nicaraguan contras. Both public- and private-sector organizations were enlisted in those efforts throughout the 1980s.

122. Miles 1986: 45. Goose 1988: 81, 98. Barry 1986: 20–26. Thompson 1989: 19. For more detailed information on the Special Operations Forces (SOF), see U.S. Special Operations Command 1993. Almost all SOF activities fit into the category of low-intensity conflict, although low-intensity conflict is not reducible to special operations alone.

123. This list is drawn from Goose 1988: 102–103 (for LIC forces); Kupperman and Trent 1979: 86–91. The latter source is devoted to the topic of defending against terrorism (i.e., antiterrorism), rather than to low-intensity conflict per se. It was written shortly before the development of contemporary LIC doctrine, of which terrorism counteraction (encompassing defensive and offensive measures against terrorism) is a mission area. Kupperman went on to write a key LIC doctrine document in the early 1980s. For a more detailed listing of equipment and technology used by U.S. Special Operations Forces (key actors in low-intensity conflict), see U.S. Special Operations Command 1993: app. A.

2. THE IMMIGRATION & NATURALIZATION SERVICE DURING THE CARTER & REAGAN ADMINISTRATIONS, 1978–1988

1. The Enforcement Division of the INS comprises the following units: Border Patrol, Detention and Deportation, Inspections, Investigations, and Antismuggling.

2. These figures have not been adjusted for changes in inflation rates. Nevertheless it is clear that the proportional increases far outstripped the cumulative effects of inflation during this period. These figures also do not include substantial fee-generated income and staff positions for 1987 and 1988 (discussed later).

3. House Committee on Appropriations 1979: 506, 515, 519; 1980: 541; 1981: 1011; 1982: 772; 1983: 622; 1984: 1405; 1985: 1110; 1986: 497; 1987: 1123; 1988: 1285; 1989b: 1397.

4. Bustamante 1978: 522–523. Acuña 1988: 376.

5. Acuña 1988: 357.

6. Cockcroft 1986: 218.

7. U.S. Select Commission on Immigration and Refugee Policy 1981. The commission was chaired by Reverend Theodore Hesburgh, president of the University of Notre Dame. Its recommendations, which were quite similar to those made in Carter's 1977 proposal, helped lay the foundation for the landmark 1986 Immigration Reform and Control Act (IRCA). For an overview, see Commission Chairman Hesburgh's introduction (especially pages 1–12) and the comments of Senator Alan Simpson (especially pages 407–408), commission member and a 6 author of IRCA. Both authors took a strong law-and-order line, especially Simpson, who also appeared to express a thinly veiled nativism. For a dissenting commission member's view, see the comments of Rose Matsui Ochi (especially page 383), who feared that the "enforcement tenor" of the report would "promote the use of abusive tactics and excessive force and violence in enforcement" against people who were "foreign looking."

8. For a general overview of the evolution of the political climate surrounding the debates on immigration in the late 1970s and early 1980s, see Cornelius 1982, Craig 1981.

9. U.S. Select Commission on Immigration and Refugee Policy 1981: 4. Chairman Hesburgh recognized the sense of urgency and hostility aroused in the public by the Mariel boatlift. He noted that the boatlift had heightened concern regarding the implications of immigration for the "national interest," a focus considered lacking in U.S. immigration policy.

10. DeWind 1990: 123. Weingarten 1989. Weingarten provides the lower figure, quoting INS officials, while DeWind provides the higher figure, which includes both Haitians apprehended by the INS and those not apprehended but known by the INS to have entered Florida without immigration documents. I thank Josh DeWind for bringing his and other articles on Haitian immigration to my attention.

11. Whereas the communist Cuban regime was seen as politically hostile and Cuban migrants were treated as political refugees fleeing oppression, the rightwing Haitian dictatorship was a U.S. ally. Thus, Haitian migrants by and large were not readily accepted or treated by the U.S. government as political refugees legitimately fleeing oppression and persecution.

12. House Committee on Appropriations 1979: 506; 1980: 541; 1981: 1011. Again, the dollar figures are unadjusted, and in this case do not appear to have exceeded inflation; they may not even have kept up with it.

13. House Committee on Appropriations 1979: 591; 1980: 578. There are nine Border Patrol sectors along the 1,950-mile U.S.–Mexico border. They are,

from east to west: McAllen (Texas), Laredo (Texas), Del Rio (Texas), Marfa (Texas), El Paso (Texas), Tucson (Arizona), Yuma (Arizona), El Centro (California), and Chula Vista (California). The sections of fence in the El Paso, Chula Vista, Yuma, and Tucson sectors only extended across portions of high-traffic, mainly urban areas within each sector. Also, it should be noted that approximately half of all undocumented border crossings in recent years took place along the San Diego–Tijuana stretch of the border (in the Chula Vista sector). The location with the second highest (though much lower) number of undocumented crossings was the El Paso–Ciudad Juárez border area.

14. House Committee on Appropriations 1979: 548. House Committee on the Judiciary 1981b: 69; 1982: 45. These three sources are somewhat contradictory on the number of helicopters deployed, with one reporting that the INS had three helicopters in 1979, while the other two indicate that only two were in use between 1978 and 1980. The Border Patrol initiated its helicopter use in 1976 and by early 1977 had two posted in the Chula Vista sector. They were Hughes 500C observation helicopters, a model widely used by the United States in the Vietnam War. All three of the initial pilots had served in Vietnam as helicopter pilots. Former military general turned INS commissioner Leonard Chapman encouraged the Border Patrol to begin using helicopters (Watson 1977: 19–20).

15. House Committee on the Judiciary 1982: 80–82. The various types of sensors deployed included infrared, seismic, magnetic, cable, and others. Electronic sensors act as labor-saving devices for the Border Patrol, because they enable agents to monitor much more territory than would be possible using only standard patrolling tactics. Initially developed for use in the Vietnam War, such sensors were first made available to the INS in 1970 and were deployed in the nine southwestern Border Patrol sectors from 1973 through 1977. The next generation of replacement sensors, deployed starting in 1979, were likely an upgrade, given the technological advances in electronics during the intervening period.

16. House Committee on Appropriations 1981: 1053. The five detention facilities were located in El Paso, Port Isabel, San Antonio, Los Angeles, and El Centro.

17. House Committee on Appropriations 1980: 578; 1981: 1024.

18. House Committee on Appropriations 1979: 532; 1980: 577. House Committee on the Judiciary 1981b: 69.

19. House Committee on Appropriations 1979: 506, 542; 1981: 1011, 1025. The dollar figures are unadjusted.

20. House Committee on Appropriations 1981: 1025. House Committee on the Judiciary 1982: 129.

21. House Committee on Appropriations 1980: 578–579. This source does not list all four of the full-time detention centers, but rather three of them, as well as several others not listed subsequently.

22. House Committee on Appropriations 1979: 542, 549; 1981: 1025, 1027.

23. House Committee on Appropriations 1981: 1015, 1025.

24. House Committee on Appropriations 1979: 578.

25. House Committee on Appropriations 1978: 1039; 1979: 515, 517–519; 1980: 550–552; 1981: 1011. The dollar figures are unadjusted. The Carter administration also tried unsuccessfully to cut 269 Border Patrol positions for 1980 in an effort to reduce its overall budget requests during a period of growing budget deficits and hard economic times.

26. House Committee on Appropriations 1979: 541–542; 1981: 1015, 1021.

27. House Committee on the Judiciary 1985: 196. One of the world's premier international police organizations, INTERPOL facilitates collaboration among law enforcement officials in 136 nations through such activities as sharing data bases and ongoing communication. See Anderson 1989.

28. House Committee on Appropriations 1980: 856. House Committee on Appropriations 1981: 1030–1031. EPIC was established in 1974. It is unclear when the INS began to participate in EPIC, though it was participating by 1979, if not earlier.

29. Crewdson (1983) details and summarizes these press accounts of Border Patrol misconduct and abuse, many instances of which he originally reported as a *New York Times* correspondent.

30. Senate Committee on the Judiciary 1980: 623. The convicted agents were from the Chula Vista (San Diego) sector. Such public candor from a top INS official was rather extraordinary, and was not found in subsequent years.

31. Senate Committee on the Judiciary 1980: 688–695. House Committee on the Judiciary 1981b: 274. See also U.S. Commission on Civil Rights 1980. The House source listed above notes that, according to the INS Office of Professional Responsibility, the number of INS misconduct cases grew from 334 in 1979 to 387 in 1980.

32. For example, see Baker 1990, Fix 1991.

33. House Committee on Appropriations 1981: 1011; 1982: 772; 1983: 622; 1984: 1405; 1985: 1110; 1986: 497; 1987: 1123; 1988: 1285; 1989b: 1397. Again, the dollar figures are unadjusted, though it is clear that the proportional increases far outpaced the cumulative inflation rate for the period.

34. The year 1982 is taken as the chronological starting point, because "Enforcement Division" per se did not exist as a category in the INS budgets of the preceding years (1978–1981). In previous years, enforcement efforts were divided in INS budget documents between "Interior Enforcement" and "Border Enforcement."

35. The new immigration inspection fee was $5 for each passenger arriving at a port of entry aboard a commercial aircraft or vessel, excluding persons arriving from Canada, Mexico, and adjacent islands (House Committee on Appropriations 1987: 1193). The IRCA legalization program application fee was levied on those applying for legalization.

36. House Committee on Appropriations 1988: 1342–1343, 1350, 1353–1354, 1358; 1989b: 1469, 1476, 1480, 1485. Significantly, these fee resources were not fully incorporated into the itemized, summarized INS budget submitted to Congress, but were detailed separately at the end of the lengthy budget document. For examples of this, compare information from the above citations with House Committee on Appropriations 1988: 1277–1285 and House Committee on Appropriations 1989b: 1389–1397, which present the itemized, summarized INS budget (minus fee income and staff), at the beginning of the INS budgets submitted to Congress.

37. House Committee on Appropriations 1983: 707; 1990a: 1682. House Committee on the Judiciary 1982: 45; 1983b: 10, 127; 1985: 118. House Select Committee on Narcotics Abuse and Control 1987b: 165. *INS Reporter* 1989: 11.

38. House Committee on the Judiciary 1982: 45. House Committee on Appropriations 1981: 1014. The deployment of helicopters to intimidate would-be undocumented border crossers at night was from the outset a key element of the Border Patrol's use of helicopters in 1976. See Watson 1977: 22–23.

39. *INS Reporter* 1989: 11. The five new helicopters were obtained in October 1988.

40. House Committee on Appropriations 1984: 1410. It should be noted, however, that because helicopters were expensive to operate, the INS was frequently unable to make full use of its fleet.

41. House Committee on the Judiciary 1982: 79. House Committee on Appropriations 1990b: 1682.

42. House Committee on Appropriations 1987: 1128.

43. House Committee on the Judiciary 1985: 122.

44. House Committee on the Judiciary 1982: 81–82. There were 1,221 electronic sensors deployed on the border during the first year of the Reagan administration (1981), approximately the same number as in 1980. Of these, it appears that approximately one third (400) were located in the Chula Vista sector (House Committee on the Judiciary 1981a: 5).

45. House Committee on Appropriations 1984: 1410; 1986: 523. The sectors were El Paso, Laredo, Del Rio, Yuma, Tucson, and Chula Vista (San Diego). The El Paso sector was outfitted first, in 1983, reportedly with 11 low-light-level television systems covering 12 miles of the border. The Tucson and Yuma sectors received low-light-level television systems in 1985, and arrangements were made for the Laredo, Del Rio, and San Diego sectors to receive systems shortly after.

46. House Committee on Appropriations 1986: 535.

47. House Committee on Appropriations 1987: 1149.

48. *INS Reporter* 1985–86: 5. However, later INS reports indicate that by 1991 only seven sectors were outfitted with CADRE (House Committee on Appropriations 1991: 1671).

49. House Committee on Appropriations 1982: 806–807; 1983: 660–661, 690–691; 1984: 1419–1420, 1489; 1985: 1147; 1986: 509, 536–540; 1987: 1156,

1179; 1988: 1326–1327. Note that the Oakdale detention center was partially complete and usable. This center, though located outside the border region, was designed to free up border-area detention space by serving as a backup and overflow facility.

50. House Committee on Appropriations 1981: 1011; 1982: 772; 1983: 622; 1984: 1405; 1985: 1110; 1986: 497; 1987: 1123; 1988: 1285; 1989b: 1397. Again, the dollar figures are unadjusted, though it should be noted that the proportional increase was much greater than the cumulative inflation rate.

51. House Committee on the Judiciary 1983a: 2. Senate Committee on the Judiciary 1983: 84. The degree to which this general policy was followed is open to debate, however. For example, chapter 7 of Samora's *Los Mojados* (1971) showed that in South Texas during the late 1960s, undocumented Mexican immigrants were routinely held briefly in detention camps after being apprehended.

52. House Committee on the Judiciary 1983a: 67. This harsh detention policy was combined with a 1981 agreement between the Reagan administration and the Duvalier dictatorship in Haiti allowing the U.S. Coast Guard to interdict Haitian immigrants on the high seas. These measures drastically reduced Haitian immigration to the United States. See Frelick 1992; DeWind 1990; Weingarten 1989; Helsinki Watch 1989: 50–53; Domínguez 1990.

53. House Committee on the Judiciary 1982: 86.

54. Undocumented immigration is a misdemeanor when there is no evidence of prior illegal entry (*González v. City of Peoria*, 722 F. 2d 468 [9th Cir. 1983], as cited by Americas Watch 1992: 3). See also "Entry of Alien at Improper Time or Place" (sec. 1325).

55. DeWind 1990: 128.

56. House Committee on Appropriations 1983: 634; 1985: 1219. In 1982 the INS was at one point detaining 2,000 Haitians. And of the 2,159 people held by the INS on April 14, 1984, 706 were Salvadoran, 195 were Haitian, and 112 were Guatemalan. These figures (along with a great many other reports) suggest that INS detention efforts in the early and middle 1980s were disproportionately focused on detaining Haitian and Central American refugees and immigrants (see Dewind 1990, Koulish 1992, U.S. Committee for Refugees 1989, Helsinki Watch 1989).

57. Melrood 1989. Rodríguez and Urrutia-Rojas 1990. Many of these children had suffered psychological trauma in their home countries or en route to the United States and needed professional mental health care, which they rarely received.

58. Helsinki Watch 1989: 57. The author refers to the landmark case of *Orantes-Hernández v. Meese and INS*, April 1988. See also Koulish 1992: 535, 540. The Orantes case was originally brought to court in 1982. A similar conclusion regarding INS treatment of Haitians was reached in 1980 by a federal district court judge (DeWind 1990: 125).

59. U.S. General Accounting Office 1992: 32–33.

60. Helsinki Watch 1989: 80–81. The author cites INS data.

61. House Committee on the Judiciary 1983b: 138. House Committee on Appropriations 1983: 632, 690–691; 1984: 1419, 1420; 1985: 1213; 1986: 509; 1987: 1136; 1988: 1296–1297, 1326. *INS Reporter* 1985–86: 11–12. This 1988 total includes the seven INS-run detention centers (New York City; Boston; Miami; El Paso and Port Isabel, Texas; Florence, Arizona; and El Centro, California) with a total capacity of 2,239.

62. House Committee on Appropriations 1983: 633.

63. House Committee on Appropriations 1983: 690–691; 1984: 1419–1420; 1986: 509; 1988: 1297, 1376. Mariel Cuban detainees in the Oakdale center (as well as those held in a federal prison in Atlanta) rioted to protest their unjustifiably long imprisonment and virtually hopeless situation. Most if not all had been convicted of some crime. Yet even after completing their sentences, they faced the prospect of further detention of undetermined length, because the United States wanted to keep them imprisoned until they could be deported to Cuba. However, Cuba refused to accept them, following another breakdown in relations with the United States. Thus the detainees had little prospect of being released. It should be noted that although Mariel refugees were generally derided as criminals in the U.S. media, most of them were law-abiding residents. Only some 3,800 out of a total of 125,000 were imprisoned in the United States, being held until deportation. See House Committee on the Judiciary 1989b: 27–28.

64. House Committee on the Judiciary 1982: 131.

65. Official sources vary on the number of private-contract facilities in use at any one time and on their respective capacity. One source lists the six private-contract detention centers with a 940-person total capacity (*INS Reporter* 1985–86: 11). Other sources list from four to six private-contract detention centers, with a total capacity of 621–700 persons (House Committee on Appropriations 1984: 1419; 1985: 1213; 1986: 510; 1988: 1296). All of the private-contract detention centers listed were located in the Southwest: San Diego, Houston, Los Angeles, Denver, Las Vegas, Laredo, El Paso, and El Centro.

66. *INS Reporter* 1985–86: 11–12. Volunteer-agency housing was probably used not for strict detention but for what the INS would later refer to as "soft" detention.

67. House Committee on Appropriations 1984: 1482; 1985: 1193. Detainee labor was used in minor construction, cooking, grounds work, and cleaning. In 1985 the INS proposed raising detainees' wages to $4 a day; it is unclear if this was enacted.

68. These figures were obtained by adding 940 (the high-end figure for the private-contract facility capacity) to 3,239 and 8,239 (figures listed previously for the normal and the emergency capacities, respectively, of the INS detention centers). Note that the normal and emergency capacity totals of 4,200 and 9,200

presented here are very close to the 4,179 normal INS capacity plus the additional emergency capacity of 5,000 (at the Oakdale, Louisiana, site) reported by the INS in 1986 (House Committee on the Judiciary 1988: 91, 93). Still, these figures may have been an underestimate, as the INS has ample extra emergency capacity at its own facilities that goes unlisted, and it has not always reported every instance of contract-facility use, especially the more temporary ones. This became obvious during the INS crackdown against Central Americans in the Lower Rio Grande Valley in 1989 (discussed in chapter 3).

69. House Committee on Appropriations 1983: 633; 1985: 1122–1123, 1213; 1986: 509–510; 1987: 1136–1137; 1988: 1295–1296; 1989b: 1408.

70. House Committee on Appropriations 1983: 633; 1985: 1123; 1987: 1137; 1988: 1295; 1989b: 1408.

71. House Committee on Appropriations 1982: 785; 1983: 634; 1986: 509–510. The 1982 and 1983 sources list the number of Cuban detainees (1,300 and 1,400, respectively) along with other detention statistics, but the 1986 source does not mention the number of Cuban detainees in the detention statistics. The fallout from the 1987 Mariel Cuban prisoner uprising, however, made it clear that the INS counted some 3,800 Mariel Cubans among its detainee population (House Committee on the Judiciary 1989b: 27–28.)

72. INS Detention and Deportation officer (anonymous), San Antonio district, interview with author, 18 June 1990. Patrick Hughes, immigration attorney, Laredo, Texas, interview with author, 18 June 1990. Also, see Markley 1990, Koulish 1992.

73. "Entry of Alien at Improper Time or Place" (sec. 1325), and as determined in *González v. City of Peoria*, 722 F. 2d 468 (9th Cir. 1983), cited by Americas Watch 1992: 3. The first offense is a misdemeanor; repeat offenses are considered felonies.

74. House Committee on Appropriations 1981: 1011; 1982: 772; 1983: 662; 1984: 1405; 1985: 1110; 1986: 497; 1987: 1123; 1988: 1285; 1989b: 1397. Again, the dollar figures are unadjusted, but the proportional increase is in general much greater than the cumulative inflation rate for this period.

75. "Immigration Reform and Control Act of 1986": sec. 111.

76. House Committee on Appropriations 1988: 1463.

77. U.S. General Accounting Office 1991: 3, 9, 10.

78. The only readily available source found with information on the Border Patrol's employment of Latino agents indicated that "Hispanics" made up approximately half of the Border Patrol in 1992, although few were in top-level posts (Salopek 1992). Further information on this topic could probably be obtained from the INS, though they do not routinely report such data in the documents available in library government depositories.

79. House Committee on Appropriations 1983: 627; 1985: 1114; 1987: 1127; 1988: 1289; 1990b: 1630.

80. House Committee on Appropriations 1988: 1371.

81. House Committee on Appropriations 1984: 1408–1409; 1985: 1113–1114; 1986: 500–501; 1987: 1127; 1988: 1288–1290, 1436. Interdicting drug smugglers (along with potential terrorists and criminals) was added to the list of "major objectives" for the Border Patrol in the 1987 and 1988 sources identified here. Also, implementing portions of the employer-sanctions program was included in the Border Patrol's base program description in 1987 and 1988. Furthermore, Commissioner Nelson stated in 1988 that the Border Patrol would be used to detect and apprehend "criminal aliens" within the United States. For a contrast, see the House Committee on Appropriations sources from 1984 to 1986; the "major objectives" for the Border Patrol listed there are solely focused on the apprehension of undocumented immigrants.

82. Contradictory interpretations can be based on the same statistical data. The present work maintains that the collection of such data by the INS is shaped by a variety of political and institutional agendas (see Cárdenas 1979 and also appendix 4). For an opposing view, see the thorough quantitative study by Bean, Espenshade, White, and Dymowski (1990). These authors assume that over time there is a fairly constant relationship between INS apprehensions and actual undocumented immigration flows—that is, they assume that INS apprehension data is a relatively objective measure of undocumented immigration flows (Bean, Espenshade, White, and Dymowski 1990: 113).

83. Crane et al. 1990: 16.

84. *INS Reporter* 1985–86: 4. Such patrols had already existed for the previous five years in the western region, mainly along the border in California and Arizona.

85. *INS Reporter* 1985–86: 5–6. House Committee on Appropriations 1987: 1128. Such efforts in the San Diego area by local police date back to 1976 with the formation of the Border Alien Robbery Task Force. See Wambaugh 1984.

86. House Committee on Foreign Affairs 1990a: 50–60. This area of the border was particularly dangerous. Nonetheless, the documented use of deadly force by the joint patrols and the Border Patrol appeared excessive, and at least some incidents occurred when agents were not in imminent danger, and appeared to be retaliatory in nature.

87. José Moreno, director of the Migrant and Refugee Services Office of the Catholic Archdiocese of El Paso, interview with author, 1 June 1990.

88. House Committee on Appropriations 1985: 1203–1204. It seems that BORTAC was expanded to 100 officers by at least 1988, as the INS Commissioner reported that the agency was acquiring 100 sets of "voice activated, hands-free communication devices" for the unit. House Committee on Appropriations 1988: 1427. Otherwise, BORTAC was rarely mentioned in INS documents and testimony submitted to Congress.

89. Border Patrol agent (anonymous), McAllen sector, interview with author, 26 October 1990.

90. House Committee on Appropriations 1985: 1204.

91. *INS Reporter* 1988: 24.

92. See House Select Committee on Narcotics Abuse and Control 1987a: 153–154; 1987b: 89–90. See also House Committee on Appropriations 1987: 1127; 1988: 1288–1289. In the latter two sources, interdicting drug smugglers was for the first time listed among the Border Patrol's "major objectives." Compare these sources with the listings of the unit's "major objectives" from earlier years. See House Committee on Appropriations 1985: 1113–1114; 1986: 500–501.

93. Former Border Patrol agent (anonymous), McAllen sector, interview with author, 26 October 1990. He reported that the shift toward drug enforcement in the McAllen sector began during the 1983–1985 period.

94. House Committee on Appropriations 1987: 1128. Other sources indicate that until 1985 there was a Customs Service horse patrol along some stretches of the border. However, by 1986 the Border Patrol was virtually the only agency regularly patrolling the border between ports of entry, often in rugged, off-road areas. (U.S. Customs Service agents [anonymous], McAllen, interview with author, 26 October 1990.)

95. See "Anti–Drug Abuse Act of 1986"; "Anti–Drug Abuse Act of 1988": secs. 6151, 6161–6162. Despite the lack of mention in the 1986 act, INS officials were apparently eager to affiliate themselves with the politically popular drug enforcement effort. See House Select Committee on Narcotics Abuse and Control 1987b: 149–154.

96. *INS Reporter* 1988 (January): 23–24. House Committee on Appropriations 1987: 1128.

97. Jiménez 1988: 5. See also Senate Committee on Appropriations 1990b: 52. The latter passage refers to Border Patrol agents' being armed in some instances with semiautomatic and fully automatic weapons, although it does not specifically mention M-14 or M-16 rifles by name. In March 1992 I saw a (McAllen sector) Border Patrol station's stock of some forty M-16s, under lock and key at the time.

98. House Committee on the Judiciary 1988: 56. The Louisiana camp referred to in this passage was probably the Oakdale detention center run jointly by the INS and the Bureau of Prisons.

99. House Committee on the Judiciary 1988: 61–63. Identifying all the agencies participating in the ABCC is impossible, because several lines under one listing of "participating components" were blacked out.

100. House Committee on the Judiciary 1988: 63. The other three subcommittees of the ABCC were focused on preventing known terrorists from entering the United States, on developing visa restrictions for aliens from certain countries or categories of people thought likely to be supportive of terrorist activity in the United States, and on the expeditious deportation of aliens supportive of terrorism, all carried out in a manner that would protect classified material and sources used as evidence.

101. House Committee on the Judiciary 1988: 64–65.

102. House Committee on the Judiciary 1988: 70, 74–78, 81–84.

103. House Committee on the Judiciary 1988: 89.

104. House Committee on the Judiciary 1988: 88, 92–93. Also, recall that plans for Oakdale to have an emergency capacity of 5,000 persons had been in existence since at least 1983. See House Committee on Appropriations 1983: 690–691.

105. Commissioner Nelson was responding to Congressman Harold Rogers of Kentucky.

> *Rogers:* And you started what is called the Alien Border Patrol [*sic*] Committee to coordinate efforts with Customs, the FBI, and the intelligence community?
> *Nelson:* That is correct. There are a number of subcommittees and working groups with all the different agencies involved evaluating procedures. We are strictly in the early stages of planning.
> (House Committee on Appropriations 1987: 1240.)

106. Senate Committee on the Judiciary 1988: 178. House Committee on the Judiciary 1982: 156. In 1982, these plans were initially dropped because the Department of Defense could not make any of its sites available for alien detention on a permanent basis.

107. See Reynolds 1990: 55–56; Weinberg 1987: 19-A, 20-A, 21-A. Reynolds cites extensively FEMA and DOD documents that she obtained through Freedom of Information Act requests as well as through other routes. She is working on a book on the subject, which should shed more light on the details of the immigration emergency plans. Reynolds shared with me a copy of an internal FEMA memorandum, dated June 30, 1982, to Louis Giuffrida, director, from John R. Brinkerhoff, acting associate director, National Preparedness Programs, on the subject "Martial Law." The memorandum debates the pros and cons of declaring martial law, pointing out the numerous potential problems with enacting such a measure in the United States, and concludes that alternatives such as deploying troops to assist civilian authorities in emergency situations and carrying out FEMA's and other departments' "peacetime action programs" and a "fully implemented civil defense program" could have the effects for which martial law is intended, but in a more manageable and politically acceptable fashion.

108. See Weinberg 1987: 18-A, 20-A, 21-A; Gelbspan 1991: 184; Linfield 1990: 165–167. These sources differ on some details. However, all point out that a question on this issue was put to Lieutenant Colonel Oliver North of the National Security Council by Representative Jack Brooks (a Democrat from Texas) during the televised Iran-contra hearings, but Committee Chairman Daniel Inouye (a Democrat from Hawaii) interrupted abruptly before North could respond. Linfield reports that FEMA's martial law plans were written into an executive order signed by Reagan, but the details remain unknown. Weinberg points out that North was the National Security Council liaison to FEMA dur-

ing the 1982–1984 period and contends that at that time North drafted a secret contingency plan to suspend the constitution and turn control of the government over to FEMA in the event of widespread public opposition to a U.S. military invasion of Nicaragua. Reportedly, the opposition of then–Attorney General William French Smith effectively squelched contingency plans to suspend the Constitution (see Novick 1987). Gelbspan, Weinberg, and Linfield all draw extensively on a *Miami Herald* article by Alfonso Chardy, "Reagan Aides and the 'Secret Government'" (5 July 1987). Linfield also extensively cites an article in *Datamation* by Charles Law Howe, "The Disaster Dossier: The Federal Government Has a Secret Plan to Take over Users' Computers in Case of National Emergency" (15 October 1984). It should be noted that Louis Giuffrida, the director of FEMA during Reagan's first presidential term, had an extensive background in designing such draconian contingency plans. During Reagan's tenure as governor of California, Giuffrida headed both the California Specialized Training Institute (a counterterrorism training center) and the California National Guard, playing a key role in drawing up and conducting readiness exercises for Operation Cable Splicer. This was a contingency plan to impose martial law in California and to carry out a mass roundup of anti–Vietnam War activists and radical Black nationalists in the event that they joined forces to challenge the authority of the state. I thank Eric and Don Devereux for providing the Weinberg and Novick articles.

109. House Committee on Appropriations 1982: 866.

110. House Committee on Appropriations 1983: 714–715.

111. Senate Committee on the Judiciary 1983: 21–22. It is important to note that the term "substantial number" was intended to be flexible enough to refer to "only a few thousand aliens," although daily undocumented land border crossings (which considerably exceed this lower limit) would not have led to the declaration of an emergency.

112. Senate Committee on the Judiciary 1983: 20, 26–28.

113. "Immigration Reform and Control Act of 1986": sec. 113.

114. House Committee on Appropriations 1990b: 1763–1764.

3. THE IMMIGRATION AND NATURALIZATION SERVICE DURING THE BUSH ADMINISTRATION, 1989–1992

1. House Committee on Appropriations 1989b: 1397; 1990b: 1624; 1991: 1644; 1992: 10; 1993: 13. Again, the dollar figures are unadjusted. However, it seems that the proportional increase in the INS finances derived from Congress approximately equaled or slightly exceeded the cumulative effects of inflation rates during this period.

2. The Enforcement Division of the INS comprises the following units: Border Patrol, Detention and Deportation, Inspections, Investigations, and Anti-smuggling.

3. House Committee on Appropriations 1992: 124, 161. The examinations fee was added in 1989, and a land border-crossing fee was implemented on a pilot basis in 1991 at the Blaine, Washington, crossing near Vancouver, British Columbia. Also, the Adjudications and Naturalization unit of the INS was moved from congressional funding to examination-fee funding (House Committee on Appropriations 1990b: 1641; 1992: 129–131). The two previously imposed fees were for particular immigration inspections and the IRCA legalization program (see chapter 2), although the latter was reduced dramatically by 1992.

4. House Committee on Appropriations 1989b: 1469, 1477, 1480, 1485; 1990b: 1694, 1702, 1705, 1709, 1713, 1718; 1992: 79, 91, 98, 121, 128–129, 1664; 1993: 74, 76, 88, 93, 120, 126, 177, 182, 185. Total fee revenues and staff levels over the 1988–1992 period were as follows: 1988, $280.7 million and 2,831 staff positions; 1989, $315.6 million and 2,844 staff positions; 1990 (estimated), $248.4 million and 4,016 staff positions; 1991, $406.6 million and 4,445 staff positions; 1992, $484.9 million and 5,101 staff positions.

5. For example, fee resources were not combined and accounted for along with congressional appropriations. Rather, in the annual INS budget documents submitted to Congress, INS officials presented the two categories of resources in a bifurcated fashion, and never provided an overall itemization of total, combined resources. In other words, the agency kept two budgets.

6. On these institutional growing pains, see House Committee on the Judiciary 1991, Juffras 1991. Also, House Committee on Appropriations 1991 contains more critical questioning of INS officials by committee members than any other document in recent years (e.g., see pages 1845–1847). The impetus for much of this questioning was a series of General Accounting Office reports in 1989 through 1992 that found serious management problems and budgetary chaos in the INS. Those reports are listed in House Committee on Government Operations 1993a: 21, and are summarized in the GAO representative's immediately preceding testimony.

7. In addition to IRCA in 1986, the other major piece of immigration legislation passed during this period was the Refugee Act of 1980, which took the INS over 10 years to implement, often in a highly politicized and unsatisfactory manner. For a discussion of how these problems came to the fore in South Texas with regard to Central American refugees, see Koulish 1992.

8. It should be noted that, in contrast to the case presented here, most assessments of INS border enforcement equipment during this period commonly emphasized its shortcomings and the agency's lack of adequate resources (e.g., see U.S. General Accounting Office 1991). The opposite stance is taken here to counterbalance that tendency, in large part because of the ever increasing resources granted to the INS throughout this period. Nonetheless, many equipment problems no doubt were not adequately addressed.

9. McDonnell 1990b, 1991b. Kamen 1992. The Pentagon's border antidrug group, Joint Task Force 6 (see discussion in chapter 4), coordinated the mili-

tary's participation in these projects. The Seabees reportedly considered arming themselves while they built the wall (on which they worked only during daylight hours).

10. McDonnell 1990b. The emphasis on drug enforcement over immigration enforcement to justify the wall and road construction projects may have been related to the involvement of the military, whose participation in border enforcement was supposed to be limited principally to drug enforcement (see chapter 4).

11. The construction of the wall was part of a larger INS enforcement strategy that also included increasing the number of Border Patrol agents, expanding the use of night-vision equipment, employing better aircraft, and increasing the amount of detention space.

12. Romney 1992 details the increase in undocumented border crossings in rural areas immediately east of the new wall. This area was patrolled by agents from the Campo Border Patrol Station, which covered some 45 miles of border east of the Otay Mountain (which is approximately where the wall would eventually end once it was expanded to 14 miles in 1993–94). While most of the increase in undocumented border crossings consisted of vehicle crossings—a large portion of which were presumed to be related to drug smuggling—apprehensions of undocumented immigrants crossing by foot were also up 21% in the area. Davidson reports that the California National Guard units had previously conducted armed reconnaissance patrols in the same general area (near Tecate), as part of its antidrug efforts (1991: 406).

13. See, for example, Bustamante 1992a. He notes, "We are viewed as a potential trade partner on one hand, as an enemy, on the other." He asserts that the wall was built to contain political damage in the United States during the current recession, by scapegoating Mexican immigrants yet again.

14. California Legislature 1990: 50–54. This proposal was put forth in June 1990 by a spokesperson for the Alliance for Border Control, based in San Diego.

15. García 1989c, 1989e. House Committee on Appropriations 1990b: 1755, 1764.

16. "Immigration Act of 1990": sec. 542.

17. García 1989e. Like the ill-fated San Diego "drainage ditch," this project caused some controversy. INS Commissioner Alan Nelson issued a qualified denial to the question of whether or not the INS had participated in the project.

18. Border Patrol agent (anonymous), Laredo sector, interview with author, 18 June 1990.

19. Border Patrol agent (anonymous), Laredo sector, interview with author, 18 June 1990. Border Patrol agent (anonymous), McAllen sector, interview with author, 26 October 1990. See also House Committee on Appropriations 1990b: 1796–1797.

20. House Committee on Appropriations 1989b: 1460–1463; 1990b: 1657–1661, 1675–1676; 1991: 1679–1680, 1694–1696; 1992: 55–56. The detention

centers that were expanded, or were scheduled to be expanded, were those in El Centro, California; El Paso and Port Isabel, Texas; and Florence, Arizona.

21. House Committee on Appropriations 1990b: 1682; 1993: 61.

22. House Committee on Appropriations 1992: 64, 66. The upgrade plan is consistent with the previously noted acquisition in 1988 of five new, much more sophisticated helicopters.

23. Ostrow 1992. This equipment expansion, along with a 300-agent increase in the Border Patrol and the addition of hundreds of other INS agents, was announced in Southern California by U.S. Attorney General William Barr as a way to reduce the level of undocumented immigration in the recession-ravaged state during an election year.

24. U.S. General Accounting Office 1991: 22. For example, a Laredo Border Patrol agent remarked that three agents and several low-light-level television cameras could cover the same amount of area previously patrolled by 25 agents. This is consistent with what I observed while accompanying Border Patrol agents in South Texas on March 17 and 18, 1992. It was obvious that electronic sensor systems played an extensive labor-saving "eyes and ears" role for the Border Patrol.

25. House Committee on Appropriations 1992: 32.

26. House Committee on Appropriations 1990b: 1629.

27. House Committee on Appropriations 1991: 1678.

28. McDonnell 1990a.

29. House Committee on Appropriations 1989b: 1397; 1990b: 1624; 1991: 1644; 1992: 10; 1993: 13. Again, it is important to note that the dollar figures were unadjusted and both the financial and staff figures include only congressional appropriations figures and do not include any resources derived from user fees. However, only a small portion of those fees was devoted to the Detention and Deportation program, as most fee-generated resources were devoted to more service-oriented units, particularly Inspections (though technically part of the Enforcement division), Adjudications and Naturalization, and Information and Records Management.

30. In recent years the INS has taken criticism for its high staff-overtime costs. Moreover, it has made use of private-contract guards (i.e., less costly, non-union) at INS facilities since at least 1982 (House Committee on the Judiciary 1982: 131), principally to reduce labor costs. I observed extensive use of this strategy at the large Port Isabel INS detention center, during a visit there in October 1990. Local INS detention officials confirmed that private-contract guards were used there.

31. House Committee on Appropriations 1990b: 1636–1637; 1992: 22; 1993: 24.

32. U.S. General Accounting Office 1992: 15–16.

33. House Committee on Appropriations 1991: 1883; 1992: 24.

34. House Committee on Appropriations 1992: 182. The five border-region INS detention centers were located in Port Isabel and El Paso, Texas; El Centro

and San Pedro, California; and Florence, Arizona. The other four were located in Boston, New York City, Miami, and Aguadilla, Puerto Rico.

35. House Committee on Appropriations 1991: 1883; 1992: 24.

36. U.S. General Accounting Office 1992: 12, 19, 20–21. The research for this report was conducted in 1991, hence the GAO's data are for 1991. The GAO examined and provided data on only seven of the nine INS detention centers. Two detention centers were not examined but were apparently included in the total of nine mentioned and in the overall detention capacity. The two unexamined INS detention centers were apparently those newly opened (in 1991) in San Pedro, California, and Aguadilla, Puerto Rico.

37. House Committee on Appropriations 1990b: 1637; 1992: 23.

38. U.S. General Accounting Office 1992: 12, 20–21. On page 12 the GAO lists 653 spaces at five private-contract detention facilities. Yet on page 20 the GAO presents a list of 13 detention centers, six of which appear to be private-contract detention centers (determined by comparing the GAO list with the list in note 33 and in House Committee on Appropriations 1992: 23, 182) that have a cumulative capacity of 853 persons, according to the GAO. Moreover, the GAO acknowledges (in a footnote on page 21) that it excluded another private-contract center in El Centro, which is included in other INS lists (see House Committee on Appropriations 1990b: 1637; 1992: 23). The seven private-contract facilities on the GAO list were in Laredo, Houston, Los Angeles, El Centro, Denver, Seattle, and New York City (the Wackenhut facility). Note that five of the seven were located in the Southwest.

39. This estimate of the capacity of the four "soft" private-contract detention facilities in South Texas is based on my tour of two of them in late April 1990, as well as discussions with local human rights advocates (particularly Rogelio Núñez, the executive director of Proyecto Libertad in Harlingen). Also, INS officials in South Texas later confirmed the agency's use of four facilities (South Texas INS officials, interview with author, 25 October 1990). Gentry (1989) also discusses one of the private detention centers that was run by the Red Cross.

40. The estimate of 750 missing regular spaces was arrived at by adding 200 (for the 200 additional private-contract detention center spaces found in the GAO's own listings), 100 (for the private detention center the GAO entirely skipped), 300 (the low estimate of private-contract "soft" detention spaces available in the Lower Rio Grande Valley), and 168 (to bring the estimate of available Bureau of Prisons spaces up to 1,000, assuming it is the Oakdale facility). The estimate of 5,700 spaces of uncounted emergency detention is based on adding the extra 5,000 places in emergency detention capacity at Oakdale to an estimated 700 additional slots of emergency space in at least four private-contract "soft" detention facilities in South Texas between 1989 and 1991.

41. The estimate of emergency capacity is undoubtedly conservative, given that it does not include the 5,000 spaces at the Port Isabel detention center that could be added on very short notice by erecting tents, according to an INS

announcement made in 1989 during a detention crackdown in the Lower Rio Grande Valley (Phillips 1989, Delgado and Phillips 1989). The actual capacity at the Port Isabel facility peaked during early 1989 at some 2,400 persons detained (Pinkerton 1989, "Tents Erected" 1990). It is unclear if the INS had similar emergency capacity at its other detention centers, but it seems quite plausible for those centers located on sites with available makeshift space and surrounding land. Moreover, as noted in chapter 2, the INS had previously drawn up contingency plans to use U.S. military facilities to provide detention space in the event of an immigration emergency.

42. U.S. General Accounting Office 1992: 3–4.

43. U.S. General Accounting Office 1992: 23–24. The 24% figure for the Central American share of the total detention population was obtained by combining the data from Central American nations, including El Salvador (13%), Honduras (6%), and Guatemala (5%). If there were additional Central American countries represented (e.g., Nicaragua), their presence was obscured in the heterogeneous "other" category. Also, the figure for Haitians in detention obviously excluded those Haitians held in the massive holding camp established in late 1991 at the U.S. military base in Guantánamo, Cuba.

44. INS Detention and Deportation officer (anonymous), San Antonio district, interview with author, 18 June 1990.

45. U.S. General Accounting Office 1992: 25. On the increase in the number of "criminal aliens" held at the Port Isabel detention center in 1992, see "Changing Scene at the Corralón" 1992. "Excludable aliens" are those who are apprehended before they formally enter the United States (e.g., when they are at sea or arrive at international airports or formal land border points of entry). "Deportable aliens" are those who are apprehended after they have formally entered the United States, but are not easily expellable through "voluntary departure" (e.g., non-Mexican undocumented immigrants).

46. House Committee on Appropriations 1992: 233. It is not clear whether McNary was referring only to INS detention centers or to the total detention space available to the INS from various sources.

47. House Committee on Appropriations 1991: 1661–1662.

48. U.S. General Accounting Office 1992: 17.

49. "Entry of Alien at Improper Time or Place" (sec. 1325). *González v. City of Peoria*, 722 F. 2d 468 (9th Cir. 1983), as cited by Americas Watch 1992: 3. The misdemeanor status applies if it is a first offense. Subsequent illegal re-entry is a felony offense. See also Kesselbrenner and Rosenberg 1994: 5-17. I thank the noted immigration attorney Barbara Hines for bringing this source to my attention.

50. U.S. General Accounting Office 1992: 25.

51. U.S. General Accounting Office 1992: 17. "Anti–Drug Abuse Act of 1988": sec. 6151. "Immigration Act of 1990": secs. 501, 510, 602. "Definitions" (sec. 1101): par. 43.

52. House Committee on Appropriations 1989b: 1488. INS Detention and Deportation officer (anonymous), San Antonio district, interview with author, 18 June 1990.

53. "Immigration Act of 1990": sec. 602. "Deportable Aliens" (sec. 1251). Immigrants can be deported if, within their first five years of residence in the United States, they are convicted of just one such crime and sentenced to a confinement of a year or more, or if they are convicted of two or more crimes of "moral turpitude" stemming from more than one episode of criminal activity, at any time, regardless of whether or not the convictions are obtained in a single trial and regardless of whether or not they are subsequently imprisoned.

54. Kesselbrenner and Rosenberg 1994: 6-5 – 6-8. Cynthia Leigh, immigration attorney, Political Asylum Project of Austin, interview with author, 3 August 1992. Leigh felt that it was likely that an attorney could prevent a deportation if one or both "moral turpitude" offenses were misdemeanors, however.

55. Patrick Hughes, immigration attorney, Laredo, Texas, interview with author, 18 June 1990. Dave Rabine, immigration attorney, El Centro Asylum Project, El Centro, California, interviews with author, 1 June and 8 June 1990.

56. Gary Silbiger, immigration attorney, Los Angeles, interview with author, 2 June 1990. For examples of crimes generally considered to constitute "moral turpitude," see Kesselbrenner and Rosenberg 1994: 6-9 – 6-13. Included in this category are crimes involving fraud, avoidance of reporting of financial transactions, bribery, possession of altered immigration documents, theft, possession of stolen goods, rape, voluntary manslaughter, murder, larceny, and aggravated assault. In contrast, involuntary manslaughter, simple assault, and violations of regulatory statutes are generally not considered to be crimes of moral turpitude. Nonetheless, definitions of what constitutes a crime of moral turpitude vary widely.

57. INS Detention and Deportation officer (anonymous), San Antonio district, interview with author, 18 June 1990. INS investigations agent (anonymous), San Antonio district, interview with author, 29 July 1992.

58. Juffras 1991: 33–34. Juffras notes that the provision cited by the INS for its "criminal alien" enforcement efforts is in section 701 of IRCA. This section was included in IRCA as an amendment by Representative Buddy McKay of Florida during debate on the floor of the House of Representatives. Citing legislative histories, Juffras states, "No one had expected this provision to be important in the implementation of IRCA" (1991: 33). Juffras also shows that the INS identified criminal aliens as an enforcement priority in 1983 and says that the agency had been planning an Alien Criminal Apprehension Project in 1986, prior to the passage of IRCA.

59. U.S. General Accounting Office 1992: 14.

60. Koulish 1992. Patrick Hughes, immigration attorney, Laredo, Texas, interview with author, 18 June 1990. Hughes noted that when the INS was short on funds at certain times of the year, it was less restrictive in its detention practices.

61. Markley 1990: 97–101, 113–116.

62. U.S. General Accounting Office 1992: 31. Tactaquin 1992: 28. This provision granted a stay of deportation and work permits to Salvadorans who registered with the INS. A lengthy effort by advocates to gain the same status for Guatemalans in the Immigration Act of 1990 was unsuccessful.

63. U.S. General Accounting Office 1992: 32. Tactaquin 1992: 28. The lawsuit was originally brought by the American Baptist Churches (ABC) against the INS in 1985. The ABC settlement protections applied only to those eligible Salvadorans and Guatemalans who were in the country and had applied for political asylum before October 1, 1990.

64. Nicaraguans were among those who faced declining fortunes with the INS, as they lost their preferential treatment—previously formalized in 1987 (see chapter 2)—following the 1990 election victory of U.S. political allies in Nicaragua. Subsequently, new arrivals from Nicaragua were likely to face deportation and detention, despite the fact that after the elections tense conditions in Nicaragua gave rise to numerous episodes that provided people with reasonable grounds for seeking political asylum in the United States. The most egregious case of exclusion during the Bush administration was that of Haitian refugees following the 1991 military coup that removed Haiti's first democratically elected government. Despite widespread human rights violations in Haiti, the United States interdicted some 30,000 Haitians on the high seas and detained them at the U.S. naval base at Guantánamo Bay in Cuba. See Frelick 1992. The Clinton administration continued and expanded these practices.

65. The 1990 immigration act called for appropriations for fiscal year 1991 to be used to increase the number of authorized full-time–equivalent (FTE) Border Patrol positions by 1,000 over the previous fiscal year ("Immigration Act of 1990": sec. 541). Another act called for appropriations for fiscal year 1989 to be used to increase the number of authorized FTE Border Patrol positions by 435 ("Anti–Drug Abuse Act of 1988": sec. 6162). However, through 1992, Congress had not authorized additional positions for these mandated increases, nor had the Bush administration or the INS pressed hard for them—perhaps due to mounting federal budget constraints. For example, INS Commissioner McNary did not even mention the mandated 1,000-position increase in Border Patrol staff in his 1992 report to Congress on the implementation of the Immigration Act of 1990. However, McNary did attempt to push through a 500-agent increase for the Border Patrol in the 1993 budget, but this apparently failed, as the 10% staff increase did not show up in the budget documents submitted the following year, in spite of a 10% increase in funding (House Committee on Appropriations 1992: 201, 232–233; 1993: 13). Meanwhile, the INS apparently did respond at least in part to the antidrug legislation in its budget request for 1991, as the agency sought a 200-position increase in Border Patrol staff, which it specifically justified in terms of the unit's expanding drug-interdiction efforts. This attempt was apparently only partially successful, however, as the unit's autho-

rized staffing level was expanded by just 81 positions (a 1.7% increase) from 1990 to 1991, despite a 13% increase in funds. See House Committee on Appropriations 1990b: 1618, 1624; 1991: 1644; 1992: 10.

66. House Committee on Appropriations 1989b: 1397; 1990b: 1624; 1991: 1644; 1992: 10; 1993: 13. Again, the dollar figures are unadjusted, though it is clear that the rate of increase was far greater than the cumulative inflation rate during this period.

67. For example, see U.S. General Accounting Office 1991: 3, 9–11. On page 11 the authors claim that the Border Patrol lacked adequate funds to fill its congressionally authorized positions. However, they had previously noted on pages 3 and 10 that Border Patrol funds rose 61% from 1986 through 1990, and that the INS provided the Border Patrol with 97% of the funds requested for the unit in the president's budgets to Congress during this period. Thus, the INS received ever greater funding from Congress for the Border Patrol, and the INS, in turn, forwarded almost all of these funds to the Border Patrol. This raises the following question: Why were these rapidly expanding funds insufficient to remedy the purported chronic underfunding of congressionally authorized Border Patrol staffing levels, which were starting to be cut back by 1990?

68. For example, see House Committee on Appropriations 1991: 1907. Total INS overtime costs were in excess of $92 million in 1990 and were estimated to exceed $104 million in 1991. There is no breakdown of this figure indicating what proportion was for the Border Patrol. See also McDonnell 1991a. In this article the San Diego Border Patrol chief indicated that he used overtime funds to concentrate personnel at traffic checkpoints. However, overtime work did not seem to be as lucrative in the Border Patrol as in other unionized jobs. For example, several South Texas agents told me that they could only earn up to one fourth above their annual salaries in overtime wages, despite the fact that they often worked extra hours (20 or more per week) far exceeding one fourth of their regularly scheduled hours (Border Patrol agents [anonymous], McAllen sector, interview with author, 17 March 1992). They were not compensated for their overtime work by the standard time-and-a-half overtime pay rate commonly found in jobs in the primary labor market.

69. U.S. General Accounting Office 1991: 3, 9, 11. For only three years— 1985, 1986, and 1990—the GAO provides precise data on the percentages of congressionally authorized Border Patrol posts devoted to the southwestern border that were actually filled (94% in 1985, 102% in 1986, and 87% in 1990). For these percentages in 1987 through 1989, however, the GAO does not give precise figures. Instead, the data for these years is shown in bar graph form. The figures appear to be about 70% in 1987, 87% in 1988, and 80% in 1989.

70. U.S. General Accounting Office 1991: 3, 9, 11. Ostrow 1992. The GAO found that the actual number of Border Patrol agents in the Southwest border region had risen from 3,222 in 1986 to 3,669 in 1990 (an increase of 14%). However, the actual number of Border Patrol agents in the border region in

1990 was 13% short of the total number (4,240) of congressionally authorized posts for the region for the year, according to the GAO report. Ostrow presented the lower figure (2,500) in his report of the announcement of Border Patrol staff increases by U.S. Attorney General William Barr. The possibility that the Bush administration understated the actual staffing level to make the 300-agent increase announced by Barr sound more impressive ought not to be categorically ruled out, especially given that 1992 was an election year.

71. U.S. General Accounting Office 1991: 9. House Committee on Appropriations 1988: 1463.

72. Based on GAO data for 1990 cited in the previous notes, this estimate assumes that the INS continued to deploy 84% of all Border Patrol agents in the U.S.–Mexico border region and that in 1992 actual staff levels in the region were below authorized staff levels at a rate similar to that reported for 1990 (i.e., 13% low, or 87% filled).

73. U.S. General Accounting Office 1991: 2, 11–12. The GAO authors did not provide an overall annual attrition rate for Border Patrol staff. Rather, they reported that the annual attrition rate was 21% for first-year agents (down from 30% in the recent past), and 12% for all other Border Patrol staff. I derived an estimate of approximately 13% for the overall Border Patrol attrition rate through a series of estimates that amounted to a mathematical weighting of the GAO's two attrition rates. I began by estimating the average annual proportion of the Border Patrol that was made up of first-year agents as 10.6% (see the next note for an explanation), which left an annual average of 89.4% for non–first-year agents. Next I multiplied these proportions by their respective attrition rates, that is, 10.6 x 21% for first-year agents and 89.4 x 12% for all others. The result of these multiplications was 2.226 and 10.728, respectively. I added these two weighted figures, for a total of 12.954, which I rounded up to 13 to get my estimated overall attrition rate for the Border Patrol as a whole.

74. House Committee on Appropriations 1988: 1303; 1989b: 1419–1420, 1545; 1991: 1666; 1992: 28. INS Commissioner Nelson reported in 1989 that three years after IRCA's passage, the Border Patrol's actual staffing levels had increased from 3,238 to 4,097 agents, which was far below the 50% increase mandated by IRCA. In addition, for the entire 1986–1991 period, the INS completed training and instruction for some 2,771 Border Patrol agents (though only 289 agents were trained during the last two years of this period). This resulted in an average of 462 new agents per year, which was approximately 10.6% of the average annual total force for the same period. It is significant that this proportion is less than the previously estimated overall Border Patrol annual attrition rate of 13%. The 10.6% estimate for the proportion of first-year agents was derived by dividing 462 (the average number of new agents each year from 1986 through 1991) by 4350 (the average number of Border Patrol agents each year during the same period). The latter figure was derived by multiplying 5,000 by 87%. Eighty-seven percent is an estimate of the proportion of Border Patrol posts

actually filled, based on the GAO's data for 1990 on the actual number of Border Patrol agents in the Southwest border sectors (3,669) and on the number of Border Patrol authorized for the region for that year (4,240). Five thousand is the approximate average number of Border Patrol positions authorized annually by Congress from 1986 through 1991 (see appendix 1 for those figures).

75. House Committee on Appropriations 1988: 1303; 1989b: 1419–1420; 1991: 1666; 1992: 28.

76. House Committee on Appropriations 1990b: 1630; 1992: 14; 1993: 18.

77. House Committee on Appropriations 1989b: 1401; 1990b: 1630; 1991: 1650.

78. INS investigations agent (anonymous), San Antonio district, interview with author, 29 July 1992. This agent described these prison-to-INS inmate transfers as apprehensions. The 1992 GAO report on INS detention efforts implies the same (U.S. General Accounting Office 1992: 16–17). Moreover, "criminal aliens" are highlighted as an apprehension category in the discussion of the Border Patrol's workload. However, annual apprehensions of criminal aliens increased by only 10,619 between 1989 and 1992, rising from 18,500 to 29,119 (House Committee on Appropriations 1993: 18).

79. House Committee on Appropriations 1991: 1844; 1992: 224–225.

80. U.S. General Accounting Office 1991: 13. The drop in the percentage of time spent on border-control activities was even sharper in the Border Patrol's busiest sector for undocumented immigration: in the Chula Vista sector this percentage declined from 67% in 1985 to 47% in 1990.

81. U.S. General Accounting Office 1991: 2. Juffras 1991: 42–44.

82. House Committee on Appropriations 1989b: 1402.

83. House Committee on Appropriations 1991: 1826, 1836–1837. The 150-mile deployment limit was to apply in the case of large cities in the border region; otherwise the agents were to be redeployed within 100 miles of the border.

84. For example, the Border Patrol in the Tucson sector appears to have placed a particularly strong emphasis on drug interdiction in their border linewatch efforts. See Senate Committee on Appropriations 1990b: 24.

85. House Committee on Appropriations 1989b: 1401; 1990b: 1628; 1991: 1649; 1992: 13. In its "Base Program Description" in budget documents submitted to Congress, the Border Patrol is listed as having this responsibility. Prior to 1989 this responsibility was not listed in the unit's "Base Program Description," although its drug enforcement efforts were increasingly noted elsewhere as the 1980s wore on, especially in 1987 and 1988 (see House Committee on Appropriations 1984: 1409; 1985: 1114; 1986: 500–501; 1987: 1127; 1988: 1289).

86. U.S. General Accounting Office 1991: 1.

87. "Immigration Act of 1990": sec. 503. INS officers were authorized to make arrests for any offense under U.S. law that was committed in their presence and, more broadly, for any felony under U.S. law whenever they had reasonable grounds to suspect that such a crime had been committed. This

expanded authority was centered in the Border Patrol, as the main enforcement arm of the INS.

88. Bruce 1991. Wong 1991. The Border Patrol reportedly actively sought this increased arrest power in all border states, although a Border Patrol spokesman denied such an effort.

89. Bruce 1991. Wong 1991. Also, see the text of Texas House Bill 51, filed November 12, 1990, by Representative Henry Cuéllar (Democrat-Laredo). All three bills were filed by Mexican American legislators. The most comprehensive was House Bill 51, which would have granted the Border Patrol authority for felony and misdemeanor arrest. I attended and observed the February 13, 1991, hearing on House Bill 51 held by the Texas House Public Safety Committee, in which a number of civil rights activists from across the state (most of whom were Mexican American) testified, expressing strong opposition to House Bill 51 due to the Border Patrol's record of abusive practices and its lack of public accountability. Following this blistering testimony, Representative Cuéllar stated that he had filed the legislation in response to requests from local Border Patrol officials in Laredo. The two similar bills were filed by Representative Irma Rangel of Kingsville and Senator Carlos Truán of Corpus Christi.

90. Border Patrol agent (anonymous), McAllen sector, interview with author, 26 October 1990.

91. McDonnell 1992e.

92. McDonnell 1992b.

93. Jehl and Broder (1992) report that the federal police contingent sent to Los Angeles included "special border patrol units." On the introduction of Border Patrol agents from Texas into Los Angeles, see Davis 1992b: 743–746. Davis relies on secondhand reports from the streets on this issue, so this assertion is not entirely certain. McDonnell 1992e reports on the deployment of Border Patrol agents from various parts of California as well as from Yuma, Arizona.

94. House Committee on Appropriations 1989b: 1402, 1514; 1990b: 1630; 1992: 14.

95. Senate Committee on Appropriations 1990b: 30. Border Patrol agent (anonymous), McAllen sector, interview with author, 26 October 1990. The Explorer Scout program is affiliated with Boy Scouts of America.

96. House Committee on Appropriations 1989b: 1514.

97. Former Border Patrol agent (anonymous), Lower Rio Grande Valley, interview with author, 26 October 1990.

98. For a theoretical discussion of the conflict between state authorities' role in enforcing immigration laws and their duty to uphold the human rights of undocumented immigrants, see Nickel 1983.

99. For several detailed examples, see U.S. Commission on Civil Rights 1980; Samora 1971: chap. 7. Also, rights abuses were more common during Operation Wetback and the mass deportations of the Great Depression (see chapter 1 of this work).

100. For examples of this, see Chávez 1992, Nathan 1991, Conover 1987, Crewdson 1983.

101. Jiménez 1992: 30.

102. See Americas Watch 1992; Immigration Law Enforcement Monitoring Project 1990, 1992; House Committee on Foreign Affairs 1990a; House Committee on Government Operations 1993b; House Committee on the Judiciary 1992; California Legislature 1990; U.S. Commission on Civil Rights 1992, 1993; Mexican National Commission for Human Rights 1992; Rotella 1992a, 1992d; Dubose 1992; Salopek 1992, 1993; Palmer 1990; McDonnell 1992a, 1992b, 1992c, 1992d; McDonnell and Rotella 1993a; Kahn 1990; Thatcher 1991; Guevara 1991; Davidson 1990; Wilkinson 1991. Please note that the press articles listed above represent only a fraction of the press reports of INS abuses published during the Bush administration. Compiling a complete list is a large project that exceeds the scope of the present work. Also, this compilation of sources does not include any that cover the infamous rights abuses committed by the INS against the Central American sanctuary movement in the United States during the 1980s, a large topic in and of itself.

103. Americas Watch 1992: 1.

104. Immigration Law Enforcement Monitoring Project 1992: 35–39. In addition to the 971 rights abuses reported in four areas of the border region, some 303 abuses were also recorded in the Miami area. Moreover, Americas Watch reported that federal-court public defenders in San Diego documented that, from 1985 to January 1991, 331 of their clients were severely beaten by Border Patrol and Customs agents at the time of their arrest (1992: 31). These cases came to light only because the victims were brought into contact with the federal court system—a relatively rare circumstance for those apprehended by the Border Patrol.

105. Salopek 1993: 7. It is significant that this less-than-flattering information about the INS was not readily available. The author reports that he had a very difficult time over a period of several months obtaining Justice Department statistics on the number of rights-abuse cases pending against the INS.

106. Jorge Bustamante, presentation to a seminar on international migration, University of Texas at Austin, 26 September 1990. The survey reported by Bustamante was an ongoing effort conducted among would-be undocumented immigrants waiting on the Mexican side of the border to cross into the United States. The survey was conducted in a variety of locales along the border, though principally in the Tijuana area, by researchers from the highly regarded Colegio de la Frontera Norte (of which Dr. Bustamante was the president).

107. Santibáñez, Valenzuela, and Velasco 1993: 23–24. Two of the three authors were affiliated with Colegio de la Frontera Norte. The third was the director of Grupo Beta, a police force in Tijuana (discussed later).

108. For a discussion and examples of this dilemma, see Nathan 1992; Mexican National Commission for Human Rights 1992: 51–52. For a discussion of

the pitfalls of cooperation between local police and the INS, see Immigration Law Enforcement Monitoring Project 1990: 6, 12; Immigration Law Enforcement Monitoring Project 1992: 33–35; Americas Watch 1992: 47–50. Without external public reporting and review mechanisms, government authorities are in a decidedly disadvantageous position to know of and document thoroughly human rights abuses by their own police agencies. The ability of nongovernmental human rights groups to gather information and conduct such investigations, however, is limited by their lack of resources, the lack of cooperation by governmental authorities, and the unprecedented nature of such work in the border region.

109. Palmer 1990. House Committee on Foreign Affairs 1990a: 13, 26–29. Salopek 1992, 1993. Border Patrol officials repeatedly defended their record by reporting that the unit had an extremely low complaint ratio of one public complaint per 17,000 arrests. However, all three sources illustrate that the official complaint process was highly inaccessible, confusing, and virtually nonexistent in practice. Vulnerable undocumented immigrants fearful of encounters with legal authorities were unlikely to search it out. Moreover, Border Patrol agents have, at least on occasion, used coercive measures to prevent insistent immigrants from filing an official complaint, and, not infrequently, they have flatly refused to take complaints from legal residents and citizens.

110. See Immigration Law Enforcement Monitoring Project 1990: 33–34; Immigration Law Enforcement Monitoring Project 1992: 12, 45–46, 57–59; Americas Watch 1992: 2–3, 14–17.

111. Immigration Law Enforcement Monitoring Project 1992: 10. See also chapter 4 of this monograph.

112. INS official (anonymous), South Texas, interview with author, 25 October 1990. See also Senate Committee on Appropriations 1990b: 52–53. Here, a Border Patrol official from the Tucson sector echoes a similar statement.

113. On the propensity of police officers to use force against those they perceive as challenging their authority and against those categories of criminal suspects who symbolize a threat to the moral order of society, see Hunt 1985. (I thank Tracy Steele for sharing this article with me.)

114. These particular areas were identified in 1984 by a leading border-region federal drug enforcement official as the principal drug-smuggling zones on the border (Senate Committee on Appropriations 1990b: 45). Each of these, especially the El Paso and Brownsville areas, was also the site of significant levels of undocumented immigration.

I witnessed a high-anxiety instance with significant potential for rights abuses while accompanying several Border Patrol agents on night patrol near the Rio Grande, on the outskirts of a fairly densely populated area in South Texas on March 18, 1992. The agents had entered a zone where prepositioned electronic intrusion-detection ground sensors had indicated some sort of significant movement nearby. The agents were tense and had their guns drawn as they proceeded down a dark path in the woods to intercept whoever had set off the sensors. They expected to encounter drug smugglers trying to carry their loads across the river under the cover of darkness, because the area was known as a crossing point for drug traffickers on foot. They later acknowledged, however, that others besides drug smugglers, including undocumented immigrants, crossed there as well, although less frequently. No one appeared on this occasion, but the agents remained noticeably on edge for the remainder of their shift that night. While their anxiety and the subsequent precautions they took were certainly understandable, such a tense setting in the midst of darkness appeared rife with possibilities for mishap, perhaps tragic in nature. Moreover, the tension seemed to lead at least one of the agents to continue being noticeably more agitated than he had been earlier in the evening, as he acted much more aggressively than his colleagues did in handling an entirely separate, low-key immigration enforcement encounter shortly after the drug enforcement stakeout.

115. Border Patrol agent (anonymous), McAllen sector, interview with author, 26 October 1990.

116. Hernández 1990c. The quote is from a caption for a photo accompanying the story. I would like to thank Miriam Davidson for bringing to my attention and sharing copies of Rubén Hernández's informative articles from a series on drug enforcement measures in Southern Arizona (see references).

117. Hernández 1990d. House Committee on Appropriations 1989b: 1488.

118. Borden 1992d. Hernández 1992b. Two of the immigrants reported that they heard yelling and shots fired on them from a hill behind them. The shouts directed at the group were insults and a command to "drop the pot." At least one man was carrying a bag of belongings, which the agent mistook for a drug-laden pack. The shooting ended after one minute, during which the group dropped to the ground. Part of the group was then arrested by Border Patrol agents, while others (including the wounded man) got away but later turned themselves in to Border Patrol agents on a nearby road. The wounded man later said that he received no medical attention but was merely given some salve for his wound before being returned to the border and expelled.

119. McDonnell 1992a, 1992c, 1992d. Pedersen 1992b. I would like to thank Rubén Hernández for sharing his extensive clippings on the Elmer trial from the two Tucson daily newspapers.

120. Hernández 1992b. Borden 1992b. Brooks 1992a.

121. McDonnell 1992c.

122. Brooks 1992b. Hernández 1992a. Borden 1992a. Miranda's family maintained that he was crossing the border to obtain day labor in Tucson, as he had periodically done before. Border Patrol agents assumed that he was acting as a scout for drug smugglers waiting to cross the border. A coroner's report stated that traces of marijuana and cocaine were found in his blood, which does not in and of itself prove involvement in drug trafficking, although it was used to imply such during the trial.

123. Coile and Hernández 1992. Elmer was acquitted of second-degree murder, manslaughter, and obstruction of justice. The judge had previously dropped the first-degree murder charge.

124. Hernández 1992a.

125. Pedersen 1992b.

126. Coile and Hernández 1992.

127. Pedersen 1992a.

128. Borden 1992c. While one agent said that warning shots were the safest way to get drug couriers to drop their loads and flee, and thereby avoid a direct confrontation with smugglers, another agent quoted by Borden maintained that warning shots were dangerous because they can put agents "'in the wrong frame of mind' if they don't know where the shots are coming from." This danger was clearly illustrated in the Elmer case.

129. Borden 1992c, 1992d. Nathan 1993.

130. Immigration Law Enforcement Monitoring Project 1992: 14. Americas Watch 1992: 17. Both reports cite a September 1991 report by the Inspector General of the Department of Justice, entitled *Audit Report: Immigration and Naturalization Firearms Policy.*

131. House Committee on Foreign Affairs 1990a: 50–60. Miller and McDonnell 1990. The House document listed 34 shootings (in which 19 people were killed and 15 wounded) by the Border Patrol and its joint unit with the San Diego police in the 1986–1989 period, while Miller and McDonnell described four Border Patrol shootings (with one person killed and three wounded) in 1990. Both sources give details on the highly questionable circumstances under which some of these shootings took place.

132. McDonnell 1991a.

133. House Committee on Foreign Affairs 1990a: 29–30.

134. For detailed information on events related to the INS crackdown on political asylum seekers in the Lower Rio Grande Valley, congressional documents include House Committee on the Judiciary 1989a. Newsletters include *Proyecto Libertad* (by the group of the same name), Harlingen, Texas; *Rio Grande Defense Committee* (by the group of the same name), Harlingen, Texas; *BARCA* (by the Border Association for Refugees from Central America), McAllen, Texas. Academic studies and additional human rights advocacy sources include the U.S. Committee for Refugees 1989, Núñez and Nelson 1990, Koulish 1992, *The Border: United States and Mexico* 1989, *The Border: Immigration and Issues* 1990 (the last two are special issues of the periodical *¡Basta!*). Extensive, detailed coverage of the INS crackdown was also provided by the local, regional, and even national press during the first half of 1989 (especially in February and March) and early 1990. In particular, see articles in the *Brownsville Herald, McAllen Monitor, Valley Morning Star, Austin American-Statesman, Houston Chronicle, Houston Post, San Antonio Express-News, San Antonio Light,* and *Dallas Morning News,* as well as in the *New York Times, Washington Post,* and *Los Angeles Times.*

135. I wish to thank Rogelio Núñez, executive director of Proyecto Libertad, for providing me with a copy of this report. The plans outlined in it correspond almost entirely to reports from the press and refugee rights advocacy groups of what occurred during the period (see previous note).

136. U.S. Immigration and Naturalization Service 1989: 2.

137. U.S. Immigration and Naturalization Service 1989: 9–10. García 1989a.

138. U.S. Immigration and Naturalization Service 1989: 11.

139. U.S. Immigration and Naturalization Service 1989: 16–17. The dispatching of INS personnel to Mexico for intelligence gathering was apparently not unique to this case. Former Border Patrol agents from El Paso reported that Border Patrol agents periodically engaged in similar activities in the Mexican state of Chihuahua during the early and middle 1980s. See Salopek 1992.

140. U.S. Immigration and Naturalization Service 1989: 18.

141. At least six different detention facilities were used by the INS in the Valley during the 1989–1990 period. These included the INS detention center in Port Isabel; a Red Cross–run "soft" detention facility for families in Brownsville (which was eventually turned over to another private agency); a county juvenile detention center in Raymondville; two private-contract "soft" detention facilities for unaccompanied minors (one in Los Fresnos and one in Mission); and another "soft" detention facility for families in San Benito. (The last three were administered by the Texas Key Corporation.) Several of these "soft" detention facilities were still in use during the fall of 1990, though at a reduced level. Numerous people were also sent to detention facilities outside the Valley (in Laredo and El Paso, among other places). This conclusion is based on my April 1990 visit to two of the privately run detention centers, as well as interviews with local human rights advocates (particularly Rogelio Núñez, executive director of Proyecto Libertad in Harlingen) and an October 25, 1990, interview with South Texas INS officials. The Red Cross's involvement in detention is also discussed in Gentry 1989.

142. For an excellent overview of the problems and rights violations associated with the asylum application process in South Texas, see Koulish 1992. Much of his discussion centers on the 1989–1990 period. See also García 1989b, U.S. Committee for Refugees 1989.

143. Sister Norma Pimentel, director, Casa Romero, interview with author, 27 October 1990. Resident of Casa Romero (anonymous), interview with author, 27 October 1990. True 1990. Murray 1990. This was the first INS raid inside the shelter grounds since it opened in 1982. None of the 35 people arrested were from Iraq. Five were from India, 2 from Pakistan, and 24 of the remaining 28 were from Mexico and Central America. A number of people were roughed up during the raid, as 50 INS agents descended on the shelter grounds and chased down refugees, while a helicopter hovered closely overhead. Other agents secured the perimeter with weapons drawn. Several of these agents were armed with M-16 rifles and positioned near the back of the shelter grounds.

144. Núñez and Nelson (1990) discuss this crackdown and interpret it as a move on the part of the INS to counter unprecedented and growing public support in the Valley for Central American refugees who had been victimized by the arbitrarily shifting, visibly harsh INS policies that had left thousands trapped in the Valley, homeless and without assistance.

145. U.S. Immigration and Naturalization Service 1989: 17.

146. House Committee on Appropriations 1989b: 1500.

147. U.S. Committee for Refugees 1991: 2–4. "Operation Hold the Line" 1990. Both sources quote at length internal INS documents regarding collaboration between INS officials and various Mexican authorities. The first source also quotes the INS district director for Mexico City.

148. U.S. Committee for Refugees 1991: 1.

149. Sontag 1993.

150. U.S. Committee for Refugees 1991: 14–15.

151. U.S. Committee for Refugees 1991: 12. This practice was also confirmed for me in June 1990 by an anonymous informant from Austin, Texas. While he was traveling in northern Mexico during the previous spring, his bus was stopped in the middle of the night in a remote area, at what seemed to him to be a military checkpoint. Personnel dressed in camouflage and armed with high-powered rifles boarded the bus to search for drugs and also sought out Central American passengers, ostensibly to check their immigration documents. The Mexican consul in Tucson acknowledged in 1990 that the Mexican military sometimes assisted police by staffing the drug enforcement checkpoints (Hernández 1990d).

152. House Committee on Foreign Affairs 1990b (especially pages 6, 26, 36–37). See also Americas Watch 1990a, 1991b; U.S. Committee for Refugees 1991: 12–15.

153. Rotella 1992e. Scott 1992. Golden 1992. See also House Select Committee on Narcotics Abuse and Control 1991b: 29–30. This source provides INS testimony that alludes to an increase in Border Patrol collaboration with local Mexican law enforcement agencies on "unique border crime problems." On the widespread extortion of bribes from immigrants by Mexican police, see Mexican National Commission for Human Rights 1992: 36–48; Bustamante 1991.

154. Rotella 1992b, 1992c. The dramatic tactic of mass rushing through official ports of entry was apparently in part a response to stepped-up Border Patrol enforcement efforts between the ports of entry, including the newly constructed wall and increased patrolling.

155. For example, while accompanying two Border Patrol agents on March 18, 1992, I witnessed one instance of direct collaboration between two U.S. Border Patrol agents and a Matamoros mounted police agent. The reactions of both parties suggested that this was not the first such incident. The details of the incident are as follows. A group of four young men fled, swimming back across the river to Matamoros, from two Border Patrol agents who were chasing them.

They verbally taunted the Border Patrol agents, and one would-be crosser made an obscene gesture at them. The Border Patrol agents were quite upset about this and anxious to see him punished. So they called out to a nearby Matamoros mounted police agent to arrest the most insubordinate of the four border crossers, which the agent did with no hesitation. As he led away the disrespectful border crosser, the Border Patrol agents observed with satisfaction that the suspect was likely to be subjected to much harsher punishment by the Matamoros police than they themselves could have imposed upon him.

156. Firsthand observation, 4 July 1992. The wall consists of five feet of concrete topped by five feet of chain-link fence posted into the concrete. A truck route was also installed alongside the wall between the bridges, and extended several miles up the river toward an industrial park.

4. THE WAR ON DRUGS IN THE U.S.–MEXICO BORDER REGION, 1981–1992

1. See Craig 1989, Bagley 1992, Isenberg 1992.

2. For example, see Isikoff 1992.

3. Klare 1988: 72. Bagley 1992: 131.

4. There are, of course, various perspectives on whether or not the U.S. government's antidrug efforts in the U.S.–Mexico border region in the late 1980s and early 1990s constituted "border militarization." For example, Craig (1989) and Williams and Coronado (1994) do not think that the U.S.–Mexico border has been militarized, though they all recognize militarization as at least a potential danger. In contrast, Sandoval (1991a, 1991b), Ramos (1991), Barry, Browne, and Sims (1994), and Bagley (1992) all adopt, to varying degrees, the notion that the border has been militarized. This work presents this thesis more forcefully, probing the topic in greater depth, or at least in greater detail.

5. House Committee on Government Operations 1990: 5–6.

6. Senate Committee on the Judiciary 1991: 25–26. According to officials from the Office of National Drug Control Policy, total border antidrug funding figures presented here included the border-region-focused spending of a variety of federal agencies, including the U.S. Customs Service as well as the INS and its Border Patrol.

7. Carlson 1991: 92. The author cites the DEA figure from a briefing by the U.S. Army–U.S. Air Force Center for Low-Intensity Conflict, "Illicit Drugs and National Security: An Executive Summary of the Threat and a Rational Response" (undated).

8. House Committee on Appropriations 1990b: 1745, 1783–1784. This estimation of the methods of drug smuggling into the United States was provided by INS Commissioner Alan Nelson, citing the DEA's El Paso Intelligence Center. The DEA estimate reported by Commissioner Nelson is consistent with what several anonymous Border Patrol agents from the McAllen sector told me on

March 18, 1992. They said that they almost never seized any cocaine on their river-border linewatch patrols, which were a key element of their ongoing anti–drug smuggling efforts in the area. Rather, on these patrols between official ports of entry they caught only marijuana smugglers—and usually small-time ones at that, who (according to these agents) are the type of drug smuggler most likely to engage in shoot-outs with law enforcement agents. Meanwhile, the largest seizures of cocaine and drugs by the Border Patrol in this area of South Texas occurred at inland highway checkpoints and on special antismuggling operations that typically did not involve linewatch patrolling activities between official ports of entry.

9. While it is impossible to determine precisely the extent to which information is withheld regarding antidrug activities, there are indications of such practices, especially regarding specific details of the military's support for these efforts, because such information was considered to be sensitive for national security. Most obvious is the case in which Lieutenant General Dean Tice (director, DOD Task Force on Drug Enforcement) was specifically questioned in writing by several congressional committee members about various aspects of DOD support for drug-interdiction efforts; 11 of his responses were deleted from the public record (Senate Committee on Appropriations 1985: 33–37, 39, 41). (Four additional examples of deletions in congressional hearing records about military involvement in drug enforcement efforts can be found in House Committee on the Armed Services 1989a: 25; 1989b: 16.) In addition, congressional hearing records show that military witnesses preferred to divulge more specific as well as classified information about the armed services' antidrug efforts in closed "executive sessions" with congressional committee members, which kept the information out of the public record. See House Committee on Appropriations 1989a: 1; House Committee on Government Operations 1985: 187; House Committee on the Armed Services 1989b: 9, 20.

10. It is important to note that the text of the 1982 Defense Authorization Act does not specifically refer to or amend the text of the Posse Comitatus statute itself (which is section 1385 of Title 18 of *U.S. Code*). Rather, the relevant sections of the 1982 act amend substantially the area of U.S. law devoted specifically to military matters (Title 10 of *U.S. Code*). Nonetheless, the official legislative history of the 1982 DOD Authorization Act states that the new text was intended to address and modify the Posse Comitatus statute ("House Report 9771" 1982: 1785).

11. "House Report 97-71" 1982: 1786. The Air Force was added in an amendment in 1956. "Posse comitatus" literally means "power of the country," which was defined in common law as all persons over the age of 15 whom the sheriff could call upon for assistance in preventing any civil disorder. Prior to 1981, no one had been charged or prosecuted under the statute in the more than 100 years since its enactment. (Its passage was apparently bound up with the political strife during Reconstruction after the U.S. Civil War.) There had

been, however, some attempts to enforce the statute indirectly by defendants seeking to have government evidence or charges against them dropped because the Posse Comitatus statute had been violated by the government's activities. The most recent cases of this type arose from the Wounded Knee occupation and standoff there between the American Indian Movement (AIM) and the federal government ("House Report 97-71" 1982: 1787–1789).

12. For example, active-duty federal troops have been used to quell urban unrest only in a few cases in modern times, such as in Detroit in 1967 and, most recently, in Los Angeles in 1992. National Guard troops have been used far more frequently (see also note 21).

13. "Department of Defense Authorization Act, 1982": sec. 905. This new section was chapter 18, to be added as a rather lengthy amendment to Title 10 of *U.S. Code,* which deals with military matters under U.S. law. The new chapter contained eight new sections (371–378) to be added to Title 10. In addition, it should be noted that these new guidelines for military cooperation with civilian law enforcement agencies detailed in section 905 of the 1982 act were listed under Title IX of the bill, which was entitled "General Provisions"—hardly a drug enforcement–specific heading.

14. "Department of Defense Authorization Act, 1982": sec. 905 (new sections 372 and 374 of Title 10 of *U.S. Code*).

15. "Department of Defense Authorization Act, 1982": sec. 905 (new section 375 of Title 10 of *U.S. Code*). The only other serious restriction placed on military assistance to civilian police officials is that it not adversely affect military preparedness.

16. "Department of Defense Authorization Act, 1982": sec. 905 (new section 372 of Title 10 of *U.S. Code*).

17. "Department of Defense Authorization Act, 1982": sec. 905 (new section 371 of Title 10 of *U.S. Code*).

18. "Department of Defense Authorization Act, 1982": sec. 905 (new section 373 of Title 10 of *U.S. Code*).

19. "Department of Defense Authorization Act, 1982": sec. 905 (new section 374 of Title 10 of *U.S. Code*).

20. House Committee on Government Operations 1986a: 251; 1986b: 199–200.

21. Wolfe 1978: 102–103. Between 1919 and 1968 the National Guard was called out to put down civil unrest over 400 times, and was *not* called out in only 4 of the 51 years surveyed.

22. House Committee on Government Operations 1990: 9. However, it is important to note that these DOD regulations can be altered with much less public debate and disclosure than U.S. law.

23. House Committee on Government Operations 1986a: 199.

24. House Committee on Appropriations 1990a: 333.

25. House Committee on Government Operations 1983: 323–325.

26. House Committee on Government Operations 1985: 143–144, 238.

27. *Rand McNally* 1976. The breakdown by state of military bases located in the border region (within approximately 150 miles of the border) is as follows: 12 in California, 5 in Arizona, 1 in New Mexico, and 10 in Texas. This count does not include the various U.S. military-weapons testing grounds.

28. House Committee on Government Operations 1985: 242–243, 302–303.

29. House Committee on Government Operations 1986a: 215–216, 227; 1986b: 198–201.

30. House Committee on Government Operations 1983: 353.

31. House Committee on Government Operations 1985: 254.

32. This quotation is from the testimony of John W. Shannon, assistant secretary of the Army. House Committee on Government Operations 1986a: 214. See also House Committee on Government Operations 1983: 476.

33. House Committee on Government Operations 1986a: 215. Senate Committee on Appropriations 1986: 72. See also House Committee on Government Operations 1983: 475–476.

34. Carlson 1991: 92.

35. House Committee on Government Operations 1986a: 219.

36. U.S. General Accounting Office 1985.

37. Excerpts included in House Select Committee on Narcotics Abuse and Control 1990: 76.

38. House Select Committee on Narcotics Abuse and Control 1990: 77. Senate Committee on the Judiciary 1991: 26, 54. Hernández 1990a. The other four HIDTA-designated sites are New York City, Miami, Houston, and Los Angeles.

39. Senate Committee on Appropriations 1988: 260. Klare 1988: 72.

40. Senate Committee on Appropriations 1988: 260, 263.

41. House Select Committee on Narcotics Abuse and Control 1987a: 79.

42. House Select Committee on Narcotics Abuse and Control 1987a: 141.

43. Senate Committee on Appropriations 1988: 263. House Select Committee on Narcotics Abuse and Control 1987a: 158–166. The military support listed in the second source was not limited to Operation Alliance, but much of it focused on the U.S–Mexico border region, where Operation Alliance was the main coordinating body for military and law enforcement agency collaboration.

44. Senate Committee on Appropriations 1990b: 36.

45. House Select Committee on Narcotics Abuse and Control 1991c: 49.

46. Senate Committee on Appropriations 1990b: 36.

47. Senate Committee on Appropriations 1990b: 33.

48. It seems that the cross-designation (i.e., deputization) of Border Patrol agents as well as state and local police to enforce contraband and drug laws enabled those agents to conduct warrantless searches when such were allowed by federal drug and contraband law. Deputization thus extended the authority of local and state police to conduct warrantless searches in the border area, and it gave the Border Patrol three legal grounds (immigration, drugs, and contra-

band) rather than just one (immigration) to conduct warrantless searches. Such authority was apparently limited to the border or its "functional equivalent," with the latter term subject to varying interpretations by the courts (e.g., checkpoints not at but relatively near to the border—how near depending on the population density in the surrounding area). See Compton and Newland 1992; National Immigration Law Center 1989: chap. 4; Compton and Wells 1988.

49. Davidson 1991: 407. Davidson attributes this characterization of the border area to an unnamed University of Arizona law professor. Other legal advocates interviewed for this project characterized the area similarly.

50. Senate Committee on Appropriations 1988: 201.

51. Senate Committee on Appropriations 1990b: 37.

52. Senate Committee on Appropriations 1988: 188, 191. House Committee on Appropriations 1990a: 394, 401. The six aerostat radar balloons lent by the Air Force to the Customs Service were supposed to be capable of simultaneous air and ground detection. They were placed near Yuma and Fort Huachuca, Arizona; Deming, New Mexico; and Marfa, Eagle Pass, and Rio Grande City, Texas. Each could cover a radius of approximately 150 miles. There were many problems with the actual operation of the aerostats (which are discussed later).

53. Senate Committee on Appropriations 1990b: 48.

54. Senate Committee on Appropriations 1990b: 38.

55. Senate Committee on Appropriations 1988: 183–184, 263–264. Of the 1,500 or so federal law enforcement agents placed in the border region during 1986 and 1987, 974 were with the Customs Service (inspectors and special agents), 300 were with the Border Patrol, and 133 were with the DEA.

56. Senate Committee on Appropriations 1990b: 34, 37.

57. Senate Committee on Appropriations 1991: 49–56. This strategy-formulation process culminated in the Border State Seminar held in Austin, Texas, May 23–25, 1990, and attended by 250 to 300 representatives from the previously listed institutions.

58. Senate Committee on Appropriations 1991: 71.

59. House Committee on Appropriations 1990a: 334.

60. See House Committee on Government Operations 1988.

61. Several Customs Service agents in the Texas-Mexico border area interviewed by author, October 1990. All the persons interviewed wished to remain anonymous. They referred to their area as the "Khyber Pass" of drug trafficking on the border and specifically likened their situation to that of troops in the Vietnam War: agents in the field report on the very difficult situations they face and on their needs, but this less-than-optimistic information is filtered out by those higher up in the chain of command and by top officials in Washington who instead proclaim to the public and the press, "We're winning." The agents who were interviewed clearly felt that this was, at best, a misrepresentation of what was actually happening in the field.

62. Sablatura 1992.

63. Once again, it is important to note that none of the legal changes discussed in this section directly amended the Posse Comitatus statute (Title 18, section 1385 of *U.S. Code*). Rather, they amended sections of U.S. law on military matters (Title 10 of *U.S. Code*), especially those sections dealing with military support for civilian law enforcement. These changes tended to focus on military support for the drug enforcement activities of civilian police agencies. This move to involve the military in one area of domestic law enforcement, however, indirectly weakened the Posse Comitatus statute's restriction of such involvement in general.

64. "National Defense Authorization Act, Fiscal Year 1989": sec. 1104. This section was entitled "Enhanced Drug Interdiction and Law Enforcement Support by the Department of Defense," and it consisted of a newly revised chapter 18 of Title 10 of *U.S. Code,* which had previously been added by the 1982 DOD Authorization Act under the title of "Military Cooperation with Civilian Law Enforcement Officials," but which was now retitled in the 1989 DOD Authorization Act with a similarly general heading, "Military Support for Civilian Law Enforcement Agencies."

65. "National Defense Authorization Act, Fiscal Year 1989": sec. 1104 (new section 374 of Title 10 of *U.S. Code*).

66. "National Defense Authorization Act, Fiscal Year 1989": sec. 1104 (new section 374 of Title 10 of *U.S. Code*).

67. "National Defense Authorization Act, Fiscal Year 1989": sec. 1104 (new section 374 of Title 10 of *U.S. Code*).

68. "National Defense Authorization Act, Fiscal Year 1989": sec. 1104 (new section 371 of Title 10 of *U.S. Code*).

69. "National Defense Authorization Act, Fiscal Year 1989": sec. 1104 (new section 375 of Title 10 of *U.S. Code*).

70. House Committee on the Armed Services 1988: 70.

71. "National Defense Authorization Act, Fiscal Year 1989": secs. 1102, 1103.

72. "National Defense Authorization Act, Fiscal Year 1989": sec. 1105. It should be noted that the National Guard was instructed to participate in drug enforcement efforts while under state, not federal, authority and command. Hence the National Guard would technically not be subject to the Posse Comitatus statute and other restrictions on the use of federally commanded military troops in domestic civilian law enforcement efforts.

73. House Committee on the Armed Services 1989a: 18–19. The breakdown of this figure was as follows: $40 million for National Guard enhancement, $60 million for the C³I integration mission, $130 million for the procurement of mostly high-tech equipment (aerostat radar balloons, etc.), $56 million for management and operations, and $14 million for research and development.

74. Johnson 1988.

75. McDonnell 1988a. The INS later reversed its opposition to the military's involvement in border-region drug interdiction activities.

76. "National Defense Authorization Act for Fiscal Years 1990 and 1991": sec. 1206. Note that, like the 1982 and 1989 DOD authorization acts, this act did not specifically address the Posse Comitatus statute. However, unlike those two previous acts, it did not make significant revisions to the various sections of chapter 18 of Title 10 of *U.S. Code* that outlined the forms of military support for civilian law enforcement agencies in general (i.e., not solely limited to drug enforcement). Rather, the 1990–1991 act specified much more clearly that the new forms of military support to civilian police were to be directed to drug enforcement. The military was still allowed, however, to provide support for other types of civilian police efforts (especially customs and immigration) under the provisions of the previously revised chapter 18 of Title 10 of *U.S. Code.*

77. "National Defense Authorization Act for Fiscal Years 1990 and 1991": sec. 1208.

78. "National Defense Authorization Act for Fiscal Years 1990 and 1991": sec. 1201. The breakdown of the $450 million is as follows: $284 million for the Department of Defense's counterdrug activities (excluding those specified in this list), $70 million for the National Guard's counterdrug activities, $27 million to integrate the communication network of the command, control, communications, and intelligence assets devoted to drug interdiction, $28 million to research and development of technologies to aid drug interdiction, $1 million to the Civil Air Patrol to conduct drug surveillance flights, and $40 million in "other assistance."

79. Jehl and Healy 1989.

80. Like all of its predecessors discussed previously, the 1991 DOD Authorization Act did not specifically address the Posse Comitatus statute. Further, like the 1990–1991 act, it did not make specific amendments to chapter 18 of Title 10 of *U.S. Code* (which deals with military support for civilian law enforcement agencies in general—i.e., not limited solely to drug enforcement). Rather, like the 1990–1991 act, the 1991 act outlines additional types of military support specifically for the drug enforcement efforts of civilian police agencies. Still, these measures did continue the process of effectively lessening the restrictions contained in the Posse Comitatus statute.

81. This provision implies that the military had counterdrug expertise beyond that of civilian law enforcement agencies. Such an implication is curious, given that the military had entered the realm of drug enforcement only relatively recently, usually as a junior partner to far more experienced civilian agencies.

82. "National Defense Authorization Act for Fiscal Year 1991": sec. 1004. The ambiguity over whether military training exercises and operations could be conducted both within and outside the United States stems from the fact that this crucial detail is not specified in the law's text, which says only that these activities may be undertaken "for the purposes of aiding civilian law enforcement agencies." At the beginning of the section of the law containing this provision, it

is stated that the military could provide support for the drug enforcement efforts of any federal, state, local, or foreign police agency. Thus it seems that military exercises and operations could be conducted both within and outside the United States, given that various of these agencies' jurisdictions cover only domestic or foreign arenas (or both in some instances).

83. "National Defense Authorization Act for Fiscal Year 1991": sec. 1001. The $1.08 billion was divided four ways: $585.6 million for maintenance and operation, $345.3 for procurement (of equipment and supplies), 447.7 million for research and development, and $105.5 million for the National Guard's antidrug efforts (a 50% increase over the Guard's 1990 antidrug funding).

84. "National Defense Authorization Act for Fiscal Years 1992 and 1993": sec. 1088. "National Defense Authorization Act for Fiscal Year 1993": sec. 1041. These two laws largely reused and made only small amendments to the section of the 1991 Defense Authorization Act that had outlined various forms of additional military support for the counterdrug activities of civilian law enforcement agencies. Beyond this continuation, drug enforcement issues received little attention in the 1992–1993 and 1992 acts. Figures for the overall funding levels authorized for the military's various counterdrug activities were not given in either of the bills' texts, which only specified the funding for one category of such activities. However, the legislative histories of these laws report that the overall counterdrug funding for the military was $1.158 billion for fiscal year 1992 and $1.263 billion for fiscal year 1993 ("House Conference Report 102-311" 1992: 1165–1166; "House Report 102-527" 1993: 1714).

85. House Committee on the Armed Services 1992: 25–26.

86. Hernández 1990b.

87. House Committee on Government Operations 1990: 9–10. It is important to note that this passage did not appear to be advocating such measures nor did the tone of the report reflect the recent congressional clamoring for continually expanding the military's domestic drug enforcement authority. Rather, the report was on the whole a very sober and critical review of U.S. military involvement in drug enforcement activities.

88. House Committee on the Armed Services 1989a: 28.

89. House Committee on the Armed Services 1989b: 8.

90. However, special-forces units such as the Green Berets that are used more frequently in LIC projects receive training in how to make such distinctions and how to interact with civilian populations more effectively. Yet one of the main purposes of this is to maintain control over targeted civilian populations without frequently employing blatantly coercive measures. This ideal notwithstanding, the human rights record of such forces is far from clean, and in some cases is far worse than that of regular military forces (see chapter 1).

91. House Committee on the Armed Services 1992: 7, 12–16, 21–25, 55, 76. The $438.8 million reported for 1989 DOD antidrug spending exceeded the $300 million called for in the 1989 DOD Authorization Act.

92. House Committee on the Armed Services 1992: 3. This information (including the quotation) and that cited in the previous note comes from the testimony of Stephen M. Duncan, coordinator for Drug Enforcement Policy and Support, Department of Defense. For more information on the military's turn in late 1989 toward greater involvement in the War on Drugs at home and abroad, see Jehl and Healy 1989.

93. House Committee on Appropriations 1989a: 32–33; 1990a: 329–330, 337. House Committee on the Armed Services 1992: 21–24, 35. Senate Committee on Appropriations 1990a: 731.

94. House Committee on Appropriations 1990a: 337.

95. House Committee on Appropriations 1990a: 335, 338. House Committee on the Armed Services 1992: 49. Funding levels exceeded those called for in the DOD authorization acts for 1990 and 1991, outlined in the previous section.

96. House Committee on Appropriations 1990a: 410. The breakdown of 1990 National Guard funding for border states was as follows: Texas, $10.9 million; California, $7.99 million; Arizona, $2.3 million; and New Mexico, $654,000.

97. Meighan 1994. In addition to heading up the Texas National Guard's antidrug task force, the implicated officer was also the Texas National Guard's director of plans, operations, and training. And even after his security clearance had been revoked due to information that he was involved in drug trafficking, state Guard officials allowed him to be promoted and have access to classified military information.

98. House Select Committee on Narcotics Abuse and Control 1991b: 26–27. House Committee on the Armed Services 1992: 24. Rohter 1988. García 1989d. Senate Committee on Appropriations 1990b: 38, 41.

99. For example, see House Committee on Appropriations 1989a: 24. Here General Stephen Olmsted (USMC) commented, "None of us would like to see soldiers in for instance El Paso handcuffing citizens. That is typical of Nazi Germany and other countries we don't admire."

100. House Committee on the Armed Services 1992: 77.

101. Senate Committee on Appropriations 1991: 9–19. The Pima County (Tucson area) sheriff who addressed the committee also expressed a desire to "modify" current restrictions on military participation in domestic intelligence-gathering efforts (especially wiretap operations) that target individuals suspected of drug trafficking. Such efforts were under the direction of civilian law enforcement agencies.

102. House Select Committee on Narcotics Abuse and Control 1991a: 76. House Committee on Appropriations 1990a: 364–365. Jehl and Healy 1989.

103. House Committee on the Armed Services 1992: 2.

104. House Committee on Appropriations 1990a: 333.

105. House Committee on Government Operations 1990: 25.

106. Zanger 1990.

107. Senate Committee on Appropriations 1991: 58.

108. Department of Defense 1989: 304.

109. Jehl 1989. House Committee on the Armed Services 1990a: 13–14. Hernández 1990c. Johnson 1989. McDonnell 1989a.

110. Senate Committee on Appropriations 1990b: 38.

111. Reza and Frammolino 1988.

112. Jehl 1989. McDonnell 1989a. Davidson 1991. The helicopter crash occurred when it hit power lines as it was attempting to move in for a closer look at what appeared to be a suspicious-looking vehicle in a remote border area. The vehicle in fact turned out to be a Border Patrol vehicle.

113. McDonnell 1989a, 1989b. See also House Committee on the Armed Services 1990a: 13–14.

114. McDonnell 1988b.

115. Reza and Frammolino 1988.

116. McDonnell 1990c.

117. Johnson 1989.

118. Meighan 1994. This was the finding of an internal Texas National Guard investigation.

119. Reuter, Crawford, and Cave 1988: xiii. (The full text of the report is included in House Committee on the Armed Services 1988.)

120. Senate Committee on Appropriations 1990b: 45.

121. House Committee on Appropriations 1990b: 1796.

122. House Committee on the Armed Services 1992: 22–23.

123. Border Patrol agent (anonymous), McAllen sector, interview with author, 26 October 1990.

124. Hernández 1990c. The September 1990 joint operation was deemed a success in that it led to 100 drug seizures involving sizeable amounts of illegal drugs. This effort stands in stark contrast to a large-scale September 1987 joint surveillance and drug-interdiction effort (called Operation Autumn Harvest) conducted by the National Guard and the Customs Service in Arizona, which yielded no apprehensions or drug seizures (see U.S. General Accounting Office 1988).

125. Healy and Davis 1989.

126. Zanger 1990. Hernández 1990c. Trainor 1989. Davidson 1991. On other difficulties in Marine–Border Patrol collaboration, such as mutual unfamiliarity as well as turf disputes, see House Select Committee on Narcotics Abuse and Control 1991a: 77.

127. Zamichow 1990. (I thank Gilberto Cárdenas for bringing this article to my attention.) See also Johnson 1990. Johnson mentions the Border Patrol exercise as an example of the use of DOD drones in civilian law enforcement activities. One evaluator of the Pentagon's use of drones noted that they are "equivalent to having a police officer 500 feet above the ground with a pair of binoculars." (I thank Gideon Sjoberg for bringing this article to my attention.)

On a related note, the drone technology used in the joint Marine–Border Patrol exercise in the Laredo sector has been considered for law enforcement activities in urban areas across the country. This case is an ominous example of how military-related law enforcement programs can be transferred from the border to the rest of the nation. It holds some disturbing implications for the status of civil rights in the United States as a whole.

128. Hernández 1992c. Of special interest to this study is that the Marine commanding officer on the scene linked his unit's reconnaissance training on the border to the U.S. military's larger efforts to be prepared to fight "little wars" in various "political hot spots" around the world, which is a clear characterization of a central form of low-intensity conflict.

129. Davidson 1991: 407.

130. Hernández 1990d.

131. Rohter 1990. Healy and Davis 1989. JTF-6 was reportedly originally devised and proposed by Army General Colin Powell, who was chairman of the Joint Chiefs of Staff during the Bush administration.

132. U.S. Army, Corps of Engineers 1994: 1-1, 1-2. I would like to especially thank María Jiménez for referring me to this exceptional and obscure document. She brought many other valuable sources to my attention—so many that I could not count them or adequately acknowledge all the ones I've used—but the document cited here was the most extraordinary.

133. Pentagon statement quoted in Mathews 1989.

134. Pentagon statement quoted in Mathews 1989.

135. Senate Committee on Appropriations 1991: 57.

136. Jehl and Healy 1989.

137. Senate Committee on Appropriations 1990a: 731–734. Zanger 1990. Conley 1990.

138. As quoted in Conley 1990.

139. U.S. Army, Corps of Engineers 1994: 4-2.

140. U.S. Army, Corps of Engineers 1994: 1-6.

141. U.S. Army, Corps of Engineers 1994: 1-8, 1-12, 1-13, 4-2.

142. U.S. Army, Corps of Engineers 1994: 1-18, 4-2.

143. U.S. Army, Corps of Engineers 1994: 1-13, 1-14, 1-15, 1-16, 4-2, 4-5. With only one exception, the information listed here for engineering activities was not divided by year in the document. Hence the information covers the entire 1990–1993 period surveyed in the document, rather than solely the 1990–1992 period .

144. Davidson 1991: 406.

145. Hernández 1992c.

146. Senate Committee on Appropriations 1990a: 737. Conley 1990.

147. Hernández 1990c.

148. As quoted in Hernández 1990c.

149. Senate Committee on Appropriations 1991: 60.

150. The larger purpose and effectiveness of Mexican drug-crop eradication programs are subject to debate. See Ruiz-Cabañas I. 1992; Craig 1989; Scott and Marshall 1991: 33–42. The first source uncritically presents some of the Mexican government's data on large-scale eradication, taking the government's reports of success at face value. The second source is somewhat less sanguine, but still relatively optimistic about the success of those efforts, while the third considers them a sham. Further, the last two sources both point out (with different degrees of emphasis) that the eradication programs provided the Mexican military and security forces with a cover for conducting operations in the countryside against antigovernment elements and fledgling guerrilla movements.

151. On the contentiousness of drug issues in U.S.–Mexico relations during the mid-1980s, see González González 1989; Craig 1989: 80–86; Toro 1990. The precipitating incident was the torture and execution of a U.S. DEA agent in Mexico in February 1985. Many critics of U.S. policy toward Mexico viewed the U.S. government's pressuring of the Mexican government on the DEA agent's killing and other drug issues as a means of punishing Mexico for other policies with which the United States disagreed, such as promoting peace negotiations in Central America.

152. See Ramos 1991: 99.

153. See "Washington's Aid Programs to Mexico" 1991.

154. House Select Committee on Narcotics Abuse and Control 1991d: 12. Jehl and Miller 1990. Miller and Jehl 1990. Miller 1992b. "Washington's Aid Programs to Mexico" 1991: 4–5. However, it should be noted that Mexican participation in binational collaborative drug-interdiction efforts was officially halted in protest for one day in June of 1992, due to the controversy surrounding the U.S. Supreme Court's decision that it was legal for the U.S. to have kidnapped a Mexican suspect (in the case of the murder of the U.S. DEA agent) in Mexico to bring him to the United States for trial.

155. House Select Committee on Narcotics Abuse and Control 1991a: 91. House Committee on the Armed Services 1992: 52–53.

156. House Select Committee on Narcotics Abuse and Control 1991d: 14.

157. Miller and Jehl 1990.

158. Noble 1992.

5. CONCLUSION

1. For example, in Somalia during 1993, dispatching U.S. military troops to help provide humanitarian aid led within nine months to their involvement in the violent suppression of civil unrest and deadly manhunt operations. A much less severe, prospective instance of "creeping militarization" in the border region occurred when the use of the military in antidrug efforts in that area was cited by Senator Barbara Boxer in 1993 as a model and precedent for her proposal to use the military in immigration enforcement in the border region.

2. Much of this conclusion was reached by identifying those enforcement measures employed by civilian law enforcement agencies in the border region that are analogous to measures advocated in LIC doctrine. However, LIC doctrine is also directly applicable in the case of the military's involvement in anti-drug efforts, as these are a specific mission area of the doctrine. In this latter case, militarization takes on a literal sense.

3. As noted in chapter 1, thus far only a few observers (Sandoval 1991a, 1991b; Ramos 1991; Barry, Browne, and Sims 1994; Bagley 1992; Calavita 1989; Bustamante 1990, 1992b) have recognized or discussed even briefly the implications of the militarization of the U.S.–Mexico border. In a distinct yet related approach, Williams and Coronado (1994) reject the characterization of border enforcement efforts as a form of militarization, but they recognize and analyze the "hardening" of the U.S.–Mexico border region.

4. It should be noted that my interpretations of border militarization go against the current of more mainstream contemporary interpretations of the nature of the U.S.–Mexico border region and of the changing roles of borders more generally. For example, see Herzog 1990, 1992. Herzog, a leading scholar of the U.S.–Mexico border, views border areas as generally becoming demilitarized as well as key sites of economic development in the world economic system. He sees the U.S.–Mexico border as a prototype of the new, more internationally integrating (rather than separating) role toward which border areas around the world are evolving. Border enforcement measures of almost any type are almost entirely absent from his interpretations, except to the extent that he proposes that the role of international boundaries as barriers is diminishing in general. Herzog apparently does not consider the possibility that growing international economic integration in border areas and the development of more restrictive border enforcement measures are not necessarily mutually exclusive phenomena, or that borders may be used simultaneously as gateways in some matters (e.g., trade and investment) and barriers in others (e.g., immigration).

5. In a similar vein, Herzog states of the U.S.–Mexico border that its "most profound meaning is that it continues to divide a Third World nation from a First World one" (1990: 252).

6. For instance, as noted previously, Ramos offers one interpretation in a similar yet more specific sense, proposing that the use of the U.S. military in civilian drug enforcement efforts in the U.S.–Mexico border region could be interpreted as a form of pressure on the Mexican government to accept bilateral accords on expanded cooperation between the two countries in antidrug operations (1991: 99).

7. Sklair 1993: 54, 63, 68, 241. The number of maquiladoras and maquiladora workers has increased dramatically over the years—from 72 plants with 4,000 employees in 1967 (two years after the maquiladora sector was established), to 585 plants with 127,048 employees in 1982, to 2,042 plants with 486,210 employees in 1992.

8. Sklair discusses the lack of domestic economic linkages, the mixed (less than positive) working conditions (including wages), and the substantial environmental problems in the maquiladora sector (1993: 197–202, 213–223, 244, 249–255). Wilson found that maquiladora operations generally have few linkages to the Mexican economy, and that the new maquiladoras using cutting-edge, "flexible production" techniques have even fewer linkages than do more "traditional" maquiladoras, while wages and opportunities for workers also tend to remain low in the new maquiladoras (1992: 48–49, 62–69, 71). On the lack of worker rights in the maquiladora sector, see La Botz 1992: chap. 7. For a detailed examination of environmental problems associated with the maquiladora sector, see Texas Center for Policy Studies 1990. It should be noted that Jorge Carrillo (of the prestigious Colegio de la Frontera Norte) is perhaps the leading researcher on the maquiladora sector; his work is heavily cited in the first three sources listed above. Unfortunately, his relevant work was unavailable to this author.

9. Russell 1994: 219–220. Russell notes that foreign private investment in Mexico jumped from $3 billion in 1989 to $12.8 billion in 1991, with 66.9% of that $12.8 billion coming from the United States.

10. Russell 1994: 162–163. From 1976 to 1982, Mexico's foreign debt more than doubled to $87 billion, as foreign bankers freely provided new loans to the Mexican government, largely on the basis of its oil reserves. However, from 1982 to 1988, while struggling under increasing interest rates and sharply declining oil prices, Mexico received few new loans, and its repayment of interest and principal exceeded total new loans by $48.53 billion.

11. Donato and Massey 1993: 539. Cornelius 1992a: 184–185.

12. Sklair 1993: 72, 213–214, 249–250. La Botz 1992. These authors detail the low wages and restricted labor rights of Mexican workers.

13. Hinojosa Ojeda and McCleery propose that U.S. immigration restrictions on Mexican laborers help, in theory, to protect Mexican capitalists from competition with the United States (capitalist employers, presumably). See Hinojosa Ojeda and McCleery 1992: 132, 134–135. A logical modification of this proposition would be that restrictive U.S. immigration enforcement generally benefits owners (whether Mexican or foreign) of firms located in Mexico, because it helps lessen the pressure on employers to pay higher wages to Mexican workers that would otherwise be necessary in order to offset the attraction of better-paying work in the United States. In a related vein, Wilson notes that two coping strategies for Mexican workers in the face of declining real wages in the 1980s (which dropped some 40% to 50% after 1982) were to withdraw from the formal labor force, and to either work in the burgeoning informal sector in Mexico or migrate to the United States (1992: 34). Hence, it seems that making the migration option less attractive through restrictive U.S. immigration enforcement during the period would have been of some benefit to the managers and owners of maquiladoras and other business operations located in Mexico.

(Wilson does not draw this conclusion herself, as she turns her attention away from the migration issue, focusing instead on the shifting of workers from the formal labor force to the informal sector as a latent threat to maquiladoras.)

14. For an insightful discussion of the links between U.S. foreign policy toward Latin America and U.S. immigration policy, see Domínguez 1990. Domínguez proposes that the relationship between the two policy realms was somewhat contradictory, with immigration-policy considerations sometimes prevailing over foreign-policy priorities, and vice versa. While agreeing that some contradictions were indeed present, I would argue that there was substantial continuity and overlap between U.S. policy toward Central America and U.S. immigration enforcement efforts along the U.S.–Mexico border directed against Central American refugees and immigrants. (Dewind [1990] makes a similar case regarding U.S. foreign policy toward Haiti and U.S. immigration policy toward Haitian refugees.) These policies and practices are viewed here not so much in terms of nation-state relations, but rather primarily as U.S. government measures against targeted civilian populations from particular countries. For example, the U.S. government actively supported the Salvadoran government and, to a lesser extent, the Guatemalan government throughout the 1980s in their campaigns of extreme violence against leftist insurgent guerrilla movements and their perceived bases of civilian support. Meanwhile, during the same period the U.S. government sought to exclude and deport refugees from Guatemala and El Salvador.

15. It is important to point out, however, that although both the Reagan and Bush administrations generally sought to impose U.S. dominion over Central America, there were important differences between the policies of the two administrations toward the region. For example, forcefully "drawing the line" against the "communist threat" in the region was a very high priority (if not an obsession) for the Reagan administration. In contrast, the Bush administration was less obsessed with maintaining U.S. domination over Central America, particularly through military means. Yet it nonetheless advanced this goal, most notably through the invasion of Panama in 1989 and the backing of successful efforts to defeat the Sandinista government in the 1990 Nicaraguan elections. However, the free-trade agreement with Mexico and the promotion of hemispheric free trade were much higher priorities in the Bush administration's policy toward Latin America.

16. This interpretation coincides in large part with that of Sandoval (1991a), who proposes that border militarization by U.S. agencies represented an attempt to reassert U.S. control (on both sides of the border) over a region that had become increasingly strategic economically. The present work extends this proposition by incorporating into the analysis the issue of potential instability in the region.

17. Herzog 1990: 28, 48–55, 163–169; 1992: 9–12. On the exceptional population growth in the border region, particularly on the Mexican side of the

border, see also Zenteno Quintero and Cruz Piñeiro 1992, Ham-Chande and Weeks 1992.

18. For examples of U.S. border cities whose economic well-being depends increasingly on that of their Mexican counterparts, see Barry, Browne, and Sims 1994: chap. 7; Herzog 1990: 55–60, 144–155.

19. For example, one particularly detailed agenda of infrastructure needs that emphasized social projects called for some $20 billion to be spent in new social and economic infrastructure on both sides of the border (Latino Summit on NAFTA 1993: 5–7). During the NAFTA debate the need for infrastructure improvements in the border area was promoted by a variety of border-region advocates. This position gained widespread acceptance. However, there were substantial differences over whether to give greater emphasis to principally economic projects (e.g., roads, bridges, and ports of entry) or social projects, and over how to reconcile the need for both (Barry, Browne, and Sims 1994: 111–119).

20. For a discussion of the comparatively low levels of public services in northern border cities versus the main interior cities in Mexico, see Guillén López 1990. On the inadequate living conditions of maquiladora workers in two border cities, see Sánchez Rodríguez 1990. In contrast, average income levels in three of the four major northern border cities (Tijuana, Ciudad Juárez, and Matamoros, but not Nuevo Laredo) were higher than in the three main urban centers in the interior (Mexico City, Monterrey, and Guadalajara), though there was considerable variation among the four border cities themselves (Browning and Zenteno Quintero 1993: 25).

21. Barry, Browne, and Sims 1994: 16–17. Sklair 1993: 214, 251.

22. See Maril 1989: 7, 11; Aguilar 1991: 5–9. For a more general overview of poverty in the U.S. border region as of 1980, see Stoddard and Hedderson 1987: 22, 56, 58, 63.

23. Barry, Browne, and Sims 1994: 15.

24. Herzog 1990: 180–184.

25. For example, in the fall of 1992 two serious disturbances took place in Mexican border cities adjacent to Texas. The first was a protest of fraud in state and municipal elections in the state of Tamaulipas. Angry protesters stormed, sacked, and burned an election office in Matamoros (Owen and True 1992). The second was a protest turned riot that included the sacking and burning of Mexican customs offices at two international bridge ports of entry in Nuevo Laredo. These latter events were sparked by frustration at a Mexican law that limited border residents' duty-free importation of American goods to just $50-worth each per day (Kleist 1992).

26. On U.S. security concerns regarding Mexico, see Aguayo Quezada 1988, 1989; Aguilar Zinser 1990: 307–311. For details of the 1988 electoral fraud, see Bartra 1990; 1993: 158–164.

27. One key expression of this hostility was a lengthy campaign in north San Diego County to remove Latino immigrant workers living in camps and shanties in the hills and fields near wealthy Anglo neighborhoods. (See Chávez 1992: chaps. 5, 6; Cornelius 1992a: 189.) Other, more openly racist expressions of Anglo hostility toward undocumented Latino immigrants included the nativist "Light up the Border" movement, as well as a growing incidence of shootings, physical assaults, and threatening harassment of Latino immigrants. See Davidson 1990; House Committee on Foreign Affairs 1990a; California Legislature 1990.

28. While the implications of NAFTA for drug enforcement are not addressed here, it is important to note that some U.S. authorities have expressed concern that the flow of illegal drugs into the United States may increase under NAFTA and the less restricted flow of commercial goods that it allows. Ramos (1995) has conducted an in-depth investigation and analysis of the relationship and tensions between U.S. antidrug and commercial customs policies in the U.S.–Mexico border region and their impact on Mexico.

29. See House Committee on the Judiciary 1994, House Committee on Foreign Affairs 1990c, Cornelius 1992b, Cornelius and Martin 1993, Weintraub 1992. These sources, while largely ignoring border-region enforcement issues, present favorable analyses of NAFTA as likely to reduce undocumented immigration flows over time. It should be pointed out, though, that immigration enforcement got some consideration in several critical discussions of NAFTA by those advocating greater freedom of mobility for labor and the protection of immigrants' rights (see Castañeda and Alarcón 1991, 1992; Jiménez 1991; Schey 1992). However, probably more widespread in anti-NAFTA circles was the view that immigration enforcement should be increased, as strongly implied by Marshall (1993: 16–17). (In fairness, it should be noted that Marshall also advocates far greater protections of immigrant workers in the United States from extreme exploitation, and throughout the same chapter he strongly advocates protecting and advancing the rights of workers more generally in both Mexico and the United States.)

30. In contrast, the noted free-trade scholar Sidney Weintraub explicitly presents NAFTA and "militarizing the border" as opposing options for reducing undocumented immigration from Mexico (House Committee on the Judiciary 1994: 178–179). He obviously favors free trade as the solution, and considers the two options to be mutually exclusive.

31. See Galbraith 1992–93, 1993; Baker 1991: 8–9.

32. See Galbraith 1992–93, 1993; Baker 1991: 8–9; Reynolds and Wagner 1990: 207–208. House Committee on Ways and Means 1990: 101, 138, 141. Weintraub 1990: 15–19, 65, 207. Of particular note, Galbraith reports that the Bush administration's national security and diplomatic leaders approved NAFTA before consulting with the administration's economists (1992–93: 324).

This suggests that the Bush administration viewed the agreement first as an issue of security and diplomacy and second as one of economic policy.

33. Bustamante 1990: 343, 353–363; 1992b: 31–40. Three of the four scenarios outlined by Bustamante involve the implementation of substantially expanded and coercive border-region enforcement measures by either U.S. or Mexican authorities. In these three negative-outcome scenarios, either Mexican political stability decreases markedly, the U.S. economy goes into a recession, or—in the worst case—both phenomena occur.

34. Jiménez 1991. Castañeda and Alarcón 1991, 1992. Schey 1991. Bustamante 1992c.

35. House Committee on the Judiciary 1994: 293–316. This section contains excerpts from the immigration provisions of NAFTA. It should be noted that the provisions do refer to a variety of professional occupations, and not just to business occupations. In addition, one potentially large loophole in the provisions, which could facilitate the cross-border movement of lower-level workers, is the allowance made for "transportation operators," which apparently includes truck drivers, among others.

36. For example, see House Committee on Foreign Affairs 1990c: 13; Cornelius 1992b. See also House Committee on the Judiciary 1994, especially pages 178–183, 141–150.

37. See Cornelius 1992b; Cornelius and Martin 1993; Hinojosa Ojeda and McCleery 1992: 138–139. However, it should be noted that Hinojosa Ojeda later largely abandoned his forecast of substantial migration flows due to the restructuring of the rural economy, because of the introduction of what he saw as significant measures to assist small-scale agricultural producers (House Committee on the Judiciary 1994: 256–257). See also Conroy and Glasmeier 1992–93: 19. While Conroy and Glasmeier do not directly address immigration issues, they predict that wages for urban Mexican workers may decline due to a large influx of rural dwellers displaced by the restructuring of the rural economy. This would seem likely to provide Mexican workers with a greater incentive to migrate to the United States. This conclusion was shared by a variety of observers, including the immigration scholar Doris Meissner, in a report she wrote before she became the commissioner of the INS in late 1993. See Mead 1993.

38. Wilson 1991; 1992: 13–14, 22–23, 27, 29–30, 34. Wilson emphasizes the importance of state intervention in "disciplining labor" and maintaining its low cost in the success of export-oriented industrialization strategies in East Asian countries (all of which were authoritarian police states for extended periods of time during the era in which they implemented these strategies). Further, she lists such measures among the "policy implications" for Mexico if it wishes to replicate the East Asian nations' economic success. She describes Mexico's "social relations" under the Import Substitution Industrialization model—which was characterized by redistributive demands from the middle class, unionized urban workers, and other popular sectors—as "a detrimental legacy" that

should be overcome (1991: 80, 94; 1992: 14, 27). (See also Sánchez Otero 1993: 18.) There is ample evidence that the Mexican government already permits a substantial level of coercive disciplinary action against laborers, and indeed itself engages in such action. See La Botz 1992.

39. See Conroy and Glasmeier 1992–93; Hinojosa Ojeda and McCleery 1992; Fernández de Castro, Verea Campos, and Weintraub 1993; Russell 1994: 354–356.

40. For a discussion of the complexity of the rebellion and its underlying context, see Davis 1992b, Kwong 1992, Jones 1992, Hazen 1992.

41. Jehl and Broder 1992. "Dispatched to Duty" 1992.

42. McDonnell 1992b, 1992e. Within two weeks after the riots, more than 700 undocumented immigrants were returned to Mexico and Central America. Many more were never formally charged with a crime and instead were reportedly pressured by INS agents into signing voluntary departure forms.

43. For an excellent overview of the militarization of Los Angeles police activities in recent years, especially its antigang and antidrug efforts, see Davis 1992a: chap. 5. See also McNamara 1992, King 1992, Cooper 1992. In addition, for details on the release of a report by Amnesty International on the actions of both the Los Angeles Police Department and the Los Angeles County Sheriff's Department, see Murphy 1992. Amnesty International accused both units of violating international standards of human rights through a pattern of unchecked excessive force that was aimed overwhelmingly at African Americans and Latinos. This report was Amnesty International's strongest indictment to date of alleged police brutality in the United States, and its first report ever to focus specifically on regional law enforcement efforts in the United States.

EPILOGUE

1. This tendency is reflected, among other places, in the recently passed crime bill, which included a series of immigration enforcement measures. See "Violent Crime Control and Law Enforcement Act of 1994": secs. 130001–130010 (all contained under "Title XIII—Criminal Aliens and Immigration Enforcement").

2. Congressional appropriations for the INS increased some 9.4% from 1992 through 1994 (an estimated 19.6% through 1995), reaching $1.051 billion in 1994 (House Committee on Appropriations 1993: 13; 1994b: 242). Note that this does not include some $600 million in expected fee-generated income or additional funds from the recently passed 1994 crime bill.

3. House Committee on Government Operations 1993a, 1993c. McDonnell and Rotella 1993b. Americas Watch 1993. Flynn and Brock 1994. McDonnell 1994. "Border Agent Pleads No Contest" 1994. Brinkley 1994. Koulish et al. 1994. This is by no means a complete listing of all the reports of INS mismanagement and misconduct over the past two years.

4. Bean et al. 1994. Fried 1994. Rotella 1994a. Gross 1994. Power 1994. "INS to Beef Up Presence" 1994. "Bloquea EU la frontera" 1994.

5. Advanced Systems Integration Department 1993. This department is part of Sandia National Laboratories in New Mexico, one of the leading military research institutions in the United States.

6. One of the most frequently cited reasons for the popularity of the blockades and walls is their perceived effect of reducing crime in U.S. border communities. However, in El Paso, the strength of the relationship between the blockade and lower crime rates (especially among more serious crimes) appears to be substantially less than is widely thought (Bean et al. 1994: 91–104).

7. See Vila (1994a; 1994b: 239–259) for an innovative analysis of the process of identity formation among Mexican Americans, Anglos in El Paso, and Mexicans in Ciudad Juárez. One of Vila's central points is that Mexican Americans on the border often strive to strongly differentiate themselves from Mexicans. The El Paso blockade appears to have greatly expanded opportunities for this sort of differentiation, as Border Patrol enforcement efforts no longer target Mexican Americans as suspected undocumented immigrants. The Border Patrol has largely eschewed random surveillance patrols in Mexican American neighborhoods and has instead focused its immigration enforcement efforts immediately on the border, literally facing Mexican would-be undocumented immigrants.

8. On the El Paso case, see Fried 1994, Nathan 1994. In San Diego, nationalist tensions were already greatly heightened by other political factors, especially the inflammatory anti-immigrant rhetoric of governor Wilson, as well as the campaign for and passage of Proposition 187.

9. See Bean et al. 1994.

10. Rotella 1994c.

11. Bean et al. 1994: 131–135.

12. Suzan Kern, Border Rights Coalition, El Paso, Texas, personal communication, 23 January 1995.

13. Rotella 1994b, 1994c. Also, in a mid-January 1995 meeting, border human rights activists from San Diego reported that they had received a greatly increased number of allegations of abuse by Border Patrol agents since the beginning of Operation Blockade. (I thank Suzan Kern for sharing this information.)

14. Sahagún 1994. Cleeland 1994.

15. House Committee on Appropriations 1993: 13; 1994b: 242, 433. Martin 1994. The number of Border Patrol positions funded by Congress rose by 486 from 1992 to 1994 (and increased by another 700 for fiscal year 1995), bringing the total number of positions funded to 5,434 in 1994 (and an estimated 6,134 in 1995), while congressional funding for the Border Patrol rose to $399.3 million in 1994 (a 23% increase from 1992 funding levels). In addition, the INS plans to expand its blockade operations in 1995, to that end reassigning 510 Border Patrol agents from support positions to line duty on the border. The new and reassigned agents will be aided by additional border fencing and lighting,

new communication and surveillance equipment, and a variety of other force-multiplying, high-tech equipment. Overall, it should be noted that with these additions in 1993 and 1994, since 1978 congressionally appropriated funding (in unadjusted dollars) for the Border Patrol shot up 411%, while authorized staffing levels grew 111% by 1994.

16. Ostrow 1994.

17. See Boxer 1993, Sandalow 1993, Green 1994. (I thank Martín Rocha for providing the Boxer document.)

18. See House Committee on Appropriations 1994a; House Committee on the Armed Services 1994a, 1994b; Senate Committee on the Judiciary 1994. Although the Clinton administration has increased resources for demand-reduction measures (such as drug treatment and education), overall antidrug funding for supply-reduction, law enforcement–oriented efforts has remained relatively constant. However, funding specifically for the military's antidrug efforts fell approximately one quarter from 1992 through 1994, and was scheduled to remain at that level in 1995. The main area of cutback was random air and sea patrolling. However, the level of funds devoted to military (including the National Guard) support activities for law enforcement agencies was relatively unchanged and remained the largest single portion of the military's antidrug efforts. Also, it should be noted that the military's border region antidrug group, Joint Task Force 6, conducted 485 missions in 1993 to support civilian law enforcement agencies, a slight increase over 1992 (U.S. Army, Corps of Engineers 1994: 4-2). Joint Task Force 6 continued its efforts in 1994, though reportedly at a somewhat reduced level; details are not currently available.

19. Marelius 1994. Military participation in immigration enforcement was the topic of an April 29, 1994, letter from Goveror Wilson to Gustavo de la Viña and Johnny Williams (Chief Border Patrol Agents of the San Diego and El Centro Border Patrol sectors, respectively). Governor Wilson sought to raise the number of California National Guard personnel aiding the Border Patrol from 47 to 177. Of these Guard troops, he proposed that 50 be funded by state funds (thereby avoiding federal restrictions on the scope of their activities) and be devoted specifically to immigration enforcement support roles, serving as drivers, translators, mechanics, camera surveillance operators, etc. (It is unclear if Wilson secured state funding for these efforts and whether or not they were actually implemented.) Meanwhile the other 127 Guard troops were to be federally funded and deployed to aid the Border Patrol's antidrug efforts. Further, an additional 83 National Guard personnel were already detailed to the U.S. Customs Service to provide inspections support at five border ports of entry. (It seems that Wilson's expansion effort was to result in a total of 260 California National Guard troops being deployed on the border in a variety of capacities.)

20. Stern 1994. Bunting 1994. Nonetheless, INS Commissioner Doris Meissner also reportedly said in her confirmation hearings before the Senate in the fall of 1993 that military units "will continue" to be used in a support role

(mainly to detect undocumented immigrants) in aid of INS immigration enforcement efforts (Jackson 1993). It should be noted, however, that Meissner's comments were made when Senator Boxer of California was actively promoting her proposal in the Senate to formally authorize the National Guard to assist the INS in immigration enforcement activities.

21. Shogren 1994. Incoming house speaker Gingrich proposed to "seal off" the border by expanding the Border Patrol to 10,000 agents. Such an expansion was provided for in the 1994 crime bill, which authorized the expansion of the Border patrol by 4,000 agents over the next four years ("Violent Crime Control and Law Enforcement Act of 1994": sec. 130006). The funding of such an expansion is far from certain, however.

APPENDIX 4

1. This position on the interrelatedness and intersection of theory and methods (and data) is advanced by Sjoberg et al. 1991: 29.

2. On state repression in the history of the United States, see Rogin 1984 and Wolfe 1978, among others.

3. Marcuse 1964: xii, xv, 3, 7, 9. It is important to point out that for Marcuse the term "advanced industrial society" refers to highly developed nations both capitalist and communist (the latter being the Soviet Union). Thus, his conceptualization of repression cuts broadly across the two competing formal ideologies of his day.

4. Marcuse 1964: 51–52.

5. Oppenheimer and Canning 1978–79: 22. Their point about the search for and creation of enemies other than communism is particularly relevant in the post–Cold War era, as the United States has lost its monolithic, totalizing "enemy," and its massive military-security apparatus is in need of new enemies and looming threats to justify its existence.

6. Oppenheimer and Canning 1978–79: 24, 27. They list numerous other indicators as well, many of which are tied to the social-welfare system.

7. West German state-security authorities may have chosen to use their border police against domestic political demonstrations because they viewed domestic leftist opposition movements as linked to the broader external security threat of communism on the other side of the Iron Curtain. A general theoretical point arising from this scenario is that wide-ranging uses of border police are more likely in settings where authorities perceive the containment of nearby foreign threats and the containment of domestic opposition as related efforts.

8. Marcuse 1971–72: 2.

9. Marcuse 1971–72: 6. On the development of the "underclass," see Wilson 1987, 1989. The term "underclass" was developed principally in reference to inner-city, poor African Americans.

10. Oppenheimer and Canning 1978–79: 4, 20–21.

11. Sjoberg and Vaughan 1993: 144–149. For a more general critique of the bureaucratization of society as having a negative impact on freedom and democracy, see Mills 1959: 165–176.

12. Wolfe 1978: xiii.

13. Wolfe 1978: 22.

14. Wolfe 1978: 9–13.

15. Wolfe 1978: 15.

16. Reich 1991: 3–9, 81–84, 114, 132–135, 198–209, 221.

17. Harvey 1989: 147, 150, 159, 179–180, 182–183, 186–187.

18. For example, in her overview of the globalization of the assembly industry and the rise of the "flexible production" strategy, Wilson certainly implies that coercive labor discipline measures are of central importance to this phenomenon. Specifically, Wilson identifies "the 'disciplining' of the labor force"— which she elsewhere terms "authoritarian control over the labor force and middle classes" (1991: 80; 1992: 14)—as the key factor contributing to the stable growth of export-oriented industrialization in the so-called Asian tigers of Hong Kong, Taiwan, South Korea, and Singapore (1991: 96; 1992: 29–30). It should be noted that all of these countries have been characterized by extended periods (some continuing through the present) of authoritarian rule during times of intense industrialization, in which labor, along with other sectors of society, has been tightly controlled.

19. Sassen 1988: 36–37.

20. In the case of the United States, although immigration policies have been comparatively liberal since 1965, they have been based largely on the principle of family reunification rather than labor recruitment and mobility. Although immigrants admitted under family-reunification guidelines have helped meet the U.S. economy's demand for low-wage immigrant labor, a substantial portion of the immigrant labor pool in the United States has nonetheless consisted of workers lacking legal status.

21. Sassen 1988. See chapter 5, especially pages 150–168. On the importance of the growth of the informal sector, downgraded manufacturing, and advanced services within first-world nations in the "flexible accumulation" strategy, see also Harvey 1989: 147–165, 186–187.

22. Sassen 1988: 6–9, 17–21, 115–119.

23. Sassen 1988: 62–65.

24. Orum, Feagin, and Sjoberg 1991: 2.

25. Sjoberg et al. 1991: 39.

26. Sjoberg et al. 1991: 57–60.

27. Sjoberg et al. 1991: 34. These authors propose the stimulation of public debate as a standard for assessing social theory, which they view as inherently embedded in methodological approaches of all types.

28. Marx 1977. See chapter 10, especially parts 5, 6, and 7. See also Cleaver 1979: 77–80.

29. Much research remains to be done on a multitude of government documents, including the *INS Statistical Year Book* and those documents pertaining to the U.S. Customs Service, the War on Drugs, and DOD involvement in the War on Drugs. Such sources are often overlooked. Nonetheless, the availability of government documents is far from complete. For example, very few internal INS documents are publicly available.

30. Notably absent from this list are Mexican sources. While some Mexican academic sources were used, Mexican government documents and press accounts were not. Contemporary Mexican government documents were simply not available to this author, and attempting to track them down would have entailed considerable expense and much additional time in an already lengthy research process. Mexican press accounts were accessible, although not those specifically from Mexican border cities. My failure to use these sources is a clear shortcoming of my research, as Mexican reports may contain much information and fresh perspectives on immigration and drug enforcement efforts on both sides of the U.S.–Mexico border. For example, the Mexican press has clearly been more critical than the U.S. press in its coverage of the INS and its treatment of Mexican immigrants.

31. This strategy for investigating bureaucracies is detailed by Sjoberg and Miller (1973: 133, 137–138).

32. Aberbach 1990: 147, 151. Aberbach proposes that the "advocacy environment" stems in large part from the fact that congresspersons' committee assignments derive much of their value and prestige from that associated with the programs and agencies under their jurisdiction.

33. Sjoberg and Miller 1973: 137.

34. Williams and Sjoberg 1993: 190.

35. Cárdenas 1979: 56–57, 77–78. Cárdenas refers specifically to INS data. The present work expands this discussion to refer to bureaucracies in general.

36. Littrell 1993 provides an insightful methodological discussion of the principle of not accepting bureaucratic information at face value, but rather viewing it critically and seeking countersources of information.

References

Aberbach, Joel D. 1990. "Relations between Organizations: Institutions, Self-Interest, and Congressional Oversight Behavior in the United States." In *Institutions in American Society: Essays in Market, Political, and Social Organizations,* edited by John E. Jackson, 135–161. Ann Arbor: University of Michigan Press.

Acuña, Rodolfo. 1988. *Occupied America: A History of Chicanos.* 3d ed. New York: Harper & Row.

Advanced Systems Integration Department 9561, Sandia National Laboratories. 1993. "Systematic Analysis of the Southwestern Border. Volume I." Prepared for the Immigration and Naturalization Service.

Aguayo Quezada, Sergio. 1988. "Mexico in Transition and the United States: Old Perceptions, New Problems." In *Mexico and the United States: Managing the Relationship,* edited by Riordan Roett, 151–177. Boulder, Colo.: Westview Press.

————. 1989. "México en transición y Estados Unidos: ¿Un problema de percepciones o de seguridad nacional?" In *México y Estados Unidos: El manejo de la relación,* edited by Riordan Roett, 203–228. Mexico City: Siglo Veintiuno.

Aguilar, Edwin Eloy. 1991. "Minority Populations Living on the Periphery of the Core: The Case of the Rio Grande Valley of South Texas." Paper prepared for delivery at the annual meeting of the Southwestern Social Science Association, March 27–30, San Antonio.

Aguilar Zinser, Adolfo. 1990. "La seguridad mexicana vista por Estados Unidos." In *En busca de la seguridad perdida: Aproximaciones a la seguridad nacional mexicana,* edited by Sergio Aguayo Quezada and Bruce M. Bagley, 295–314. Mexico City: Siglo Veintiuno.

Álvarez, Rodolfo. 1985. "The Psycho-Historical and Socioeconomic Development of the Chicano Community in the United States." In *The Mexican American Experience: An Interdisciplinary Anthology,* edited by Rodolfo O. de la Garza, Frank D. Bean, Charles M. Bonjean, Ricardo Romo, and Rodolfo Álvarez, 33–56. Austin: University of Texas Press.

Americas Watch. 1982. *Human Rights in Guatemala: No Neutrals Allowed.* New York: Americas Watch.

————. 1990a. *Human Rights in Mexico: A Policy of Impunity.* Report written by Ellen L. Lutz. New York: Americas Watch.

————. 1990b. *Messengers of Death: Human Rights in Guatemala, November 1988 – February 1990.* Report written by Anne Manuel. New York: Americas Watch.

————. 1991a. *El Salvador's Decade of Terror: Human Rights since the Assassination of Archbishop Romero.* New Haven, Conn.: Yale University Press.

————. 1991b. *Unceasing Abuses: Human Rights in Mexico One Year after the Introduction of Reform.* New York: Americas Watch.

————. 1992. *Brutality Unchecked: Human Rights along the U.S. Border with Mexico.* New York: Americas Watch.

————. 1993. "United States Frontier Injustice: Human Rights Abuses along the U.S. Border with Mexico Persist amid Climate of Impunity." *News from Americas Watch* 5 (4): 1–46.

Americas Watch and American Civil Liberties Union. 1982. *Report on Human Rights in El Salvador.* New York: Vintage Books.

Amnesty International. 1987. *Guatemala: The Human Rights Record.* London: Amnesty International Publications.

————. 1988. *El Salvador: "Death Squads"—A Government Strategy.* London: Amnesty International Publications.

Anderson, Malcolm. 1989. *Policing the World: Interpol and the Politics of International Police Cooperation.* New York: Oxford University Press.

Anderson, Thomas P. 1971. *Matanza: El Salvador's Communist Revolt of 1932.* Lincoln: University of Nebraska Press.

"Anti–Drug Abuse Act of 1986" (Public Law 99-570). 1987. *United States Code Congressional and Administrative News,* 99th Cong., 2d sess. (1986), vol. 2. Saint Paul, Minn.: West Publishing.

"Anti–Drug Abuse Act of 1988" (Public Law 100-690). 1989. *United States Code Congressional and Administrative News,* 100th Cong., 2d sess. (1990), vol. 3. Saint Paul, Minn.: West Publishing.

Archdiocese of São Paulo. Catholic Church. 1986. *Torture in Brazil: A Report.* Translated by Jaime Wright, edited by Joan Dassin. New York: Vintage Books.

Bacevich, A. J., James D. Hallums, Richard H. White, and Thomas F. Young. 1988. *American Military Policy in Small Wars: The Case of El Salvador.* Washington, D.C.: Pergamon-Brassey's.

Bagley, Bruce M. 1992. "Myths of Militarization: Enlisting the Armed Forces in the War on Drugs." In *Drug Policy in the Americas,* edited by Peter H. Smith, 129–150. Boulder, Colo.: Westview Press.

Baker, George. 1991. "Mexican Labor Is Not Cheap." *Rio Bravo* 1 (1): 7–26.

Baker, Susan González. 1990. *The Cautious Welcome: The Legalization Programs of the Immigration Reform and Control Act.* Santa Monica, Calif.: Rand; Washington, D.C.: Urban Institute.

Barnes, Rudolph C., Jr. 1988. "Civil Affairs: A LIC Priority." *Military Review* 68 (9): 38–49.

Barnet, Richard J. 1988. "The Costs and Perils of Intervention." In *Low-Intensity Warfare: Counterinsurgency, Proinsurgency, and Antiterrorism in the Eighties,* edited by Michael T. Klare and Peter Kornbluh, 207–221. New York: Pantheon Books.

Barrera, Mario. 1979. *Race and Class in the Southwest: A Theory of Racial Inequality.* Notre Dame, Ind.: University of Notre Dame Press.

Barry, Tom. 1986. *Low-Intensity Conflict: The New Battlefield in Central America.* Albuquerque: Inter-Hemispheric Education Resource Center.

Barry, Tom, Harry Browne, and Beth Sims. 1994. *Crossing the Line: Immigrants, Economic Integration, and Drug Enforcement on the U.S.–Mexico Border.* Albuquerque: Resource Center Press.

Barry, Tom, and Deb Preusch. 1986. *The Central America Fact Book.* New York: Grove Press.

Bartra, Roger. 1990. "Nacionalismo revolucionario y seguridad nacional en México." In *En busca de la seguridad perdida: Aproximaciones a la seguridad nacional mexicana,* edited by Sergio Aguayo Quezada and Bruce M. Bagley, 146–173. Mexico City: Siglo Veintiuno.

———. 1993. "Revolutionary Nationalism and National Security in Mexico." In *Mexico: In Search of Security,* edited by Bruce M. Bagley and Sergio Aguayo Quezada, 143–169. New Brunswick, N.J.: Transaction Publishers.

Bean, Frank D., Roland Chanove, Robert G. Cushing, Rodolfo de la Garza, Gary Freeman, Charles W. Haynes, and David Spener. 1994. "Illegal Mexican Migration and the United States/Mexico Border: The Effects of Operation Hold-the-Line on El Paso/Juárez." Prepared for the Commission on Immigration Reform. Population Research Center, University of Texas at Austin.

Bean, Frank D., Barry Edmundston, and Jeffrey S. Passel, eds. 1990. *Undocumented Migration to the United States: IRCA and the Experience of the 1980s.* Santa Monica, Calif.: Rand; Washington, D.C.: Urban Institute.

Bean, Frank D., Thomas J. Espenshade, Michael J. White, and Robert F. Dymowski. 1990. "Post-IRCA Changes in the Volume and Composition of Undocumented Migration to the United States: An Assessment Based on Apprehension Data." In *Undocumented Migration to the United States: IRCA and the Experience of the 1980s,* edited by Frank D. Bean, Barry Edmundston, and Jeffrey S. Passel, 111–158. Santa Monica, Calif.: Rand; Washington, D.C.: Urban Institute.

"Bloquea EU la frontera de Arizona." 1994. *Diario de Juárez,* 18 October.

Borden, Tessie. 1992a. "Drug Traces Found in Man's Body in Border Shooting." *Arizona Daily Star,* 17 July.

———. 1992b. "Elmer Says He Thought Drug Smugglers Were Firing at Him." *Arizona Daily Star,* 11 December.

————. 1992c. "Trial Mars Border Patrol's By-the-Rules Image." *Arizona Daily Star*, 15 December.

————. 1992d. "Two Aliens Tell Elmer Jury of Shooting by Agents." *Arizona Daily Star*, 5 December.

"Border Agent Pleads No Contest in Rape of Illegal Immigrant." 1994. *Phoenix Republic*, 28 July.

The Border: Immigration and Issues. 1990. Special issue. *¡Basta!* (National Journal of the Chicago Religious Task Force on Central America), February.

The Border: United States and Mexico. 1989. Special issue. *¡Basta!* (National Journal of the Chicago Religious Task Force on Central America), December.

Boxer, Barbara (Senator, California). 1993 (Oct. 15). "Comments on the Use of the National Guard to Aid the Border Patrol in Immigration Enforcement." *Congressional Record*, vol. 139, no. 139, pp. S13539–S13540. 103d Cong., 1st sess. Washington, D.C.: GPO.

Brinkley, Joel. 1994. "At Immigration: Disarray and Defeat." *New York Times*, 11 September.

Brooks, Laura. 1992a. "Border Shooting's Replay Poses Nagging Queries." *Arizona Daily Star*, 12 July.

————. 1992b. "Tucsonan Faults Border Patrol in His Brother's 'Racist' Slaying." *Arizona Daily Star*, 16 June.

Browning, Harley, and René M. Zenteno Quintero. 1993. "The Diverse Nature of the Mexican Northern Border: The Case of Urban Employment." *Frontera Norte* 5 (9): 11–31.

Bruce, Jason. 1991. "Truán Seeks to Give Border Patrol More Authority." *Corpus Christi Caller*, 22 January.

Bunting, Glenn F. 1994. "Boxer's Bid to Put National Guard at Border Is Stymied." *Los Angeles Times*, 6 August.

Bustamante, Jorge A. 1978. "Las propuestas de política migratoria en los Estados Unidos y sus repercusiones en México." *Foro Internacional* 18 (3): 522–530.

————. 1990. "México–Estados Unidos: Migración indocumentada y seguridad nacional." In *En busca de la seguridad perdida: Aproximaciones a la seguridad nacional mexicana*, edited by Sergio Aguayo Quezada and Bruce M. Bagley, 340–366. Mexico City: Siglo Veintiuno.

————. 1991. "La extorsión en la frontera norte: Violaciones de los derechos humanos." *Demos* 4: 20–21.

————. 1992a. "If There's a Recession in America, It Must Be Time to Pick on Mexico." *Los Angeles Times*, 16 February.

————. 1992b. "Interdependence, Undocumented Migration, and National Security." In *U.S.–Mexico Relations: Labor Market Interdependence*, edited by Jorge A. Bustamante, Clark W. Reynolds, and Raúl A. Hinojosa Ojeda, 21–41. Stanford, Calif.: Stanford University Press.

————. 1992c. "Mexican Labor Migration and the Free Trade Agreement." Sixth Annual Américo Paredes Distinguished Lecture. Center for Mexican

American Studies, University of Texas at Austin, 27 April.

Calavita, Kitty. 1989. "The Immigration Policy Option Debate: Critical Analysis and Future Options." In *Mexican Migration to the United States: Origins, Consequences, and Policy Options*, edited by Wayne A. Cornelius and Jorge A. Bustamante, 151–177. La Jolla, Calif.: Center for the U.S.–Mexican Studies, University of California, San Diego.

———. 1992. *Inside the State: The Bracero Program, Immigration, and the INS.* New York: Routledge.

California Legislature. Joint Committee on Refugee Resettlement, International Migration, and Cooperative Development. 1990. *Joint Hearing on International Migration and Border Region Violence.* Sacramento, Calif.: Joint Publications.

Cárdenas, Gilberto. 1979. "Critical Issues in Using Government Data Collected Primarily for Non-Research Purposes." In *Quantitative Data and Immigration Research*, edited by Stephen R. Couch and Roy Simon Bryce-Laporte, 55–98. Washington, D.C.: Research Institute on Immigration and Ethnic Studies, Smithsonian Institution.

Carlson, Craig L. 1991. "Measures of Effectiveness: The Key to a Successful National Drug Control Strategy." *Military Review* 71 (8): 90–94.

Castañeda, Jorge. 1992. "Again, People Are Mexico's Number One Export." *Los Angeles Times*, 24 March.

Castañeda, Jorge, and Rafael Alarcón. 1991. "Workers Are a Commodity, Too." *Los Angeles Times*, 22 April.

———. 1992. "Workers Are a Commodity, Too." In *Trading Freedom: How Free Trade Affects Our Lives, Work, and Environment*, edited by John Cavanagh, John Gershman, Karen Baker, and Gretchen Helmke, 88–89. San Francisco: Institute for Food and Development Policy.

"The Changing Scene at the Corralón." 1992. *Proyecto Libertad* (Newsletter of Proyecto Libertad, Harlingen, Tex.), spring-summer: 1–3.

Chávez, Leo R. 1992. *Shadowed Lives: Undocumented Immigrants in American Society.* Fort Worth, Tex.: Harcourt Brace Jovanovich College Publishers.

Chaze, William. 1983. "Invasion from Mexico: It Just Keeps Coming." *U.S. News and World Report*, 7 March.

Cleaver, Harry. 1979. *Reading Capital Politically.* Austin: University of Texas Press.

Cleeland, Nancy. 1994. "Illegal Immigration in Nogales Soars." *San Diego Union-Tribune*, 26 June.

Cockcroft, James D. 1986. *Outlaws in the Promised Land: Mexican Immigrant Workers and America's Future.* New York: Grove Press.

Coile, Norma, and Rubén Hernández. 1992. "A Juror Cites Michael Elmer's Fear for His Life in Explaining Why He Was Acquitted of the Murder of a Mexican National." *Tucson Citizen*, 17 December.

Comblin, Joseph. 1976. "La doctrina de la seguridad nacional." *Mensaje*

(Santiago de Chile) 25 (247): 96–104.

Committee of Santa Fe (L. Francis Bouchey, Roger Fountaine, David C. Jordan, Gordon Sumner, and Lewis Tambs). 1980. *A New Inter-American Policy for the Eighties*. Washington, D.C.: Council for Inter-American Security.

Compton, Nina H., and Garrett T. Newland. 1992. "The Functional Border Equivalent." *Journal of Borderland Studies* 7 (2): 73–92.

Compton, Nina H., and Del Wells. 1988. "The Constitutionality of Search and Seizure in the Extended Border Area by Border Patrol Officers." *Journal of Borderland Studies* 3 (4): 17–34.

Conley, Jim. 1990. "Special Unit Tries to Keep Low Profile." *Tucson Citizen*, 14 November.

Conover, Ted. 1987. *Coyotes: A Journey through the Secret World of America's Illegal Aliens*. New York: Vintage Books.

Conroy, Michael E., and Amy K. Glasmeier. 1992–93. "Unprecedented Disparities, Unparalleled Adjustment Needs: Winners and Losers on the NAFTA 'Fast Track.'" *Journal of Interamerican Studies and World Affairs* 34 (4): 1–37.

Cooper, Marc. 1992. "LA's State of Siege: Cops from Hell." In *Inside the L.A. Riots: What Really Happened, and Why It Will Happen Again*, edited by Don Hazen, 12–18. [New York]: Institute for Alternative Journalism.

Cornelius, Wayne A. 1982. *America in the Era of Limits: Migrants, Nativists, and the Future of U.S.–Mexican Relations*. Working Papers in U.S.–Mexican Studies, no. 3. La Jolla, Calif.: Center for U.S.–Mexican Studies, University of California, San Diego.

————. 1992a. "From Sojourners to Settlers: The Changing Profile of Mexican Immigration to the United States." In *U.S.–Mexico Relations: Labor Market Interdependence*, edited by Jorge A. Bustamante, Clark W. Reynolds, and Raúl A. Hinojosa Ojeda, 155–195. Stanford, Calif.: Stanford University Press.

————. 1992b. "The Scare Stories Don't Wash." *Los Angeles Times*, 28 February.

Cornelius, Wayne A., and Phillip L. Martin. 1993. *The Uncertain Connection: Free Trade and Mexico–U.S. Migration*. San Diego, Calif.: Center for U.S.–Mexico Studies, University of California, San Diego.

Craig, Ann L. 1981. *Mexican Immigration: Changing Terms of the Debate in the United States and Mexico*. Working Papers in U.S.–Mexican Studies, no. 4. La Jolla, Calif.: Program in U.S.–Mexican Studies, University of California, San Diego.

Craig, Roger. 1989. "U.S. Narcotics Policy toward Mexico: Consequences for a Bilateral Relationship." In *The Drug Connection in U.S.–Mexican Relations*, edited by Guadalupe González González and Marta Tienda, 71–92. La Jolla, Calif.: Center for U.S.–Mexican Studies, University of California, San Diego.

Crane, Keith W., Beth J. Asch, Joanna Zorn Heilbrunn, and Danielle C. Cullnane. 1990. *The Effect of Employer Sanctions on the Flow of Undocumented Immigrants to the United States*. Santa Monica, Calif.: Rand; Washington, D.C.: Urban Institute.

Crewdson, John. 1983. *The Tarnished Door: The New Immigrants and the Transformation of America.* New York: Times Books.

Danner, Mark. 1993. "The Truth of El Mozote." *New Yorker,* 6 December.

Davidson, Miriam. 1990. "The Mexican Border War." *Nation,* 12 November.

————. 1991. "Can Soldiers Stop Drugs?" *Nation,* 1 April.

Davis, Mike. 1992a. *City of Quartz: Excavating the Future of Los Angeles.* London: Verso Books, 1990. Reprint, New York: Vintage Books.

————. 1992b. "In L.A., Burning All Illusions." *Nation,* 1 June.

"Definitions" (sec. 1101). *U.S. Code,* Title 8. 1988 edition. Washington, D.C.: GPO.

De León, Arnoldo. 1983. *They Called Them Greasers: Anglo Attitudes toward Mexicans in Texas, 1821–1900.* Austin: University of Texas Press.

Delgado, Berta, and Jim Phillips. 1989. "Dozens Detained by INS Rules." *Austin American-Statesman,* 22 February.

"Department of Defense Authorization Act, 1982" (Public Law 97-86). 1982. *United States Code Congressional and Administrative News,* 97th Cong., 1st sess. (1981), vol. 1. Saint Paul, Minn.: West Publishing.

"Deportable Aliens" (sec. 1251). *U.S. Code,* Title 8. 1988 edition. Washington, D.C.: GPO.

DeWind, Josh. 1990. "Alien Justice: The Exclusion of Haitian Refugees." *Journal of Social Science Issues* 46 (1): 121–132.

"Dispatched to Duty." 1992. Sidebar. *Los Angeles Times,* 2 May.

Dixon, Howard Lee. 1987. *The Role of Reserve Forces in Low-Intensity Conflict.* Langley Air Force Base, Va.: Army–Air Force Center for Low-Intensity Conflict.

Doggett, Martha. 1993. *Death Foretold: The Jesuit Murders in El Salvador.* Washington, D.C.: Georgetown University Press; Lawyers Committee for Human Rights.

Domínguez, Jorge. 1990. "Immigration as Foreign Policy in U.S.–Latin American Relations." In *Immigration and U.S. Foreign Policy,* edited by Robert W. Tucker, Charles B. Keely, and Linda Wrigley, 150–166. Boulder, Colo.: Westview Press.

Donato, Katherine M., and Douglas S. Massey. 1993. "Effects of the Immigration Reform and Control Act on the Wages of Mexican Migrants." *Social Science Quarterly* 74 (3): 521–541.

Dubose, Louis. 1992. "Suing the Border Patrol: The Battle at Bowie High." *Texas Observer,* 11 December.

"Entry of Alien at Improper Time or Place: Misrepresentation and Concealment of Facts" (sec. 1325). *U.S. Code,* Title 8. 1988 edition. Washington, D.C.: GPO.

Escuela de las Américas. Ejército de los Estados Unidos de América. 1978. *Catálogo de Cursos.* Course listings in Spanish and English. Zona del Canal [Panama]: Fuerte Gulek.

Fagen, Patricia Weiss. 1992. "Repression and State Security." In *Fear at the Edge: State Terror and Resistance in Latin America,* edited by Juan E. Corradi, Patricia Weiss Fagen, and Manuel Antonio Garretón, 39–71. Berkeley: University of California Press.

Falla, Ricardo. 1994. *Massacres in the Jungle: Ixcán, Guatemala, 1975–1982.* Translated by Julia Howland. Boulder, Colo.: Westview Press.

Fason, William E. 1989. "AID's Office of Public Safety: Developing Third World Police States." Unpublished manuscript.

Fernández, Celestino, and Lawrence R. Pedroza. 1982. "The Border Patrol and News Media Coverage of Undocumented Mexican Immigration during the 1970s: A Quantitative Content Analysis in the Sociology of Knowledge." *California Sociologist* 5 (2): 1–26.

Fernández de Castro, Rafael, Mónica Verea Campos, and Sidney Weintraub, eds. 1993. *Sectoral Effects of North American Free Trade.* Austin and Mexico City: Lyndon B. Johnson School of Public Affairs, University of Texas at Austin; Centro de Investigaciones sobre Estados Unidos de América, Universidad Nacional Autónoma de México; Instituto Tecnólogico Autónomo de México.

Fishel, John T., and Edmund S. Cowan. 1988. "Civil-Military Operations and the War for Moral Legitimacy in Latin America." *Military Review* 68 (1): 36–49.

Fix, Michael, ed. 1991. *The Paper Curtain: Employer Sanctions' Implementation, Impact, and Reform.* Santa Monica, Calif.: Rand; Washington, D.C.: Urban Institute.

Flynn, Ken, and Peter Brock. 1994. "INS Worker Convicted of Bribery." *El Paso Herald-Post,* 26 February.

Foley, Douglas E. 1988. *From Peones to Políticos: Class and Ethnicity in a South Texas Town, 1900–1987.* 1st rev. ed. With Clarice Mota, Donald E. Post, and Ignacio Lozano. Austin: University of Texas Press.

Foreign Service Institute. U.S. Department of State. 1988. *Low-Intensity Conflict: Support for Democratic Resistance Movements.* Washington, D.C.: Center for the Study of Foreign Affairs, Foreign Service Institute.

"Fort Bliss Gets New General for Drug War." 1990. *Austin American-Statesman,* 14 July.

Frelick, Bill. 1992. "Haitians at Sea: Asylum Denied." *NACLA Report on the Americas* 26 (1): 34–38.

Fried, Jonathan. 1994. *Operation Blockade: A City Divided.* Report from the American Friends Service Committee's Immigration Law Enforcement Project. Philadelphia: American Friends Service Committee.

Galbraith, James K. 1992–93. "What Mexico—and the United States—Wants: What NAFTA Really Means." *World Policy Journal* 10 (1): 29–32.

———. 1993. "Labor and the NAFTA: A Short Report." *Economic Development Quarterly* 7 (4): 323–327.

García, F. Chris, ed. 1974. *La Causa Política: A Chicano Politics Reader.* Notre Dame, Ind.: University of Notre Dame Press.

García, Guillermo X. 1989a. "Border Patrol Boosts Troops in Valley to Thwart Refugees." *Austin American-Statesman,* 28 February.

———. 1989b. "Immigration Lawyers to Tackle INS in Valley." *Austin American-Statesman,* 13 March.

———. 1989c. "Plans to Build Border Ditch Cut Rift between U.S., Mexico." *Austin American-Statesman,* 9 April.

———. 1989d. "Texas Guard Joins Drug War." *Austin American-Statesman,* 22 October.

———. 1989e. "Work on Border Ditch Slated to Begin in April." *Austin American-Statesman,* 18 February.

García, Juan Ramón. 1980. *Operation Wetback: The Mass Deportation of Mexican Undocumented Workers in 1954.* Westport, Conn.: Greenwood Press.

Gelbspan, Ross. 1991. *Break-ins, Death Threats, and the FBI: The Covert War against the Central America Movement.* Boston: South End Press.

Gentry, Blake. 1989. "The Texas Border Crisis: Perceptions and Reality." *¡Basta!* (National Journal of the Chicago Religious Task Force on Central America), December: 22–26.

Golden, Tim. 1992. "Mexico Is Now Acting to Protect Border Migrants." *New York Times,* 28 June.

Gómez, Leonel. 1984. "Feet People." In *Central America: Anatomy of Conflict,* edited by Robert S. Leiken, 219–229. New York: Pergamon Press.

Gómez-Quiñones, Juan. 1990. *Chicano Politics: Reality and Promise, 1940–1990.* Albuquerque: University of New Mexico Press.

González González, Guadalupe. 1989. Introduction to *The Drug Connection in U.S.–Mexican Relations,* edited by Guadalupe González González and Marta Tienda, 1–16. La Jolla, Calif.: Center for U.S.–Mexican Studies, University of California, San Diego.

Goose, Stephan D. 1988. "Low-Intensity Warfare: The Warriors and Their Weapons." In *Low-Intensity Warfare: Counterinsurgency, Proinsurgency, and Antiterrorism in the Eighties,* edited by Michael T. Klare and Peter Kornbluh, 80–111. New York: Pantheon Books.

Green, Stephen. 1994. "House OKs Plan to Put Troops on the Border." *San Diego Union-Tribune,* 9 June.

Griswold del Castillo, Richard. 1990. *The Treaty of Guadalupe Hidalgo: A Legacy of Conflict.* Norman: University of Oklahoma Press.

Gross, Gregory. 1994. "Border Clamped Down." *San Diego Union-Tribune,* 4 October.

Guevara, Robert. 1991. "Border Patrol Accused of Torturing Guatemalans." *Valley Morning Star,* 27 March.

Guillén López, Tonatiuh. 1990. "Servicios públicos y marginalidad social en la frontera norte." *Frontera Norte* 2 (4): 95–120.

Ham-Chande, Roberto, and John R. Weeks. 1992. "A Demographic Perspective of the U.S.–Mexico Border." In *Demographic Dynamics of the U.S.–Mexico*

Border, edited by John R. Weeks and Roberto Ham-Chande, 1–28. El Paso: Texas Western Press.

Hammond Incorporated. 1989. *United States History Atlas.* New, rev., and expanded ed. Maplewood, N.J.: Hammond Incorporated.

Harvey, David. 1989. *The Condition of Postmodernity: An Enquiry into the Origins of Cultural Change.* Cambridge, Mass.: Basil Blackwell.

Harwood, Edwin. 1986. *In Liberty's Shadow: Illegal Aliens and Immigration Law Enforcement.* Stanford, Calif.: Hoover Institution Press.

Hazen, Don, ed. 1992. *Inside the L.A. Riots: What Really Happened, and Why It Will Happen Again.* [New York]: Institute for Alternative Journalism.

Healy, Melissa, and Kevin Davis. 1989. "Marines to Join Front Lines in Fight on Drugs." *Los Angeles Times,* 14 October.

Helsinki Watch. 1989. *Detained, Denied, Deported: Asylum Seekers in the United States.* Report by Karin König. New York: U.S. Helsinki Watch Committee.

Hernández, Rubén. 1990a. "Border a Drug 'War Zone.'" *Tucson Citizen,* 12 November.

———. 1990b. "Border Rancher Wary of Military." *Tucson Citizen,* 13 November.

———. 1990c. "Command Center to Be Set up at D-M." *Tucson Citizen,* 12 November.

———. 1990d. "Two Armies on Different Roads in Drug Fight." *Tucson Citizen,* 14 November.

———. 1992a. "Border Agent's Bond Set at One Million Dollars." *Tucson Citizen,* 1 July.

———. 1992b. "I 'Freaked Out,' Elmer Testifies." *Tucson Citizen,* 11 December.

———. 1992c. "Marines Aid Border Agents." *Tucson Citizen,* 31 August.

Herzog, Lawrence A. 1990. *Where North Meets South: Cities, Space, and Politics on the U.S.–Mexico Border.* Austin: Center for Mexican American Studies, University of Texas at Austin.

———. 1992. "Changing Boundaries in the Americas: An Overview." In *Changing Boundaries in the Americas: New Perspectives on the U.S.–Mexican, Central American, and South American Borders,* edited by Lawrence A. Herzog, 3–24. La Jolla, Calif.: Center for U.S.–Mexican Studies, University of California, San Diego.

Heyman, Josian M. 1991. *Life and Labor on the Border: Working People of Northeastern Sonora, Mexico.* Tucson: University of Arizona Press.

Hinojosa Ojeda, Raúl A., and Robert K. McCleery. 1992. "U.S.–Mexico Interdependence, Social Pacts, and Policy Perspectives: A Computable General Equilibrium Approach." In *U.S.–Mexico Relations: Labor Market Interdependence,* edited by Jorge A. Bustamante, Clark W. Reynolds, and Raúl A. Hinojosa Ojeda, 113–154. Stanford, Calif.: Stanford University Press.

"House Conference Report 102-311" (Legislative History, Defense Authorization Act, Public Law 102-190). 1992. *United States Code Congressional and*

Administrative News, 102d Cong., 1st sess. (1991), vol. 3: 1042–1217. Saint Paul, Minn.: West Publishing.

"House Report 97-71" (Legislative History, Department of Defense, Public Law 97-86). 1982. *United States Code Congressional and Administrative News,* 97th Cong., 1st sess. (1981), vol. 3: 1785–1876. Saint Paul, Minn.: West Publishing.

"House Report 102-527" (Legislative History, Department of Defense Authorization Act, Public Law 102-484). 1993. *United States Code Congressional and Administrative News,* 102d Cong., 2d sess. (1992), vol. 4: 1637–1768. Saint Paul, Minn.: West Publishing.

Hunt, Jennifer. 1985. "Police Accounts of Normal Force." *Urban Life* 13 (4): 315–341.

Hunt, John B. 1991. "Emerging Doctrine for LIC." *Military Review* 71 (6): 51–59.

Imerman, Vicky A. 1993. "SOA: School of Assassins." *Covert Action Information Bulletin* 44: 15–19.

"Immigration Act of 1990" (Public Law 101-649). 1991. *United States Code Congressional and Administrative News,* 101st Cong., 2d sess. (1990), vol. 4. Saint Paul, Minn.: West Publishing.

Immigration Law Enforcement Monitoring Project. American Friends Service Committee. 1990. *Human Rights at the Mexico–U.S. Border.* Second annual report. Houston: ILEMP.

———. 1992. *Sealing Our Borders: The Human Toll.* Third annual report. Philadelphia: American Friends Service Committee.

"Immigration Reform and Control Act of 1986" (Public Law 99-603). 1987. *United States Code Congressional and Administrative News,* 99th Cong., 2d sess. (1986), vol. 3. Saint Paul, Minn.: West Publishing.

INS Reporter. 1985–86. 34: 1 (fall-winter issue).

INS Reporter. 1988. 35: 1 (January issue).

INS Reporter. 1989. 36: 2 (summer issue).

"INS to Beef Up Presence at Arizona Border." 1994. *El Paso Times,* 18 October.

Isenberg, David. 1992. "Militarizing the Drug War." *Covert Action* 42: 42–47.

Isikoff, Michael. 1992. "Martínez Suffers Setbacks as Drug Control Director." *Washington Post,* 24 February.

Jackson, Robert L. 1993. "Nominee for INS Chief Says She Will Study Border Crossing Fee." *Los Angeles Times,* 1 October.

Jamail, Milton H. 1981. "Voluntary Organizations along the Border." In *Mexico–United States Relations,* edited by Susan Kaufman Purcell, 78–87. New York: Praeger.

Jehl, Douglas. 1989. "U.S. Enlisting Guard in Drug Fight." *Los Angeles Times,* 31 March.

Jehl, Douglas, and John M. Broder. 1992. "Bush Pledges Enough Force to Quell Riots." *Los Angeles Times,* 2 May.

Jehl, Douglas, and Melissa Healy. 1989. "In Reversal, Military Seeks Drug War Role." *Los Angeles Times,* 15 December.

Jehl, Douglas, and Marjorie Miller. 1990. "U.S. Military Unit in Mexico Aids Drug War." *Los Angeles Times,* 7 June.

Jehl, Douglas, and Ronald Ostrow. 1992. "Pentagon Said to Reject Bigger Anti-Drug Role." *Los Angeles Times,* 27 January.

Jiménez, María. 1988. "Police Policies and Practices: The Case of the Border Patrol." *Immigration Newsletter* (Immigration Project of the National Lawyers Guild) 17 (4): 1, 5–8.

———. 1991. "Labor Mobility and the North America Free Trade Agreement." *Immigration Newsletter* (Immigration Project of the National Lawyers Guild) 19 (4): 3–7.

———. 1992. "War in the Borderlands." *NACLA Report on the Americas* 26 (1): 29–33.

Johnson, Chip. 1990. "Techno-Cops: Police Tools of the '90s Are Highly Advanced, but Privacy Laws Lag." *Wall Street Journal,* 11 November.

Johnson, David. 1988. "Action in Congress." *New York Times,* 22 August.

Johnson, Stephen. 1989. "Texas Guardsmen Used in Clandestine Scouting." *Houston Chronicle,* 11 June.

Jones, Robert A. 1992. "A Few Hours When Our Town Hung in the Balance." *Los Angeles Times,* 3 May.

Juffras, Jason. 1991. *Impact of the Immigration Reform and Control Act on the Immigration and Naturalization Service.* Santa Monica, Calif.: Rand; Washington, D.C.: Urban Institute.

Justice, Glen. 1992. *Revolution on the Rio Grande: Mexican Raids and Army Pursuits, 1916–1919.* El Paso: Texas Western Press.

Kahn, Robert. 1990. "INS Investigates Alleged Sexual Harassment." *Brownsville Herald,* 27 September.

Kamen, Al. 1990. "Central America Is No Longer the Central Issue for Americans." *Austin American-Statesman,* 21 October.

———. 1992. "Mexicans Undeterred by Barriers on the Border." *Washington Post,* 18 February.

Kesselbrenner, Dan, and Lory D. Rosenberg. 1994. *Immigration Law and Crimes.* Produced under the auspices of the National Immigration Project of the National Lawyers Guild. Deerfield, Ill.: Clark, Boardman, & Callaghan.

King, Peter. 1992. "Notes on a Week in L.A." *Los Angeles Times,* 6 May.

Klare, Michael T. 1988. "The Interventionist Impulse: U.S. Military Doctrine for Low-Intensity Warfare." In *Low-Intensity Warfare: Counterinsurgency, Proinsurgency, and Antiterrorism in the Eighties,* edited by Michael T. Klare and Peter Kornbluh, 49–79. New York: Pantheon Books.

Klare, Michael T., and Peter Kornbluh. 1988. "The New Interventionism: Low-Intensity Warfare in the 1980s and Beyond." In *Low-Intensity Warfare: Counterinsurgency, Proinsurgency, and Antiterrorism in the Eighties,* edited by Michael T. Klare and Peter Kornbluh, 3–20. New York: Pantheon Books.

Kleist, Trina. 1992. "Tariffs Spark Riot by Almost 2,000 in Nuevo Laredo." *San Antonio Express-News*, 30 November.

Kornbluh, Peter. 1988. "The War at Home." *Southern Exposure* 16 (4): 36–39.

Koulish, Robert E. 1992. "Systematic Deterrence against Prospective Asylum Seekers: A Study of the South Texas Immigration District." *Review of Law and Social Change* 19 (3): 529–570.

Koulish, Robert E., Manuel Escobedo, Raquel Rubio-Goldsmith, and John Robert Warren. 1994. *U.S. Immigration Authorities and Victims of Human and Civil Rights Abuses: The Border Interaction Project Study of South Tucson, Arizona, and South Texas.* Working Paper Series, no. 20. Tucson: Mexican American Studies and Research Center, University of Arizona.

Kupperman, Robert H., and Darrell M. Trent. 1979. *Terrorism: Threat, Reality, Response.* Stanford, Calif.: Hoover Institution Press, Stanford University.

Kwong, Peter. 1992. "The First Multicultural Riots." *Village Voice*, 9 June.

La Botz, Dan. 1992. *Mask of Democracy: Labor Suppression in Mexico Today.* Boston: South End Press.

Landau, Saul. 1988. *Dangerous Doctrine: National Security and U.S. Foreign Policy.* Boulder, Colo.: Westview Press.

Langguth, A. J. 1978. *Hidden Terrors.* New York: Pantheon Books.

Langham, Thomas Caloway. 1984. "The Eisenhower Administration and Operation Wetback, 1953–1956: A Case Study of the Development of a Federal Policy to Control Illegal Migration." Ph.D. diss., University of Texas at Austin.

Latino Summit on NAFTA. 1993. "Latino Consensus Position on NAFTA." Position paper of summit convened by Mexican American Legal Defense and Education Fund, National Council of La Raza, and Southwest Voter Research Institute. Photocopy.

Limón, José E. 1974. "El Primer Congreso Mexicanista de 1911: A Precursor to Contemporary Chicanismo." *Aztlán* 5 (spring-fall): 85–106.

Linfield, Michael. 1990. *Freedom under Fire: U.S. Civil Liberties in Times of War.* Boston: South End Press.

Littrell, Boyd. 1993. "Bureaucratic Secrets and Adversarial Methods of Social Research." In *A Critique of Contemporary American Sociology*, edited by Ted R. Vaughan, Gideon Sjoberg, and Larry T. Reynolds, 207–231. Dix Hills, N.Y.: General Hall.

"Losing Control of the Borders." 1983. *Time*, 13 June.

"Low-Intensity Conflict Proponencies Directorate." 1991. *Military Review* 71 (6): 24–25.

Maechling, Charles, Jr. 1988. "Counterinsurgency: The First Ordeal by Fire." In *Low-Intensity Warfare: Counterinsurgency, Proinsurgency, and Antiterrorism in the Eighties*, edited by Michael T. Klare and Peter Kornbluh, 21–48. New York: Pantheon Books.

Majara, Davan, and Leslie Beckman. 1992. "Car Hits Pedestrian Near I-5 Checkpoint." *Los Angeles Times*, 22 January.

Marcuse, Herbert. 1964. *One-Dimensional Man: Studies in the Ideology of Advanced Industrial Society.* Boston: Beacon Press.

———. 1971–72. "The Movement in a New Era of Repression: An Assessment." *Berkeley Journal of Sociology* 16: 1–14.

Marelius, John. 1994. "Wilson Bolsters Troops at the Border, Sues for Aid." *San Diego Union-Tribune*, 30 April.

Maril, Robert Lee. 1989. *Poorest of Americans: The Mexican Americans of the Lower Rio Grande Valley of Texas.* Notre Dame, Ind.: University of Notre Dame Press.

Markley, Jennifer. 1990. "Bonds in the Asylum Context: The Treatment of Central American Refugees in Texas." Master's thesis, University of Texas at Austin.

Marshall, Ray. 1993. "The North American Free Trade Agreement: Implications for Workers." In *Sectoral Effects of North American Free Trade*, edited by Rafael Fernández de Castro, Mónica Verea Campos, and Sidney Weintraub, 3–34. Austin and Mexico City: Lyndon B. Johnson School of Public Affairs, University of Texas at Austin; Centro de Investigaciones sobre Estados Unidos de América, Universidad Nacional Autónoma de México; Instituto Tecnológico Autónomo de México.

Martin, Gary. 1994. "Border Patrol Fund Boost Set for Clinton Signature." *San Antonio Express-News*, 20 August.

Martínez, Óscar J. 1988. *Troublesome Border.* Tucson: University of Arizona Press.

Marx, Karl. 1977. *Capital.* Vol. 1. New York: Vintage Books.

Mathews, Mark. 1989. "Military Task Force Begins Border Duty." *Houston Chronicle*, 14 November.

McClintock, Michael. 1985a. *The American Connection.* Vol. 1, *State Terror and Popular Resistance in El Salvador.* London: Zed Books.

———. 1985b. *The American Connection.* Vol. 2, *State Terror and Popular Resistance in Guatemala.* London: Zed Books.

McDonnell, Patrick C. 1994. "Border Patrol Agent Is Charged in Auto Thefts." *El Paso Herald-Post*, 3 June.

McDonnell, Patrick J. 1988a. "INS Chief Opposes Use of Military in Role on Border." *Los Angeles Times*, 17 June.

———. 1988b. "State National Guard Wants to Join Drug War on U.S.–Mexico Border." *Los Angeles Times*, 18 October.

———.1989a. "Guardsmen at Border Armed, Alert for Aliens." *Los Angeles Times*, 2 June.

———.1989b. "Guardsmen to End Patrol Duty at Border." *Los Angeles Times*, 3 June.

———. 1990a. "INS Aims High Beams on Border to Catch Illegal Crossers." *Los Angeles Times*, 28 January.

————. 1990b. "Navy Will Fix Fence on the U.S.–Mexico Line." *Los Angeles Times*, 12 December.

————. 1990c. "State Guard Plans Larger Role in Drug War." *Los Angeles Times*, 15 January.

————. 1991a. "A Semblance of Order." *Los Angeles Times*, 7 July.

————. 1991b. "U.S.–Mexico Border Being Patched Up." *Los Angeles Times*, 6 February.

————. 1992a. "Border Agent Reportedly Told of Body." *Los Angeles Times*, 19 June.

————. 1992b. "Immigrants' Advocates Allege Mistreatment." *Los Angeles Times*, 16 May.

————. 1992c. "Official Says Border Killing Victim Might Have Lived." *Los Angeles Times*, 20 June.

————. 1992d. "Possible Cover-Up Probed in Border Killing." *Los Angeles Times*, 18 June.

————. 1992e. "Scores of Suspects Turned over to INS." *Los Angeles Times*, 6 May.

McDonnell, Patrick J., and Sebastian Rotella. 1993a. "Crossing the Line: Turmoil in the U.S. Border Patrol." Special series. *Los Angeles Times*, 22–24 April.

————. 1993b. "When Agents Cross over the Borderline." *Los Angeles Times*, 22 April.

McLemore, S. Dale. 1994. *Racial and Ethnic Relations in America*. 4th ed. Boston: Allyn & Bacon.

McNamara, Joseph D. 1992. "When Police Create Disorder." *Los Angeles Times*, 3 May.

Mead, Walter Russel. 1993. "Immigration Remains Key NAFTA Issue." *Los Angeles Times*, 11 November.

Meighan, Tyrone. 1994. "Security Breached in Guard: Report Recommends Probe into Colonel's Promotion." *Corpus Christi Caller-Times*, 13 February.

Melrood, Laurie. 1989. "Y mi madre no sabe de lo que yo sufrí . . ." *¡Basta!* (National Journal of the Chicago Religious Task Force on Central America), December: 29–31.

The Mexican Experience in Arizona. 1976. New York: Arno Press.

Mexican National Commission for Human Rights. 1992. *Report on Human Rights Violations of Mexican Migratory Workers on Route to the Northern Border, Crossing the Border, and upon Entering the Southern United States Border Strip*. Mexico City: Comisión Nacional de Derechos Humanos.

Miles, Sara. 1986. "The Real War: Low-Intensity Conflict in Central America." *NACLA Report on the Americas* 20 (2): 17–48.

Miller, Marjorie. 1992a. "Friendly Fire in Front Lines of Drug War." *Los Angeles Times*, 1 August.

————. 1992b. "Mexico Attacks Ruling, Halts Drug War Role." *Los Angeles Times*, 16 June.

Miller, Marjorie, and Douglas Jehl. 1990. "U.S. to Provide Helicopters, Radar to Mexico for Anti-Drug Effort." *Los Angeles Times,* 11 July.

———. 1992. "U.S., Mexico Ease Tensions on Court Ruling." *Los Angeles Times,* 17 June.

Miller, Marjorie, and Patrick J. McDonnell. 1990. "Rise in Violence along Border Brings Call for Action." *Los Angeles Times,* 9 December.

Mills, C. Wright. 1959. *The Sociological Imagination.* New York: Oxford University Press.

Milner, Elmer Ray. 1979. "An Agonizing Evolution: A History of the Texas National Guard, 1900–1945." Ph.D. diss., North Texas State University.

Montejano, David. 1987. *Anglos and Mexicans in the Making of Texas, 1836–1986.* Austin: University of Texas Press.

Monticone, Joseph Raymond. 1981. "Revolutionary Mexico and the U.S. Southwest." M.A. thesis, California State University, Fullerton.

Moreira Alves, Maria Helena. 1985. *State and Opposition in Military Brazil.* Austin: University of Texas Press.

Morley, Jefferson. 1991. "Gene McNary: Riding the Tiger of U.S. Immigration Policy." *Los Angeles Times,* 5 May.

Morris, Milton D. 1985. *Immigration: The Beleaguered Bureaucracy.* Washington, D.C.: Brookings Institution.

Mott, Charles P. 1989. "Realistic LIC Strategy in Latin America." *Military Review* 69 (5): 16–23.

Muñoz, Carlos, Jr. 1989. *Youth, Identity, Power: The Chicano Movement.* London: Verso.

Murphy, Dean E. 1992. "Rights Study Cites Serious Police Abuse in L.A." *Los Angeles Times,* 27 June.

Murray, Dan. 1990. "Activists Call Raid Un-American." *Valley Morning Star,* 29 September.

Nathan, Debbie. 1991. *Women and Other Aliens: Essays from the U.S.–Mexico Border.* El Paso, Tex.: Cinco Puntos Press.

———. 1992. "If We Make Waves, We'll Be Jailed." *NACLA Report on the Americas* 26 (1): 32.

———. 1993. "A Death on the Border." *Texas Observer,* 15 January.

———. 1994. "El Paso under the Blockade." *Nation,* 28 February.

"National Defense Authorization Act, Fiscal Year 1989" (Public Law 100-456). 1989. *United States Code Congressional and Administrative News,* 100th Cong., 2d sess. (1988), vol. 2. Saint Paul, Minn.: West Publishing.

"National Defense Authorization Act for Fiscal Year 1991" (Public Law 101-510). 1991. *United States Code Congressional and Administrative News,* 101st Cong., 2d sess. (1990), vol. 2. Saint Paul, Minn.: West Publishing.

"National Defense Authorization Act for Fiscal Year 1993" (Public Law 102-190). 1993. *United States Code Congressional and Administrative News,* 102d Cong., 2d sess. (1992), vol. 2. Saint Paul, Minn.: West Publishing.

"National Defense Authorization Act for Fiscal Years 1990 and 1991" (Public Law 101-189). 1990. *United States Code Congressional and Administrative News*, 101st Cong., 1st sess. (1989), vol. 1. Saint Paul, Minn.: West Publishing.

"National Defense Authorization Act for Fiscal Years 1992 and 1993" (Public Law 102-190). 1992. *United States Code Congressional and Administrative News*, 102d Cong., 1st sess. (1991), vol. 1. Saint Paul, Minn.: West Publishing.

National Immigration Law Center. 1989. *INS Misconduct: Rights and Remedies in Immigration Law Enforcement*. Los Angeles: National Immigration Law Center.

Nickel, James W. 1983. "Human Rights and the Rights of Aliens." In *The Border That Joins: Mexican Migrants and U.S. Responsibility*, edited by Peter G. Brown and Henry Shue, 31–45. Totowa, N.J.: Rowman & Littlefield.

Noble, Justin. 1992. "DPS Trains Mexican Police in Relations Effort." *Daily Texan*, 1 July.

Novick, Michael. 1987. "Secret Training of Reserves for Domestic Martial Law." *Guardian* (New York), 9 September.

"Now It's Bush's War." 1989. *Newsweek*, 18 September.

Nunca Más: The Report of the Argentine National Commission on the Disappeared. 1986. New York: Farrar, Strauss, & Giroux.

Núñez, Rogelio, and Harold Nelson. 1990. "Reflections on the Refugee Crisis: What Did and Almost Did Happen in Texas." Paper presented at the annual Southwestern Social Science Association meeting, March, Dallas.

"Operation Hold the Line: U.S. Immigration Service Involvement in Mexico." 1990. *Refugee Reports* 11 (9): 4–5.

Oppenheimer, Mark, and Jane C. Canning. 1978–79. "The National Security State: Repression within Capitalism." *Berkeley Journal of Sociology* 23: 3–33.

Orum, Anthony M., Joe R. Feagin, and Gideon Sjoberg. 1991. "Introduction: The Nature of the Case Study." In *A Case for the Case Study*, edited by Joe R. Feagin, Anthony M. Orum, and Gideon Sjoberg, 1–26. Chapel Hill: University of North Carolina Press.

Ostrow, Ronald. 1992. "U.S. to Add 300 Agents along Mexican Border." *Los Angeles Times*, 9 February.

———. 1994. "Border Has Tightened, Official Says." *Los Angeles Times*, 14 October.

Owen, Bab, and Philip True. 1992. "Protesters Sack, Burn Matamoros Election Office." *San Antonio Express-News*, 12 November.

Palmer, Louise. 1990. "Agents of Abuse." *Texas Observer*, 21 December.

Paredes, Américo. 1958. *"With His Pistol in His Hand": A Border Ballad and Its Hero*. Austin: University of Texas Press.

Pearce, Jenny. 1986. *Promised Land: Peasant Rebellion in Chalatenango, El Salvador*. London: Latin America Bureau.

Pedersen, Ann-Eve. 1992a. "After a Border Patrol Agent Is Acquitted in the Slaying of a Mexican Man, Human Rights Advocates Say the Agency Needs an Overhaul." *Tucson Citizen*, 17 December.

————. 1992b. "Bond Again Denied Border Agent." *Tucson Citizen,* 20 June.

Perkins, Clifford Alan. 1978. *Border Patrol: With the U.S. Immigration Service on the Mexican Boundary, 1910–54.* El Paso: Texas Western Press.

Phillips, Jim. 1989. "U.S. Sends 'Strong Signal' to Political Asylum Seekers." *Austin American-Statesman,* 21 February.

Pinkerton, James. 1989. "Tensions Linger after Refugee Center Disturbance." *Austin American-Statesman,* 18 March.

Power, Stephen. 1994. "Comes a Tide." *Dallas Morning News,* 27 October.

Ramos, José María. 1991. "La política de Estados Unidos hacia el narcotráfico y la frontera norte de México." *Frontera Norte* 3 (5): 85–101.

————. 1995. "Las políticas antidrogas y comercial de Estados Unidos en la frontera con México." Tijuana: Colegio de la Frontera Norte.

Rand McNally. 1976. *Major Military Installations of the United States.* Map. Chicago: Rand McNally.

Reich, Robert B. 1991. *The Work of Nations: Preparing Ourselves for Twenty-First-Century Capitalism.* New York: Knopf.

Reuter, Peter, Gordon Crawford, and Jonathan Cave. 1988. *Sealing the Borders: The Effects of Increased Military Participation in Drug Interdiction.* Prepared for the Office of the Undersecretary of Defense for Policy. Santa Monica, Calif.: Rand.

Reynolds, Clark W., and Stephen J. Wagner. 1990. "Integración económica de México y Estados Unidos: Implicaciones para la seguridad de ambos países." In *En busca de la seguridad perdida: Aproximaciones a la seguridad nacional mexicana,* edited by Sergio Aguayo Quezada and Bruce M. Bagley, 207–229. Mexico City: Siglo Veintiuno.

Reynolds, Diana. 1990. "FEMA and the NSC: The Rise of the National Security State." *Covert Action Information Bulletin* 33 (winter): 54–58.

Reza, H. G., and Ralph Frammolino. 1988. "Drug Operation Suspended after Deaths in Helicopter." *Los Angeles Times,* 27 October.

Robert H. Kupperman and Associates, Inc. 1983. *Low-Intensity Conflict.* Vol. 1. Final report prepared for the U.S. Army Training and Doctrine Command. Fort Monroe, Va.: U.S. Army Training and Doctrine Command.

Rodríguez, Néstor P., and Ximena Urrutia-Rojas. 1990. *Undocumented and Unaccompanied: A Mental Health Survey of Unaccompanied Immigrant Children from Central America.* Monograph no. 90-4. Houston: Institute for Higher Education Law and Governance, University of Houston Law Center.

Rogin, Michael Paul. 1984. "Control, Suppression, and Intimidation." In *Encyclopedia of American Political History: Studies of the Principal Movements and Ideas,* edited by Jack P. Greene, 1: 392–415. New York: Scribner.

Rohter, Larry. 1988. "National Guard Used in Test to Curb Drug Flow from Mexico." *New York Times,* 22 August.

————. 1990. "Sovereignty and Suspicion Hinder U.S.–Mexican Drug Alliance." *New York Times,* 25 February.

Romney, Lee. 1992. "The Lure of the Open Border." *Los Angeles Times*, 16 August.

Rosenbaum, Robert J. 1981. *Mexicano Resistance in the Southwest: "The Sacred Right of Self-Preservation."* Austin: University of Texas Press.

Rotella, Sebastian. 1992a. "Border Patrol Agent Indicted in Beating." *Los Angeles Times*, 31 July.

———. 1992b. "Border Patrol Calls off Plan for Bottleneck." *Los Angeles Times*, 6 February.

———. 1992c. "Border Patrol Plans Bottleneck." *Los Angeles Times*, 5 February.

———. 1992d. "INS Clears Agents in Fatal Temecula Crash." *Los Angeles Times*, 24 June.

———. 1992e. "Reducing the Misery at the Border." *Los Angeles Times*, 10 March.

———. 1994a. "Agents Begin Massive Sweep along Border." *Los Angeles Times*, 2 October.

———. 1994b. "Border Patrol Agents Accused of Abuses." *Los Angeles Times*, 5 October.

———. 1994c. "Border Patrol Push Diverts Flow." *Los Angeles Times*, 17 October.

Ruiz-Cabañas I., Miguel. 1992. "Mexico's Permanent Campaign: Costs, Benefits, and Implications." In *Drug Policy in the Americas*, edited by Peter H. Smith, 151–162. Boulder, Colo.: Westview Press.

Russel, George. 1985. "Trying to Stem the Illegal Tide." *Time*, 8 July.

Russell, Philip L. 1994. *Mexico under Salinas*. Austin: Mexico Resource Center.

Sablatura, Bob. 1992. "Radar Gaps Are Weak Link in Military's Electronic Fence." *Houston Chronicle*, 16 August.

Sahagún, Louis. 1994. "Nogales Wall Takes Toll in Injuries—and Costs." *Los Angeles Times*, 8 September.

Salopek, Paul. 1992. "Walls of Silence: Border Law and Abuse." Special report. *El Paso Times*, 6–8 December.

———. 1993. "La Migra: The Border Patrol's Wall of Silence." *Texas Observer*, 12 March.

Samora, Julián. 1971. *Los Mojados: The Wetback Story*. Notre Dame, Ind.: University of Notre Dame Press.

Samponaro, Frank N., and Paul J. Vanderwood. 1992. *War Scare on the Rio Grande: Robert Runyon's Photographs of the Border Conflict, 1913–1916*. Austin: Texas State Historical Association.

Sánchez Otero, Germán. 1993. "Neoliberalism and Its Discontents." *NACLA Report on the Americas* 26 (4): 18–21.

Sánchez Rodríguez, Roberto. 1990. "Condiciones de la vida de los trabajadores de la maquiladora en Tijuana y Nogales." *Frontera Norte* 2 (4): 153–182.

Sandalow, Marc. 1993. "Plan to Send Guardsmen to Border Gets a Boost." *San Francisco Chronicle*, 8 October.

Sanders, Sol. 1987. "Mexican Immigration: A Fortress America?" In *Central America and the Reagan Doctrine,* edited by Walter F. Hahn, 209–224. Lanham, Md.: University Press of America.

Sandos, James A. 1992. *Rebellion in the Borderlands: Anarchism and the Plan of San Diego, 1904–1923.* Norman: University of Oklahoma Press.

Sandoval, Juan Manuel. 1991a. "La frontera México–Estados Unidos en la perspectiva de la seguridad binacional." Paper presented at the international forum Las Fronteras Nacionales en el Umbral de Dos Siglos, organized by the Seminario Permanente de Estudios Chicanos y de Fronteras, July 24–28, Mexico City.

———. 1991b. "Militarización de la frontera, trabajadores migratorios, y tratado de libre comercio México–Estados Unidos." Paper presented at the Nineteenth Annual Meeting of the National Association for Chicano Studies, April 24–27, Hermosillo, Sonora, Mexico.

Santibáñez, Jorge, Javier Valenzuela, and Laura Velasco. 1993. "Migrantes devueltos por la Patrulla Fronteriza." Paper presented at the conference The Facets of Border Violence, May, University of Texas at El Paso.

Sassen, Saskia. 1988. *The Mobility of Labor and Capital: A Study in International Investment and Labor Flow.* New York: Cambridge University Press.

Schaden, Richard T. N.d. [ca. mid-1980s]. "The Strategic Implications of Immigration from Mexico and Central America: A Think Piece." Unpublished manuscript.

Schey, Peter. 1992. "Free Trade and the Human Rights of Migrant Workers." *Immigration Law Bulletin* 10 (1): 1, 4–7.

Schoultz, Lars. 1981. *Human Rights and United States Policy toward Latin America.* Princeton, N.J.: Princeton University Press.

Scott, David Clark. 1992. "Small Mexican Force Reaps Large Success in Patrolling Border." *Christian Science Monitor,* 28 May.

Scott, Peter Dale, and Jonathan Marshall. 1991. *Cocaine Politics: Drugs, Armies, and the CIA in Central America.* Berkeley: University of California Press.

Shogren, Elizabeth. 1994. "Gingrich Says He Opposes U.S. Version of 187." *Los Angeles Times,* 5 December.

Sjoberg, Gideon, and Paula Jean Miller. 1973. "Social Research on Bureaucracy: Limitations and Opportunities." *Social Problems* 21 (1): 129–143.

Sjoberg, Gideon, and Ted R. Vaughan. 1993. "The Ethical Foundations of Sociology and the Necessity for a Human Rights Alternative." In *A Critique of Contemporary American Sociology,* edited by Ted R. Vaughan, Gideon Sjoberg, and Larry T. Reynolds, 114–159. Dix Hills, N.Y.: General Hall.

Sjoberg, Gideon, Ted R. Vaughan, and Norma Williams. 1984. "Bureaucracy as a Moral Issue." *Journal of Applied Behavioral Science* 20 (4): 441–453.

Sjoberg, Gideon, Norma Williams, Ted R. Vaughan, and Andrée Sjoberg. 1991. "The Case Study Approach in Social Research: Basic Methodological Issues." In *A Case for the Case Study,* edited by Joe R. Feagin, Anthony M. Orum, and

Gideon Sjoberg, 27–79. Chapel Hill: University of North Carolina Press.

Sklair, Leslie. 1993. *Assembling for Development: The Maquila Industry in Mexico and the United States.* 2d ed. (updated and expanded). La Jolla, Calif.: Center for U.S.–Mexico Studies, University of California, San Diego.

Sloan, Stephen. 1987. "Countering Terrorism in the Late 1980s and the 1990s: Future Threats and Opportunities for the United States." Maxwell Air Force Base, Ala.: Airpower Research Institute, Air University Center for Aerospace Doctrine, Research, and Education.

Smith, Peter H. 1992. "The Political Economy of Drugs: Conceptual Issues and Policy Options." In *Drug Policy in the Americas,* edited by Peter H. Smith, 1–21. Boulder, Colo.: Westview Press.

Sontag, Deborah. 1993. "U.S.–Mexico Pact Exposed." *New York Times,* 15 July. *Austin American-Statesman,* 17 July.

Stepan, Alfred. 1976. "The New Professionalism of Internal Warfare and Military Role Expansion." In *Armies and Politics in Latin America,* edited by Abraham F. Lowenthal, 244–260. New York: Holmes & Meier.

Stern, Marcus. 1994. "National Guard Unused as a Border Tool." *San Diego Union-Tribune,* 10 March.

Stoddard, Ellwyn R., and John Hedderson. 1987. *Trends and Patterns of Poverty along the U.S.–Mexico Border.* Las Cruces: Joint Border Research Institute, New Mexico State University.

Struthers, David R. 1990. "Low-Intensity Conflict Policy in Latin America." Master's report, University of Texas at Austin.

Tactaquin, Cathi. 1992. "What Rights for the Undocumented?" *NACLA Report on the Americas* 26 (1): 25–28.

Taw, Jennifer Morrison, and Robert C. Leicht. 1992. *The New World Order and Army Doctrine: The Doctrinal Renaissance of Operations Short of War?* Prepared for the United States Army. Santa Monica, Calif.: Rand.

"Tents Erected in Advance of INS Policy Announcement." 1990. *Austin American-Statesman,* 7 February.

Texas Center for Policy Studies. 1990. *Overview of Environmental Issues Associated with Maquiladora Development along the Texas-Mexico Border.* Austin: Texas Center for Policy Studies.

Texas Legislature. House of Representatives. 1990. "House Bill 51," 12 November.

Thatcher, Rebecca. 1991. "Lawyer Charges Police Brutality Abounds in Valley." *Brownsville Herald,* 26 March.

Thompson, Loren B. 1989. "Low-Intensity Conflict: An Overview." In *Low-Intensity Conflict: The Pattern of Warfare in the Modern World,* edited by Loren B. Thompson. Lexington, Mass.: Lexington Books.

Toro, María Celia. 1990. "México y Estados Unidos: El narcotráfico como amenaza a la seguridad nacional." In *En busca de la seguridad perdida: Aproximaciones a la seguridad nacional mexicana,* edited by Sergio Aguayo Quezada and Bruce M. Bagley, 367–387. Mexico City: Siglo Veintiuno.

Trainor, Bernard E. 1989. "Drug Smugglers and the Marines Exchange Shots." *New York Times,* 15 December.

True, Pete. 1990. "Border Patrol Raids Casa Romero." *Brownsville Herald,* 28 September.

United Nations. Commission on the Truth for El Salvador (Belesario Betancur, Reinaldo Figeredo Planchart, and Thomas Buergenthal). 1993. *From Madness to Hope: The Twelve-Year War in El Salvador.* Report of the Commission on the Truth for El Salvador. New York: United Nations.

U.S. Army. 1983. "U.S. Army Operational Concept for Special Operations Forces." Draft of internal U.S. Army training document.

———. 1986. *U.S. Army Operational Concept for Low-Intensity Conflict.* TRADOC PAM 525-44. Fort Monroe, Va.: U.S. Army Training and Doctrine Command.

U.S. Army. Corps of Engineers. Fort Worth District. 1994 (April). *Programmatic Environmental Impact Statement: JTF-6 Activities along the U.S.–Mexico Border.* Draft copy.

U.S. Cabinet-Level Task Force on Terrorism. 1987. *Combatting Terrorism: The Official Report of the Cabinet-Level Task Force Chaired by Vice-President George Bush.* International Security and Terrorism Series, no. 3. Roncocas, N.J.: Defense Information Access Network.

U.S. Commission on Civil Rights. 1980. *The Tarnished Golden Door: Civil Rights Issues in Immigration.* Washington, D.C.: U.S. Commission on Civil Rights.

U.S. Commission on Civil Rights. 1992. "Joint Texas–New Mexico Advisory Committee Forum on Border-Related Civil-Rights Issues." Transcript. U.S. Commission on Civil Rights, 12 June.

U.S. Commission on Civil Rights. 1993. "Joint Meeting of the Arizona and California Committees to the United States Commission on Civil Rights." Transcript. U.S. Commission on Civil Rights, 16–17 April.

U.S. Committee for Refugees. 1989. *Refugees at Our Border: The U.S. Response to Asylum Seekers.* Report written by Bill Frelick. Washington, D.C.: American Council for Nationalities Service.

———. 1991. *Running the Gauntlet: The Central American Journey through Mexico.* Report written by Bill Frelick. Washington, D.C.: U.S. Committee for Refugees.

U.S. Congress. Arms Control and Foreign Policy Caucus. 1990. "The Atlacatl Battalion and Alleged Human Rights Abuses: Atlacatl's Record and U.S. Policy." Staff memorandum. Washington, D.C., 25 April.

U.S. Congress. House. Committee on Appropriations. 1979. *Departments of Commerce, Justice, and State, the Judiciary, and Related Agencies Appropriations for 1980.* 96th Cong., 1st sess. Washington, D.C.: GPO. [Y4.Ap6/1:st2/980/pt.5]

———. 1980. *Departments of Commerce, Justice, and State, the Judiciary, and Related Agencies Appropriations for 1981.* 96th Cong., 2d sess. Washington, D.C.: GPO. [Y4.Ap6/1:st2/981/pt.3]

————. 1981. *Departments of Commerce, Justice, and State, the Judiciary, and Related Agencies Appropriations for 1982.* 97th Cong., 1st sess. Washington, D.C.: GPO. [Y4.Ap6/1:C73/2/982/pt.6]

————. 1982. *Departments of Commerce, Justice, and State, the Judiciary, and Related Agencies Appropriations for 1983.* 97th Cong., 2d sess. Washington, D.C.: GPO. [Y4.Ap6/1:C73/2/983/pt.7]

————. 1983. *Departments of Commerce, Justice, and State, the Judiciary, and Related Agencies Appropriations for 1984.* 98th Cong., 1st sess. Washington, D.C.: GPO. [Y4.Ap6/1:C73/2/984/pt.6]

————. 1984. *Departments of Commerce, Justice, and State, the Judiciary, and Related Agencies Appropriations for 1985.* 98th Cong., 2d sess. Washington, D.C.: GPO. [Y4.Ap6/1:C73/2/985/pt.8]

————. 1985. *Departments of Commerce, Justice, and State, the Judiciary, and Related Agencies Appropriations for 1986.* 99th Cong., 1st sess. Washington, D.C.: GPO. [Y4.Ap6/1:C73/2/986/pt.7]

————. 1986. *Departments of Commerce, Justice, and State, the Judiciary, and Related Agencies Appropriations for 1987.* 99th Cong., 2d sess. Washington, D.C.: GPO. [Y4.Ap6/1:C73/2/987/pt.6]

————. 1987. *Departments of Commerce, Justice, and State, the Judiciary, and Related Agencies Appropriations for 1988.* 100th Cong., 1st sess. Washington, D.C.: GPO. [Y4.Ap6/1:C73/2/988/pt.4]

————. 1988. *Departments of Commerce, Justice, and State, the Judiciary, and Related Agencies Appropriations for 1989.* 100th Cong., 2d sess. Washington, D.C.: GPO. [Y4.Ap6/1:C73/2/989/pt.6]

————. 1989a. *Department of Defense Appropriations for 1990.* 101st Cong., 1st sess. Washington, D.C.: GPO. [Y4.Ap6/1:D36/5/990/pt.4]

————. 1989b. *Departments of Commerce, Justice, and State, the Judiciary, and Related Agencies Appropriations for 1990.* 101st Cong., 1st sess. Washington, D.C.: GPO. [Y4.Ap6/1:C73/2/990/pt.2]

————. 1990a. *Department of Defense Appropriations for 1991.* 101st Cong., 2d sess. Washington, D.C.: GPO. [Y4.Ap6/1:D36/5/991/pt.4]

————. 1990b. *Departments of Commerce, Justice, and State, the Judiciary, and Related Agencies Appropriations for 1991.* 101st Cong., 2d sess. Washington, D.C.: GPO. [Y4.Ap6/1:C73/2/991/pt.2]

————. 1991. *Departments of Commerce, Justice, and State, the Judiciary, and Related Agencies Appropriations for 1992.* 102d Cong., 1st sess. Washington, D.C.: GPO. [Y4.Ap6/1:C73/2/992/pt.2A]

————. 1992. *Departments of Commerce, Justice, and State, the Judiciary, and Related Agencies Appropriations for 1993.* 102d Cong., 2d sess. Washington, D.C.: GPO. [Y4.Ap6/1:C73/2/993/pt.2B]

————. 1993. *Departments of Commerce, Justice, and State, the Judiciary, and Related Agencies Appropriations for 1994.* 103d Cong., 1st sess. Washington, D.C.: GPO. [Y4.Ap6/1:C73/2/994/pt.2B]

————. 1994a. *Department of Defense Appropriations for 1995.* 103d Cong., 2d sess. Washington, D.C.: GPO. [Y4.Ap6/1:D36/5/995/pt.5]

————. 1994b. *Departments of Commerce, Justice, and State, the Judiciary, and Related Agencies Appropriations for 1994.* 103d Cong., 2d sess. Washington, D.C.: GPO. [Y4.Ap6/1:C73/2/995/pt.2B]

U.S. Congress. House. Committee on Foreign Affairs. 1990a. *Allegations of Abuse along the United States–Mexico Border.* 101st Cong., 2d sess. Washington, D.C.: GPO. [Y4.F76/1:V81/2]

————. 1990b. *Current Developments in Mexico.* 101st Cong., 2d sess. Washington, D.C.: GPO. [Y4.F76/1:M57/14]

————. 1990c. *Report of the Commission for the Study of International Migration and Cooperative Economic Development.* 101st Cong., 2d sess. Washington, D.C.: GPO. [Y4F76/1:M/58/24]

U.S. Congress. House. Committee on Government Operations. 1983. *Review of the Administration's Drug Interdiction Efforts.* 98th Cong., 1st sess. Washington, D.C.: GPO. [Y4.G74/7:D84/15]

————. 1985. *Continued Review of the Administration's Drug Interdiction Efforts.* 98th Cong., 2d sess. Washington, D.C.: GPO. [Y4.G74/7:D84/16]

————. 1986a. *Initiatives in Drug Interdiction.* Pt. 1. 99th Cong., 1st sess. Washington, D.C.: GPO. [Y4.G74/7:D84/17/pt.1]

————. 1986b. *Initiatives in Drug Interdiction.* Pt. 2. 99th Cong., 2d sess. Washington, D.C.: GPO. [Y4.G74/7:D84/17/pt.2]

————. 1988. *Operation Alliance: Drug Interdiction on the Southwest Border.* 100th Cong., 2d sess. Washington, D.C.: GPO. [Y1.1/8:100-562]

————. 1990. *The Role of the Department of Defense in the Interdiction of Drug Smuggling into the United States.* 101st Cong., 2d sess. Washington, D.C.: GPO. [Y4.G74/7:D36/37]

————. 1993a. *The Immigration and Naturalization Service: A Mandate for Change.* 103d Cong., 1st sess. Washington, D.C.: GPO. [Y4.G74/7:IM6/7]

————. 1993b. *Immigration and Naturalization Service and U.S. Border Patrol: Agency Mission and Pursuit Policies.* 102d Cong., 2d sess. Washington, D.C.: GPO. [Y4.G74/7:Im6/6]

————. 1993c. *The Immigration and Naturalization Service: Overwhelmed and Unprepared for the Future.* 103d Cong., 1st sess. Washington, D.C.: GPO. [Y1.1/8:103-216]

U.S. Congress. House. Committee on the Armed Services. 1988. *Narcotics Interdiction and the Use of the Military: Issues for Congress.* 100th Cong., 2d sess. Washington, D.C.: GPO. [Y4.Ar5/2:N16]

————. 1989a. *Military Role in Drug Interdiction.* 101st Cong., 1st sess. Washington, D.C.: GPO. [Y4.Ar5/2a:989-90/2]

————. 1989b. *Military Role in Drug Interdiction.* Pt. 2. 101st Cong., 2d sess. Washington, D.C.: GPO. [Y4.Ar5/2a:989-90/5]

———. 1990a. *Military Role in Drug Interdiction.* Pt. 3. 101st Cong., 2d sess. Washington, D.C.: GPO. [Y4.Ar5/2a:989-90/35]

———. 1990b. *U.S. Low-Intensity Conflicts, 1899–1990.* 101st Cong., 2d sess. Washington, D.C.: GPO. [Y4.AR5/2:UN3/3]

———. 1992. *Fiscal Year 1992 DOD Budget Submission for Drug Interdiction.* 102d Cong., 1st sess. Washington, D.C.: GPO. [Y4Ar5/2a:991-92/19]

———. 1993. *Regional Threats and Defense Options for the 1990s.* 102d Cong., 2d sess. Washington, D.C.: GPO. [Y4.Ar5/2a:991-92/73]

———. 1994a. *Hearing on National Defense Authorization Act for Fiscal Year 1994: DOD Drug Interdiction and Civil Defense.* 103d Cong., 1st sess. Washington, D.C.: GPO. [Y4.Ar5/2A:993-94/16]

———. 1994b. *Hearing on National Defense Authorization Act for Fiscal Year 1995: Counter-Drug Activities.* 103d Cong., 2d sess. Washington, D.C.: GPO. [Y4.Ar5/2A:993-94/37]

U.S. Congress. House. Committee on the Judiciary. 1981a. *Immigration and Refugee Issues in Southern California: An Investigative Trip.* 97th Cong., 1st sess. Washington, D.C.: GPO. [Y4.J89/1:Im6/10]

———. 1981b. *INS Oversight/Authorization.* 97th Cong., 1st sess. Washington, D.C.: GPO. [Y4.J89/1:97/4]

———. 1982. *Authorization/Oversight of the Immigration and Naturalization Service.* 97th Cong., 2d sess. Washington, D.C.: GPO. [Y4.J89/1:97-36]

———. 1983a. *Detention of Aliens in Bureau of Prisons Facilities.* 97th Cong., 2d sess. Washington, D.C.: GPO. [Y4.J89/1:97/81]

———. 1983b. *INS Budget Authorization for Fiscal Year 1984.* 98th Cong., 1st sess. Washington, D.C.: GPO. [Y4.J89/1:98/9]

———. 1985. *INS Budget Authorization: Fiscal Year 1986.* 99th Cong., 1st sess. Washington, D.C.: GPO. [Y4.J88/1:99/8]

———. 1988. *Legislation to Implement the Recommendations of the Commission on Wartime Relocation and Internment of Civilians.* 100th Cong., 1st sess. Washington, D.C.: GPO. [Y4.J89/1:100/19]

———. 1989a. *Central American Asylum Seekers.* 101st Cong., 1st sess. Washington, D.C.: GPO. [Y4.J89/1:101/25]

———. 1989b. *Mariel Cuban Detainees.* 100th Cong., 2d sess. Washington, D.C.: GPO. [Y4.J89/1:100/81/errata]

———. 1991. *Immigration and Naturalization Management Issues.* 102d Cong., 1st sess. Washington, D.C.: GPO. [Y4.J89/1:102/8]

———. 1992. *Operations of the Border Patrol.* 102d Cong., 2d sess. Washington, D.C.: GPO. [Y4.J89/1:102/66]

———. 1994. *Immigration-Related Issues in the North American Free Trade Agreement.* 103d Cong., 1st sess. Washington, D.C.: GPO. [Y4.J89/1:103/18]

U.S. Congress. House. Committee on Ways and Means. 1990. *United States–Mexico Relations.* 101st Cong., 2d sess. Washington, D.C.: GPO. [Y4.W36:101–108]

U.S. Congress. House. Select Committee on Narcotics Abuse and Control. 1986. *Drug Trafficking and Abuse along the Southwest Border (El Paso).* 99th Cong., 2d sess. Washington, D.C.: GPO. [Y4.N16:99-2-4]

———. 1987a. *Federal Drug Enforcement and Interdiction Provisions of the Anti–Drug Abuse Act of 1986.* 100th Cong., 1st sess. Washington, D.C.: GPO. [Y4.N16:100-1-4]

———. 1987b. *U.S. Narcotics Control Efforts in Mexico and on the Southwest Border.* 99th Cong., 2d sess. Washington, D.C.: GPO. [Y4.N16:99-2-17]

———. 1990. *Federal Drug Strategy Update.* 101st Cong., 2d sess. Washington, D.C.: GPO. [Y4.N16:101-2-4]

———. 1991a. *Federal Drug Interdiction Efforts.* 102d Cong., 1st sess. Washington, D.C.: GPO. [Y4.N16:102-1-6]

———. 1991b. *The Federal Strategy on the Southwest Border.* 101st Cong., 2d sess. Washington, D.C.: GPO. [Y4.N16:101-2-16]

———. 1991c. *National Drug Control Strategy.* 102d Cong., 1st sess. Washington, D.C.: GPO. [Y4.N16:102-1-2]

———. 1991d. *Study Mission to Brownsville, Texas, Mexico City, Mexico, and Guatemala City, Guatemala (December 9–13, 1990).* 101st Cong., 2d sess. Washington, D.C.: GPO. [Y4.N16:101-2-18]

U.S. Congress. House. Speaker's Special Task Force on El Salvador. 1990. "Interim Report of the Speaker's Special Task Force on El Salvador." 30 April. Photocopy.

U.S. Congress. Senate. Committee on Appropriations. 1985. *Department of Defense Support for Drug Interdiction.* 98th Cong., 2d sess. Washington, D.C.: GPO. [Y4.Ap6/2:S.hrg.98-1285]

———. 1986. *Drugs and Domestic Terrorism Threat to Arizona and the Southwest Border.* 99th Cong., 2d sess. Washington, D.C.: GPO. [Y4.Ap6/2:S.hrg. 99-866]

———. 1988. *Southwest Border Law Enforcement and Trade.* 100th Cong., 2d sess. Washington, D.C.: GPO. [Y4.Ap6/2:S.hrg.100-549]

———. 1990a. *Department of Defense Appropriations Fiscal Year 1991.* 101st Cong., 2d sess. Washington, D.C.: GPO. [Y4.Ap6/2:S.hrg.101-936/pt.3]

———. 1990b. *The Frontline of the U.S. War on Drugs: The Southwest Border.* 101st Cong., 1st sess. Washington, D.C.: GPO. [Y4.Ap6/2:S.hrg.101-485]

———. 1991. *Southwest Border High-Intensity Drug Trafficking Designation.* 101st Cong., 2d sess. Washington, D.C.: GPO. [Y4.Ap6/2:S.hrg.101-1109]

U.S. Congress. Senate. Committee on the Judiciary. 1980. *Department of Justice Authorization and Oversight, 1981.* 96th Cong., 2d sess. Washington, D.C.: GPO. [Y4.J89/2:96-63]

———. 1983. *Immigration Emergency Powers.* 97th Cong., 2d sess. Washington, D.C.: GPO. [Y4.J89/2:J97-147]

———. 1988. *Authorization Legislation and Oversight of the U.S. Department of Justice (Civil Rights Division and the INS).* 100th Cong., 1st sess. Washington,

D.C.: GPO. [Y4.J89/2:S.hrg.100-577/pt.4]

———. 1991. *Review of the National Drug Control Strategy.* 102d Cong., 1st sess. Washington, D.C.: GPO. [Y4.J89/S.hrg.102-334]

———. 1994. *Review of the National Drug Control Strategy.* 103d Cong., 2d sess. Washington, D.C.: GPO. [Y4.J89/2:S.hrg.103-547]

U.S. Department of Defense. Joint Chiefs of Staff. 1989. *Department of Defense Dictionary of Military and Associated Terms.* Washington, D.C.: Joint Chiefs of Staff.

U.S. General Accounting Office. 1985. *Coordination of Federal Drug Interdiction Efforts.* Washington, D.C.: GAO. [GA1.13:GGD-85-67]

———. 1988. *Drug Interdiction Operation Autumn Harvest: A National Guard–Customs Anti-Smuggling Effort.* Washington, D.C.: GAO. [GA1.13:GGD-88-86]

———. 1991. *Border Patrol: Southwest Border Enforcement Affected by Mission Expansion and Budget.* Washington, D.C.: GAO. [GA1.13:GGD-91-72BR]

———. 1992. *Immigration Control: Immigration Policies Affect INS Detention Efforts.* Washington, D.C.: GAO. [GAO/GGD-92-85]

U.S. Immigration and Naturalization Service. 1989. "Enhancement Plan for the Southern Border." 16 February. Photocopy.

U.S. Select Commission on Immigration and Refugee Policy. 1981. *U.S. Immigration Policy and the National Interest.* Final report and recommendations. Washington, D.C.: GPO. [Y3.IM6/2:2Im6/981]

U.S. Special Operations Command. 1993. *United States Special Operations Forces: Posture Statement 1993.* N.p.: Assistant Secretary of Defense for Special Operations and Low-Intensity Conflict; U.S. Special Operations Command.

Valentine, Douglas. 1992. *The Phoenix Program.* New York: Morrow, 1990. Reprint, New York: Avon Books.

Vila, Pablo. 1994a. "The Construction of Social Identities on the Border: Some Case Studies in Ciudad Juárez and El Paso." In *Sociological Explorations: Focus on the Southwest,* edited by Howard C. Daudistel and Cheryl A. Howard, 51–64. Saint Paul, Minn.: West Publishing.

———. 1994b. "Everyday Life, Culture, and Identity on the Mexican-American Border: The Cuidad Juarez–El Paso Case." Ph.D. diss., University of Texas at Austin.

"Violent Crime Control and Law Enforcement Act of 1994" (Public Law 103-322). 1994. *United States Code Congressional and Administrative News,* 103d Cong., 2d sess. (1994), no. 7. Saint Paul, Minn.: West Publishing.

Waghelstein, John D. 1985. "Post-Vietnam Counterinsurgency Doctrine." *Military Review* 65 (5): 42–49.

Waller, Douglas. 1993. "Running a 'School for Dictators.'" *Newsweek,* 9 August.

Walters, Jana. 1990. "Illegal Immigration: The Making of Myth." Research paper for graduate seminar on international immigration. Photocopy.

Wambaugh, Joseph. 1984. *Lines and Shadows.* New York: Morrow.

"Washington's Aid Programs to Mexico: Military and Anti-Narcotics Assistance." 1991. *Resource Center Bulletin* 26 (winter): 1–6.

Watson, George. 1977. "Helicopters along the Border." *INS Reporter* 26 (2): 19–23.

Webb, Walter Prescott. 1965. *The Texas Rangers: A Century of Frontier Defense.* 2d ed. Austin: University of Texas Press.

Weinberg, Bill. 1987. "The Contragate Conspiracy for a Coup d'Etat in the U.S." *Downtown* (New York), 16 September.

Weingarten, Steve. 1989. "INS Looks Back for Lesson Today: Cuban, Haitian Influx Paralleled." *Austin American-Statesman,* 26 February.

Weintraub, Sidney. 1990. *A Marriage of Convenience: Relations between Mexico and the United States.* New York: Oxford University Press.

———. 1992. "North American Free Trade and the European Situation Compared." *International Migration Review* 26 (2): 506–525.

Wilkinson, Tracy. 1991. "Mexico Consulate Speaks Out." *Los Angeles Times,* 11 January.

Williams, Edward J., and Irasema Coronado. 1994. "The Hardening of the United States–Mexico Borderlands: Causes and Consequences." *IBRU Boundary and Security Bulletin* 1 (4): 69–74.

Williams, Norma, and Andrée F. Sjoberg. 1993. "Ethnicity and Gender: The View from Above versus the View from Below." In *A Critique of Contemporary American Sociology,* edited by Ted R. Vaughan, Gideon Sjoberg, and Larry T. Reynolds, 160–202. Dix Hills, N.Y.: General Hall.

Wilson, Patricia A. 1991. "The Global Assembly Industry: Maquiladoras in International Perspective." *Journal of Borderlands Studies* 6 (2): 73–101.

———. 1992. *Exports and Local Development: Mexico's New Maquiladoras.* Austin: University of Texas Press.

Wilson, William Julius. 1987. *The Truly Disadvantaged: The Inner City, the Underclass, and Public Policy.* Chicago: University of Chicago Press.

———, ed. 1989. *The Ghetto Underclass: Social Science Perspectives. Annals of the American Academy of Political and Social Science,* vol. 501.

Woerner, Fred F. 1991. "The Strategic Imperatives for the United States in Latin America." In *Uncomfortable Wars: Toward a New Paradigm of Low Intensity Conflict,* edited by Max G. Manwaring, 57–68. Boulder, Colo.: Westview Press.

Wolfe, Alan. 1978. *The Seamy Side of Democracy: Repression in America.* 2d ed. New York: Longman.

Wong, Jennifer. 1991. "New World Border." *Texas Observer,* 19 April.

Young, Elliott. 1994. "Deconstructing *La Raza:* Identifying the *Gente Decente* of Laredo, 1904–1911." *Southwestern Historical Quarterly* 98 (2): 227–259.

Zamichow, Nora. 1990. "Marine Drones Used in Drug War." *Los Angeles Times,* 8 March.

Zanger, Maggy. 1990. "Planes, Trains, and Automatic Weapons." *Tucson Weekly,* 4–10 April.

Zenteno Quintero, René M., and Rodolfo Cruz Piñeiro. 1992. "A Geodemographic Definition of the Northern Border of Mexico." In *Demographic Dynamics of the U.S.–Mexico Border,* edited by John R. Weeks and Roberto Ham-Chande, 29–42. El Paso: Texas Western Press.

Index

CMAS BOOKS

The Militarization of the U.S.–Mexico Border, 1978–1992: Low-Intensity Conflict Doctrine Comes Home was designed by Jace Graf and Víctor J. Guerra. The text was composed by CMAS Books, primarily in Minion, with Hiroshige used for the title page and chapter titles. The book was printed and bound by Edwards Brothers, of Ann Arbor, Michigan.